BLACK ZION

Recent titles in
RELIGION IN AMERICA SERIES
Harry S. Stout, General Editor

SAINTS IN EXILE
The Holiness-Pentecostal Experience in African American Religion and Culture
Cheryl J. Sanders

DEMOCRATIC RELIGION
Freedom, Authority, and Church Discipline in the Baptist South, 1785–1900
Gregory A. Wills

THE SOUL OF DEVELOPMENT
Biblical Christianity and Economic Transformation in Guatemala
Amy L. Sherman

THE VIPER OF THE HEARTH
Mormons, Myths, and the Construction of Heresy
Terryl L. Givens

SACRED COMPANIES
Organizational Aspects of Religion and Religious Aspects of Organizations
Edited by N. J. Demerath III, Peter Dobkin Hall, Terry Schmitt, and Ryhs H. Williams

MARY LYON AND THE MOUNT HOLYOKE MISSIONARIES
Amanda Porterfield

BEING THERE
Culture and Formation in Two Theological Schools
Jackson W. Carroll, Barbara G. Wheeler, Daniel O. Aleshire, Penny Long Marler

THE CHARACTER OF GOD
Recovering the Lost Literary Power of American Protestanism
Thomas E. Jenkins

THE REVIVAL OF 1857–58
Interpreting an American Religious Awakening
Kathryn Teresa Long

AMERICAN MADONNA
Images of the Divine Woman in Literary Culture
John Gatta

OUR LADY OF THE EXILE
Diasporic Religion at a Cuban Catholic Shrine in Miami
Thomas A. Tweed

TAKING HEAVEN BY STORM
Methodism and the Rise of Popular Christianity in America
John H. Wigger

ENCOUNTERS WITH GOD
An Approach to the Theology of Jonathan Edwards
Michael J. McClymond

EVANGELICALS AND SCIENCE IN HISTORICAL PERSPECTIVE
Edited by David N. Livingstone, D. G. Hart and Mark A. Noll

METHODISM AND THE SOUTHERN MIND, 1770–1810
Cynthia Lynn Lyerly

PRINCETON IN THE NATION'S SERVICE
Religious Ideals and Educational Practice, 1868–1928
P. C. Kemeny

CHURCH PEOPLE IN THE STRUGGLE
The National Council of Churches and the Black Freedom Movement, 1950–1970
James F. Findlay, Jr.

TENACIOUS OF THEIR LIBERTIES
The Congregationalists in Colonial Massachusetts
James F. Cooper, Jr.

BLACK ZION

African American Religious Encounters with Judaism

EDITED BY

Yvonne Chireau

Nathaniel Deutsch

New York Oxford

Oxford University Press

2000

Oxford University Press

Oxford New York
Athens Auckland Bangkok Bogotá Buenos Aires Calcutta
Cape Town Chennai Dar es Salaam Delhi Florence Hong Kong Istanbul
Karachi Kuala Lumpur Madrid Melbourne Mexico City Mumbai
Nairobi Paris São Paulo Singapore Taipei Tokyo Toronto Warsaw

and associated companies in
Berlin Ibadan

Published by Oxford University Press, Inc.
198 Madison Avenue, New York, New York 10016

Library of Congress Cataloging-in-Publication Data
Black Zion : African American religious encounters with Judaism / edited by
Yvonne Chireau, Nathaniel Deutsch.
p. cm.—(Religion in America series)
Includes bibliographical references and index.
ISBN 0-19-511257-1—ISBN 0-19-511258-X (pbk.)
1. Afro-Americans—Relations with Jews. 2. Afro-Americans—Religion.
3. Black Hebrews. 4. Black Muslims. 5. Judaism—Relations—Christianity
I. Chireau, Yvonne Patricia, 1961– II. Deutsch, Nathaniel.
III. Religion in America series (Oxford University Press)
E184.36.A34 B53 1999
296.3'9'08996073—dc21 99-039278

1 3 5 7 9 8 6 4 2

Printed in the United States of America
on acid-free paper

To our parents
Dorothy and Roland Chireau
Sue and Zvi Deutsch

Acknowledgments

This book is the product of a sustained conversation between two friends and colleagues around the issues of religion, race, and identity in America. In time, we extended our dialogue to include a broader circle of participants. Our intellectual commitment to religious studies led us to explore the issues in a more structured and meaningful format. We gratefully acknowledge all of those who helped as those initial conversations developed into the present book.

First and foremost we wish to thank our contributors. Without their willingness to participate in this collaborative effort, this book would not be possible. Special thanks to Cynthia Read, our editor at Oxford, who was enthusiastic about this project from the beginning; and to Nina Sherwin, our editorial assistant, who deserves mention for her skillful efficiency in moving the book through its various phases.

We would like to express our gratitude to faculty and staff at Swarthmore College, including Provost Jennie Keith, for her interest and encouragement. A Faculty Research Grant from the College provided crucial funding. We also acknowledge the members of the Department of Religion, including Don Swearer, Jerry Frost, Mark Wallace, Ellen Ross, Vera Moreen, Steven Hopkins, Cynthia Baker, and Ruqayya Khan; thanks also to Eileen McElrone for her valuable administrative assistance.

Yvonne Chireau would like to thank Randall Burkett and Richard Newman for their suggestions and advice; also Monique Wubbenhorst and Dorothy and Roland Chireau (to whom this book is dedicated) for their high expectations. My appreciation goes to Michael and Gabrielle Rodriguez for their patience and unconditional love. And thanks to God and the Forces for their guidance and inspiration.

Nathaniel Deutsch would like to thank members of the Hebrew Israelite communities of Dimona, Israel, and Accra, Ghana, for the warmth and hospitality shown to him on research visits in the summer of 1998. Special thanks to Moriel ben Asiel for his insight and friendship during the journey. Jack Salzman and participants in the Northeastern Seminar on Black Religion made helpful comments on earlier drafts of the essay on the Nation of Islam. Finally, without the love and encouragement of the following people this project could not have been completed: Sue and Zvi Deutsch, Yael Deutsch, Shai Levi, David Deutsch, Aliza Deutsch, Max Deutsch, and Miriam Greenberg.

Contents

Contributors xi
Introduction 3

PART ONE AFRICAN AMERICAN JEWS AND ISRAELITES

1. Black Culture and Black Zion: African American Religious Encounters with Judaism, 1790–1930, an Overview 15
   Yvonne Chireau
2. African American Jews: Dispelling Myths, Bridging the Divide 33
   Bernard J. Wolfson
3. Symbolic Identity Formation in an African American Religious Sect: The Black Hebrew Israelites 55
   Merrill Singer
4. Another Exodus: The Hebrew Israelites from Chicago to Dimona 73
   Ethan Michaeli

PART TWO AFRICAN AMERICAN MUSLIMS AND JUDAISM

5. The Proximate Other: The Nation of Islam and Judaism 91
   Nathaniel Deutsch
6. The Nubian Islaamic Hebrews, Ansaaru Allah Community: Jewish Teachings of an African American Muslim Community 118
   Kathleen Malone O'Connor

PART THREE AFRICAN AMERICAN CHRISTIANITY AND JUDAISM

7. Remembering Nehemiah: A Note on Biblical Theology 153
   Allen Dwight Callahan
8. Theological Affinities in the Writings of Abraham Joshua Heschel and Martin Luther King, Jr. 168
   Susannah Heschel

9. This Is the Gateway to the Lord: The Legacy of Synagogue Buildings for African American Churches on Cincinnati's Reading Road 187
Karla Goldman
10. "The Jew" in the Haitian Imagination: Pre-Modern Anti-Judaism in the Postmodern Caribbean 203
Elizabeth A. McAlister

Selected Bibliography 229
Index 237

Contributors

Allen Dwight Callahan is associate professor of New Testament and Horace Dey. Lentz Lecturer at the Harvard Divinity School. Professor Callahan has taught theology at Boston College and the language and literature of the New Testament at Holy Cross College, Andover-Newton Theological School, and Harvard University, where he is a member of the New Testament Department faculty at the Divinity School.

Elizabeth A. McAlister is assistant professor of religion at Wesleyan University, and holds a Ph.D. in American studies and African American studies from Yale University. She has published in the *Journal of Caribbean Studies*, in *Sacred Arts of Haitian Vodou* (Los Angeles: Fowler Museum of Cultural History, 1995), and *Gatherings in Diaspora: Religious Communities and the New Immigration* (Philadelphia: Temple University Press, 1998), and has produced an album for Smithsonian Folkways called *Rhythms of Rapture: Sacred Musics of Haitian Vodou.*

Karla Goldman is associate professor of American Jewish history at the Hebrew Union College–Jewish Institute of Religion in Cincinnati, Ohio. She is the author of *Beyond the Gallery: Finding a Place for Women in American Judaism*, forthcoming from Harvard University Press.

Merrill Singer is associate director and chief of research at the Hispanic Health Council. He is the co-author of several books, including *African American Religion in the Twentieth Century* (U of Tennessee Press), *Critical Medical Anthropology* (Baywood Publishing), and *Medical Anthropology and the World System* (Greenwood). Dr. Singer is a member of the executive committee of the Center for Interdisciplinary Research on AIDS at Yale University and the executive committee of the National Society for Medical Anthropology.

Bernard J. Wolfson holds a B. A. in history from the University of California at Berkeley, and an M.A. in international studies from the Johns Hopkins University.

For the past thirteen years, he has worked as a journalist in Washington, D.C., Paris, London, Mexico City, and Boston. He is currently a staff writer at the *Orange County Register* in Santa Ana, California.

Kathleen Malone O'Connor is currently a lecturer in the religious studies program at the University of California, Davis, and recently completed a postdoctoral fellowship (1995–1998) with a concurrent assistant professorship (Near Eastern Studies Department) at the University of Michigan. She is currently working on a book entitled *The Worlds of Interpretation of African American Muslims* that studies the intersections between the exegetical techniques of the Moorish Science Temple, the Nation of Islam, the Ansarullah Community, the Five Percent Nation of Gods and Earths, and the larger Islamic tradition.

Nathaniel Deutsch is a historian of religions who received his training in America, Israel, and Russia and is currently assistant professor of Religion at Swarthmore College. He has written and lectured on a wide range of topics including Jewish mysticism, Gnosticism, Mandaeism, the Nation of Islam, and Hasidism. He is the author of *The Gnostic Imagination: Gnosticism, Mandaeism, and Merkabah Mysticism* and of *Guardians of the Gate: Angelic Vice Regency in Late Antiquity*, and is currently working on a book entitled *An Other Hasidism.*

Susannah Heschel holds the Eli Black Chair in Jewish Studies at Dartmouth College. She is the author of numerous studies on modern Jewish thought, including *Abraham Geiger and the Jewish Jesus*, published by the University of Chicago Press, and *Insider/Outsider: American Jews and Multiculturalism*, co-edited with David Biale and Michael Galchinsky, published by the University of California Press.

Yvonne Chireau is associate professor in the Religious Studies Department at Swarthmore College, and holds a Ph.D. in religious studies from Princeton University. She has written on a variety of topics in African American religious history and is currently completing a book on black religion, magic, and supernaturalism.

Ethan Michaeli is a 1989 graduate of the University of Chicago, with a Bachelor of Arts in English language and literature. Founder and editor-in-chief of *Residents' Journal*, a bi-monthly magazine for and by Chicago public housing residents, he also directs the Urban Youth International Journalism program, which trains public housing teenagers in journalism skills. He previously was an investigative reporter with the *Chicago Daily Defender*, where he covered public housing, politics, crime, environment, and community issues. His articles have also appeared in the *Forward*, *Afrique Newsmagazine*, the *JUF News*, and *New City Magazine.*

BLACK ZION

Introduction

Yvonne Chireau and Nathaniel Deutsch

Black Zion grows out of a joint interest in religious diversity and a deep concern over the absence of religion in conversations involving blacks and Jews in American society. This book addresses shared elements in black and Jewish sacred life, as well as the development and elaboration of new religious identities by African Americans. These essays explore the creative ways that African Americans have interacted with Jewish beliefs, Jewish traditions, and Jewish institutions. Black religious encounters with Judaism—and the contexts and circumstances that have shaped these encounters—have produced a spectrum of forms that are as varied and complex as the religious experience itself.

Black Zion does not purport to be a book on "black–Jewish relations" as social scientists, academics, and politicians currently use that phrase. Nor is it particularly concerned with African American and Jewish "dialogues" or "alliances," which, in our opinion, are paradigms with limited use for comprehending the interactions between the two groups. Indeed, such paradigms may actually obscure a better understanding of the historical relationship between African Americans and Jews. Rather than focus our discussion on dialogues and alliances or, conversely, on any disappointment and anger between blacks and Jews, we seek to explore the critical role of religion in defining and shaping the relationship between the two peoples.[1]

Blacks have encountered Jewish traditions in myriad forms and under a number of historical circumstances. Until now, studies concerned with African American religions and Judaism have dealt primarily with the theological impact of biblical texts on black Christian traditions and, to a lesser degree, on the emergence of "black Jewish" groups in the United States.[2] While these subjects are also given consideration in this text, they do not begin to exhaust the wealth of African American religious encounters with Judaism. There is no normative model, no typical relationship between African American religions and Judaism. Because African Americans have had such a rich and complex relationship with Jewish traditions, the essays in this volume employ a wide variety of methodological approaches drawn from a number of disciplines, including cultural studies, theology, anthropology, sociology, and the history of religions. They offer new possibilities for viewing black American religious institutions, faith traditions, and life experiences. Nevertheless, the volume—despite its wide selection of essays—still represents a suggestive sample rather than an exhaustive survey.

Although the essays in *Black Zion* address the ways in which African American religions have interacted with Jewish traditions, texts, and spaces, this does not mean that Jewish groups and individuals have been unaffected by their contact with African American religious culture. In some cases the impact has been quite dramatic, as Susannah Heschel illustrates in her essay on her father, Abraham Joshua Heschel, whose relationship with Martin Luther King, Jr., profoundly affected both men's religious thinking. Indeed, many Jewish individuals and congregations were spiritually transformed by their involvement in the civil rights movement and by the African American religious leaders who were at its vanguard. There are also numerous African American Jews whose religious identities have been shaped by their participation in both cultures, as Bernard Wolfson shows in his essay on the Alliance of Black Jews and Rabbi Capers Funnye. In other cases, such as that of the Hebrew Israelites, a sect of black Americans who emigrated to Israel in 1969, religious influences on Jews may be more difficult to detect or may become more apparent with time, but at least one Israeli Jew has already become a member of the group. The Hebrew Israelites are examined by Merrill Singer and Ethan Michaeli in two separate chapters. Notwithstanding these examples, it may be argued that the undeniably powerful influence of African American culture on Jewish groups and individuals occurs less in the realm of religious beliefs and practice and more in the realms of secular culture, political activism, and ethnic identity construction.

By concentrating on the ways in which African Americans have encountered Judaism, we do not mean to imply that Judaism has had a greater impact on African American religiosity than have Christianity, Islam, or African traditional religions. Rather we hope to illuminate one thread in the intricate tapestry of black religious experiences by exploring the manifold and ingenious ways in which African Americans have incorporated Judaism into their religious identities.

As we have indicated, *Black Zion* is not specifically about black–Jewish relations—or at least in the way those relations have traditionally been understood. Previous works have typically focused on the social and political relationship between the two groups while almost totally ignoring the religious dimension. *Black Zion*, by contrast, places religion at its center, thereby illuminating an obscured—but critically significant—area of black–Jewish encounters in America. For example, Nathaniel Deutsch's essay on the Nation of Islam treats the group as first and foremost a religious movement whose political and social activism grows out of a complex religious ideology—one espoused in the group's own sacred texts. Examining the writings and speeches of two critical figures in the movement's history, Elijah Muhammad and Louis Farrakhan, Deutsch presents a picture of the ambivalence of the Nation of Islam's thought regarding Judaism, which is expressed alternately, in social condemnation and spiritual identification. Without an appreciation of the religious significance of the Nation of Islam's mythology and scriptural interpretation, he argues, an informed understanding of their attitudes toward Jews and Judaism is impossible.

The paucity of studies on the religious dimension of black–Jewish relations in America is particularly striking, and egregious, given the critical importance of religion to both communities. In part this neglect reflects an unfortunate tendency of some academics and intellectuals to overlook the vital role of religion in American culture. Generally, when religion does receive attention by writers, coverage focuses on mainstream groups and denominations, while smaller or lesser-known groups are disregarded, unless they are perceived to be dangerous or deviant, as with the case of David Koresh and the Branch Davidians in Waco. This lack of appreciation for religion in the lives of ordinary Americans has had devastating effects, as Waco also illustrates. If people had made greater efforts to understand the religious beliefs and motivations of the Branch Davidians, instead of treating the situation as a "secular" hostage standoff, unnecessary bloodshed might have been avoided. Only recently has scholarly interest turned to an appreciation of the power of religion in Americans' lives, particularly as it shapes popular opinion and civic behavior.[3]

We believe that there is another important reason why the religious aspects of black–Jewish relations have received such scant attention. The dominant view (at times promulgated by social scientists, academic writers, and the media) is that relations between the two groups are in crisis. In examining black–Jewish relations, it is important to avoid what the historian Salo Baron called a "lachrymose" view of history. Baron was referring to the tendency among Jewish historians to focus entirely on the negative episodes in Jewish history rather than presenting a well-rounded picture. Because of the traumatic events in both African American and Jewish history, a lachrymose perspective is easy to adopt. Yet this historiographical method obscures the positive experiences of both peoples, including the constructive interactions that they have shared.[4]

Ironically, the "crisis view" of black–Jewish relations is also problematic in that it suggests that a halcyon period once existed between the two groups. In fact, along with the positive and neutral exchanges, there have always been tensions in the joint social and political endeavors of African Americans and Jews. From the establishment of the National Association for the Advancement of Colored People (NAACP) at the start of the twentieth century to the contemporary civil rights struggle, some African Americans have welcomed the participation of Jews while others have viewed Jewish involvement as patronizing at best and self-serving at worst—a view espoused by Malcolm X in *The Autobiography of Malcolm X*:

> I gave the Jew credit for being among all other whites the most active, and the most vocal, financier, "leader" and "liberal" in the Negro civil rights movement. But I said at the same time that the Jew played these roles for a very careful strategic reason: the more prejudice in America could be fo-

> cused upon the Negro, then the more the white Gentiles' prejudice would keep diverted off the Jew. [5]

In this statement, Malcolm X, a Muslim, expresses a deep suspicion of Jews' intentions vis-à-vis blacks, as well as an acute awareness that historically, Jews, like blacks, have been marginalized in relation to "white Gentile" society. His words capture an important element of the paradoxical relationship of blacks and Jews in America, one in which accusation and identification have gone hand in hand. It is within the religious realm that the most intense identification of blacks with Jews has occurred.

The essays in this collection illustrate the fluid nature of cultural categories as well as the shifting meanings of race and ethnicity in the historical experiences of the African American people. By exploring the ways in which blacks have identified with and as Jews *religiously*, this book problematizes the very category of "black–Jewish relations" insofar as this term implies a dichotomous relationship. As the essays in this volume dramatically indicate, "black" and "Jewish" are not mutually exclusive. Many individuals and communities in the United States have embraced both identities.

Although this book focuses on African American religions, it also raises important questions for the meaning of Judaism. Certainly one of the most vexing of these questions is whether one can even speak of a single Judaism. In fact, it may be argued that the popular image of a unified Judaism does not accurately reflect any historical period, let alone our own. Scholars increasingly refer to "Judaisms" when they discuss the religious landscape of 2,000 ago. Closer to the present, the rise of Hasidism and the Reform movement both triggered great controversy and changes within the body of Judaism. Despite a few notable but ultimately unsuccessful attempts to create a Jewish creed or dogma, Jews—unlike Christians and Muslims—have traditionally eschewed a set of defining beliefs. As the millennium draws to a close, the question of "Who is a Jew?" has become a lightning rod for debate. The identification of African Americans with and especially *as* Jews expands the parameters of this debate and highlights issues of race, ethnicity, and self-definition in determining who is a Jew.

If a group of African Americans who were raised as Christians form a new community and declare themselves to be Jews, does this act make them Jewish? Must they first be converted by one of the "official" branches of Judaism? Are these branches any more valid than another group that claims Jewish origins? Moreover, what about a group of African Americans who claims that they are legitimately Jewish and that others who call themselves Jews (i.e., Orthodox, Conservative, etc.) are imposters or "so-called Jews"? Finally, what happens when a group of African Americans who identify with biblical Israel but reject the label "Jews" as inaccurate emigrate to the modern state of Israel and establish a community? These scenarios, far from being heuristic, are part of the current reality in America and Israel and are explored by the contributors to *Black Zion*.

For some African Americans, identification with the biblical nation of Israel has assumed allegorical or metaphorical significance; other blacks have considered themselves to be the only true physical descendants of Israel; still others have affirmed their connection to ancient Israel as members of the Jewish community. Thus it is important to distinguish between those groups and individuals who identify with the biblical Israel and those who identify with contemporary Jews, although there is some overlap.

Several essays in this volume examine a cross-section of African American groups and individuals that embrace some form of Jewish or Hebrew/Israelite identity. Yvonne Chireau's essay investigates the religious and historical developments that culminated in the genesis of black Jewish groups at the turn of this century. Chireau shows how the earliest groups combined Christian rituals and symbols with Jewish traditions, such as a Saturday Sabbath and Passover celebrations, and later some African Americans were more directly influenced by their contact with Jews of European background. By contrast, black Hebrew groups such as the Commandment Keepers Congregation of Harlem, currently the largest African American Jewish community in New York City, claimed an organic relationship to the Jews of Ethiopia, the *Beta Yisroel*.[6]

Those African Africans who identify as Jews present a particularly striking challenge to the American notion of what constitutes Jewish culture and ethnicity, and they form part of a broader contemporary awakening within both Jewish and non-Jewish communities to the wide variety of Jewish experiences. By their very existence, African American Jews also undermine the image of Jews as a race unto themselves or as belonging to a single race, be it white, Semitic, or Asiatic. Bernard Wolfson's essay illuminates a very different but equally important group of African Americans: those who identify as members of the larger Jewish community. Some have a Jewish and an African American parent while others have converted to Judaism; some belong to predominantly African American congregations, others identify with the Orthodox movement. Wolfson also examines the Alliance of Black Jews, a group whose mission statement is "to bring together people of African descent who believe in Torah and its mandates and/or who are culturally affiliated with Judaism."

Although Jews have generally avoided defining Judaism by a single creed or dogma, for millennia they have drawn inspiration and strength from a common set of religious themes, rituals, and beliefs. These include identification as the chosen people of Israel, a reverence for the Law, and belief in a covenantal relationship with God. Occupying an equally important place in the history of the Jewish people and their religious imagination are the concepts of exile and redemption. In the Jewish tradition, chosenness, Law, Covenant, Exile, and Redemption all originate in the

Hebrew Bible. It is therefore no accident that Jews in all periods and places have employed biblical exegesis as a primary means for self-understanding and self-renewal. Several essays in this volume focus on the constructive use of biblical interpretation in black religious cultures. Allan Callahan examines the significance of the book of Nehemiah to contemporary African American Christians. He begins by tracing the exegetical history of Nehemiah in ancient Jewish sources. Ultimately, Callahan argues, Nehemiah was almost forgotten by Jewish exegetes and by the African American slaves who created the tradition of the spirituals. Callahan shows how in the past two decades black Christian leaders such as John Perkins and Johnny Ray Youngblood have recovered the postexilic book of Nehemiah and drawn inspiration from its message of community restoration.

In his essay, Nathaniel Deutsch explores the attitudes of Elijah Muhammad and Louis Farrakhan toward Jews and Judaism, illuminating a profound structural affinity between Muhammad's biblical exegesis and the style of rabbinic biblical interpretation known as midrash. Both Muhammad and the Rabbis employed ingenious and imaginative methods of biblical interpretation as a form of resistance to religious and political oppression, transforming biblical exegesis into a powerful tool for self-definition and affirmation. The use of midrashic-type exegesis is also a distinctive characteristic of the Holy Tabernacle Ministries (also known as Nubian Islaamic Hebrews/Ansaaru Allah). Kathleen Malone O'Connor reveals the ways in which the group's leader, Malachi Z. York, employs biblical interpretation—informed by his knowledge of Semitic languages—to define the group's worldview. O'Connor places the Holy Tabernacle Ministries within the historical context of African American Muslim (Moorish Science Temple, Nation of Islam, Five Percent Nation of Gods and Earths) and Jewish (Moorish Zionist Temple, Commandment Keepers, Hebrew Israelites) groups. Her analysis of the movement's history reveals how the Holy Tabernacle Ministries has combined Muslim, Jewish, and Christian elements, sometimes emphasizing one heritage, sometimes another, according to the changing orientation of their leader.

The roots of African American identification with, and transformation of, Israelite and Jewish traditions are to be found in the central narrative of the Hebrew Bible: a lowly people is chosen by God, suffers slavery and exile, and is ultimately redeemed and returned to its Promised Land. This story resonated profoundly with the African slaves and their descendants who cried by the rivers of their own Babylon—America—during centuries of oppression and exile. Blacks have consistently offered their own liberatory exegesis of biblical traditions by emphasizing the chosenness of African Americans and the promise of redemption for their suffering.

The various modes of black identification with Judaism and Jewish texts share a critically important element: they all subvert the racist image of blacks as a damned people, an image cultivated over the years by white religious figures employing scriptural justification for slavery and other forms of racist oppression. In her essay, Elizabeth McAlister explores a fascinating variation of this phenomenon in which practitioners of Haitian Vodou symbolically assume the role of Jews vis-à-vis Catholics in order to subvert the latter group's religious authority. As McAlister writes: "When Rara members [Vodou practitioners and participants in the seasonal festival of Lent] embrace the negative cultural category of the Jew, the mythology they generate may be understood as a repressed people's subversion of the ruling order. This class resistance to Catholic hegemony is a form of theatrical positioning on the part of the peasants that says 'We are the Jews, the enemy of the French Catholic landowners.'"

In addition to identification—whether metaphorical or literal—with biblical Israel or Jews, many African Americans have also transformed particular Jewish traditions, symbols, and rituals. Other essays in this volume consider a wide variety of these transformations. Karla Goldman examines the mental reconfiguration of Jewish symbols and architecture by African American Christians. The theme of constructing community is central to her discussion of black congregations that have moved into former synagogues on Cincinnati's Reading Road. Goldman draws upon interviews as well as her own architectural observations of these sacred spaces. She examines how members of several congregations, Jewish and African American, have interpreted the transition from synagogue to church. The phenomenon that Goldman identifies is widespread throughout the United States but has not received sufficient attention from either urban historians or scholars of religion. Goldman's analysis reveals another dimension of the complexity of race and religion in contemporary America and sheds new light on one of the most important chapters in the history of black–Jewish relations: the transformation of urban Jewish neighborhoods into African American ones.

Whereas the relationship of African American and Jewish congregations is the subject of Goldman's piece, Susannah Heschel examines the friendship and theological affinities of two individuals: Martin Luther King, Jr., and Abraham Joshua Heschel. Although Heschel and King came from dramatically different cultural backgrounds, they shared a number of profound bonds. Susannah Heschel argues that "[w]hat linked Heschel and King theologically was their reading of the Bible, particularly of the prophets, and the understanding of God they drew from their biblical readings." Writings and speeches reveal that Heschel and King were spiritually enriched by their friendship and their work in the civil rights movement. After the men marched arm in arm in Selma, Alabama, Heschel wrote in his diary that King had described the march as "the greatest day in his life," while Heschel "thought of having walked with Hasidic rabbis on various occasions. I felt a sense of the Holy in what I was doing."

The structure of *Black Zion* mirrors the mosaic of African American religions, both contemporary and past. Many black groups and individuals that identify on some level with Judaism also consider themselves to be Christians, Muslims, or—as the example of the Vodouisants illustrates—members of African-based religions. The book is divided into three sections, each exploring a different cluster of groups and traditions. The first section examines those African Americans who identify themselves as the physical descendants of ancient Israel or as members of the contemporary Jewish community. These include black converts to Judaism, children of Jewish and African American parents, early figures such as Prophet Cherry in Philadelphia and Arnold Josiah Ford of Marcus Garvey's Universal Negro Improvement Association (UNIA), as well as currently active groups such as the Hebrew Israelites (also known as the Black Hebrew Israelites). The second section explores the relationship between African American Muslims and Judaism. Two groups are examined—the Nation of Islam and the Nubian Islaamic Hebrews, also called the Ansaaru Allah Community, and more recently, the Holy Tabernacle Ministries. The third section, on African American Christianity and Judaism, reveals how blacks have interacted with Jewish traditions, spaces, and religious leaders through the medium of Christianity and Christian-based traditions. The essays in this section examine the use of the biblical book of Nehemiah by black evangelicals; the relationship of Martin Luther King, Jr., and Abraham Joshua Heschel; how African American congregations have transformed synagogue spaces into churches; and the symbolic role of Jews in the Haitian religious imagination.[7]

Even as the theoretical scope of *Black Zion* is expansive, it was not possible to include all areas of the African Diaspora, such as the Rastafarian movement in Jamaica, which has many deep connections to Judaism, or the influences of Sephardic Jewish communities on African slaves in the Caribbean and coastal regions of Central America. Furthermore, we have not included some of the more interesting recent developments in the United States, such as the rise of the Nation of Yahweh, a messianic movement based in Miami, or the establishment of Hatzaad Harishon, an organization concerned with black and Jewish relations in the 1960s and 1970s. Indeed, the number of topics to which we could devote attention would fill an additional volume. We hope, however, that the essays we have included here will stimulate future considerations of the vital significance of racial and ethnic identities in American religion. The unique products of the encounter between African American religions and Judaism provide ample evidence of the creative spiritual capacities of the African American people and the enormous diversity that is embodied in black religious life.

Notes

1. On black–Jewish relations, see Seth Forman, *Blacks in the Jewish Mind: A Crisis in Liberalism* (New York: New York University Press, 1998); Jack Salzman and Cornel West, eds., *Struggles in the Promised Land: Toward a History of Black–Jewish Relations in the United States* (New York: Oxford University Press, 1997); Michael Lerner and Cornel West, *Jews and Blacks: A Dialogue on Race, Religion and Culture in America* (New York: Penguin, 1996); Hasia Diner, *In the Almost Promised Land: American Jews and Blacks, 1915–1935* (Baltimore: Johns Hopkins,

1995); and Paul Berman, ed., *Blacks and Jews: Alliances and Arguments* (New York: Delacorte, 1994).

2. See, for example, Howard Brotz, *The Black Jews of Harlem: Negro Nationalism and the Dilemmas of Negro Leadership* (New York: Schocken, 1964); Israel Gerber, *The Heritage Seekers: American Blacks in Search of Jewish Identity* (Middle Village, N.Y.: Jonathan David, 1977); Yosef A. A. ben-Jochannan, *We the Black Jews* (Baltimore: Black Classic Press, 1993); Graenum Berger, *Black Jews in America: A Documentary with Commentary* (New York: Federation of Jewish Philanthropies, 1978); Elly M. Wynia, *The Church of God and the Saints of Christ: The Rise of Black Jews* (New York: Garland Publishing, 1994); and Sydney Freedberg, *Brother Love: Murder, Money and A Messiah* (New York: Pantheon, 1994).

3. For two important statements, see Stephen Carter, *The Culture of Disbelief: How American Law Trivializes Religious Devotion* (New York: Basic Books, 1993), and Robert Bellah et al., *Habits of the Heart: Individualism and Commitment in American Life* (Berkeley: University of California Press, 1985).

4. See Salo W. Baron, "Ghetto and Emancipation," *Menorah Journal* 14 (June 1928), pp. 515–26.

5. Malcolm X, with Alex Haley, *The Autobiography of Malcolm X* (New York: Ballantine Books, 1992), p. 372.

6. Several contemporary African American Hebrew congregations are featured in a photographic essay by Chester Higgins, Jr., "In the Spirit of Abraham," *CommonQuest* 3.1 (Winter 1998), pp. 20–31. On the current adoption of Jewish traditions by a Guyanese Christian church in New York, see Nadine Brozan, "Finding Room for More Than One Faith at Passover Table," *New York Times*, April 2, 1999, p. 6.

7. The objection may be raised that some subjects do not belong in the same section; after all, how much does a black convert to Orthodox Judaism share with a Hebrew Israelite, and what connection does Martin Luther King, Jr., have with either a Voudouisant or a Catholic in Haiti? Yet we have chosen to combine these disparate subjects precisely in order to show the complexity and fluidity of religious categories that may appear to be fixed. We hope that after one reads the essays in this volume it will be more difficult to define simply and narrowly what it means to be Jewish, Christian, or Muslim.

PART I

African American Jews and Israelites

After the turn of the twentieth century, blacks began to transform one of the most deeply rooted tropes in African American religiosity: the spiritual identification with biblical Israel. Historically, black Christians had embraced a typological or metaphorical relationship with Israel but did not claim to be physical descendants of the ancient Israelites. This position changed with the establishment of African American sects like the Church of God and the Saints of Christ in 1896, and later, Prophet Cherry's Church of the Living God, Pillar of Truth for All Nations. These and other groups heralded a new phenomenon in African American religion, popularly known as "black Judaism." The essays in this section explore a cross-section of African American groups and individuals that embrace some form of Jewish or Hebrew/Israelite identity.

In some traditions the identification initially assumed allegorical dimensions, as is discussed by Yvonne Chireau in her piece on African American religious encounters with Judaism from 1790 to 1930. Later, black Americans began to affirm their connection to ancient Israel as members of a larger, worldwide Jewish community. Bernard Wolfson describes more recent expressions of this affiliation in his chapter on African Americans in the Alliance of Black Jews. The final two essays in this section examine a contemporary community, the Original Hebrew Israelites of Jerusalem or the Hebrew Israelites, who have established a thriving community in Israel, where they began to settle in 1969 after a sojourn in Liberia.

Merrill Singer conducted his research in the 1970s, at a time when the Hebrew Israelites believed that they were the only true descendants of biblical Israel and that Jews were "imposters." Singer argues that although the Hebrew Israelites succeeded in creating an empowering alternative to the racist environment of 1960s America, they also established a community with an inegalitarian hierarchy of its own. The author of the second essay, Ethan Michaeli, visited the Hebrew Israelite community in Dimona, Israel, nearly twenty years later and discovered a dramatically different situation; in the intervening years the Hebrew Israelites developed a more inclusive ideology. Michaeli also found a community that has improved its relations with the Israeli government and addressed its own internal tensions. Whereas the leadership had once been suspicious of white Jews and denied their legitimacy, they now included some white Jews in their collective "Chosen People."

1

Black Culture and Black Zion

African American Religious Encounters with Judaism, 1790–1930, an Overview

Yvonne Chireau

The time has come, it seems to me . . . for an earnest propaganda of Judaism: and I would earnestly plead for Africa . . . and entreat Israel to remember that land of their sojourn and early training, to assist Ethiopia to stretch forth her hands unto God.

The Jewish Question (1898)

These words, written by the illustrious pan-African intellectual Edward Wilmot Blyden, echo one of the most prominent themes in black religious thought from the nineteenth century onward: Ethiopianism, the prophesied redemption of Africa, a mission that was to be accomplished through the efforts of black Americans. Blyden, who in his later years became a passionate defender of Islam, initially found in the Jewish doctrine of Zionism an implicit affirmation of his belief in the spiritual destiny of African Americans. To Blyden, the sons and daughters of Africa everywhere in the diaspora—like the Jews—possessed a special charge as religious exemplars for the rest of humanity. Believing that Jewish aspirations for nationhood were comparable to those of blacks, Blyden hoped that some day African Americans would return to their motherland in order to aid, uplift, and restore her to her former glory. As for Zionism, Blyden argued that the significance of that movement extended far beyond the worldly promise of Jewish statehood. The Jews were "qualified by the unspeakable suffering of ages to be the leaders," he wrote, "not in politics but in religion," and best suited at "propagating the international religion" by which persons of "all races, climes, and countries [could] call upon the one Lord." Advocating a kinship between blacks and Jews, Blyden went so far as to suggest that Africa might be a productive site for both to begin the "higher and nobler work" of the uplift of humankind to which both peoples had been called.[1]

Edward Wilmot Blyden envisioned a corresponding role for blacks and Jews in the fulfillment of an unfolding, divine plan. But even he did not foresee the innovative relationships that would be forged as African Americans appropriated ideas and resources from Judaism for the construction of their own religious identities. This essay considers black–Jewish encounters in the United States from 1790 to 1930, a significant period in the formation of new religious traditions and institutions in Afro-America. The products of these black–Jewish encounters were quite varied, ranging from black Christians' identification with the enslaved "Hebrew Children" in the eighteenth and nineteenth centuries to the typological association of African American Jews as the descendants of the twelve tribes of Israel in the twentieth. In these and other aspects of black belief and practice, Judaism contributed significantly to the character of African American religious life.

With regard to the variety of religious encounters between African Americans and Judaism, one must consider two recurring themes. The first is analogies in the experiences of blacks and of the Jewish people, including their common histories of dispersion, bondage, persecution, and emancipation. These analogies facilitated the various adaptations of Judaism within black religion, including the adoption of the language and symbols of the Hebrew Scriptures, and the unique formulations of ritual within Afro-Jewish practices. The second theme concerns the self-delineation of black people as Jews, either by an inherited bicultural heritage or by the appropriation of Jewish accoutrements, underscoring the significance of Judaism as a viable source of black American identity. Although these themes may not represent all manifestations of the historical relationship between black religion and Judaism, they do acknowledge the convergence of these traditions, often occurring in experiences that are more complex and multifaceted than is suggested by the designation "black Jews."[2]

Allegorical Associations

Analogies in the experiences of blacks and Jews have produced important models for the study of African American religion. Parallels can be seen in the language describing the two groups' respective histories. The concept of diaspora, for example, which has traditionally referred to the global dispersion of the Jews among the gentile nations, also describes the voluntary and involuntary migrations of blacks from Africa to Asia, the Middle East, Europe, and the Americas for over four centuries in the modern era. Whereas interpretations of the black diaspora as analogous to that of the Jews can be seen in American writing as early as the nineteenth century, conventional uses of the term coincide with the establishment of African and African American history as fields of academic study in the 1970s. Yet during this time few texts utilized what could be considered a diasporic approach to black American religion.[3]

Although both Africans and Jews would face dispersion, exile, and persecution in the modern period, earlier episodes in the Jewish past assumed particular significance for the descendants of African peoples in the United States. Unlike Jewish immigrants, the Africans who were brought to North America did not possess a unified spiritual heritage or a single sacred myth of their origins. It was in part the influence of Christianity that brought African bondspersons, who represented diverse ethnic backgrounds, into a recognition of what they perceived to be a shared, communal history. Christianity provided what E. Franklin Frazier, in *The Negro Church in America* (1964), termed a new "basis of social cohesion" for enslaved Africans, who had been torn from their lands of origin, their kin, and their indigenous religious institutions. The conversion of numbers of slaves during the Protestant revivals in late eighteenth- and early nineteenth-century America facilitated the formation of cultural frameworks by which black people began to construct a collective identity. As they made Christianity their own, African Americans gave meaning to the ordeal of slavery by highlighting the correspondences between their own experiences and those of the biblical Jews. These analogies would have very real implications for the development of black religion in the United States.

African American religion in this early stage was informed by ideas, images, and characters appropriated from the Hebrew Bible. Interpretations of the Hebrew Bible provided the substance for many of the innovations that distinguished Afro-Christianity from its white counterparts. While all Protestants adhered to a faith tradition that was nurtured by an understanding of the Old and the New Testaments as holy Scripture, African American Christians possessed a special affinity for the canon of Hebrew texts, including the Psalms and Proverbs, the apocalyptic books of the prophets, and the narrative accounts of Israel's formative history. Enslaved and free black converts to Christianity in the antebellum period engaged these biblical sources through practices such as prayer, preaching, and devotional song.

Studies from a variety of academic disciplines—from theology and history to ethnomusicology and religious studies—have given attention to the profound influence of the Old Testament in the lives of black Americans.[4] Lawrence Levine, in *Black Culture and Black Consciousness: Afro-American Folk Thought from Slavery to Freedom* (1978), argues that the Bible was central to the creation of African Americans' sacred world. In a discussion of the spirituals, Levine writes that "the essence of slave religion cannot be fully grasped without understanding [the] Old Testament bias":

> Daniel and David and Joshua and Moses and Noah, all of whom fill the lines of the spirituals, were delivered in this world and delivered in ways which struck the imagination of the slaves. Over and over their songs dwelt upon the spectacle of the Red Sea opening to allow the Hebrew slaves past before inundating the mighty armies of the Pharaoh. They lingered delightedly upon the image of little David humbling the great Goliath with a stone.... They retold in endless variation the stories of the blind and humbled Samson bringing down the mansions of his conquerors; of the ridiculed Noah patiently building the ark which would deliver him from the doom of a mocking world; of the timid Jonah attaining freedom from his confinement

> through faith. The similarity of these tales to the situation of the slaves was too clear for them not to see it. . . . "O my Lord delivered Daniel," the slaves observed, "O why not deliver me, too?"[5]

Religiously inventive, enslaved black Christians selected those parts of the Hebrew Bible that affirmed their experiences both as persons of faith and as an oppressed race. The slaves believed themselves to be another Israel, a people who toiled in the "Egypt" of North America but who were providentially guided by the same God who had led the Jews into the Promised Land. Projecting their own lives into Old Testament accounts, African Americans recast their destiny in terms of the consummation of a divine drama, the event of the Exodus. For African Americans, notes historian of religions Charles Long in *Significations: Signs, Symbols, and Images in the Interpretation of Religion* (1986), the Exodus was powerfully invested with religious meaning. "The deliverance of the Children of Israel from the Egyptians," Long observes, "became an archetype which enabled the slave to live with promise." Looking ahead to their ultimate day of deliverance, African Americans participated in a reenactment of the Jewish past, claiming Jewish history as *their* sacred history, a history in which the biblical world was inextricably bound with the present, in which the future carried the promise of freedom.[6]

Enslaved black Christians also fashioned vernacular practices out of Old Testament sources, expressing their most ardent beliefs and ultimate concerns in oral traditions. The spirituals, for example, forged in the oral cultural milieu, made consistent use of biblical imagery. In song, bondspersons declared the dual hardships of enslavement and the burdens of the believer's walk. The spiritual "Wrestling Jacob" testified of endurance and struggle as the keys to righteousness; "Didn't My Lord Deliver Daniel" recognized human suffering and God's presence therein; "Blow Your Trumpet, Gabriel" celebrated the promise of future rewards, and "Steal Away" and "I Am Going to Canaan Land" imparted conspiratorial allusions to freedom to otherworldly lyrics. Finally, the classic spiritual "Go Down, Moses" provided the quintessential explication of the slaves' identification with Israel, alluding to the history that both shared, as retold in the Exodus narrative:

> Go down Moses
> Way down in Egyptland
> Tell old Pharaoh
> To let my people go.[7]

Old Testament imagery also infused African American ritual experiences. Black Christians brought the Hebrew Bible to life in African-based practices that had been preserved for generations within the slave community. In liturgical traditions such as the Ring Shout—the circular, ecstatic performance that often accompanied slave prayer and worship meetings—bondspersons revisited African practices of spirit possession and ceremonial dance. In the Ring Shout, Levine has argued, time was ritually abolished and recreated, and the present was extended back to the past and into the mythic realm of the Old Testament. "[t]he slaves created a new world," he notes, "by transcending the narrow confines of the one in which they were forced to live." In these moments of transcendence, the boundaries between sacred and profane were effaced, as black worshippers dramatized pivotal events in early Jewish history, such as the Israelites' liberation and triumphant departure out of Egypt, their momentous crossing over the River Jordan, and their victorious, martial procession around the walls of Jericho. Long after slavery had ended, African Americans continued to enshrine events and persons from the Bible in their vernacular traditions. The Hebrew leader Moses has been perhaps the most frequently appropriated Old Testament personality in black folk thought. Moses was valorized in the life of Harriet Tubman, the "Moses of her people"; he was immortalized in the legacy of Marcus Garvey, the "Black Moses" who was to lead and uplift the entire African race; and he was mythologized in African American folklore as a powerful conjurer of the supernatural arts. Moses' prominence derived from the correspondence of his biblical role as a liberator with that of numerous hero figures in black culture.[8]

The Old Testament also provided important referents for the creation of written verse, as seen in the voluminous antislavery writings of African American clergy and laypersons prior to the antebellum era. By the late 1700s black Americans were engaged in a tradition of producing letters known as *black jeremiads*, a form of protest literature that challenged racial injustice with predictions of divine judgment, impending disaster, and strident calls for repentance. Wilson Moses, in *Black Messiahs and Uncle Toms* (1983), argues that the African American jeremiadic tradition, which was named for the sixth-century Hebrew prophet, manifested elements of an insurgent nationalist ideology. African Americans who adopted the rhetorical formulary of the black jeremiad included Prince Hall, the eighteenth-century founder of the black Freemasons; the Afro-feminist lecturer Maria Stewart; and clergy such as Absalom Jones and Richard Allen of the African Methodist Church, the first independent black denomination in the United States. Frequently utilized by African American orators, the jeremiad was a vehicle of protest in late eighteenth- and early nineteenth-century America, rivaled only by later appropriations of the prophet Isaiah, whose messianic proclamations were linked to redemptive suffering in twentieth-century black Christian theology.[9]

Although the Exodus account provided an enduring model for black Americans, there were other analogies with Jewish experience that were given prominent expression in African American religious thought. In particular, the concept of "chosenness" captured the spiritual imagination of blacks. Enslaved African American Christians in the antebellum era had conceived of themselves as a chosen people through their identification with the biblical Jews. The idea of chosenness was further reinforced in the decades following Emancipation, when it appeared that the Promised Land would remain perpetually out of reach. By the end of the nineteenth century, black chosenness would be conflated with African American understandings of historical destiny, as articulated in the text of Psalm 68:31, "Princes shall come out of Egypt and Ethiopia shall soon stretch forth her hands unto God." This ancient biblical prophecy became the paradigm by which an entire generation of clergy and theologians fathomed God's providential design in allowing the oppression of the black race, and it became, according to Albert Raboteau, "the most quoted verse in African American religious history."[10]

The notion of chosenness, or divine favor of a particular people, would be articulated in a variety of ways by African Americans in the United States and abroad during the late nineteenth and early twentieth centuries. Ethiopianism—the name that was given to this racialist discourse—gave a powerful philosophical impetus to movements as diverse as Marcus Garvey's Universal Negro Improvement Association, the Nation of Islam, and the Ras Tafarian Brethren in Jamaica. At the heart of Ethiopianism was the belief that the descendants of the inhabitants of Africa (Ethiopia) were specially selected to effect God's great plan of redemption. This variation on the Jewish idea of the chosen people allowed for a unique understanding of history and the agonizing injustices that African Americans had endured. Yet in a departure from the Jewish conception of chosenness, the Ethiopian doctrine did not posit that the sufferings of African Americans had been brought upon them as a consequence of their unfaithfulness, or by their breach of the divine covenant. The meaning of Psalm 68:31 was interpreted according to the exceptional mandate that it gave African Americans, for out of their afflictions would come greatness, the restoration of Africa to its former glory among nations, and the spiritual and social uplift of the entire black race. The unification and redemption of African people was to be accomplished through the sustained labors of New World blacks, who would return to the motherland as preachers and teachers, carrying with them the elevating power of Christianity. Ethiopianism thereby provided the theological rationale for the endeavors of numerous African American churches and missionary associations in the latter part of the nineteenth century, and it undergirded the ideology of secular black nationalism in the century to come.[11]

Interpretations of the Ethiopian prophecy vacillated between particularistic ideas of black people as the chosen elect, to universalistic perspectives that suggested that all of humankind would be saved during the advent of a new millennial phase of history in which blacks would play a vital role. The theme of choseness was given a distinctive slant within African American formulations of Judaism. In the traditions of black Jewry that would emerge in the early twentieth century, the emphasis upon chosenness fostered a definition of race which allowed blacks to counter the assaults of Anglo-American supremacy and the stigma of African American inferiority. Ultimately, the Old Testament, which had been the principal resource for African American appropriations of Judaism, came to be understood by many blacks as a literal presentation of the history of the African people—as the true Jews.

Blacks as Jews

Directly before the turn of the twentieth century, African Americans' identification with Judaism acquired additional elements. In black American religious discourse, the rhetoric of chosenness that had pervaded biblical Ethiopianism was supplemented with several important features. After 1900 a plethora of groups who characterized themselves as black Jews, black Hebrews, and black Israelites expanded the metaphorical kinship between black religion and Judaism so as to encompass racial dimensions. In many of these new black–Jewish religious groups, not only were the symbols and images of Judaism employed allegorically, but Jewish practices led to the construction of new identities by which blacks literally *became* Jews.

One of the first communities to which the designation "black Jews" was applied was the Church of God and the Saints of Christ (also known as the Temple Beth-el congregations), established in Lawrence, Kansas, in 1896 by William Saunders Crowdy. Crowdy, a former Baptist preacher, called his congregations "tabernacles" and embedded select Jewish beliefs and practices within a format that was similar to that of a Christian church. This group's appropriation of Judaism constituted what some writers have characterized a Hebraic-Christian or Judeo-Christian formation, in which aspects of Old Testament tradition were integrated with Christian elements. Like several other African American groups that were organized shortly after the turn of the twentieth century, such as Prophet Frank S. Cherry's Church of the Living God—Pillar and Ground of Truth for All Nations in Philadelphia, and Elder Warren Robinson's Temple of the Gospel of the Kingdom, Ever Live and Never Die Church in New York City,[12] the Church of God adopted Jewish customs that may have been based upon a literal interpretation of Old Testament rites. Members of the Church of God, for instance, maintained the office of the rabbinate, celebrated Passover, and observed a Saturday sabbath while incorporating New Testament principles, emphasizing the works of Jesus Christ and his teachings, and practicing rituals such as baptism. This pattern of selecting components of Judaism and preserving theological and doctrinal perspectives from Christianity was typical of a number of groups in the the early establishment of black Jewish communities in the United States.[13]

Many of the early black Jewish groups encouraged their followers to make a conscious break with certain aspects of their heritage while retaining others. Name transformation, or the rejection of the terms "Negro" and "black" in favor of "Hebrew," was one strategy by which some blacks signified Judaism as a racial classification. African Americans who identified as Jews defined themselves not only in opposition to whites, but against other blacks, and especially black Christians. Prophet Cherry, for example, leader of the Church of the Living God in Philadelphia, frequently castigated black clergy, calling them "damn fools" and "vultures," while Rabbi Wentworth Matthew of the Commandment Keepers Congregation in Harlem ridiculed what he called "niggeritions," religious activities such as shouting and speaking in tongues, which were seen as the stereotypical mannerisms of Afro-Christian revivalists. While such practices were repudiated as incompatible with African American Jewish identity, other unique elements appearing in black Jewish worship, such as oral preaching and instrumental rhythm (with Cherry), or Conjure healing practices (Matthew), revealed a creative synthesis of Jewish styles with compatible religious cultural traditions that were readily familiar to many black Americans.[14]

A number of African American Jewish congregations were established between 1908 and 1925, a period coinciding with the Great Migration, when vast numbers of black southerners relocated to northern urban centers in the United States. Prior to this period many black Americans had had little or no personal interaction with Jews or Jewish culture. Although there is evidence that relationships between African Americans and Jews during the slavery period resulted in a few conversions by blacks—such as "Old Uncle Billy," a bondsman in antebellum Charleston, South Carolina, whose experiences were widely documented—most African American encounters with the Jewish religion during the nineteenth century, as we have seen, consisted of figurative interpretations of biblical sources. By the second decade of the twentieth century, however, black appropriations of Judaism showed evidence of contact with members of a larger, international Jewish community that included Sephardic, Ashkenazic, and Ethiopian Jews. These contacts played an important role in revitalizing African American Jewish traditions and helping to create the new religious identities that further distinguished black Jews from their white counterparts.[15]

In the mid-1920s African American Jewish congregations were formed in the cities of Washington D.C., Philadelphia, Chicago, and New York, and in New Jersey. Converging patterns of emigration may have contributed to the proliferation of black Jewish groups in the cities. It is possible that black migrants arriving from South America and the West Indies carried Jewish beliefs and practices from countries where Judaism had been established long before European Jews entered the United States in any significant numbers. As early as the seventeenth century, for example, Sephardic Jews from Spain, Portugal, and the Netherlands had founded settlements in the northern regions of Latin America, Central America, and the Caribbean. Intermarriage between diasporic Jews, black slaves, and freepersons were not uncommon in these areas; out of these unions emerged some of the first African American converts to Judaism in the Western hemisphere. The influx of West Indian and South American blacks, and later migrations of Jews from Eastern Europe, may have resulted in greater exposure of black Americans to Judaism, especially given the close residential proximity of all of these groups in urban ghettos during the first few decades of the twentieth century.[16]

Some black Jews in the new urban communities were consistent in their understanding of Judaism as a religion with a special appeal to African American people. This emphasis may have derived from the strong nationalist orientation of some black Jewish leaders and their constituents. Rabbi Mordecai Herman, a member of

FIGURE 1.1 *Rabbi Arnold J. Ford with members of the UNIA choir and Congregation Beth B'nai Abraham, 1925. Courtesy Corbis/Underwood and Underwood.*

Marcus Garvey's Universal Negro Improvement Association (UNIA) and organizer of the Moorish Zionist Temple of New York, was one of the first African Americans to endorse the establishment of a shared homeland for black Jews and others in Palestine. Another African American rabbi, Arnold Josiah Ford (fig. 1.1), was particularly active in the Garvey movement at Liberty Hall, the New York headquarters of the UNIA. Both Herman and Ford recruited Garveyites into their respective congregations, which included a sizable contingent of West Indian immigrants. Racial exclusivism, informed by Garvey's brand of black nationalism and the older ideals of Ethiopian destiny, came to be a dominant feature of African American Judaism during this formative period.[17]

Some African Americans self-identified as Jews by claiming ties to an exclusive lineage whose roots, many alleged, were in Africa, the spiritual source from which Judaism had emerged. A corollary to these assertions was the claim that Africa was the geographical foundation—the land that had produced the Jewish religion—and that black people had lost knowledge of their ancestral heritage because of the traumas of slavery and social intermixture. Possessing a hereditary right to Judaism, all blacks were therefore obligated to reclaim their religion and their culture. A variety of embellishments on the theme of African Hebrew origins were advanced within black Jewish traditions. Some leaders conjectured that the African lineage of the Jews could be identified in the "Hebrewisms" in African culture, such as the symbol of the shield of David, found inscribed on West African artifacts, or could be traced to similar linguistic elements or to parallels between indigenous African and Jewish rituals and concepts of law. Others provided biblical explanations for their claims. Prophet Cherry cited his interpretation of disparate verses from the Old Testament that attested to the primacy of blacks in Judaism with a racialized theology, which conceived of both God and Jesus Christ as black. Yet unlike others who came after him, Cherry did not teach of the Jews' African origins but conjectured, according to one of his followers, that black people "were chased out of Palestine by the Romans into the west coast of Africa" and ultimately were "captured and sold" as slaves to America.[18]

It appears that denial of the veracity of "white" Jewish traditions was requisite to the construction of a new, racialized religious identity for many African American Jews. The assertion that Judaism was uniquely suited to black people went hand in hand with the claim by some black Jews that Jews of European ancestry were in fact frauds or "interlopers." Prophet Cherry, for example, often quoted Revelation 3:9 ("Behold, I will make those of the synagogue of Satan who say that they are Jews and are not, but lie, behold, I will make them come and bow down before your feet and learn that I have loved you") in support of his belief that white Jews were religious impostors. Rabbi Arnold Ford taught that the "real" Jews were black people, while Jews of European descent were said to be "offshoots" of the original lineage of black Jews or converts who had received the religion secondhand from Africans. Black Jewish dogma, as represented by the statements of these leaders, expounded tenets of spiritual and cultural provenance that foreshadowed the beliefs of later religious movements with racially exclusive, nationalist concerns, such as the Nation of Islam.[19]

The idea that black American Jews were descendants of the ancient tribes of Israel was corroborated by an elaborate schema that chronicled the beginnings of humanity, the genealogy of the Hebrew people, and the origins of racial categories. Focusing on etiological elements of biblical texts, some black Jewish interpreters formulated mythologies that explained color difference. While detailing the "anthropology of the Ethiopian Hebrews," Rabbi Wentworth Matthew once described how according to the Bible, blacks were directly descended from Abraham. "Isaac, son of Abraham, was father of Esau, he explained, "whose skin was hairy, like the white man's . . . and of Jacob . . . whose skin was smooth, like the black man's." Similarly, Prophet Cherry explicated a passage in II Kings 5:27, his interpretation of the story of a leprous curse placed by God upon the first white man, Gehazi, an act that resulted in his pale skin coloring. This interpretation directly countered one of the most widely held myths in Western Christianity—the so-called Curse of Ham—which told of Noah's condemnation of his grandson Canaan (Genesis 9 and 10), an account that was seen by many as providing divine sanction for the enslavement of blacks. African American Jews expounded their own myths, which had specific application to the situation of black people in the United States. Their beliefs were informed by internally produced values and the communal recognition of their cultural distinctiveness.[20]

The premise that the original Israelites were Africans was reflected in early twentieth century scholarly literature. Some of these studies, such as Joseph Williams's *Hebrewisms of West Africa from the Nile to the Niger with the Jews* (1930) and Allen Godbey's *The Lost Tribes: A Myth* (1930), established the African roots of Judaism by demonstrating commonalities between the religion of the Israelites and that of indigenous peoples in sub-Saharan African societies.[21] The veneration of Africa as the source of Judaism was informed not only by the historical significance of Africa in black American thought, but by the discovery of Ethiopian Jews, whose presence had been documented as early as the eighteenth century. For black Jews in the United States, it would appear that the Ethiopians provided the vital link that substantiated many of their claims to racial and religious solidarity with Africa. Both black and white Jews in the United States would seek to establish relations with the Ethiopian *Beta Yisroel*, known also as the Falashas, whose practice of Judaism, it was believed, was so ancient as to have predated the compilation of the Mishnah and the Talmud.[22]

To be sure, the self-understanding of one of the largest and best-known black Jewish congregations in New York City, the Commandment Keepers Congregation of Harlem, was inspired by the legacy of Ethiopian Judaism. Rabbi Wentworth Arthur Matthew, founder of the Commandment Keepers and its associated lodge, the Royal Order of Ethiopian Hebrews, viewed the Ethiopians as the progenitors of the black Jews in America. An implicit link between African Americans and the ancient heritage of the Ethiopian Jews provided the basis of Matthew's identification. Matthew, a West Indian citizen who was himself born in Africa, held that black Jews in America were actual kin to the Jews of Ethiopia, who had descended from the lineage established by King Solomon and the Queen of Sheba, as related in the biblical account of 1 Kings 10 and II Chronicles 9. Armed with the knowledge of an indigenous, African-based Judaism, Matthew and other black Hebrews in the United States would strive to legitimate their Jewish heritage in response to critics and outsiders who had expressed skepticism and hostility toward them and their claims.

The discovery of the *Beta Yisroel* stimulated hope among some black Jews in the possibility of creating an African American colony in Africa. Although alluding to all of Africa and not just the modern East African state, the idea of "Ethiopia," as we have seen, had been the locus of black American visions of destiny in the nineteenth century. In the early twentieth century Marcus Garvey sharpened the rhetoric of Ethiopianism by producing a broadly appealing vision of "Africa for Africans," in order to mobilize an international movement. But it was Arnold Ford, the African

American rabbi who was instrumental in the formation of several black Jewish congregations in New York in the 1920s, who would successfully pull together the disparate strands of cultural and religious sentiment into a practical program. Sustained by his dedication to Judaism as well as his political commitment to Garveyism, Ford would be the first black American to emigrate in order to found a homeland, a black Jewish Zion, in Ethiopia.[23]

Arnold Josiah Ford was one of black Judaism's most influential leaders. Born and raised in Barbados, he migrated to the United States at the end of the First World War, as did many other Afro-Caribbeans during the heyday of the Garvey movement. He immersed himself in the cultural milieu of postwar black New York, performing as a jazz artist, serving as choirmaster for the UNIA, and authoring the Universal Ethiopian Hymnal for the Garvey movement (fig. 1.2). Ford's compositions displayed his diverse linguistic skills, showing influences from Jewish, Christian, Islamic, and African sources. Many of his hymns also evoked the biblical analogies between black Americans and the Jews and promoted the doctrine of Ethiopianism, as was evident in several lyrics in which the redemption of Africa was a prominent theme. But Ford's interests extended far beyond his artistic talents. In 1923 he accepted the rabbinate of Beth B'nai Abraham (House of the Sons of Abraham), a black Hebrew congregation in Harlem. Fluent in Hebrew and Yiddish, Ford studied the Torah and the Talmud under the tutelage of some white Jews who were liberal patrons of the modest network of integreted synagogues and Hebrew schools in New York City. Ford would eventually devote his full energy to his emigration plan, which had developed partly as a natural extension of his pan-African sensibilities and partly out of his ardent desire to establish a black Jewish homeland. He organized two associations to help further this goal: the Progressive Corporation, a business enterprise aimed at supporting African American industry and technical development in Africa, and the Aurienoth Club, which was comprised of black professionals who supported African emigration.[24]

In November 1930, with the financial backing of Beth B'nai Abraham, the Aurienoth Club, and members of the Commandment Keepers congregation, Ford set out as an official delegate to the coronation of Emperor Haile Selassie in Ethiopia. Reestablishing himself in the Ethiopian capital of Addis Ababa, over the next three years Ford persisted in his efforts to secure territory for the black Jewish community. Between 1931 and 1932 some 60 members of Beth B'nai Abraham would follow him to Africa, many hoping to settle an 800 acre area north of Lake Tana, in the province inhabited by the *Beta Yisroel*, which had been set aside by the Ethiopian government. However, even as his status as unofficial leader of the emerging community of African Americans in Ethiopia was confirmed, Ford was not able to realize his dream of creating a black Jewish colony. In 1934, after a brief illness, he died, on the eve of the outbreak of the Italo-Ethiopian War. In New York Rabbi Wentworth Arthur Matthew would take up the mantle of leadership among the black Jews, and for nearly four decades he continued to teach his community of their

FIGURE 1.2 *Arnold Ford. From the frontispiece from the Universal Ethiopian Hymnal, 1922. Courtesy of the Schomburg Center for Research in Black Culture, Manuscripts, Archives and Rare Books Division, New York Public Library, Astor, Lenox and Tilden Foundations*

Ethiopian heritage, promoting the vision of Judaism that he and Ford had shared among white and black American rabbis, their congregations, and other religious organizations.[25]

Black and Jewish religious interactions provide evidence of the eclectic strategies utilized by African Americans in the creation of new traditions. African American understandings of Judaism were informed by the social and political orientations of black people in the United States and were often embedded in African Americans' responses to the discrimination, violence, and exploitation that they had suffered in American society. Blacks understood and experienced the Jewish faith, as they did other religions, on their own terms. They made use of Jewish traditions, drawing upon their collective historical experiences as well as their own cultural resources. Whether African American identifications with Judaism were allegorical, as with the eighteenth- and nineteenth-century black Christians who assimilated the Hebrew Scriptures into their own sacred world, or were exegetical, as with the pervasive myth of Ethiopianism, they demonstrated selective, self-conscious, and creative appropriations of Jewish sources. Ultimately these appropriations facilitated the construction of alternative religious and racial identities.

As for Arnold Ford, as the first person to synthesize the themes that had historically characterized black and Jewish religious interactions, he had proven himself a pioneer. The issues of biblical interpretation, cultural identity, racial politics, black nationhood, and spiritual destiny that he engaged during his life would be continually revisited by African American Jews into the late twentieth century. As one historian has observed, "Ford's teachings were not only an interesting amplification of preceding traditions, but [they] were to mark the conceptual world of following generations." Arnold Ford and his party of black Hebrews returned to Africa, the promised land and the putative source of Judaism, in order to help Ethiopia "stretch forth her hands unto God." With their departure, black American encounters with Judaism had come full circle.[26]

Notes

1. Edward Wilmot Blyden, *The Jewish Question* (Liverpool, England: Lionel Hart, 1898), pp. 8, 21. On Blyden's understanding of "international religion," see Hollis Lynch, *Edward Wilmot Blyden, Pan-Negro Patriot, 1832–1912*, (New York: Oxford University Press, 1967); on Blyden and Judaism, see Lynch, "A Black Nineteenth-Century Response to Jews and Zionism: The Case of Edward Wilmot Blyden," in Joseph Washington, ed., *Jews in Black Perspectives: A Dialogue* (Boston: University Press of America, 1989), pp. 42–54. Blyden's recommendation of Africa as a potential location for Jewish settlement was revisited in a different context in 1903, when the British government offered 6,000 square miles of land in western Uganda to the Zionist movement. See Robert Weisbord, *African Zion: The Attempt to Establish a Jewish Colony in the East African Protectorate* (Philadelphia: Jewish Publication Society of America, 1968).

2. The historian James Tinney maintains that a distinction should be drawn between "Black Jews", "Black Hebrews," and "Black Israelites" as three representative forms of African American Judaism in the United States. He argues that "Black Jews" refers to those groups who adopt Jewish practices and traditions while maintaining a Christological perspective; "Black Hebrews" are more orthodox in their orientation to Judaism; and "Black Israelites," the most nationalist in their ideology, are, according to Tinney, "the farthest from traditional Judaism in beliefs and practices." See James Tinney, "Black Jews: A House Divided," *Christianity Today*, December 7, 1973, pp. 52–54.

3. An exception would be the work of the anthropologist Melville Herskovits, who adopted a diasporic or hemispheric perspective in his treatment of black religion in the United States. Herskovits considered continuities of African culture in the African American experience by formulating a "baseline" of African cultural retentions. See Melville Herskovits, *The Myth of the Negro Past* (Boston: Beacon Press, 1945), and *The New World Negro* (Bloomington: Indiana University Press, 1966). For a current consideration of black and Jewish "diasporas" see Paul Gilroy, *The Black Atlantic: Modernity and Double Consciousness*, Cambridge, Mass.: Harvard University Press, 1993), pp. 205–12. Other than "diaspora," a term that has been adopted from the Jewish experience and applied to black America is "holocaust," used recently in reference to the destruction of African cultures in the New World slave environment. See, for example, Jon Butler, *Awash in a Sea of Faith: Christianizing the American People* (Cambridge, Mass.: Harvard University Press, 1993), p. 154. On the diaspora model in historical research, see especially George Shepperson, "The African diaspora—or the African Abroad," *African Forum: A Quarterly Journal of Contemporary Affairs* 2 (1966), 76–93; and St. Clair Drake, "The Black Diaspora in Pan-African Perspective," *Black Scholar* 7 (September 1975), 2–14. For an essay that considers models of diaspora studies in religion, see Albert Raboteau, "African Religions in America: Theoretical Perspectives," in Joseph Harris, ed., *Global Dimensions of the African Diaspora* (Washington, D.C.: Howard University Press, 1993), pp. 65–79.

4. See Gayraud Wilmore, *Black Religion and Black Radicalism* (Garden City, N.Y.: Doubleday, 1973); Albert Raboteau, *Slave Religion: The Invisible Institution in the Antebellum South* (New York: Oxford University Press,1978); Cain Felder, *Stony the Road We Trod: African American Biblical Interpretation* (Minneapolis: Ausburg Fortress Publishers 1990); and Theophus Smith, *Conjuring Culture: Biblical Formations of Black America* (New York: Oxford University Press 1994) for approaches to Old Testament traditions as they have appeared in black Christian belief and practice.

5. Lawrence Levine, *Black Culture and Black Consciousness: Afro American Folk Thought from Slavery to Freedom* (New York: Oxford University Press, 1978), p. 50. On the spirituals as the "oral bible" of the slaves, see Harold Courlander, *Negro Folk Music, U.S.A.* (New York: Columbia University Press, 1963), pp. 36–43.

6. Charles Long, *Significations: Signs, Symbols, and Images in the Interpretation of Religion* (Philadelphia: Fortress Press, 1986), p. 179. The Hebrew Bible was also a source of inspiration for black resistance, as seen in the conspiracies of Gabriel Prosser, Nat Turner, and Denmark Vesey, in which Old Testament verses were read and interpreted by African Americans for their subversive antislavery meanings. See Timothy L. Smith, "Slavery and Theology: The Emergence of Black Christian Consciousness in Nineteenth-Century America," *Church History*, 41, no. 4, 1972; Vincent Harding, "Religion and Resistance Among Antebellum Negroes, 1800–1860," in *The Making of Black America*, vol. 1, ed. August Meier and Elliot Rudwick (New York: Athenaeum Press, 1969), pp. 179–97.

7. Early scholarly works that examined the black sacred musical tradition of the spirituals include W. E. B. DuBois' *The Souls of Black Folk* (New York: Saint Martins Press, 1997), and James Weldon and J. Rosamond Johnson's *Books of American Negro Spirituals* (New York: The Viking Press, 1925–1926); and R. Nathaniel Dett, *Religious Folk-Songs of the Negro as Sung at Hampton Institute* (Hampton, Va.: Hampton Institute Press, 1927). More recently, see Miles Mark Fisher, *Negro Slave Songs of the United States* (Ithaca: Cornell University Press,1953); Harold Courlander, Negro Folk Music, U.S.A. (New York: Columbia University Press, 1963); John Lovell, *Black Song: The Forge and the Flame* (New York: Macmillan, 1972); Dena Epstein, *Sinful Tunes and Spirituals* (Champaign: University of Illinois Press, 1977) and James Cone, *The Spirituals and the Blues* (Maryknoll: Orbis Books, 1991). As folklorists, ethnomusicologists, and historians have shown, African American spirituals are an unparalleled source for comprehending the interior modes and meanings of black religion.

8. Levine, *Black Culture and Black Consciousness*, p. 32. On time transposition in the black slave visionary experience, see Mechal Sobel, *Trabelin On: The Slave Journey to an Afro-Baptist Faith* (Princeton, N.J.: Princeton University Press, 1979), pp. 125–26. On the figure of Moses in black culture, see John Roberts, *From Trickster to Badman: The Black Folk Hero in Slavery and Freedom* (Philadelphia: University of Pennsylvania Press, 1989).

9. On the black jeremiad, see Wilson J. Moses, *Black Messiahs and Uncle Toms: Social and Literary Manipulations of a Religious Myth* (University Park, Penn.: Pennsylvania State University Press, 1982), pp. 30–48.

10. Albert J. Raboteau, "Ethiopia Shall Stretch Forth Her Hands: Black Destiny in Nineteenth Century America," in *A Fire in the Bones: Reflections on African American Religious History* (Boston: Beacon Press, 1995), p. 42.

11. On the confluence of Christianity, black nationalism, and the chosenness doctrine in biblical Ethiopianism, see St. Clair Drake, *The Redemption of Africa and Black Religion* (Chicago: Third World Press, 1970); Wilson Moses, *The Golden Age of Black Nationalism*, 1850–1925, (New York: Oxford University Press, 1988); Albert Raboteau, "Exodus, Ethiopia, and Racial Messianism: Texts and Contexts of African American Chosenness," in William Hutchinson and Hartmut Lehmann, *Many Are Chosen: Divine Election and Western Nationalism* (Minneapolis: Fortress Press, 1993). For an essay that considers the overlap of black and Jewish historical experiences and their similar conceptions of providential destiny, see also St. Clair Drake, "African Diaspora and Jewish Diaspora: Convergence and Divergence," in Joseph Washington, ed., *Jews in Black Perspectives: A Dialogue* (Lantham, Md: University Press of America, 1989).

12. Cherry's church was established in 1912, and the Temple of the Gospel of the Kingdom, Ever Live and Never Die was founded in 1917. Arthur Huff Fauset, *Black Gods of the Metropolis: Negro Religious Cults of the Urban North* (Philadelphia: University of Pennsylvania Press, 1944), pp. 31–40. On Elder Roberson, see Ruth Landes, "The Negro Jews of Harlem," *Jewish Journal of Sociology* 9, no. 2, (December 1967), 178–80. For a recent compilation of bibliographic sources on black Jewish sectarianism, see Sherry Sherrod DuPree, *African American Holiness Pentecostal Movement: An Annotated Bibliography* (New York: Garland Publishing, 1996), pp. 354–65.

13. The founding dates of the earliest black-Jewish congregations are in dispute. Shapiro notes that F. S. Cherry's Church of God was organized in Tennessee in 1886, but other sources do not confirm this date. Another group, the Moorish Zion Temple, founded in 1899 by a Rabbi Richlieu of Brooklyn, New York, was one of the earliest black Jewish congregations that did not combine Jewish and Christian beliefs, as did the Church of God and the Saints of

Christ. For a discussion of the origins of black Judaism in America, see Deanne Shapiro, "Factors in the Development of Black Judaism," in C. Eric Lincoln, ed., *The Black Experience in Religion* (Garden City, N.Y.: Anchor Doubleday, 1974); see also Howard Brotz, *The Black Jews of Harlem: Negro Nationalism and the Dilemmas of Negro Leadership* (London: The Free Press of Glencoe, 1964), p. 51. On Crowdy and the Church of God and the Saints of Christ, see Elly M. Wynia, *The Church of God and the Saints of Christ: The Rise of Black Jews* (New York: Garland Publishing, 1994); and Raymond Julius Jones, "A Comparative Study of Religious Cult Behavior Among Negroes with Special Reference to Emotional Group Conditioning Factors" (Washington, D.C.: Graduate School for the Division of the Social Sciences, Howard University, 1939).

14. Howard Waitzkin, "Black Judaism in New York," *Harvard Journal of Negro Affairs* 1, no. 3 (1967), 12–44; Brotz, *Black Jews of Harlem*, pp. 34–35; Fauset, *Black Gods of the Metropolis*, pp. 31–38.

15. On "Old Uncle Billy," see Ralph Melnick, "Billy Simons: The Black Jew of Charleston," *American Jewish Archives* 32 (1980), 3–8; Julius Eckman, "Old Billy: A Jewish Rechabite," *American Jewish Archives* 15 (April 1963), 3–5; Charles Reznikoff and Uriah Engleman, *The Jews of Charleston* (Philadelphia: Jewish Publication Society, 1950), p. 78, cited in Bertram Wallace Korn, "Jews and Negro Slavery in the Old South, 1789–1865," in Leonard Dinnerstein and Mary Dale Palsson, eds., *Jews in the South* (Baton Rouge: Louisiana State University Press, 1973), p. 115. On other cases of black converts to Judaism in the nineteenth century, see Graenum Berger, *Black Jews in America: A Documentary with Commentary* (New York: Commission on Synagogue Relations, Federation of Jewish Philanthropies of New York, 1978), pp. 11, 29–37.

16. Jacob Marcus, *The Colonial American Jew, 1492–1776* (Detroit: Wayne State University Press, 1970). On African American and Jewish social proximity, see Hasia Diner, *In the Almost Promised Land: American Jews and Blacks, 1915–1935*, (Baltimore: Johns Hopkins University Press, 1995).

17. Theodore Vincent, *Black Power and the Garvey Movement* (Berkeley, Cal.: Ramparts Press, 1971), pp. 134–35; Brotz, *Black Jews of Harlem*, p. 11. Randall Burkett notes that Prophet Cherry of the Church of the Living God in Philadelphia was also "directly linked" to the UNIA. See Burkett, *Garveyism as a Religious Movement: The Institutionalization of a Black Civil Religion* (Metuchen: Scarecrow Press, 1978), p. 182. The UNIA would be a consistent ideological influence upon the black Jews. However, a possible genealogical connection to African American Islam can also be seen, especially in the advent of the black Jewish congregations that were called "Moorish," similar to the immediate forerunner of the Nation of Islam, the Moorish Science Temple, a black Islamic sect founded in Newark, New Jersey, in 1913. In 1899 Rabbi Leon Richlieu established the Moorish Zion Temple in Brooklyn, and in 1921 Mordecai Herman or Mordecai Joseph reformed the Moorish Zionist Temple in Harlem, with affiliate branches in Newark and Philadelphia. See Shapiro, "Factors in the Development of Black Judaism," p. 266, and Landes, "The Negro Jews of Harlem," p. 181.

18. Kenneth King, "Some Notes on Arnold J. Ford and New World Black Attitudes to Ethiopia," in Randall K. Burkett and Richard Newman, eds., *Black Apostles: Afro-American Clergy Confront the Twentieth Century* (Boston: G.K. Hall, 1978), pp. 49–55; Fauset, *Black Gods of the Metropolis*, p. 115.

19. Elias Farajaje-Jones, *In Search of Zion: The Spiritual Significance of Africa in Black Religious Movements* (Bern: Peter Lang, 1990), p. 167; Deanne Shapiro, "Factors in the Development of Black Judaism," p. 268; Brotz, *The Black Jews of Harlem*, p. 56.

20. Brotz, *The Black Jews of Harlem*, p. 20; Roi Ottley, *New World A-Coming* (New York: Arno Press and The New York Times, 1969), p. 144; Fauset, *Black Gods of the Metropolis*, p. 34; Farajaje-Jones, *In Search of Zion*, p. 168. On the Curse of Ham, see Winthrop Jordan, *White Over Black: American Attitudes Toward the Negro* (New York: W.W. Norton, 1968), pp. 17–20.

21. More recent works that argue for widespread Judaic and Israelite influences in African religion include Yoseph A. A. ben-Jochannan, *We the Black Jews*, vols. 1 and 2, (Baltimore: Black Classics Press, 1993); Jose V. Malcion, *How the Hebrews Became Jews* (New York: UB Productions, 1978); Rudolph Windsor, *From Babylon to Timbuktu* (New York: Exposition Press, 1969); Rudolph Windsor and Steven Jacobs, *The Hebrew Heritage of Our West African Ancestors* (Wilmington, Del.: Rose-Lee, Inc., 1971); and Steven Jacobs, *The Hebrew Heritage of Black Africa* (Philadelphia: Boldlee Publishing, 1976).

22. Wolf Leslau, *Falasha Anthology: The Black Jews of Ethiopia* (New Haven, Conn.: Yale University Press, 1951), p. x. In 1949 Leslau first published his research on Ethiopian Judaism, called "The Black Jews of Ethiopia," in *Commentary* 7 (1949), 216–24, and later, *Falasha Anthology*, which made available to an English-speaking readership the writings of the Ethiopian Jewish community, including the Torah and other apocryphal literature written in Ge'ez, the ancient language of Ethiopia.

23. The desire to reclaim Africa had been present in the UNIA from its inception, and as early as 1919 the organization had begun to investigate the prospects of purchasing land for the colonization of Liberia. See John Henrik Clarke, ed., *Marcus Garvey and the Vision of Africa* (New York: Vintage Books, 1974). On Garvey and Ethiopianism, see Burkett, *Garveyism as a Religious Movement*.

24. William Scott, "Rabbi Arnold Ford's Back-to-Ethiopia Movement: A Study of Black Emigration, 1930–1935, *Pan African Journal* 8, no. 2 (Summer 1975), 191–202; Kenneth King, "Some Notes on Arnold J. Ford," pp. 50–53. The intersecting social and cultural worlds of black and white Jews within interracial synagogues, such as the Moorish Palestinian Talmud Torah Congregation in East New York or Rabbi Richlieu's Moorish Zionist Temple Society, is given brief attention in Arthur Dobrin, "A History of the Negro Jews in America" (unpublished paper, City College of the City University of New York, 1965; Schomburg Collection, New York Public Library), and in Landes, "Negro Jews in Harlem," pp. 184–187. More recently, black Jewish congregations that are recognized by the larger Jewish community include Adat Bayt Moshesh in New Jersey and Mount Horeb Congregation in New York City.

25. Scott, "Rabbi Arnold Ford's Back-to-Ethiopia Movement," pp. 194–200, and Scott, *Sons of Sheba's Race: African-Americans and the Italo-Ethiopian War, 1935–1941* (Bloomington: Indiana University Press, 1993), p. 183; Joseph E. Harris, *African American Reactions to War in Ethiopia, 1936–1941* (Baton Rouge: Louisiana State University Press, 1994), pp. 11–14; Landes, "Negro Jews in Harlem," pp. 184–85.

26. Farajaje-Jones, *In Search of Zion*, p. 171.

African American Jews

Dispelling Myths, Bridging the Divide

Bernard J. Wolfson

ON THE SECOND weekend of November in 1995, Rabbi Capers Funnye hosted a momentous meeting at his synagogue on Chicago's south side. He and a small group of other black Jews from around the country gathered there for a two-day conference to launch a new national organization. Funnye had met many of his visitors two years earlier at a symposium on black Jews sponsored by the California African-American Museum in Los Angeles.[1] They had remained in close contact since then, frequently lamenting their shared sense of isolation—but also contemplating their tremendous possibilities—in a society where hostility between blacks and Jews was widely viewed as the natural state of affairs. This weekend was the culmination of their ongoing conversations. The main idea was simply to have a kind of national coming out—a "Black Jews' debutante ball," as Funnye put it—to tell the world that being black and being Jewish were not mutually exclusive.[2] Funnye and his guests hoped to establish a permanent forum in which black Jews could simply find each other, share their experiences, and begin to foster a sense of common identity. The mere existence of such a group, they believed, would defy the prevailing notion that Jews were all white people of European descent. It would also challenge the conventional wisdom that blacks and Jews were mutually antagonistic, for that perception, while certainly not without some grains of truth, was based on the erroneous assumption that the two groups were entirely separate.

The black Jews who gathered at Funnye's synagogue that weekend all shared a strong commitment to both the black and the Jewish communities, as well as a desire to foster better communication between them. Yet they believed that white Ashkenazi Jews in the United States were fundamentally racist and had wrongly claimed Judaism as their own exclusive domain. They resented the idea that Jewishness could be circumscribed by skin color or by cultural trappings that were, after all, largely traceable to an accident of geography. They would stand up and declare that Judaism belonged to all those who embraced it. But there were significant differences, both cultural and religious, among the members of this group. Some were secular Jews, others were Reform or Conservative, one was an Orthodox convert.

There were children of marriages between white Jews and black non-Jews; others were Jewish on both sides of the family going back countless generations. And while Funnye's Beth Shalom B'nai Zaken Ethiopian Hebrew Congregation had a strong African American identity, most of his out-of-town guests belonged to more mainstream white Jewish congregations.

Those who were active in white Jewish communities lived in a kind of cultural limbo. They often felt excluded by fellow Jews who doubted their authenticity and by other blacks who viewed their Jewishness as a betrayal. Funnye's case was different. He had also been subjected to the probing skepticism of white Jews, but he did not experience a sense of tension between his black and Jewish selves. After all, he was regularly surrounded by other black Jews. His congregation had descended from a movement of self-proclaimed black Jews that formed in the 1920s and 1930s, rejecting Christianity as the religion of slavery. Funnye believed that his ancestors in Africa had been Jews before they were uprooted and forced to become slaves. By observing Judaism, he was simply reclaiming what was rightfully his. His Judaism was thus a reaffirmation and a celebration of his African heritage. For the others, however, being both black and Jewish was a kind of cultural dualism, with the two parts sometimes difficult to reconcile.

Clearly, then, those who attended the Chicago meeting came to the table with very different perspectives on what it meant to be black and Jewish. Indeed, it seemed quite possible that their religious, cultural, and political diversity might ultimately weigh them down and prevent their organization from blossoming. But they intended to bridge those differences. Their group would be a voice for all blacks who identified themselves as Jews.

After two days of meetings, punctuated by Sabbath services at Funnye's synagogue, the group announced that they had formed the Alliance of Black Jews. They held a small, impromptu press conference in the synagogue's main chamber, although only two reporters showed up for the event. Robin Washington, a Boston journalist who had been named executive chairman of the new alliance, read its rather broad mission statement: "To bring together people of African descent who believe in Torah and its mandates and/or who are culturally affiliated with Judaism." The alliance would be a forum for communication and self-education, reaching out to black Jews not only in the United States but worldwide. The group had originally planned to make the organization domestic in scope and name it the National Conference of Black Jews, but they changed their minds at the behest of Lily Golden, a rather imposing woman who defied classification. Golden was a black Russian Jew who had grown up in the Soviet Union and was now teaching African history and music at Chicago State University. She convinced her colleagues that they should reach out to black Jews throughout the world, so they changed the name of the organization to eliminate the implied geographical limits.

Golden, who wore a bright red pants suit and gray fur hat, was a tall, stout woman, not quite elderly yet slightly beyond middle age. She was the Soviet-born daughter of a black Mississippi agronomist and his Polish Jewish emigre wife, who had met in the American communist movement in the 1920s, moved to Uzbekistan in 1933, and never returned to the United States. Golden's father, a former student of George Washington Carver at the Tuskegee Institute in Alabama, had been invited by the Stalin government to advise the Uzbek republic on cotton production techniques. He and his wife decided to go, in large part because of the poisonous state of race relations in America. Lily Golden was thus a Soviet citizen of American descent, whose parents had emigrated to escape racial intolerance in the United States. She was born and raised in Uzbekistan and lived most of her adult life in Moscow, where she had taught before going to Chicago after glasnost.[3]

Growing up under Stalinism, Golden had never set foot in a synagogue, because they were all closed down about the time she was born. Funnye's Sabbath service was the first one she had ever attended. In her thick Russian accent, Golden explained how isolated she had felt growing up black and Jewish in Uzbekistan. "I felt I was unique. I didn't have an identity," she said. But during the weekend at Funnye's synagogue she had begun to feel she was not alone. "When we started talking, I found that a lot of these people felt the same way. It's important to find other people who are black Jews like you." Golden said she knew black Jews in Western and Eastern Europe who would be interested in joining the group, and she planned to contact them. There had also been inquiries from black Jews in Canada and New Zealand. In her view, the purpose of the alliance should be "to build bridges between people—all people." That meant whites and blacks, blacks and Jews, Jews and Jews. "There are a lot of differences among black Jews, too," she said. The founding members of the alliance believed they would demonstrate by their example the heterogeneity of Jewry worldwide. "There are more than just Jews of African descent," said Gabrielle Foreman, a professor of ethnic studies at Occidental College in Los Angeles, who was designated as one of two co-chairs for education. "There are many Latino Jews, Iranian Jews, Asian Jews—and we don't usually imagine that when we say Jewish. So we hope that our existence also opens up minds."

Bridging the Divide

The alliance would be a repository of information and a channel of communication not only for black Jews but for white Jews and black non-Jews as well. Its mere existence would help facilitate communication between the broader black and Jewish communities. "When we speak to black groups and we tell them what Jews think, those black groups don't think we're making it up," said Robin Washington, the newly appointed executive director. "We have no reason to be lying to them; we're black just like they are. And in a meeting with the American Jewish Committee, I told them what black folks were thinking. No one argued with me about the validity of that thought; a fellow Jew was in the room talking to them."

On that first day of its existence, the alliance issued a statement calling for dialogue between the white Jewish establishment and its arch-nemesis, Louis Farrakhan, the head of the Nation of Islam. Farrakhan had been dominating the headlines because of his Million Man March in Washington, D.C., a few weeks earlier, and the alliance unanimously endorsed the march. Rabbi Funnye was the group's conduit to the Nation of Islam. He and Farrakhan had a personal relationship dating back to when Funnye had publicly criticized the Nation of Islam leader for calling Judaism a "gutter religion." Funnye said he had felt "a great disdain" for Farrakhan until a Christian minister who knew both men brought them together to hash out their differences. "I expected to meet a guy with sweat and wild looking eyes, ready to pounce on me because how dare I call myself a Jew, and what am I doing with those Jews, and all that good stuff," Funnye recounted. "But that wasn't the case at all. We got past our rough spots. I told him I didn't appreciate Judaism being called a gutter religion, because Islam was the daughter of Judaism, as was Christianity, and if your momma's in the gutter, where can your daughter be? He laughed when I made that statement to him." Funnye said he and Farrakhan had maintained a regular dialogue ever since that first encounter. "When I sit at Louis Farrakhan's table and we break bread together, I'm Rabbi Funnye; he's Minister Farrakhan. And we are sitting and talking. Those members of the Nation of Islam whom I've met respect me as a rabbi," Funnye said. He claimed that Farrakhan had evolved to a more conciliatory stance and was ready for dialogue with the broader Jewish community. Funnye fervently believed it was incumbent on the Jewish establishment to meet the Nation of Islam halfway.

Although the alliance adopted Funnye's conciliatory approach, some of its members felt distinctly squeamish about Farrakhan. Michelle Stein-Evers, one of the driving forces behind the creation of the alliance,[4] was uncompromising in her hostility toward him. In lengthy conversations many months before the Chicago meeting she had condemned Farrakhan as harshly as any white Jew would have. "He's got an interesting tailor, but the structure of his soul needs working on," said Stein-Evers, who became the alliance's co-chair for membership. "Farrakhan is a street politician. He says what he has to say to keep his job," she added. "He went last summer and had dinner with some group of reform rabbis in order to 'facilitate dialogue,' and the same week he was doing that his newspaper was spewing out the same spew."

Stein-Evers's opinion of Louis Farrakhan may have borne some relation to the fact that, despite her chocolate brown skin and curly black hair, she felt in many ways more attuned to the white Jewish world than to the black non-Jewish one. Michelle was the daughter of an Ethiopian Jew and his southern white Jewish wife. Her mother's family had emigrated from Germany to the antebellum South in 1804, and her great-grandfather, a white German Jew, had been notorious for beating slaves to death on his Mississippi plantation during the middle decades of the nineteenth century. After her parents divorced, Stein-Evers was reared by her mother and maternal grandmother, and she spent most of her life among whites. In a brief narrative of her life, which she wrote for the 1993 symposium on black Jews, Stein-Evers recalled how her grandmother had given her "the proper southern but Prussian Jewish education for young ladies. I had piano lessons and deportment lessons and letterwriting, and visited the sick in hospitals and served old ladies iced tea."[5] Stein-Evers had had a rough go of it among blacks, because she made so few concessions to the trappings of African American culture. She laced her speech with Hebrew and Yiddish expressions and didn't, as she put it, "talk street." When she was a student at the University of Pennsylvania, she lived in a black section of Philadelphia and was threatened by neighbors who thought she was being "uppity." Luckily, a black friend intervened to protect her. "All my life I've been told, 'Why don't you talk like black people; why don't you dress like black people; why don't you believe like black people,'" Stein-Evers said. "There's an Orthodoxy about these things, and because I didn't conform to the Orthodoxy they would say, 'Hey, she's trying to be white.' But I wasn't trying to be white. I was just trying to be myself."

In this respect, there was clearly a stark contrast between the life experience of Stein-Evers and that of Rabbi Funnye, who was born into a family of African Methodist Episcopalians in South Carolina and grew up in black Chicago. Funnye identified strongly with black America, while Stein-Evers did not. And unlike Stein-Evers, Funnye was quick to defend Louis Farrakhan against the attacks of white Jewish groups. He condemned the Anti-Defamation League (ADL), which had recently taken full-page ads in the *New York Times* and other newspapers criticizing Farrakhan and the Million Man March. Funnye considered the ads to be racist and inflammatory. "It's beginning to get dangerous when the ADL starts comparing the Nation of Islam with the Ku Klux Klan," he said. "The KKK was an organization with a mission given to the destruction of the black people, and they physically did that. The Nation of Islam has never attacked any Jew; they've never castrated any Jewish man; they've never bombed any synagogue; they've never desecrated any Jewish cemetary. So for the ADL to make that kind of comparison is dangerous." Not only was Jewish fear misplaced, Funnye contended, but it was Farrakhan himself who was most likely to be the victim of any violence. "He's still a black man, an American black man who says some things that a lot of other people in America do not like. And because they don't like him and what he says, he's an endangered black man." But Funnye also made clear that Farrakhan did not speak for the whole black community and should not be allowed to set the agenda in black–Jewish or black–white relations. "His alienation cannot be our alienation," he said. By the same token, Jews should not let the presence of Farrakan obscure the essential meaning of the Million Man March. It wasn't about Farrakhan. "It was about the need felt by massive numbers of black men to say, 'Are we as bad as we're reading in the newspapers? Is all we do rape, plunder, and pillage in our communities? Is everybody a shiftless lazy ass, who won't work and care for the families they're making? Is the only thing we're fit for the penal system?' The picture that has been painted of the black man in America is not who the black man is, and that's why those men went to

Washington." Funnye hoped the Alliance of Black Jews could help bridge that perception gap. He also hoped it would facilitate a dialogue between Jewish and black leaders, including Farrakhan and the ADL. He said he would insist on a place at that table, "because the ADL is not the entirety of the Jewish community or of Jewish thought."

The Jewish Population Survey

In order to have the kind of influence its members hoped for, the alliance would need to grow beyond its embryonic size of little more than twenty individuals (fig. 2.1). Not only might their widely diverging perspectives slow their momentum, but they also faced some formidable logistical obstacles. For one thing, they were dispersed across the country—from Los Angeles to Chicago to Boston to New York. They were all busy with their own full-time pursuits and would have to squeeze the alliance into their crowded schedules. They would also need grants and other sources of financing to keep the organization going. Nonetheless, they expressed confidence that their ranks would swell over time. They all knew other black Jews who would be interested in joining. Robin Washington recalled that the Association of Black Journalists, to which he belonged, had started out with only a handful of pioneers and had grown to 3,000 members twenty years later. "And there are a lot more black Jews than black journalists," he said.

There certainly appeared to be a large pool of potential alliance members. Funnye and Robinson put the number of black Jews in the United States as high as 250,000, but that was probably an inflated figure. According to the Council of Jewish Federations' (CJF) 1990 National Jewish Population Survey, 2.4 percent of self-identified Jews, approximately 132,000, listed their race as black. A broader measure in the survey turned up 239,000 blacks who had some personal connection to Judaism.[6]

In many ways, this overlap between black and Jewish identities was quite natural. Through the 1960s, at least, there had been a sense of shared experience and identity between blacks and Jews. For both groups, the experience of living under constant threat from a hostile majority weighed heavily on the collective conscience.[7] Reuben Greenberg, the black Jewish police chief of Charleston, South Carolina, recalled that he had first been drawn to Judaism in the early 1960s, when he attended civil rights meetings in San Francisco that were frequently held in the synagogues of white Jewish congregations. "The civil rights movement in San Francisco, and in perhaps most other urban areas outside the South, was almost as much a Jewish movement as it was a black movement," Greenberg wrote. "It was both natural and, given the history of the Jews, logical for Jews to be involved in civil rights projects in proportions far exceeding their ratio to the overall population."[8] In fact, the civil rights movement facilitated intimate unions between blacks and Jews that ultimately spawned a whole generation of black Jews. Barry Kosmin, who directed the CJF's 1990 National Jewish Population Survey, esti-

FIGURE 2.1 *Rabbi Capers Funnye (center rear) and founding members of the Alliance of Black Jews. Photograph by Bernard Wolfson.*

mated that there might be as many as 20,000 to 30,000 of these black Jewish "civil rights babies."[9]

ENCOUNTERING RACISM

Still, many white Ashkenazi Jews resisted the idea that blacks could be Jewish. Virtually every member of the alliance complained of having been treated disrespectfully by white Jews who found it hard to accept the idea of a black face in synagogue or, worse yet, in the family. They had all been questioned at one time or another about their Jewishness. "If I enter a predominantly white synagogue with a well-worn yarmulke, a well-worn prayer book, and a well-worn prayer shawl, inevitably somebody will ask me if I'm really Jewish," said Rabbi Funnye, a tinge of anger in his voice. "Yet a white person, even if he or she is clearly confused and has no idea what to do, will not get the same question." His voice swelled with sarcasm as he mocked the mercifully short conversations he was accustomed to having with white Jewish questioners: "'Are you really Jewish'? 'Nah, I just wear this stuff.'"

Michelle Stein-Evers, despite her cultural affinity with the Ashkenazi community, also had had her share of problems. She recalled being at a Bar Mitzvah where one of the other guests approached her to ask whose family she cleaned for. "I don't clean for anybody," she replied acidly. "I'm a Jewish girl."

Yona Avraham, a convert to Orthodox Judaism, found it virtually impossible to have a happy, fulfilling social life in her predominantly white Jewish community. Avraham had been born into a black Baptist family in a lower-middle-class neighborhood of Compton, California. But sometime in the 1970s she began to feel her destiny was pulling her toward Judaism. She had studied Christianity for many years, with both Baptists and Seventh Day Adventists, and was deeply religious, but she always felt something standing in the way of her spiritual fulfillment. She ultimately realized that the Christian values and ideas that most appealed to her were really Jewish ones. That's when her spiritual odyssey began. After scraping together enough money, Avraham went to Jerusalem in 1979, where she learned Hebrew, converted to Judaism under the supervision of the Orthodox rabbinate, and took Israeli citizenship. After returning from Israel, she settled in an Orthodox community of West Los Angeles and took a part-time job teaching Hebrew to schoolchildren. Avraham hoped her membership in the alliance would help attract other Orthodox black Jews who might be shy about joining a group of such mixed membership and secular orientation.

But there were virtually no other blacks in Avraham's own community. The white Ashkenazi Jews with whom she worshipped and socialized didn't quite know what to make of her black skin. She said she often felt as if they just didn't see her. She resented their lack of interest in the major figures of African American literature about whom she cared so passionately: Langston Hughes, James Baldwin, Maya Angelou, Toni Morrison, and others. Aside from teaching Hebrew, Avraham also worked at the California Afro-American Museum, a job she valued because it gave her daily contact with other African Americans. But although she felt a strong sense of connection with the black community, her strict faith made it difficult to maintain regular social contact with other blacks. If she ate out, the restaurant had to be kosher, a requirement that restricted her to a few sections of town. And on Friday nights and Saturdays—prime time for socializing—she was busy observing the Sabbath. So she spent a lot of her time with other religious Jews, all of them white. They cared about her and looked after her as they would any other member of the community, Avraham said. But they acknowledged only half of who she was—the Jewish half. The dilemma was particularly painful, Avraham said, when it came to the question of marriage. Orthodox Jews put great emphasis on having children, and they were always nudging other members of the community about starting families. But when it came to her, they would just grow silent and shrug their shoulders. "The matchmakers are always going around trying to fix people up, but they never came knocking on my door," Avraham said. Of course, the unspoken assumption was that no white member of the community would want to marry a black—even a nice Orthodox Jewish one.

Yona's story rankled Rabbi Funnye, drawing his ire at the racism so prevalent in

American Jewry. In an ideal world, he said, Jewish parents should tell their children: "I'd much rather you marry another Jew—and I don't care if he is pink—than see you married to a non-Jew. The color of the person has nothing to do with it. The fact that he or she is a Jew is the most compelling point, and if you can find someone to love like that, all the better, because that will ensure Jewish continuity." But that was not the way things were, he lamented. "And that's why Yona, in the Orthodox community in Los Angeles, is still single, and a lot of other women too. Because, oh they're Jews, all right. They're good Jews. But they're not the kind of Jews you should bring home to Aba and Ema—to Daddy and Mommy. And you definitely don't want to take them to grandma and grandad."

But racism was not a one-way street, as Courtenay Edelhart, another alliance member, attested. Edelhart was the mixed-race daughter of a white Jewish father and a black Methodist mother who had met as social workers in Chicago. When Edelhart was studying journalism at Northwestern University, she became heavily involved in black activism on campus and met a man whom she began dating. "He had this image of me as his sister in the struggle, and then a few months later he found out I was Jewish," Edelhart recounted. "To him, the two couldn't exist in the same person, so he started pulling away from me. I never could make him understand that I felt the same commitment he did; I just had a different religion than he did. That's very common."

A "Peculiar Status"

Many black Jews, particularly those with ties to white Jewish communities, were living in a cultural and demographic no-man's land. They had one foot in the black community and the other in the Jewish community, but they never really felt completely at home in either one. Stein-Evers wrote about this dilemma for the symposium on black Jews: "All my life, I have heard from others in the Jewish community about my peculiar status: it has been defined as marginal at best, and while I have always been an active member of the community, there have always been those who looked at me either as not quite a Jew or as a type of synagogue pet," she wrote. "Ironically, the same was true in the black community: if I was a Jew, then I was an Oreo, or a female Uncle Tom. In other words, a race traitor. I was neither as authentically black as other blacks nor as authentically Jewish as other Jews."[10]

Complicating things further was the relationship of black Jews to the white gentile world, a world in which both blacks and Jews were historically marginalized and insecure minorities. Robin Washington illustrated this sense of double jeopardy with a story from his adolescence. In a telephone conversation more than a year before the meeting at Funnye's synagogue, Washington recounted the time he had been clowning around in the playground with a high school acquaintance, who accidentally jammed a pitchfork through Washington's foot. As

Washington screamed in pain and as blood gushed from the wound, his playmate, horrified at what he had done, hoisted him onto his shoulders and carried him to the doctor. Washington had to stay home and rest for a few days. But meanwhile, he later learned, the boy who had stabbed him was bragging to his school chums, "I got the nigger; I got the nigger." Robin returned to school three days later, and as he stepped off the bus he saw his tormentor pointing at him and saying, "That's the nigger I got." A third young man, who also knew Robin, quickly corrected him: "That's not a nigger; that's a kike." Washington was a "civil rights baby," the son of a white Jewish mother and black Baptist father. His parents had been active in the civil rights movement, and they began taking their son to marches and rallies when he was still a toddler. Washington, with light brown skin and short-cropped, curly black hair, said people often had difficulty figuring out his ethnicity.

Cultural Judaism vs. the Torah

Washington, like Stein-Evers, had both genetic and cultural connections to Judaism. They were both religious in their own ways, though neither of them was strictly observant. Washington, for example, said he kept kosher, "with an inexplicable exception for clams." Stein-Evers confessed that "When I get depressed, I have to eat lobster." But despite these transgressions, they were both Jewish and always would be. They had not chosen to be Jews; it was just a part of who they were.

Funnye and Avraham, on the other hand, had chosen to be Jews. For them, Judaism was not a question of culture or blood ties. It was about following the dictates of Jewish law—the Torah. Avraham said she had no interest in learning Yiddish or eating chopped liver, only in doing God's will. And she neatly separated her blackness from her Jewishness. "If for some reason I woke up in the morning and no longer believed in God, I would no longer be a Jew," she said. "But I would still be black."

Rabbi Funnye complained that many Ashkenazi Jews put too much emphasis on their own cultural forms, neglecting the Torah as the one truly universal prescription for Judaism. He said there were always some white Jewish visitors to his synagogue who questioned the customs of his congregation. "We had one visitor once around Passover, who said, 'Oh rabbi, what about the rice?' I said, 'Listen, the Ashkenazi custom is that they don't eat rice and corn and peas and things of that nature during the days of unleavened bread. That's not Torah law. That's not halakhic law. Those are customs that developed in Europe. And that's fine. But I don't care if it's a 200- or 300-year-old custom that evolved in Europe, it's still not halakhah. So you can't make it halakhah.'" In fact, this was not so much a conflict between white and black Jews as between Ashkenazim and Sephardim. Ashkenazi custom prohibits the consumption of rice, beans, peas, and corn during the seven days of Passover, but those foods are allowed by the Sephardim. The Beth Shalom B'nai Zaken Ethiopian Hebrew congregation followed Sephardic customs. Funnye said there was no specifically black Jewish food. "What black Jews have done is to kosherize what would be called soul food," he said. That might mean collard greens with kosher smoked turkey instead of pork, or with no meat at all. It also meant lots of corn bread, which Funnye's congregation ate during Passover in addition to matzoh. Then there was baked chicken and chicken soup, which Funnye said belonged as much to blacks as to white Jews. "I'm not going to give the Ashkenazi community preeminence with homemade chicken soup. Black folks have been making chicken soup for years," he said.

Funnye and his Synagogue

Funnye's synagogue stands in an ethnically mixed working-class neighborhood, surrounded by faded two-story brick and shingle houses packed tightly together. The streets have virtually no grass or trees, but there are several vacant lots heaped high with mounds of earth. The synagogue towers over the surrounding homes, with its facade of brown and yellow brick crowned by a large green Star of David high above. On either side of the structure rises a brick turret capped by a green dome, the right one listing sharply toward the center. Above the synagogue's arched doorway are the words *Agudath Achim–Bikur Cholim*. Those were the two congregations, both of white European descent, that inhabited the synagogue before Funnye's group arrived.

Bikur Cholim, chartered in 1888, was a congregation of Orthodox German Jews who had worked in the now-defunct steel mills nearby. They erected the building in 1902, which made it Chicago's oldest continuously used synagogue. Bikur Cholim was in decline by the 1970s, when Agudath Achim, an Orthodox congregation of Eastern European origins, took over the building. Funnye's congregation arrived in 1993, as the ranks of Agudath Achim were dwindling. For the first several months the two congregations prayed separately, but in 1994 they began joint services, and Agudath Achim dissolved soon afterward.

Funnye is not only the spiritual and intellectual leader of his congregation; he also serves as the synagogue's maintenance man. On the Thursday morning before the big weekend meeting he was inside the building, busily applying a white wax polish to its lumpy brown vinyl floor. He wore a white prayer shawl with blue stripes, and a blue, full-skull yarmulke with gold leaf design weaved over the sides and top. After finishing the floor, he descended the stairs to his basement office, a windowless, white-walled rectangle with a large wooden desk and four green cloth chairs. His desk was covered with books, papers, and letters, many in Hebrew. It was there that he spent the better part of four hours sharing his views on Judaism, black Jews, and race relations in America.

No Such Thing as the Jewish "Race"

Funnye looks to be in early middle age, of medium height and build, with ebony skin, dark luminescent eyes, and a goatee that trails off in thin wisps toward the back of his cheekbones. He radiates a fiery intensity and irresistible charisma with his piercing gaze and resonant baritone. His passion was particularly palpable as he lamented the racism that had crept into American Judaism, and he envisioned a time when Jews of all ethnicities and nationalities would unite around the Torah even while maintaining their cultural distinctions. "The prophets declare that my house shall be a house of prayer for all people, and I'm not going to try to change the workings of the Torah," Funnye said. "I take all people to mean all people. There is no such thing as the Jewish race. There never has been such a thing as the Jewish race, and race never had any role in antiquity as far as restricting an individual from coming into the House of Israel."

In Funnye's view, white Europeans have no monopoly on Judaism, but they believe they do because the society they live in is fundamentally racist and eurocentric. "Listen, you shouldn't be surprised. The media is much more concerned with what goes on in America, Great Britain, France, Russia, and even Luxembourg, than they are with African countries or South America or India," he said. "And I think it's racism, not counting people of color as being as relevant as white people. I see the Olam Ha-Bah, the world beyond, as a very different place. The chief rabbi may be a black guy. I see it as a very mixed place of all ethnicities and things from every walk. I don't think it's going to resemble or be reflective in any way, shape, or form of Western society as it's described and laid out." As Funnye noted, the realities of ethnic geography made it seem rather unlikely that the original Jews had been fair-skinned. "When we look at the location of the state of Israel and its proximity to the continent of Africa, it makes sense to me that those people may not have been as black as me, but they sure weren't as white as the next guy, okay?"

"Reverting" to Judaism

Funnye, drawing on the teachings of earlier black Jewish movements, argues that well before the Common Era, Jews migrated south along trade routes into sub-Saharan Africa, spreading their Hebrew language and customs while interbreeding with black Africans, so that their physical features gradually became indistinguishable from those of the local people. He speaks of numerous Hebraic or Hebrew-influenced settlements that existed for many centuries in parts of central, southern, and western Africa.[11] He believes that his ancestors, and those of many black Americans, came from those groups and continued to practice Judaism in some form until the day they were shipped off to America as slaves. Funnye thinks of himself not as a convert to Judaism, but as a "revert," returning to what he has always been. He was born into a family of African Methodist Episcopalians in South Carolina and first came to Judaism in 1971, when he joined the House of Israel under Rabbi Robert Devine, a black Jewish leader in Chicago who mixed observance of Torah with a belief in Jesus Christ as the Lord and savior. Funnye later rejected the Christian teachings and left the House of Israel to join the Ethiopian Hebrews. He has gone way beyond most other black Jewish leaders in forging ties to the white Jewish mainstream. In 1985, the same year he was ordained as an Ethiopian Hebrew rabbi, Funnye underwent formal conversions to Judaism under both Conservative and Orthodox rabbis. He also sits on the board of the American Jewish Congress, and the Jewish Council of Urban Affairs.

Funnye works with two Conservative white rabbis in a Beth Din, or rabbinical court, helping with conversions, divorces and other Jewish communal matters. Gentiles who join his congregation are converted in the Conservative tradition, and in accordance with all the requirements of Jewish law. Despite this, the mainstream rabbinical groups have been slow to accept Funnye as a bona fide rabbi, because they do not recognize the Ethiopian Hebrews' Israelite Rabbinical Academy in Queens, New York, where he was ordained.[12] But his committment and adherence to the Torah are good enough for him. "No, I didn't graduate from the Jewish Theological Seminary, and I didn't graduate from Yeshiva University, nor from Hebrew Union College," he said. "But I tell you, in my mind your ordination don't carry no more weight before the creator than does mine. I never professed to be the talmudist or the halakhist that some of these great-minded rabbis are. But I'm dedicated to it, and I'm committed to it, and I burn the midnight oil, and I have questions about things, and try to learn and try to teach and try to guide the community." Funnye said whites are perfectly welcome in his community, and despite the strong black identity of his congregation, he hoped for the day when it would be completely integrated. The congregation did have a handful of white members, he said, including five left over from the now-defunct Agudath Achim and two from the Bikur Cholim congregation that preceded it. There were also two whites who married black members of the congregation and converted to Judaism under Funnye's supervision. The oldest member of the congregation was a 90-year old white woman from Bikur Cholim. Funnye said she once told his wife during a synagogue celebration of Sukkot, "This place has never had so much fun."

But many members of Funnye's congregation did not share his enthusiasm for mixing with the white Jewish community. He tried to negotiate for an associate membership in the Union of American Hebrew Congregations, the Reform branch of Judaism, but in the end his own members rejected the idea. The majority felt that Reform Judaism was not a good match for their more traditional congregation. Significant differences arose over such questions as the separation of genders during services, treatment of gays and lesbians, and the ordination of women rabbis. On all three issues, Funnye's congregation came down on the socially conservative side. But race also played a part in his congregation's decision. Some members simply weren't ready for a substantial opening to the mainstream Ashkenazi Jewish community.

Many harbored feelings of mistrust and resentment toward white Jewish groups, whom they viewed as exclusive and imperious in their approach to Judaism. Some members said they preferred to be called Hebrew Israelites rather than Jews, in order to distinguish themselves from the mainstream white Jewish community.[13] Funnye conceded that many in his congregation probably would not join the Alliance of Black Jews, at least initially, in part because of its overlap with the white Jewish community. Funnye himself, though far more open to the white Jewish community, was also acutely aware of the inextricable link between his Judaism and his identity as an African American. "I was a Black Jew before I was a Jew Jew," he said.

Funnye's Sabbath Service

Funnye infuses his Sabbath service with a strong sense of black American and African identity, palpable both in his sermon and in the music that followed it. He began the service inside an elevated prayer box at the center of the synagogue chamber, his book spread out before him. The chamber is a wide open rectangular space with no pillars. It has a high ceiling and large arched windows that allow the daylight to flood in, making it a strikingly cheerful place of worship. After leading the congregation in prayer for more than an hour, Funnye called male members up to read from the Torah. Then he went up to the altar to deliver his sermon. He talked about how Abraham was described in the Torah as welcoming strangers into his home, giving them sustenance and a bowl of water to wash their feet. Modern society, he said, had strayed far from that sense of generosity to strangers. Now we stick to our own, are wary of strangers, afraid to let them into our lives. He extended the metaphor to include relations between the races and between different ethnic groups, who all too often treat each other with fear and suspicion. Funnye spoke in the fire-and-brimstone style more often associated with Baptist preachers than rabbis, beginning a sentence in quiet, understated tones, then ratcheting up the volume to underscore his authority as he surged toward the booming, emotive crescendo. His voice rose as his words punctured the air, and he sprinkled his delivery with black English, calling biblical figures "brother" and "sister," and even referring to Sarah as "homegirl." After the sermon, the synagogue band struck up and the congregation sang along. The music was played on congo drums and an electric keyboard, with the syncopated rhythms and pentatonic scales characteristic of purely African music, free of European influences. The voices of the congregation soared to the melodies as they romped joyously through "Marching to Zion," a selection from their songbook: "We're marching to Zion, beautiful, beautiful Zion. We're marching to Zion, that beautiful city of God."[14]

For Funnye and his congregation, being Jewish represents a return to selfhood and a celebration of black pride. Another song from their songbook, entitled "What's My Name," powerfully expresses this intersection between their black and Jewish identities:

I've roamed this whole world over,
Been immersed in sin and shame,
No man's feet I've not been under,
What's my name?
I've been chained, whipped, and beaten,
Slavery's my only fame,
Even my soul the nations plunder,
What's my name?
What's my name, who could care?
For none doth stand with me,
I alone have to bear my grief and misery.
Comes the day my God is tired,
'Way the heathens use His name,
And he'll tear my bonds asunder,
Then you'll hear when I proclaim,
Yisrael, Yisrael, Yisrael is my name.[15]

Funnye's Spiritual and Intellectual Lineage

That blacks should find such powerful symbolism in Judaism is not surprising. Slavery has been an important unifying theme for blacks and Jews, while Hebrew bible narratives, especially the Exodus, have played a prominent role in black American religious life. Some black leaders, both during slavery and in the decades that followed, drew inspiration from Judaism's practical here-and-now approach to human life. The message it held for an impoverished and heavily burdened people was that they could take charge of their own destiny. Booker T. Washington, for example, pointed to the group pride and self-reliance of Jews as a worthy model for American blacks.[16]

Rabbi Arnold Ford, the musical director of Marcus Garvey's Universal Negro Improvement Association, fused his brand of Judaism with the black nationalism of Garvey's "Back to Africa" movement, which flourished and then collapsed in the 1920s. More than once Ford tried to convince Garvey to adopt Judaism as the movement's official religion, but without success. Ford was one of the leading lights among black Jews in New York, and in 1923 he established a congregation called Beth B'nai Abraham, House of the Children of Abraham. He left New York in the early 1930s for Ethiopia, and it is unclear what happened to him after that. Some believe he remained in Africa until his death in 1935; others say he went to Detroit instead, assumed a new identity, and became one of the early leaders of the Black Muslim movement.[17] In any event, Ford's mantle fell on the shoulders of his disciple, Rabbi Wentworth A. Matthew, who had founded the Commandment Keepers Congregation in Harlem sometime in the mid-1920s. Matthew taught that he and the members of his congregation had descended from the original Israelites through Menelik

I, the son of King Solomon and the Queen of Sheba. According to Matthew's teachings, Menelik I was born in Ethiopia but moved to Jerusalem at the age of 12 and lived there with his father until he was 25, when Solomon, fearing a plot against his son's life, sent him back to Ethiopia for his own safety. Menelik I then ascended to the throne, and became the first in a long line of Ethiopian Hebrew kings ending with Emperor Hailie Selassie. Matthew believed Selassie was a covert Jew and that he had embraced the Coptic Christian church under pressure from Britain.[18] To bolster his claim of Hebrew heritage, Matthew taught that Solomon, as well as the Hebrew patriarchs, had been black.[19] The Commandment Keepers thought of Ethiopia as an extension of Israel and often referred to the two interchangeably.

Matthew claimed to have received his rabbinical ordination in Ethiopia from the chief rabbi of the Ethiopian Jews, or Falashas. But Graenum Berger asserted that "the first and only contact Matthew had directly with Ethiopia was when he attended a reception for Emperor Hailie Selassie at the Waldorf Astoria in New York in 1954."[20] Berger also wrote that Matthew was in fact an ordained Protestant minister, registered in New York as Bishop W. A. Matthew, pastor of the Church of the Living God, Pillar and Ground of Truth and Faith of Jesus Christ. At least until 1929, Berger reported, the following inscription could be found inside Matthew's church sanctuary: "People prepare to meet thy God. Jesus Saves!"[21]

Eventually Matthew jettisoned the Christian trappings, although some black Jewish groups have preserved them to this day. In the 1940s Matthew founded the Ethiopian Hebrew Rabbinical College, where he ordained over twenty black rabbis, who went on to head black Jewish congregations around the United States. Matthew maintained cordial ties with white Ashkenazi Jewish leaders and often invited them to pray at his synagogue. He hoped to gain their official recognition of his rabbinic status, applying at least twice for membership on the New York Board of Rabbis. But his applications were turned down, because the board did not consider him to be a bona fide halakhic Jew. When Matthew died in 1973, he was succeeded by Rabbi Levy Ben Levi, who continues to head the movement as chief rabbi of the Israelite Rabbinical Academy in Queens. Capers Funnye was ordained by Rabbi Ben Levi in 1985, and his Beth Shalom B'nai Zaken Ethiopian Hebrew congregation is thus a direct descendant of Matthew's Commandment Keepers.

Funnye's desire to be accepted within the white Jewish mainstream was in keeping with Matthew's legacy. But Funnye also maintained close ties to other offshoots of the early black Jewish movements—ones more hostile to white Jews. He considered them partners in Judaism, although some were theologically light years away from his own Jewish creed. One of these figures was Gaston Sample, who heads the Tabernacle of Israel, a descendant of Devine's House of Israel, where Funnye started out. Sample has a broad, round face covered with whitening whiskers, and a full-skull purple cloth cap pulled snugly over his forehead. His business card identifies him as "Minister Yehoshua," the Hebrew name for Joshua. He said he used the title of minister, not rabbi, because it was more easily understood within the predominantly Christian black community. Sample said his congregation followed "the ways of the Jew," but he rejected the word Judaism, because "when you say Judaism, you're cutting out my main man—Jesus." Christ, he said, was "the king of Israel, and he'll last forever, spiritually speaking." But he said his congregation observed all the Jewish holidays and no Christian ones, because "Jesus didn't tell anybody to go and celebrate Easter or anything else." Sample also said he adhered to the Jewish dietary laws of *kashrut*, in his own way: he wouldn't eat pork or shellfish, but he did mix meat and dairy products. The Jewish prohibition against cooking the kid in its mother's milk had been "misinterpreted," he said.

Sample had an associate membership on the Israelite Board of Rabbis in Queens, which oversees the Ethiopian Hebrew movement. But he did not attend the meeting at Funnye's synagogue that gave birth to the Alliance of Black Jews. It seemed highly unlikely he could ever come to a meeting of the minds with the founders of the alliance, since almost all of them were active in white Jewish communities.[22] Like some members of Funnye's congregation, Sample considered himself a Hebrew Israelite, not a Jew, because "If I said Jewish, they'd associate us with those other people." By that, he meant white Jews. "A lot of Hebrew Israelites are kind of fearful of the Caucasian people, because they think they're going to come in and take over and run things," he said. He pointed to the *Protocols of the Elders of Zion*, the infamous anti-Semitic work that circulated widely in Europe around the turn of the century, which alleged there was a Jewish conspiracy to take over the world. Asked if he really believed what it said, Sample responded by talking about how Israel had built itself up into a strong nation with massive aid from the United States. How, he asked, could America have been persuaded to pour so much money into a foreign country so far away when her own people were hungry and homeless and unemployed? "I think the Jews are some of the smartest people in the world." When Sample said "Jews," he was talking about a subset of the "Caucasian people."

The Farrakhan Litmus Test

Sample's remarks put black anti-Semitism in a new light: it wasn't aimed at Jews per se, but at white Jews. That, at least in part, seemed to explain Rabbi Funnye's conciliatory, if somewhat conflicted, feelings toward Louis Farrakhan. As a Jew, Funnye didn't feel targeted by Farrakhan, perhaps because he knew that when Farrakhan criticized Jews, he was talking about *white* Jews. And as a black American, Funnye clearly empathized more with Farrakhan than with his white Jewish detractors. His voice betrayed a certain defensiveness as he spoke of the Farrakhan–Jewish rift, and at times he referred to Jews in the third person. "If Jews have problems with the Catholic Church, they don't attack it in the newspaper. They seek out the cardinal and other leadership of that particular archdiocese, and they try to get to a table to talk. And they owe that to Farrakhan," Funnye said. But he claimed that the ADL and other Jewish groups weren't really interested in dialogue, because Farrakhan served their purposes just fine. His irony surfaced as he mocked white Jewish leaders recoiling from Farrakhan: "'Oh, no, we ain't gonna talk.' Come on! You want him there. You want him as a force so you can say that's the reason you can't get along with black people. And that's bullshit, okay?"

But Rabbi Funnye also clearly felt considerable ambivalence toward Farrakhan, who he said must stop his rhetoric about Jews and apologize for past offenses. At first Funnye described the problem as one of semantic imprecision rather than anti-Semitism. He said that when Nation of Islam ministers had started talking about the Jews controlling Hollywood, he told Farrakhan: "I'm a Jew, and I've never been to Hollywood, don't know nothing about Hollywood, don't get a nickel of what's earned in Hollywood, and I know hundreds of Jews who are white, who have nothing to do with Hollywood, who don't know anything about Hollywood, whose families don't have anything to do with Hollywood. So when you say Jews, that is a misstatement. If you have a problem with Mr. Goldwyn or Mr. Mayer, or some producer or director of a particular film, you have got to be more specific."

Yet Funnye later acknowledged that the Nation of Islam leader in fact knew precisely what he was saying and had no intention of being more specific. "Farrakhan is a student of history, and in how many societies and cultures have Jews been scapegoats? You can't name a European country where they haven't been scapegoated. So, yeah, it's calculated. He knows it's going to get him full-page coverage in the *New York Times* and the *Washington Post*. He knows there are elements in the Jewish community who are going to react, and it broadens his persona as the only black guy in America willing to stand up against evil and those who would hurt black people." But Funnye resented Jewish leaders who he said used Farrakhan as a kind of litmus test to decide which blacks they could trust. "'Yeah, we'll talk to you, but first tell me how you feel about Louis Farrakhan. And if you don't feel the way I want you to feel about him, then I don't know.' That's wrong. Absolutely, unequivocally wrong," Funnye said.

Judaism as a Joy, Not a Burden

Another unfair litmust test often administered by the Jewish community, Funnye said, was the Holocaust. "The leadership in the Jewish community here gets mad because there are some black professors who say that there was an African holocaust. They get mad, because they think that the term Holocaust is reserved exclusively for Jews." But why dwell so singularly on the Holocaust, Funnye asked, when so many other people have suffered just as much? What about the Gypsies who were killed in Nazi death camps, or the Cambodian genocide of the Pol Pot years, or the recent ethnic killings in Bosnia?

Here was yet another example of white European Jews asserting their preeminence in Jewish life, Funnye suggested: "The Torah tells us that every Jew who is here with us today, or that will ever be, should see themselves as connected to the experience at Sinai. But it seems to me that many of my Jewish brothers and sisters think that if you cannot connect to the Holocaust, or you did not lose someone in the Holocaust, your Jewishness is not authentic or your suffering has not been as bad. And suffering and pain, no group has a monopoly on."

Funnye believes that in the minds of many Jews, dwelling on the Holocaust creates a negative association with Judaism. "Many Jews border on that line where their Jewishness is intrinsically tied to the Holocaust," he said. "We have to look at the Holocaust as an affliction of pain upon humanity and not use it as a rallying cry—just as when blacks want to use slavery as their rallying cry, I don't answer that rallying cry. I'm not going to go to that ultimately ugly, negative, demoralizing, dehumanizing experience and call that our rallying point."

For Rabbi Funnye and his congregation, being Jewish isn't a burden; it is an unmitigated joy. "Judaism is a well," he says, "and the water is so sweet and the taste is never tiring." Funnye views Judaism as a powerful force for the liberation of the human spirit—and of black Americans. He argues that the black Jewish movements of the early twentieth century—his spiritual and intellectual forefathers—were in the vanguard of black self-realization and were the forerunners of black nationalism and black power. "Black Jews were saying in 1900 that Jesus was not a white guy with blond hair and blue eyes," Funnye said. "It's only been within the last five or ten years that many black Christians have started asking questions that black Jews have been asking for a long time."

Notes

1. On December 5, 1993, the California African-American Museum in Los Angeles sponsored a symposium entitled "Where Worlds Collide: The Souls of African-American Jews." The event was split into two panel discussions, in which African-American Jews from around the country shared their differing perspectives on what it meant to be both black and Jewish. Funnye was one of the speakers, as were four others who attended the Chicago meeting two years later: Lily Golden, Robin Washington, Michelle Stein-Evers, and Yona Avraham.

2. This and all other quotes from Funnye are based on numerous in-depth interviews with him, both by telephone and in person, over most of 1994 and 1995, as well as remarks he made at a press conference in his synagogue on November 12, 1995, following the conclusion of the meeting described in this chapter. Except where otherwise noted, quotes and profiles of all individuals in the chapter are similarly based on numerous conversations with them over the same period of time, and on remarks they made over that weekend in November 1995. All characterizations of their experiences, perspectives, similarities, and differences are based on my interpretations of those conversations. I first profiled many of the same people in "The Soul of Judaism," *Emerge*, September 1995, pp. 42–46 and later in the *Miami Herald*, November 23 1995. In this chapter, however, I have drawn on those articles only in very limited instances.

3. The details of Golden's life history are taken from Yelena Khanga, *Soul to Soul* (New York: Basic Books, 1990). Khanga, Golden's daughter, unravels the rich, complicated story of her family, spanning four generations and three continents.

4. Stein-Evers had been heavily instrumental in putting together the 1993 symposium at the California African-American Museum and was one of its moderators. She was tireless in her efforts to find black Jews from all over the country and bring them together. She was a key figure from the very beginning in the discussions with Funnye, Robin Washington, and others that led to the creation of the Alliance of Black Jews.

5. In an unpublished brochure distributed at the symposium, Stein-Evers compiled brief narratives of the lives of several panel participants, including herself.

6. Barry A. Kosmin, Sidney Goldstein, Joseph Waksberg, Nava Lerer, Ariella Keysar, and Jeffrey Scheckner, *Highlights of the CJF 1990 National Jewish Population Survey* (New York: Council of Jewish Federations), pp. 5–10. Kosmin, an English-born Jew who is director of research at CJF and a professor of sociology at the City University of New York, cautioned in a 1994 interview that the survey's margin of error was plus or minus 3 percent—greater than the percentage of Jews who said they were black. In statistical terms, this meant that the number of black Jews might actually have been anywhere from zero to over 260,000. Kosmin also said the survey could have exaggerated the size of the black Jewish population, because a certain number of foreign-born Iranian, Hispanic and Yemenite Jews, not knowing what to say about their race, probably listed themselves as black. But he conceded that when his survey team went back to double-check a number of responses that at first seemed dubious, nearly all turned out to be genuine. This finding, along with evidence from other surveys, interviews, and Jewish congregations around the country, suggested that 100,000 African American Jews was a "reasonable figure," Kosmin said.

7. Many prominent black writers and thinkers identified quite closely with Jewish experiences of persecution. See, for example, James Baldwin, *The Fire Next Time* (New York: Dell, 1962), pp. 74–75. Baldwin described how he had felt an ominous sense of foreboding for black Americans upon learning of the Nazi death camps in Europe. "For my part, the fate of the Jews, and the world's indifference to it, frightened me very much," he wrote. "I could not but feel, in those sorrowful years, that this human indifference, concerning which I knew so much already, would be my portion on the day that the United States decided to murder its Negros systematically instead of little by little and catch-as-catch can." See also Dick Gregory, *No More Lies: The Myth and the Reality of American History* (New York: Harper & Row, 1971), pp. 257–258. "The Jew in America deludes himself about his status in society," Gregory wrote. "But he should paint his face as black as mine one day and come with me to hear what the gentile says about him everyday. Then the Jew will recognize that he is in the same trick bag with the rest of us."

8. See Reuben Greenberg, *Let's Take Back Our Streets* (Chicago: Contemporary Books, 1989), 186.

9. From my 1994 interview with Kosmin, referenced above.

10. From Stein-Evers's introduction to the brochure she compiled for the California African-American Museum's symposium on black Jews.

11. Funnye bases his argument in part on the work of Joseph J. Williams, *Hebrewisms of West Africa: From Nile to Niger with the Jews* (New York: Biblo and Tannen, 1930). Williams theorized that sometime after the first exile in 722 BCE, Jewish refugees made their way south along the Nile and then westward across the width of Africa to the Niger River and beyond. A great Hebrew or hebraically influenced empire of the Songhois tribe arose along the Niger, making its capital first at Timbuktu then at Gao, both in modern-day Mali, Williams argued. Eventually this Hebrew culture spread to the Ashantis, along the Gold Coast in what is now Ghana, he said. Most vestiges of these civilizations were eradicated with the coming of Islam

many centuries later, Williams wrote, but the Hebrews left their imprint on the entire African continent. There are groups in Africa today that observe Jewish customs and believe themselves to be descendants of the ancient Hebrews. In Mali, in and around Timbuktu, a group of a few thousand people claimed in 1995 to have discovered their Israelite roots and published a manifesto declaring their loyalty to Judaism. See Sennen Andriamirado, "Juifs, Noirs et Maliens," *Jeune Afrique* 1879 (January 8, 1997), 20–22. In southern Africa, members of the Balemba tribe, numbering approximately 150,000, practice a number of Jewish customs and believe they are the descendants of ancient Hebrews who fled Israel about 2,500 years ago. See Immanuel Suttner, "Members of the Tribe," *The Jerusalem Report* 3:31 (July 15, 1993), 34–35. But Jews frequently dismiss claims of Hebrew roots in Africa as myth and hearsay. See, for example, Joseph Telushkin, *Jewish Literacy* (New York: William Morrow, 1991), p. 88: "Because we lack any precise information on the Ten Tribes' fate . . . a large body of legends has grown up speculating on what became of them. As a rule, any nation that has acted sympathetically to the Jews . . . or practiced any ritual that corresponds to some ritual in the Torah (as do some American Indian tribes) has been rumored to be descended from the Ten Lost Tribes."

12. In October 1997 the Chicago Board of Rabbis voted to give Funnye an associate membership, a position created especially for him. Rabbi Ira Youdovin, the board's executive vice president, said the decision was meant to acknowledge his contribution to the Jewish community while recognizing that "his seminary training is not the same as other members of the board." See *Chicago Sentinel Forward,* October 10, 1997.

13. Based on conversations with congregation members following the Sabbath service on November 13, 1995.

14. From the *Beth Shalom B'nai Zaken Ethiopian Hebrew Congregation Song Book* (unpublished), p. 21.

15. Ibid, p. 20.

16. See Booker T. Washington, *The Future of the American Negro* (Boston: Small, Maynard, 1899), pp. 182–83. "We have a very bright and striking example in the history of the Jews in this and other countries," Washington wrote. "There is, perhaps, no race that has suffered so much, not so much in America as in some of the countries in Europe. But these people have clung together. They have had a certain amount of unity, pride, and love of race; and, as the years go on, they will be more and more influential in this country—a country where they were once despised, and looked upon with scorn and derision. It is largely because the Jewish race has had faith in itself. Unless the Negro learns more and more to imitate the Jew in these matters, to have faith in himself, he cannot expect to have any high degree of success."

17. See Graenum Berger, *Black Jews in America* (New York: Federation of Jewish Philanthropies of New York, 1978), pp. 77–84; and Howard Brotz, *The Black Jews of Harlem: Negro Nationalism and the Dilemmas of Negro Leadership* (New York: Schocken Books, 1964), pp. 11–12.

18. See Brotz, *Black Jews of Harlem*, pp. 15–45. In a chapter on the Commandment Keepers, Brotz reprinted a small handbook that Matthew had written for his congregation, setting forth his views on the origins of the black Jews.

19. Brotz, *Black Jews of Harlem*, p. 18. As proof of Solomon's black skin, Matthew pointed to the Song of Songs 1:5, in which Solomon wrote, "I am black but comely, O ye daughters of Jerusalem." But Matthew said the correct translation should have been "black *and* comely." According to Brotz, the original Hebrew allows either alternative. However, in the original Hebrew, the adjectives are in the feminine form, indicating that the person speaking is not meant to be Solomon himself.

3

Symbolic Identity Formation in an African American Religious Sect

The Black Hebrew Israelites

Merrill Singer

SINCE THE CIVIL WAR, African American communities have witnessed the emergence of an array of religious sects that claim some form of Hebraic or Jewish identity, that adhere to a set of religious rituals derived at least in part from the Old Testament or contemporary Jewish practice, and that embrace an assemblage of symbols, such as the Star of David, suggesting affinity with Judaism. Some of these groups have been large enough or sufficiently flamboyant to attract media or even scholarly attention, but most have been obscure and relatively short-lived. Among the most distinctive African American sects that have claimed a Judaic identity is a group called the Black Hebrew Israelites.[1] The uniqueness of this group lies in several factors, including its prominence in the mass media (the group has been the subject of hundreds of newspaper articles and television and radio reports in the United States, Europe, and Israel), its position at the nexus of African American/Jewish relations within the United States and between the United States and Israel, and its attempt to merge black Jewish identity and religious symbolism with the Return-to-Africa ideology that has been a major theme in African American culture since its inception. Born in the highly segregated inner city of Chicago, the Black Hebrew Israelite group migrated to Liberia in 1967 and then to Israel (which they define as part of Africa) several years later. The group has established a growing community in several development towns in the Negev Desert in southern Israel. The purpose of this essay is to present an interpretation of black Hebrew symbolism within the context of group history and the encompassing political economy of the African American community, that is, in terms of power, class, and race.

THE HISTORIC CONTEXT OF THE BLACK HEBREW ISRAELITES

Black Judaism is an example of a religious type that has been termed messianic nationalism.[2] Groups of this sort combine religious expectation of divine deliverance from oppressive conditions with a strong sense of nationhood. Indeed, Judaism itself could be described as having such an orientation. Among African Americans, messianic nationalism has found a number of expressions, including groups that variously embrace politico-religious Christian, Islamic, and Jewish identities and associated symbols. Among the latter, as Landing points out:

> The terminology is as varied as their numbers, some referring to themselves as Israelites others as Jews, Hebrews, Canaanites, Essenes, Judaites, Rechabites, Falashas, and Abyssinians. Although the terminology differs, all such groups perceive themselves as lineal descendants of the Hebrew Patriarchs.[3]

Several writers have suggested that the ultimate roots of black Judaism lie in the identification of African American slaves with the Egyptian servitude and liberation of the biblical Hebrews.[4] Notes Jones, "The religious imagery of [African American] Christianity is full of references to the suffering and hopes of the oppressed Jews in Bible times."[5] This natural empathy found its earliest expression in the spiritual music of the slaves.[6] Above all, it was "the compelling sense of identification with the children of Israel, and the tendency to dwell incessantly upon and to relive the stories of the Old Testament that characterized the religious songs of the slaves."[7] As Raboteau concludes, through spiritual music, "The slaves' identification with the children of Israel took on an immediacy and intensity which would be difficult to exaggerate."[8] Given their respective day-to-day experiences, "Songs about Moses and Joshua must have had a much more personal and immediate meaning to the Afro-American than to his white master."[9]

Similarly, folk preachers among the slaves were conversant with biblical stories and used them regularly in their sermons. For example, Genovese records the case of John Jasper, a popular African American preacher from Virginia who regularly was asked to give his sermon on Joshua to both slaves and whites.[10] As Drake and Cayton note:

> A good preacher must "know The Book." Among the most popular Bible stories are "The Prodigal Son," "The Three Hebrew Children in the Fiery Furnace" and "The Parable of the Virgins," together with the exploits of Moses, Samson, David, Ester, Solomon, and other Jewish heroes.[11]

For some slaves biblical stories offered a political message in addition to the spiritual comfort they provided. Uya argues that "[a]mbitious slaves saw in the Mosaic tradition an invitation to dress themselves in messianic garments and a justification for revolt against their oppressors."[12] Herein lay the potential of Hebraic identity to furnish a messianic nationalist response to white oppression. It is noteworthy that slave rebellion leaders like Gabriel Prosser, Denmark Vesey, and Nat Turner all took inspiration from the Bible. Vesey, for example, interpreted several verses from Zechariach and Joshua as heavenly calls to battle against the sin of slavery.[13] Adds Marable:

> The black faith of a Nat Turner posed a crucial problem for slave culture. If Moses was a deliverer of the Israelites from slaveholders in Egypt, could not a black messiah lead his people from bondage into a new Canaan land?[14]

The exact route of transition from metaphoric or politically coded use of Old Testament figures, place names, and events to express the harsh conditions experienced by the slaves and their hoped-for liberation to an actual adoption of Hebraic identity and alleged kinship is historically unclear. Brotz, for one, maintains:

> As early as 1900, Negro preachers were traveling through the Carolinas preaching the doctrine that the so-called Negroes were really the lost sheep of the House of Israel. There is no reason to think, however, that such reflections did not begin much earlier, in fact within slavery itself, when the more imaginative and daring of the slaves began to wonder about the very human question of who they really were and where they really came from.[15]

The source for Brotz's assertion about the message of itinerant preachers in the Carolinas in 1900 is unknown. One intriguing possibility is that their work began during a postbellum South Carolina gubernatorial race. According to Genovese, "After the war black preachers took the political stump to tell the freedmen in South Carolina that the Republican gubernatorial candidate, Franklin J. Moses, was none other than the man himself [i.e., the biblical Moses], who had come to lead them to the Promised Land."[16] Given the deep intimacy African Americans during this era commonly felt toward the ancient Hebrews, this confusion of the biblical Moses with his mortal namesake is not hard to understand. Certainly, many African Americans in the South had been awaiting Moses' arrival since before the Civil War. In fact, some slaves had concluded "that the abolitionists and Union troops were agents of Moses."[17] Belief in the actual appearance of Moses in South Carolina may well have helped finalize identification with the Children of Israel for some individuals.

The first efforts to organize distinct black Jewish congregations began just before or after the turn of the twentieth century.[18] Some have suggested that the origin of the earliest black Jewish groups might be traced either to the slaves of Jewish slave owners or to individual African American converts to Judaism prior to the turn of the century, although Bertram Korn, who studied African American and Jewish relations in the antebellum South, discounts both of these possibilities because of limited available evidence.[19] Although there is record of a number of African American members of southern Jewish congregations prior to and after the Civil War, there is no historic record that any of these individuals attempted to organize distinct black Jewish groups.[20] Instead, the earliest black Jewish sects were organized by working-class men who, as far as is known, lacked a clear-cut involvement with white Jewish congregations (fig. 3.1).

The oldest known black Jewish sect was called the Church of the Living God, the Pillar Ground of Truth for All Nations. Organized by a widely traveled African

FIGURE 3.1. *Rabbi Wentworth Matthew and members of the Moorish Zionist Temple, one of the earliest black Hebrew congregations in New York. Photo by James Van Der Zee. Donna Van Der Zee collection.*

American seaman and railroad worker named F. S. Cherry, the sect was founded in Chattanooga, Tennessee, in 1886, although little information exists about the church from this period.[21] Cherry later moved the group to Philadelphia, where it was studied by Fauset in the early 1940s.[22]

Cherry taught his followers that, in a vision, God called him to establish a church and bring to the world the message that the true descendants of the biblical Hebrews were African Americans. Moreover, he insisted that both God and Jesus, as well as Adam and Eve, were black. White people, in his interpretation, were the offspring of the servant Gehazi, who was cursed by the prophet Elisha with skin "as white as snow" (II Kings 5:27). Moreover, Cherry preached that white Jews were interlopers and frauds.[23]

What is probably the second oldest black Jewish group was called the Church of God and Saints of Christ. William S. Crowdy, a cook on the Sante Fe Railroad, was the founder of this group. Crowdy proclaimed that he was called by God to lead his people back to their historic religion and identity. In 1896 he established his church in Lawrence, Kansas, among former slaves who had fled westward in search of land and freedom from the rising wave of white oppression. Following Cherry's example, Crowdy moved his church to Philadelphia in 1900 but then moved again in 1905 to Belleville near Portsmouth in Nansemond County, Virginia, where the group prospered. Branches of the church were established in a number of cities in the United States and overseas as well.

In Crowdy's formulation, African Americans were described as heirs of the ten lost tribes of Israel, while white Jews were seen as the offspring of miscegenation with white Christians. Crowdy adopted various Jewish rituals and symbols, such as circumcision of newborn boys, use of the Jewish calendar, wearing of skullcaps, observance of Saturday as the Sabbath, and celebration of Passover, including smearing animal blood on the outside of their homes in commemoration of God's method for differentiating Jewish from Egyptian homes in the book of Exodus. These were blended with Christian practices, including baptism, consecration of bread and water as the body and blood of Christ, and foot washing, to form a unique ritual synthesis.

A number of the beliefs and symbols of both of these black Jewish groups, as well as others that were to spring up over time, can be traced to a broader set of developments in the African American community. After the Civil War a number of prominent African American leaders began urging their followers to use the Jews as a model for overcoming their abundant hardships. Benjamin Tucker Tanner, editor of the leading African American magazine of the day, the *African Methodist Episcopal Church Review*, urged his readership to emulate European Jews who had overcome great adversity to achieve a measure of economic success.[24] A similar message was offered by Booker T. Washington, who claimed that unless the African American "learns more and more to imitate the Jew . . . he cannot expect to have any high degree of success."[25] Enhancing the older identification with biblical Hebrews, the prompting by recognized leaders to model their lives after contemporary Jewry probably helped to strengthen African American interest in Jewish identity.

In addition, in response to the worsening social conditions in the South, toward the end of the nineteenth century there developed a strong nationalist upsurge among African Americans. As Edwin Redkey's review of this period indicates:

> The collapse of Republican Reconstruction had demoralized many who believed, with much justification, that the violence and economic oppression that had threatened them throughout Reconstruction would soon become intolerable. The discontent that grew from political and economic changes provided fertile soil for black nationalism.[26]

The first flames of this nationalist sentiment were kindled in a reborn Back-to-Africa movement that swept across South Carolina in 1877. The leadership of this new movement was soon assumed by Bishop Henry M. Turner of the African

Methodist Episcopal Church, "without doubt the most prominent and outspoken . . . advocate of black emigration in the years between the Civil War and the First World War."[27] Turner's numerous fiery speeches at church conventions helped to focus African American discontent and disillusionment. Central to Turner's philosophy, and later to that of most black Jewish groups, was the idea that African Americans have as much right biblically and historically to maintain that God is black as do white people who portray both Jesus and God as white.

Despite abundant oratory skill and tremendous effort, Turner was unable to build a successful emigration movement. Redkey identifies an important reason:

> American blacks, cut off from most of their African memories and immersed in a nation that refused to acknowledge that blacks could have a cultural background, have had a difficult time fashioning a cultural identity other than the tradition of oppression. Bishop Turner was unable to find or create a mythical structure of the Afro-American past that would inspire his people.[28]

In the Old Testament accounts of the biblical Israelites, men like F. S. Cherry, William Crowdy, and those who came after them found such a mythical charter and potent symbols which they used to found black Jewish groups that have endured throughout the twentieth century. Included among the offspring of the groups started by these men is the Black Hebrew Israelite group, which did succeed in leading several thousand African Americans out of the United States to their current residence in Israel.

In Chicago: Emergent Group Symbols and Identities

The early 1960s was a period of significant upsurge in attempts to reshape African American identity and culture, as well as a time of widespread expansion of alternative African American religious orientations, nationalist sentiments, and African identification. It also was a period when a number of often competing black Jewish groups were active in the south-side and west-side African American neighborhoods of Chicago. Among these diverse "camps," as they were known as by participants, was a group called the Abeta Hebrew Israel Cultural Center. This group, housed in a rented hall on the south-side of the city, was under the leadership of a number of "elders" or Righteous Teachers, men in their forties and fifties who had a long involvement in black Judaism. Central to the ideology of this group, born of the Return-to-Africa urging fostered by Bishop Turner (whose writings were studied by group members), was a belief in African repatriation. To achieve this aim, the elders sought to acquire land grants in Africa for the eventual relocation of the group.

Such beliefs and activities were not unique to Abeta; similar ideas were being expressed by the leaders of some of the other black Jewish camps. But among Abeta members, perhaps as a result of intense intergroup rivalry and the need to assert distinction in a highly competitive sectarian environment, migration to Africa became a particularly pressing issue. Intertwined with this belief was the expectation of divine deliverance and of punishment for wrongdoers. Abeta leaders began to make claims that the hour of heavenly retribution was nearing. Eventually this belief led to the prophecy by group leaders that on the Passover holiday of 1967, on the evening of April 24, Abeta members would be miraculously led back to Africa. On the expected day, group members gathered at the Abeta center with their bags packed and ceremoniously locked the doors to await the miracle, which they had likened to the Exodus of the ancient Israelites from Egypt. But nothing happened. Rather than cause disillusionment, this turn of events only helped to further consolidate the commitment of group members.[29] Thwarted in their attempt to activate divine intervention through force of will, they set upon a more practical course for achieving their primary objective.

In May 1967 three leaders of Abeta flew to Liberia, a country founded by former American slaves, to investigate the possibility of relocating to the African continent. One of the men chosen for this task was a young foundry worker by the name of Ben Carter, who, like other Abeta members, had adopted a Hebrew name in the process of identity transformation. Carter was known to his fellow Abeta members as Ben Ammi (Son of my People). Though he was just one of a number of younger leaders at Abeta before the migration, he eventually was to become the group's undisputed head.

In Liberia, Ben Ammi and his Abeta compatriots were surprised to discover that only citizens were allowed to own real estate and that, despite Liberia's history, citizenship was not automatically awarded to African Americans. However, in Monrovia, the Liberian capital, the trio met a black expatriate from Cincinnati who had been granted Liberian citizenship, and he agreed to purchase land for the Abeta members. Ultimately, 300 acres of thickly forested land in Bong County were purchased at fifty cents an acre.

The return of the Abeta emissaries was a spirited event. Now, unlike rival claimants to spiritual leadership in the black Jewish milieu of Chicago, Abeta could assert its possession of land in Africa. Individuals who felt strongly about leaving "Babylon" (i.e., America) and returning to Africa, the idealized homeland of their ancestors, flocked to the Abeta Center. Activists within the group spread throughout the African American community and to the meeting places of other black Jewish groups with flyers announcing their imminent return to Africa. Their object was to attract as many new members as possible.

Religious symbols, according to Clifford Geertz, represent (and thus help to create) a general order of worldly and spiritual existence for believers, an order that is clothed in an "aura of factuality" (as ultimate and compelling truth rather than as human intellectual creation), and hence these symbols are capable of sparking some of the deepest emotions and most consequential behaviors (including life-or-death decisions). In the case of the Black Hebrews, joining the group and taking on this new identity often results in the severing of kinship and friendship relations and ultimately in giving up worldly possessions and traveling to Israel—actions of no small measure.

Willingness to undergo such a dramatic life change reflects the needs and emotional states of individuals attracted to the Black Hebrew group. Life history interviews conducted with 110 members of the group suggest that they shared several attitudinal, experiential, and emotional characteristics at the time of joining the Black Hebrew Israelites. The most important of these are (1) acceptance of a strong moralistic orientation, (2) expressed desire for upward social mobility, (3) experience of blocked goal-fulfillment and self-reported stress associated with inability to achieve personal life objectives, (4) resulting alienation from mainstream society, and (5) adoption of a religious seeker orientation as a means of resolving conflicted life experience. Group members repeatedly expressed feeling ill at ease with the style of living they saw around them prior to their affiliation with the group. This dissatisfaction stemmed from what they experienced in the general society as well as in the black community. As one member commented, "When I was older and the fellows would go and steal or do something else that was wrong, I would always hurt inside. I just couldn't go along with those kinds of things because of what I'd learned from my grandparents." Another noted, "It used to be like I was a misfit.... You got to go through too much filth to get anywhere in the States. You got to get low. You got to do things you don't want to do, things against your moralism." This moral orientation led these individuals to feel conflicted and distraught as they came to realize that achieving their goals would entail compromises or even wholesale violation of their personal values. Moreover, because of racial discrimination, future group members encountered significant, at times insurmountable, barriers to goal fulfillment. As one member said, "All my life was failure in the sense of trying to achieve my goals there. It was a total disaster.... I was struggling but never seeming to reach a goal.... So it would keep you in a state of frustration.... Every black man in America has suffered at one time in his life or experienced discrimination." Another lamented, "I knew how America was built. Unless you was a thief or had a certificate saying you were qualified to do a certain kind of work, you wasn't going to make it. Then that certificate didn't mean you were going to make anything because the average black coming out of college was making what the average white was coming out of high school.... In college they give you a champagne kind of appetite, but when you hit the world they're drinking gin and vodka." In response to these kinds of experiences, members became increasingly alienated, sometimes violently so. Explained one member, "I wanted to do something, explode that world. If I hadn't [joined the Black Hebrews], I might have hurt someone." A similar sense of disaffection was expressed by another member in the following way: "I was always a good citizen in America, but it didn't seem to matter what I did; America is just a terrible place. I worked, I supported myself; my brothers went into the army. I even lost a brother in the army. Even so, America treated me terribly. America killed my spirit."

Intensely frustrated, deeply in conflict with the life they saw around them, and emotionally injured by discrimination and blocked goal-fulfillment, the individuals who would join the Black Hebrews could find little that was meaningful in their lives. Prior to encountering the Black Hebrews, they had entered into a phase of "religious seekership," which Lofland and Stark have defined as the search for a satisfactory system of religious meaning to interpret and resolve significant internal discontent.[30]

The ideology of the Black Hebrews offers a set of powerful symbols concerning the "true" identity and divine mission of African Americans, conceptions that stand in sharp contrast to the damaging messages (e.g., being seen as culturally and socially deprived, lazy, dirty, a national burden, inferior, ignorant, polluted, criminals, drunks, drug addicts, failures, welfare recipients, miserable, wretched, odor-ridden, pest-ridden, rat-infested, contaminated with disease, oversexed, undermotivated, violent, uncouth, crude, and immoral, as itemized by Williams) that are incorporated into racist diatribe and conveyed more subtly in day-to-day assaults in a society that devalues, distrusts, and demeans African Americans.[31] Around the Black Hebrew set of symbolic conceptions, which fix blame for the problems and suffering of African Americans on a diabolical conspiracy to hide the true identity of the descendants of the biblical Hebrews, members of the group are able to formulate personal restitutive narratives and thereby to take on a new identity that is free of the damaging effects of feeling like a failure and the weight of self-blame. As part of this process, the prior suffering and disillusionment of members are placed "in a meaningful context, providing a mode of action through which it can be expressed, being expressed understood, and being understood, endured" or even transcended.[32]

From Chicago to Liberia

Within a few months of the return of the Abeta emissaries from Africa, group members began selling their possessions and holding fund-raisers to pay for passage to Liberia. Believing themselves to be the first of hordes of African Americans who would escape the coming destruction of America for its oppressive treatment of the Chosen People, contingents of Black Hebrew Israelites began leaving for Monrovia, Liberia, in July 1967 (although some members remained in the United States to continue recruitment and fund-raising efforts). In addition to various supplies and personal possessions, they brought with them a pioneering spirit and high hopes for their adventurous undertaking. While they recognized that few group members had farming skills, they felt, as one Black Hebrew expressed it at the time, that "it doesn't take much to live on dedication."[33] After arriving in the capital, each contingent rented taxies and traveled for several hours along the rough dirt road that led to their destination, an underdeveloped area called Gbayea near the Kpelle village of Gbatala in the central region of the country.

Although the land was completely forested, the Black Hebrews, almost all of whom were raised in the city, looked upon their new home as a refuge from their suffering in America. As one member recalled:

> Liberia was freedom. It wasn't like the streets of America, where you are always afraid, afraid of your neighbor, afraid of your brother, afraid of your sister. . . . In Liberia, it was freedom. You didn't have to hide from nobody. You were just free.[34]

Buoyed by this newfound sense of emancipation and lofty aspirations, the Black Hebrews set about the arduous task of transforming their land, which they came to call "The Camp," into a prosperous and, they believed, growing settlement.

Initial clearing of the dense forest was hampered by heavy rains characteristic of the Liberian summer. Using machetes and other hand tools, the men of the group with the aid of their Kpelle neighbors cut back the lush vegetation until enough ground was freed for the construction of temporary dwellings and the planting of vegetables. Later the group would begin work on more permanent structures, but tents and woven mats provided their initial homes. Despite the hard work, throughout the first weeks morale remained high, and the Black Hebrews anxiously awaited the apocalyptic events that would send millions of African Americans hastening to the fledgling settlement.

Throughout this period, leadership in the group remained fairly dispersed. The Righteous Teachers were the nominal leaders, but all adult male members were free to express their views, and most decisions were made by consensus of this group. However, because most Black Hebrews were women and children, the decision-making group was not large. As one member explained:

> We had spokesmen, Teachers of Righteousness, that we respected. But all the decisions was made by the brethren. . . . We didn't have a council. We'd just call all the brethren together, every brother.

As the months passed, the initial euphoria of the group began to subside. Before long, the realities of jungle life sapped the enthusiasm of the struggling community, allowing underlying tensions to boil to the surface. Recalling some of the physical difficulties, one member noted:

> In the land of captivity [the United States], you light a match and you have a gas flame.
>
> In Liberia, if you wanted to eat you had to chop your tree down, bring it back, chop it up, build a fire. Even the fire was hard and it was smoky. We didn't know how to build no fire. . . . In the rainy season, the shelters wasn't properly covered. It was snake infested where we lived at. A snake was as

> common a sight as you drink a cup of water. To get our water, it wasn't turning on no faucet. . . . We ran into many difficulties.

During this period the Black Hebrews underwent what one woman described as "a big struggle in our minds." Unable to fully severe their emotional ties to the United States, members anxiously awaited letters from relatives and friends. Some members began to complain bitterly about their primitive existence and to reminisce about the life and comforts they left behind. According to one member, those who were most disgruntled complained "that they were starving, no food, the way they were living, the rain coming in on them. They were talking about that they were better off in the land of captivity, at least they would be dry."

Adding to the deteriorating morale, interpersonal conflicts began to mount. When the community was given a number of hens, the egg distribution system broke down because members were keeping any eggs they found for themselves. Similarly, the group's communal kitchen system fell apart because of bickering among the women who worked there. Additionally, the group ran low on money to purchase necessities and amenities, and their limited cash reserves were squandered on trips to Monrovia to purchase expensive imported food from the United States. Impure drinking water caused additional problems. Soon illnesses began sweeping through the camp, further sapping the strength needed to build up the settlement. Several accidents, including an explosion that destroyed the group's generator, caused still more problems. Ultimately some individuals began leaving the camp and moving to Monrovia. As conditions worsened, it became increasingly clear to even the most dedicated members that the group was approaching a crisis point. Although several efforts were made to overcome their problems, including an attempt to start several businesses in Monrovia, in the eyes of group members their difficulties came to a head during Passover.

In line with their identity as the direct descendants of the ancient Hebrews, the group attempted to follow the laws recorded in the Old Testament, including the sacrifice of a lamb during Passover (based on Exodus 12:3–11). The first spring, this ritual was conducted in accord with biblical stipulations, but the following year, as other problems began to multiply, the Black Hebrews had great difficulty locating a lamb or kid that was "without blemish." At the last moment a goat was found, but the owner, learning that the settlers were in no position to refuse, charged double the going rate for the animal. Then, shortly before the sacrifice was to take place, it was discovered that the goat had become ensnared in its rope and had died of strangulation. Group members interpreted the death as an ominous sign and fearfully speculated that their Liberian settlement had lost divine favor. None of the leaders could offer an acceptable explanation that was consistent with Black Hebrew ideology. At this critical juncture, Ben Ammi reported that he had received a divine revelation. He informed group members that God never desired animal sacrifices. What God craved instead, he explained, was the strict obedience of the Israelites as indicated in Proverbs 21. Thus Ben Ammi preached that the Black Hebrews were the true offering in the modern era; it was their loyalty that God desired. This speech, which incorporated a creative reconfiguration of several Black Hebrew key symbols, allowed Ben Ammi to begin a process of consolidating his position as the singular leader of the group.

Israel: The Promised Land

Ben Ammi proposed that he and another member travel to Israel to investigate the possibility of relocating the settlement. Given the identification of group members with the ancient Hebrews, Israel held considerable appeal. The idea of migrating to Israel had been discussed among black Jews in the United States since the founding of the Israeli state in 1948. Several black Jewish groups had long advocated that Israel was their rightful homeland. Even in Liberia the Black Hebrews were reminded of Israel. An eye clinic in Monrovia and several other medical aid projects in the country were staffed and funded by Israelis.

Once in Israel, Ben Ammi discovered that it was much more developed than Liberia. He saw that there would be opportunities for employment and for more comfortable housing than their tents in Liberia. Leaving his compatriot in Israel to learn the language and get better acquainted with the country, Ben Ammi then returned to the United States to gather new recruits and funds for the next stage of the Black Hebrew journey.

In July 1969, after his return to Liberia, Ben Ammi sent a letter to the Israeli embassy requesting permission and assistance to immigrate to Israel, "our land and the land of our forefathers" (quoted in an undated statement issued by the Consulate General of Israel, New York, p. 3). Israeli officials maintained that the embassy answered Ben Ammi's letter and explained that Israel's Law of Return did not apply to the Black Hebrews. The group denies this assertion, insisting that their letter was never answered. An any rate, shortly after Ben Ammi sent his letter, he instructed five group members to travel to Israel and seek admission under the Law of Return. While the status of these individuals was left undecided, they did receive the kind of benefits offered to Jewish immigrants, including apartments and employment in the Negev development town of Arad. In December 1969 a second contingent of 39 Black Hebrews, mostly women and children, traveled to Israel. This time immigration officials were more hesitant to admit group members. After 24 hours of deliberation, during which the new arrivals remained in the airport, they were given temporary visas, assigned apartments in Dimona, another Negev development town, and extended various other privileges that are usually accorded new immigrants. The permanent status of the Black Hebrews was left unresolved, however. When the chief rabbi of Dimona visited the Black Hebrews, he concluded that they were not Jews and had no legitimate claim to Israeli citizenship, but he offered to begin *giyur* (conversion) procedures. After considering the idea for several months, the Black

Hebrews informed the chief rabbi that, as the true descendants of the biblical Hebrews, they would be happy to begin conversion procedures. Thus began many years of conflict between the Black Hebrews and Israeli religious and political officials.

The event that appears to have triggered the rejection of the conversion offer from the chief rabbi was the arrival in Israel, in March 1970, of Ben Ammi and his remaining 70 followers, all the other Black Hebrews from the Liberian settlement, including the original leaders. Upon his arrival, Ben Ammi insisted that they were not Jews but were Hebrews, a distinction that, though meaningless to Israelis, was now a central component of group ideology. Explained Ben Ammi:

> Our customs are different from yours. We believe only in the Torah, not what was added later. What man has the right to add anything to the Torah. . . . Don't be like the rich man giving alms to the poor and asking for their souls in return.[35]

Further, Ben Ammi asserted that the Black Hebrews and not the Jews were the "true inheritors" of Israel. White people could not be genuine Hebrews because Abraham and Moses were black. The term "Jew," according to Ben Ammi, was a seventeenth-century corruption of the word "Judah," and whites who call themselves Jews were usurpers of a black land and culture.

The new set of arrivals were admitted to Israel on tourist visas and were not offered any benefits by the Israeli government. Instead, they crowded into the apartments of the group members in Arad and Dimona. Several months later a new contingent of Black Hebrews arrived in Israel—nine individuals who had not lived in Liberia but had been recruited by Black Hebrew missionaries who remained in the United States for this purpose. During the next year 150 to 200 new members arrived from the United States. One group, which arrived in early 1971, applied for and received housing from the government in the isolated Negev town of Mitzpe Ramon.

The rapid influx of new members from the United States, individuals who had not undergone the trials and faith-testing experiences of the Liberian settlement, had a dramatic impact on the Black Hebrew group. Because they were admitted into Israel on temporary tourist visas and were not provided with jobs or housing, the new waves of Black Hebrews moved into the increasingly overcrowded apartments. In some apartments as many as three families were pressed together, overtaxing the utilities and causing unsanitary living conditions. Additionally, several of the new arrivals began stealing from their Israeli neighbors, including one who was convicted of robbing a gas station. When these errant members were chastised by Ben Ammi, they began to question his authority. As a member who was loyal to Ben Ammi explained:

> We came to the land of Israel to establish the Kingdom of God. It wasn't to recreate America or any ghettos. There were those who yet didn't understand and came and they began to rebel and backslide in certain ways. . . .

> They were terrible. They were lying and stealing and doing various other things.... But we didn't come to do these things, neither did we come to have these kinds of labels attached to us.

Those who questioned Ben Ammi's authority complained that the leader "broke up the husbands and wives and families, and the women weren't allowed to say anything."[36] Further, they asserted that they had been beaten on several occasions by Ben Ammi's henchmen when they failed to comply with the dictates of the leader.

Fearing that the group was splitting into warring factions, Ben Ammi initiated a final consolidation of power. On October 24, 1972, he called a gathering of all members on a hilltop overlooking Dimona and announced a new set of rules for the group. Included in these "National Guidelines" was a list of punishments for violations of the new social order of what was now called the Black Hebrew Israelite Nation, with disobedience of group leaders being the gravest transgression. Also at this time Ben Ammi instituted a number of formal leadership positions in which he installed his closest supporters. As in the past, Ben Ammi bolstered these changes with a claimed reception of divine revelation. According to one member:

> On that day... is when it was made clear to all the nation, unto all those that had come out of America and out of Liberia unto the land of Israel what our divine purpose and mission was and those things that would not be tolerated.... That's when all the guidelines were set forth and the divine appointments of the princes and the ministers took place. This was done in order to set the Nation in order that we might be about our divinely appointed work.... Those that stood firm, having been called by the spirit of God to oversee the Nation, made it plain that those who were not to stand for God would be on their way. You could say it was a separation because the stand had to be made, it had to be taken.

Individuals who resisted the new regime were expelled and forced to leave their apartments. Only those dissenters who had come to Israel in 1969 and had been given apartments by the Israeli government were allowed to stay in their homes (they continue to live next to but apart from the Black Hebrews). The climax of these events occurred on January 29, 1972, when three dissident Black Hebrews returned to Dimona to speak with some of their friends and relatives still in the group. In front of the municipal bus stop they were confronted by five of Ben Ammi's supporters and a fight ensued, during which one of the dissenters was killed.[37] The five who were loyal to Ben Ammi were tried by the Israeli government, convicted of manslaughter, and sentenced to 6–24 months in prison. When the recipient of the harshest sentence was released from prison and returned to the Black Hebrew community, he was rewarded for his loyalty by having the title *Ha-Gibbor* (the Warrior or Hero) added to his name.

In subsequent years Ben Ammi's position, not only as the political and religious leader of the group but as a messiah figure revered by members, was fully consolidated. Ben Ammi explains this transformation in the following way:

> My anointing did not come until after we had arrived in Israel. The Father sent a prophet to anoint me and to let me know the further off or great portion of my mission. . . . At the time he anointed me. . . . I received the name Nasi Hashalom [The Prince of Peace]. . . . Later on this same prophet came again to tell me according to the word of God that at a later date someone would be sent to anoint me to sit on the throne of David in the spirit and to fulfill the prophecies of he that was to sit on the throne of David. The words of a true prophet, they certainly came to pass, and it took place just as he said. Afterwards, from Nasi Hashalom my name was changed to Rabbey and Adoni Rabbey [My Lord and Master].

As an expression of the group's veneration for Ben Ammi, his picture adorned at least one wall in every group apartment, and when he entered a room, all members immediately stood. Further, Ben Ammi was allotted privileges not enjoyed by the average member. Despite overcrowding, the group maintained two private homes, one in Jerusalem and the other in Arad, largely for Ben Ammi's private use. Ben Ammi, following biblical example, had four wives. Most of the men he appointed to the position of prince also had multiple wives, whereas most of the rank-and-file men in the group did not. In this sense, a clear-cut hierarchy developed within the group, with unequal access to the creation of symbols, the holding of positions of social esteem, and the distribution of material wealth and privilege.

Black Hebrew Symbols in Social Context

Within the Black Hebrew community, as has been noted, Ben Ammi has on several critical occasions reshaped basic tenets and symbols that form group ideology, and these changes, whatever other impact they may have had, served to shore up or consolidate Ben Ammi's position as leader. Over time, Ben Ammi's status was redefined several times, moving from being one among several co-leaders to the unchallenged and near-deified head of the Black Hebrew Israelites. As the arbiter of the increasingly skewed distribution of group knowledge, Ben Ammi and his closest supporters derived both social and material benefits unavailable to others. While most members readily accepted such a hierarchy, this acceptance was not universal. At critical points in the group's history, individuals, families, and small clusters have broken away (or been ejected), some of them becoming openly disparaging of the symbolic and structural changes implemented by Ben Ammi.[38]

Beyond the unequal participation in acquiring knowledge, the social embeddedness of Black Hebrew symbols is reflected in their emergence as a messianic nationalist response to racism and social subordination. Ironically, while the ideology of the group affirms the legitimacy of internal inequality, Black Hebrew beliefs express profound rejection of the gross, racially based disparities of U.S. society. The counterhegemonic features of Black Hebrew ideology include (1) rejection of the denigrated image of African Americans as a subservient people; (2) disdain for various social patterns found disproportionately in the inner city black community, including family instability and female-headed households; (3) substitution of an alternative African American identity founded on a belief in a glorious group history; (4) adoption of various millenarian rites and beliefs; (5) vocal criticism of American society; (6) assertion of black sovereignty through the development of a national flag, anthem, and unique costume, a separatist economic base, and commitment to emigration from the United States; and (7) chiliastic and messianic expectations of a brighter future. In this sense, Black Hebrew symbols construct a world of deliverance for group members. While providing motivation to make dramatic life changes, including suffering various emotional and material losses, and supporting passive integration into a hierarchical community, Black Hebrew symbols offer a sense of personal salvation, a coherent explanation for painfully oppressive realities, and unfettered hope of future redemption.

In short, Black Hebrew symbols weave simultaneous webs of signification and mystification. On the one hand, they construct a meaningful world that shields adherents from the worst insults and injuries of the dominant ideology. On the other hand, they encourage group members in an understanding of the world that subordinates them to a messiah figure while clinging to the expectation of divine intervention as the means of overcoming racial oppression. As Good aptly concludes, the study of the work of symbols has "the potential to awaken us to the presence of the solteriological in human culture, as well as the potential for its exploitation."[39]

Notes

1. The group currently refers to itself as the Hebrew Israelites. Unless otherwise indicated, quotes from the group are from Merrill Singer, *Saints of the Kingdom: Group Emergence, Individual Affiliation, and Social Change among the Black Hebrews of Israel*, doctoral dissertation, Department of Anthropology, University of Utah, 1979, and are based on one year of ethnographic research with the Black Hebrews in Israel.

2. Hans Baer and Merrill Singer, *African American Religion in the Twentieth Century: Varieties of Protest and Accommodation* (Knoxville: University of Tennessee Press, 1992).

3. James Landing, "The Spatial Expression of Cultural Revitalization in Chicago," *Proceedings of the Association of American Geographers* 6 (1974), p. 51.

4. Howard Brotz, *The Black Jews of Harlem* (New York: Schocken, 1970); Deanne Ruth Shapiro, "Double Damnation, Double Salvation," MA thesis, Department of Philosophy, Columbia University; Singer, *Saints of the Kingdom*.

5. Le Roi Jones, *Blues People: Negro Music in White America* (Westport, CT: Greenwood Press, 1963), p. 40.

6. Merrill Singer, "'Now I Know What the Songs Mean!': Traditional Black Music in a Contemporary Black Sect," *Southern Quarterly* 23 (1985), 125–40.

7. Lawrence Levine, *Black Culture and Black Consciousness* (New York: Oxford University Press, 1977), p. 23.

8. Albert Raboteau, *Slave Religion* (New York: Oxford University Press, 1978), p. 250.

9. Harold Courlander, *Negro Folk Music U.S.A.* (London: Jazz Book Club, 1966), p. 42.

10. Eugene Genovese, *Roll Jordan Roll* (New York: Vintage Books, 1974).

11. St. Clair Drake and Horace Cayton, *Black Metropolis* (New York: Harper, 1962), p. 623.

12. Okon Edet Uya, "Life in a Slave Community," *Afro-American Studies* 1 (1971), 289.

13. Gayraud Wilmore, *Black Religion and Black Radicalism* (Garden City, NY: Orbis, 1972).

14. Manning Marable, *Blackwater: Historical Studies in Race, Class Consciousness and Revolution* (Dayton, Ohio: Black Praxis Press, 1981), pp. 18–19.

15. Brotz, op. cit., p. 1.

16. Genovese, op. cit., p. 252.

17. Marable, op. cit., p. 26.

18. Merrill Singer, Freddie Valentín, Hans Baer, and Zhongke Jia, "Why Does Juan García Have a Drinking Problem? The Perspective of Critical Medical Anthropology," *Medical Anthropology* 14 (1991), pp. 77–108.

19. Bertram Korn, "Jews and Negro Slavery in the Old South 1789–1865," *Publications of the American Jewish Historical Society* 1 (1961), pp. 151–201.

20. David Bleich, "Black Jews: A Halakhic Perspective," *Tradition* 15 (1972), 47–49; Graenum Berger, *Black Jews in America* (New York: Commission on Synagogue Relations, 1978).

21. Shapiro, op. cit.

22. Arthur Huff Fauset, *Black Gods of the Metropolis* (Philadelphia: University of Pennsylvania Press, 1971).

23. Ibid., p. 34.

24. August Meier, "The Emergence of Negro Nationalism," *The Midwest Journal* IV (1963), 95–111.

25. Booker T. Washington, *The Future of the American Negro* (Boston: Smally, Maynard and Company, 1902), p. 7.

26. Edwin Redkey, *Black Exodus* (New Haven, CT.: Yale University Press, 1969), p. 22.

27. Ibid., p. 24.

28. Ibid., p. 301.

29. Leon Festinger, Henry Riecken, and Stanley Schachter, *When Prophecy Fails* (New York: Harper and Row, 1956).

30. John Lofland and Rodney Stark, "Becoming a World-Saver: A Theory of Conversion to a Deviant Perspective," *American Sociological Review* 30 (1965), 862–75; Singer, "The Social Context of Conversion to a Black Religious Sect," *Review of Religious Research* 30 (1988), 177–92.

31. Melvin Williams, *On the Street Where I Lived* (New York: Holt, Rinehart, and Winston, 1981); Baer and Singer, op. cit.; Singer, "Life in a Defensive Society: The Black Hebrew Israelites," in Jon Wagner, ed., *Sex Roles in Contemporary American Communes* (Bloomfield: Indiana University Press, 1982), pp. 45–81.

32. Clifford Geertz, *The Interpretation of Cultures* (New York: Basic Books, 1973), p. 105.

33. Quoted in Delores MacCahill, "Black Hebrews Cook Up a Land of Promise in Liberia," *Chicago Sun Times*, April, 11, 1969, p. 38.

34. Quoted in Singer, *Saints of The Kingdom*.

35. Quoted in Emmet Wigoder, "America's Black Jews in Israel," *Israel Magazine* 3 (1970), 43

36. Quoted in Tony Griggs, "Angry Black Jews Return Here," *The Chicago Defender*, September 27, 1972, p. 3.

37. Herbert Ben-Avdi, "Witness 17 Describes Black Hebrew's Fight," *The Jerusalem Post*, February 22, 1972.

38. Singer, "Now I Know What The Songs Mean!"

39. Byron Good, *Medicine, Rationality and Experience* (Cambridge: Cambridge University Press, 1994), p. 181.

4

Another Exodus

The Hebrew Israelites from Chicago to Dimona

Ethan Michaeli

From their birthplace in the ghettos of Chicago's South Side to their current home in the modern state of Israel, the Hebrew Israelites have been propelled by a powerful combination of religious and racial identity. In this essay I will examine recent developments within the Hebrew Israelite community. My work is based on a series of interviews I conducted with Hebrew Israelite leaders in the United States and Israel (many while I was a reporter for the *Chicago Defender*), on my visit to the Dimona community in 1996, and on my attendance at a number of Hebrew Israelite events in Chicago over the course of the 1990s. Though limited to official sources, my research reveals that the Hebrew Israelites are currently experiencing a number of significant political and ideological shifts, including a better relationship with the Israeli government and a more inclusive attitude toward Jews.

My insights into the Hebrew Israelites were both enhanced and limited by my role as a reporter for the *Chicago Defender*, an African American–owned daily newspaper which has been published for nearly a century. Because of the newspaper's historic role within the African American community, I was privileged with unique access to the Hebrew Israelite leadership and their supporters throughout African American Chicago and when I traveled to Israel. The readership and editorial staff of the *Defender*, moreover, were highly interested in continuing coverage of the Hebrew Israelites, allowing me to revisit the topic over a period of several years. My research was largely defined, however, by the constraints of daily newspaper reporting in that I had relatively little access to rank-and-file Hebrew Israelites or to the group's literature, nor is my perspective that of a scholar of religion but rather that of a journalist with long experience in the African American community.

In 1969 the Hebrew Israelites began arriving in Israel—which they referred to as Northeast Africa—from Liberia, where they had established a community during the 1960s. The Hebrew Israelites claimed the right to Israeli citizenship under the nation's Law of Return, which guarantees automatic citizenship to any Jewish individual. Like many immigrants to Israel at the time, the Hebrew Israelites requested settlement in Jerusalem. However, using policies designed to expand the Israeli presence in outlying areas with new immigrants, the Israeli government instead settled them in the Negev Desert town of Dimona. In 1973, Israeli officials ruled that the Hebrew Israelites did not have the right to Israeli citizenship and denied the group work permits and state benefits.

The Hebrew Israelites retaliated with a campaign in the United States which accused the Israeli government of racist discrimination against the group. Throughout the 1970s and 1980s Prince Asiel Ben Israel, the Hebrew Israelites' "International Ambassador" and the highest-ranking Hebrew Israelite in the United States, organized protests and enlisted black political figures, community activists, and other figures—including Nation of Islam leader Louis Farrakhan—in the Hebrew Israelites' cause. Ben Ammi, the leader of the Hebrew Israelites, claimed publicly that Jews had usurped the mantle of being "God's chosen" from African Americans. American Jewish organizations—in particular the Anti-Defamation League of B'nai Brith—responded to the Hebrew Israelites' actions with a media campaign which portrayed the Hebrew Israelites as a racist movement in the same vein as the Nation of Islam and various white supremacist groups.

Though the Israeli government never officially moved to deport the Hebrew Israelite community as a whole, a number of individuals were returned to the United States after being arrested for working illegally. Ultimately, the Hebrew Israelites renounced their American citizenship in an effort to prevent further deportations. During the same period the Hebrew Israelites faced other challenges. For example, in 1986 the U.S. Attorney's Office in Chicago brought charges of various financial misdealings against Prince Asiel Ben Israel. He and three others were found guilty and served several years in prison.

In October 1990, Illinois state legislators brokered an agreement with the Israeli government that settled—albeit temporarily—the Hebrew Israelites' legal status in Israel. They are now permitted to hold jobs and receive access to social services and housing. Members of the group reclaimed their American citizenship and received support from the American government that allowed them to build a school and expand housing.

Hebrew Israelite settlements in Dimona and Arad, another Negev town, have a combined population of over 2,000. The Hebrew Israelite gospel choir tours throughout Israel, and the community owns restaurants in several Israeli cities. The settlement with the American and Israeli governments has allowed the Hebrew Israelites to expand their housing and develop a specialized school that combines an education in modern Hebrew, science, math, and Israeli civics with Hebrew Israelite spiritual tenets. Within its compound, the group operates a clinic, communal kitchen, and organic farm.

The rhetorical conflict that marked the previous decades of the Hebrew Israelites' tenure in Israel appears to have evaporated. According to Israeli government sources, the community's two decades in Israel have dispelled Israeli fears that acceptance of the Hebrew Israelites would encourage an exodus of millions of African Americans. Despite aggressive proselytizing in African American neighborhoods across the country, Hebrew Israelites have little more than trickled into Dimona and the other, smaller communities.

In the United States the Hebrew Israelites have established communities in a number of major cities, including Chicago, St. Louis, and Washington, D.C. In addition to bringing in new members, the group's American branches seek to play a grass roots political role in many African American neighborhoods. Characteristic of these efforts was their part in brokering a truce between rival street gangs in Chicago's infamous public housing developments in the fall of 1993.

Beliefs and Rituals

The distinct identity forged by the Hebrew Israelites—visible in their beliefs, rituals, and lifestyle—fuses their particular interpretation of biblical religion with aspects of African American culture. Hebrew Israelite clothing, for example, combines West African styles with biblical traditions. Men wear long African print shirts with the biblically prescribed fringes known in Hebrew as *tsitsit*, as well as head coverings called *kippot*. Women wear long, modest dresses and follow the biblical rules concerning menstruation, known as *niddah*. Following the biblical example—one that was also accepted in some Jewish communities into the twentieth century—Hebrew Israelite men are allowed to have more than one wife.

The community has a strictly vegan diet, which it derives from its exegesis of Genesis 1:29, "And God said: Behold, I have given you every herb-yielding seed, which is upon the face of all the earth, and every tree, in which is the fruit of a tree yielding seed—to you it shall be for food." The Hebrew Israelites refer to their diet as "Edenic" (derived from the Garden of Eden) and consider dietary prescriptions that appear later in the Bible, such as the rules of Leviticus, as concessions or accommodations to human weakness and not binding on their own community. The Hebrew Israelites also characterize their diet as an antidote to the unhealthy lifestyle they associate with African American inner city communities. Reflecting their own roots in these communities, however, the Hebrew Israelite communal kitchen in Dimona serves vegan versions of traditional African American dishes, such as corn bread and gravy, along with tofu products the group makes in its own factory.

The community considers its leader, Ben Ammi, to be the messiah and view themselves as locked in an apocalyptic struggle with the forces of evil. In this struggle the Hebrew Israelites play a biblically ordained, redemptive role and will eventually gather in the righteous to Jerusalem. Although they do not have a substantial physical presence in Jerusalem, members of the group visit the city often. In addition, the community's ritual leaders are known as *kohanim*, the Hebrew word for the priests who served in the ancient Temple in Jerusalem. Unlike contemporary Jewish *kohanim*, who claim to be actual descendants of the biblical priests, the Hebrew Israelites choose individuals to become priests on the basis of their spiritual characteristics rather than ancestry.

The Hebrew Israelites observe the Sabbath from Friday to Saturday night and celebrate other biblically ordained holidays such as Yom Kippur and Passover. Following another biblical tradition, the group celebrates the New Year in spring rather than in the fall, when contemporary Jews celebrate the New Year festival of Rosh Hashanah. The Hebrew Israelites combine African American religious traditions, such as gospel songs and call and response, with prayers in Hebrew composed by members of the community, often employing biblical verses, in particular the Psalms. The Hebrew Israelites characterize their history in biblical terms and depict their journey from the ghettos of the United States to Israel as a reenactment of the ancient Israelites' Exodus from Egypt.

In a 1995 interview in Chicago, Ben Ammi said he knew Liberia was an interim stop for the group. He described the Hebrew Israelites' abbreviated tenure there as a tropical, coastal metaphor for Moses' 40-year sojourn in the Sinai desert. Ben Ammi emphasized that the travails of the last quarter century had tested, transformed, and finally revised key doctrines of the Hebrew Israelites' faith. Most notably, he recently modified his earlier assertions that African Americans are the only true descendants of biblical Israel and that Jews are "imposters." In an April 1996 interview with me in Dimona (fig. 4.1), Ben Ammi explained that the quarter century of contact with Israeli Jews was necessary to free his mind from the narrow vision of Jews and Judaism that he had brought with him from Chicago.

Ben Ammi and other Hebrew Israelite spokespeople currently espouse the view that not all African Americans or all Jews are physical descendants of biblical Israel but that many members of both groups, as well as some individuals from other groups, can trace their ancestry to the tribes of Israel who were exiled from the land of Israel. In current Hebrew Israelite ideology, an individual's righteousness, rather than his or her skin color or ethnic origin, is the true sign of Hebrew Israelite ancestry. Reflecting this new ideological development, the Hebrew Israelites now have a number of non-African American members.

Ben Ammi: Return to Chicago

In 1993 Ben Ammi traveled to Chicago and appeared at a South Side church whose pastor had long been involved in black nationalist causes. As a reporter for the *Chicago Defender*, I covered his appearance. The chill from the brisk Sunday morning and the desolate surroundings of Garfield Boulevard belied the enthusiastic, colorful crowd inside the church. Craig Hodges, a former Chicago Bulls basketball star, joined dozens of community activists and local leaders. The crowd included men in their Sunday suits and women in resplendent outfits as well as numerous individu-

FIGURE 4.1. *Ben Ammi with the author. Dimona, Israel, 1996.*

als in African style clothes. By the time Ben Ammi began to speak, the church was filled to capacity.

Ben Ammi took the podium dressed in robes and turban. A thin, graceful man with blazing blue-gray eyes and a sparse beard, he began his speech slowly and methodically. As he delved deeper into religious topics from both the Hebrew Bible and the New Testament, Ben Ammi began to rock forward and make stiff, powerful gestures. He traced the origin of all religious life to the Middle East and discussed a number of prophets, from Ezekiel to Jesus. He described the Hebrew Israelites' Dimona settlement as a community that had freed itself from the evils of African American urban life—no drugs, no crime, no drive-by shootings. He encouraged African Americans to accept their destiny as God's chosen people and begin a new life in the Middle East. Ben Ammi listed the names of dozens of individuals who had been to Dimona and could testify that it was an idyllic, moral community of devout African Americans in the Holy Land.

In 1995 Ben Ammi visited Chicago again and made high-profile appearances in both the African American and Jewish communities. During his visit I interviewed him for the *Chicago Defender*. Ben Ammi declared that the political settlement had allowed the Hebrew Israelites in Dimona to stabilize and thrive. Although the original Hebrew Israelite settlers all came from Chicago, new waves of immigrants had arrived from African American communities across the United States. The community now included members who had been reared in Detroit, Atlanta, Washington, D.C., and New York City.

According to Ben Ammi, the agreement between the Hebrew Israelites, the American government, and Israeli officials paved the way for the community to expand in both concrete and philosphical terms. The years of conflict with the Israeli government had been hard years, Ben Ammi admitted. His people were not allowed to work legally, and those who worked and were caught were deported. They lived in a few extremely crowded apartments and suffered even as a new generation of Hebrew Israelites was being born in the Holy Land. The group's morale was low and the tensions sometimes turned to anger. Ben Ammi emphasized that only the kindness and generosity of Dimona's Israeli residents had ensured that the Hebrew Israelites did not starve; Israelis respected the Hebrew Israelites' determination to stay in a nation that was still developing.

"We have never had a problem with the people," Ben Ammi said. "The differences we have had have always been political differences."

In addition to solidarity with the Israelis, Ben Ammi said his community had emerged from the hard years in Dimona with an increased strength in their resolve. The community had not descended into drug abuse, violence, and despair, characteristics of the neighborhoods that they had left. The Dimona Hebrew Israelites had maintained the diet, lifestyle, and faith that had brought them across the ocean. Ben Ammi saw this success as evidence of the righteous nature of the community.

In the spring of 1995 Ben Ammi and Prince Asiel attended the Israeli Independence Day celebration in Chicago. Held every year in the elegant Cultural Center in the heart of Chicago's business district, the event typically saw the gathering of a variety of Jewish leaders and intellectuals, Israeli residents of the area, and politicians demonstrating their solidarity with the State of Israel. Ben Ammi and Prince Asiel, dressed in African-style robes and carrying wooden staffs, mingled easily with the crowd, greeting journalists, dignitaries, and well-wishers amid trays of pita bread, humus, and babaganoush. The party-goers included many of the state legislators, both Jewish and black, who had brokered the deal that legitimized the Hebrew Israelites' presence in Israel.

Privately, Israeli government officials from the local consulate expressed general satisfaction with the Hebrew Israelites, but they also revealed that they had learned that during his current tour of America, Ben Ammi had met with Louis Farrakhan and other African American figures whom they considered to be hostile to Jews and the State of Israel. Ben Ammi's public statements had nevertheless remained friendly to Israel and Jews in general, the consulate officials said, and the Israeli government had not regretted its decision to support the Dimona community.

Ben Ammi repeatedly described his group as uniquely qualified to serve as a bridge between African Americans and traditional Jews on both sides of the ocean.

Unlike the Ethiopian Jews, who had been brought to Israel in dramatic airlifts during the 1980s and 1990s, for example, the Hebrew Israelites had roots within the African American community. Buoyed by the success of his visit to America, Ben Ammi was ebullient about the prospects of playing a central role in improving relations between African Americans and Jews.

Dimona

I visited the Hebrew Israelites' Dimona community on the last day of Passover in the spring of 1996. Since the Hebrew Israelites' arrival in Israel, the country had become a prosperous, industrialized state. Development had not, however, occurred evenly throughout the nation. Whereas Tel Aviv, Haifa, and other coastal areas had become thriving cosmopolitan centers, smaller towns in the Negev like Dimona had not benefited proportionately.

The road to Dimona from Tel Aviv demonstrates the diversity of the Israeli geography. The fecund, humid coast of Tel Aviv gives way to the farms and orchards of central Israel. Minutes later the greenery evaporates along the gradual decline into the sun-baked Negev. Mountains of red and gold stone, barren in their lunar beauty, spread out through the horizon. The last stop before Dimona is Beer Sheva, Israel's desert metropolis, a one-time Bedouin market that has sprouted businesses, factories, and apartment high-rises.

Dimona is located several kilometers beyond Beer Sheva. The main street is lined with Israeli low-rise dwellings, many with red-tiled roofs. When I arrived, the boulevard's only other traffic was a lone donkey, lazily driven in a slow meander by a youth with a twig. At the periphery of the Hebrew Israelite compound I was greeted by a young Hebrew Israelite boy wearing a knitskull cap and African-print robes.

I asked him in Hebrew, "Excuse me, where is Ben Ammi's house?"

The boy looked at me and pointed into a complex of houses. "Over there," he answered in Hebrew, "through those houses."

The gateway to the Hebrew Israelite compound was ringed by a waist-high wall of khaki round stones. I walked along a stone-paved path through the small, one-level houses that typify Israeli immigrant settlement communities. A group of tall, thin young men, dressed in crisp white robes and wearing white knit skullcaps, stood in the shade of a tall tree. I explained to them that I had an appointment with Ben Ammi, and one of the youths quickly guided me to the home of another community leader.

Elegant in his comfortable cotton robe, Prince Elkannan stroked his luxuriant white beard as he offered me a cold, sweet fruit drink. The living room was spare: concrete, cool, and airy as most Israeli homes are, though Elkannan's home lacked the air conditioner and television set that are common in Israeli homes. A native of one of Detroit's most impoverished neighborhoods, Elkannan said his decision to become a Hebrew Israelite arose from a desire to shed a life destined for corruption, poverty, and misery in favor of everlasting paradise. African Americans from similar places around the country—ghettos in New York, Baltimore, Philadelphia, and other cities—had come for similar reasons. All of them believed that the Hebrew Israelite lifestyle would afford them immortality. Elkannan assured me that no one had ever died in the Hebrew Israelite community. He saw everlasting life as the product of the Hebrew Israelite's comprehensive, philosophic approach to life, a matrix that coded their daily behavior.

The land of Israel was the only environment in which the Hebrew Israelite community could thrive, according to Elkannan. He continued to emphasize that the Hebrew Israelite community had never seen and would never see a funeral; illness and malnutrition had been eliminated in Dimona, he insisted. Moreover, the Hebrew Israelites had eliminated the violent deaths that claim a disproportionate number of young African Americans. Elkannan said that the illegal drug trade and its consequences—addicts, dealers, drive-by shootings, and incarceration—were all unknown to those members of the Dimona community who had grown up there. The Hebrew Israelites had developed a quasi-Zionist ideology that made living in Israel a precondition to eliminating the perceived evils of the African American world they had left behind.

All of the inhabitants of the Dimona Hebrew Israelite community dressed in gender-indicative African print cloth. The women wore ankle-length robes and layered head scarves, while older men wore two-piece suits with brimless cylindrical caps. Younger men tended to wear knit caps. My guides through the Dimona community informed me that space was extremely tight. Although the community's yards and homes maintained a neat outward appearance, families were packed into the few houses. The guides said the community was quiet because of Passover, but the stone paths between the homes teemed with groups of young children playing in groups. The children bowed and greeted the adults who passed them. In general, the community was gender-segregated, with strict separation between unmarried young people and even between unaccompanied married adults of the opposite sex.

The Dimona community contained a number of communal facilities. The Conquering Lion of Judah Health Center was operated by Crown Brother Abir. Abir described a training curriculum that included martial arts and yoga, weights, and isometric equipment as well as use of a Jacuzzi and massage facilities. The physical regimen included intensive stretching, breathing, and other holistic exercises, Abir explained, with separate classes and schedules for men and women. The Hebrew Israelite health clinic was staffed by a team of midwives and spiritual physicians who dealt with a wide variety of illnesses and conditions. The midwives boasted that over 600 children had been born successfully through their techniques. Serious injuries such as broken bones were treated at local hospitals, however.

The school compound, financed through the arrangement with the U.S. and Israeli governments, had been built at the edge of the Hebrew Israelite settlement. Although only Hebrew Israelite children attended the school, Israeli school system teachers were employed there as instructors of modern Hebrew, with Russian immigrants as science and math teachers, and Hebrew Israelite teachers for religion and culture.

Many of the community's services were organized along the lines of communal Israeli settlements known as *kibbutzim*. The community's cafeteria was known as a *chadar ochel* after the dining space in the *kibbutzim*. The cafeteria's head cook explained that the community's younger children ate two meals daily at the *chadar ochel*, prepared according to the strict vegan diet prescribed by Hebrew Israelite beliefs. Like many agricultural *kibbutzim*, much of the food used in the *chadar ochel* was grown in communal plots. At the community's clothing store, Hebrew Israelite seamstresses assembled and sold robes, dresses, and turbans that the community members wore, but they also geared their designs for sale to Israeli and foreign consumers.

Hebrew Israelites referred to Ben Ammi as *abba*, the Hebrew word for "father." Ben Ammi received me in the Prince Asiel International Spiritual Center, a modest office decorated with newspaper and magazine articles and photographs depicting the African American singer Stevie Wonder's tour of the Dimona community, along with magazine articles about the community in *Teva Dvarim*, the Israeli version of *National Geographic*. Several of the articles featured the Hebrew Israelites' talented choir.

Ben Ammi described a Hebrew Israelite community that was planted firmly in the modern nation of Israel and the politics of the Middle East. Ben Ammi proclaimed that the Hebrew Israelites had changed their orientation and needs after a quarter century spent in Israel. He referred to Israel as "The Land," a translation from the Hebrew *ha'aretz*, the word employed by Israelis. Ben Ammi acknowledged that geography and experience had created a set of concerns entirely different from those of other African American leaders.

"I would be more concerned with getting an audience with [then Prime Minister Shimon] Peres than with getting an audience with Bill Clinton. The position of Peres is more essential to my life and well-being than the position of Bill Clinton. Naturally, that puts us in a very unique position," Ben Ammi said. "No intended disrespect but it's a question of priorities. Our destiny is tied to the State of Israel."

Ben Ammi emphasized that the Hebrew Israelites' experience in Israel had transformed their perspective concerning Jews. Where he had once been suspicious of Jews and denied their legitimacy, Ben Ammi now included at least some Jews in his collective "Chosen People." Ben Ammi attributed part of the change in perspective to the political agreement that had eased their living conditions. But the single most powerful agent of the Hebrew Israelites' change was the conduct of the Israeli residents of Dimona. Dimona residents had provided food, work, and other necessities for the Hebrew Israelites when the political situation prevented official support of any kind.

"Our problems have always been political. Our people have always been great. In

Dimona, we've never had any problems. No one has ever lifted up a finger against us. We haven't lifted a finger against anyone. In times of emergency, we all go out together.

"We're very thankful because, once again, we want to become more involved with what's taking place here."

The Hebrew Israelites' appreciation for their Israeli neighbors was heightened during the Persian Gulf War. When the notoriously imprecise Iraqi SCUDS targeted the Dimona nuclear reactor, the Hebrew Israelites hid in bunkers alongside their Israeli neighbors. In Ben Ammi these experiences generated a feeling of solidarity, inclusion, and loyalty. Ben Ammi contrasted these feelings with the exasperation and helplessness that he had experienced in Chicago.

"We were ready to go to Iraq. Anything that we could have done to stop those SCUDS, we would have been ready to do that and we view that differently from the violence in the neighborhood. We don't want violence in Chicago neighborhoods, but our priorities are quite different here because, again, we're part of the state of Israel," Ben Ammi said. He emphasized that the Hebrew Israelites were committed to pursuing full citizenship and would recognize military and other obligations.

"We want the whole load. When it's time to cry, we will weep together. When it's time to rejoice, we will rejoice together."

Ben Ammi's priorities have placed the Hebrew Israelites on the right of Israeli politics. He supports continued Israeli occupation of the West Bank on religious grounds and urges all Jews to adhere to biblical principles and morals.

"Our priorities are quite different from those of African American communities. These are the things that we seek in our vision. We see the redemption of our people there, in Israel, and all humanity as coming via the achievements and the redemption of the children of Israel," he said. "We were chosen to be a light unto the nations."

Ben Ammi saw a distinct, grand role for the Hebrew Israelites and for himself in modern Israel. Theologically oriented, Ben Ammi saw himself as the broker for the salvation of both Jews and blacks. Arguing that many blacks and Jews were descended from a common heritage, Ben Ammi said that his role would be to catalyze this realization in both communities. He hoped to serve as the "spiritual prime minister" of an Israel that would welcome both Jews and African Americans.

The Hebrew Israelites alone had the ability to exploit this potential alliance, Ben Ammi argued. He saw the Hebrew Israelites as the only group capable of bridging the considerable gaps between Jews and African Americans. Conscious that most Jews and African Americans do not believe that they share a common ancestry and birthright, Ben Ammi said the Hebrew Israelites' unique understanding of both cultures was the necessary ingredient to forge a union of Zionist Jews and Pan-Africanist blacks.

"We represent another paradigm and we are telling all Jews, Israelites, that you're Africans. They're not really ready to accept yet that Israel is a part of Africa historically. That means that if you're a Jew, an Israelite, you're not a European," Ben Ammi told me.

"I'm not trying to make you like me. I'm an Israelite. I'm an African. Israelites are, were, and always will be African as far as the continent. Because of the old indoctrinations, there is a fear of that."

I asked Ben Ammi to reflect on the country and community he had left behind. Ben Ammi was disappointed in the conditions in poor African American neighborhoods, which he felt were far worse than at the time of his departure. The efforts of African American leaders—albeit well intentioned—had failed to disrupt a tide of poverty, drug abuse, and depravity, Ben Ammi argued. To Ben Ammi, African Americans' circumstances would not improve until they acknowledged their Israelite identity and sought out the Promised Land.

Sound and the Kidnapped Afrikan

From disparate, sometimes contradictory motivations and experiences, the Hebrew Israelites have developed a complex worldview. The Hebrew Israelites have followed their religious vision—which combines traditional African American identification with biblical Israel and Pan-African philosophy—to the modern state of Israel. The Hebrew Israelites believe that the redemption of African Americans can be accomplished only through an exodus to the Promised Land. In trying to motivate other African Americans to join their exodus, the Hebrew Israelites have articulated their worldview in literature, music, and other creative endeavors.

Perhaps most compellingly, since 1995 the Hebrew Israelites have toured the United States with a musical drama called *Sound and the Kidnapped Afrikan*. The play depicts the harsh conditions of life in inner city communities as divine punishment. Like the Old Testament Israelites, African Americans are portrayed as a chosen people temporarily out of favor. The play traces African American history from a time of regal prosperity in Africa, to slavery on Southern plantations, to self-destructive behavior on the streets of Northern cities. In the play, musical ability functions as a metaphor for divine selection. In each scene of the performance, African Americans perform music to transcend their miserable circumstances. The songs reflect the continuous ability of the African people to produce beauty, even during the agony of their exile.

In Chicago *Sound and the Kidnapped Afrikan* was performed on several weekends in February 1997 at the AFC Theater on 79th and Ashland, the desolate heart of the Englewood neighborhood. Once a thriving commercial district, Englewood today is a lonely landscape of vacant lots, long-abandoned storefronts, and run-down single-family homes. Originally built as a movie theater, the AFC Theater now serves mainly as the headquarters of an evangelical Protestant church. Although the play had taken over the actual performing space, most of the building's storefronts were in use as prayer halls even on the night of the play. The building's corner store, which must have been in a prime location in the theater's heyday, now housed a store selling religious paraphernalia.

On the night I attended *Sound and the Kidnapped Afrikan*, the audience's many affluent-looking members appeared to have come from beyond blighted Englewood. The parking lot was filled with late-model, expensive vehicles. Well-dressed men in long leather coats escorted women in furs and boots through the howling Chicago winds into the theater's lobby. Prince Asiel stood at the theater's entrance, greeting many of the arriving community leaders. Entrance to the theater was controlled by a phalanx of large, tight-suited security men. In the hallway immediately outside the theater, Hebrew Israelites from Dimona offered books by Ben Ammi as well as clothing and jewelry.

The theater's interior typified the once-grand style of Chicago's inner-city neighborhoods. The previous weekends' performances had been sold out, although the performance I attended was approximately three-fifths filled with an entirely African American crowd. The start of the play was delayed by a quarter hour, apparently to facilitate the arrival of a special guest. Just before the lights dimmed, a small group of suited men hustled to the front two rows. At their center was Nation of Islam Leader Louis Farrakhan, dressed in a white fur coat, a bowler cap, and his trademark amber-tinted, gold-framed glasses. Farrakhan glanced quickly back at the crowd and flashed a broad smile.

Farrakhan's presence at the performance of *Sound and the Kidnapped Afrikan* suggested that the Nation of Islam and the Hebrew Israelites continued to enjoy at least a cordial relationship since the days when Farrakhan had lent support to the Hebrew Israelites in their lobbying efforts. This view was supported by an earlier event I attended in June 1996, in which Ben Ammi gave a lecture entitled "Our Prophetic Geo-Political Position: Israel–America–Africa: Hebrewism, Christianity, and Islam," at Kennedy-King College, a public institution on Chicago's South Side. Farrakhan's wife, Khadijah, was one of several African American community leaders who joined a group of prominent Hebrew Israelites on stage.

During my interview with Ben Ammi in Dimona, I had asked him about the Million Man March organized by Farrakhan in Washington, D.C. Ben Ammi took exception to the Nation of Islam's description of the event as a "A Day of Atonement." Referring to the Jewish holy day Yom Kippur, Ben Ammi said the march's theme was a misappropriation of an Israelite tradition and therefore, despite the march's positive aspects, he was unable to endorse it:

"The Day of Atonement—that's a special kind of event. [The Million Man March] wasn't the Day of Atonement and the danger would have been for me to give the impression that it was the Day of Atonement.

"You know what's going to happen now. That's going to become a tradition and I've been warned about the traditions of men.

"They need a Day of Atonement but that wasn't it.

"The Muslim world is looking for some inroads to form an alliance between the

Muslim community and the African American community and to move into the political arena—Muslims, African Americans, and Arabs.

"And we look up and see it is working. First of all, they gave an address. In the midst of the African American community, they said, here is the address to make inroads.

"They're making inroads because the African American community again is lacking in understanding. First of all, lacking in understanding of the problems that are there and lacking in understanding of the tools that they have at their disposal to neutralize the multiplicity of problems that exist today between the African American and the Jewish communities."

From his comments, it was clear that Ben Ammi felt a connection to Farrakhan because of their shared goal to improve the spiritual and material conditions of African Americans. He also respected the Nation of Islam's efforts to raise the issues of responsiblity and atonement within the African American community. Yet, because of the Hebrew Israelites' position within the State of Israel, Ben Ammi was concerned about any alliance between African American, Muslim, and Arab groups that might jeopardize the security of Israel and, by extension, the Hebrew Israelite community. Moreover, Ben Ammi appeared troubled by the tension between the Nation of Islam and the American Jewish community and hoped that African Americans would awaken to the positive role that the Hebrew Israelites could play in improving relations between the two groups.

After watching Farrakhan enter the theater, I greeted Zockriel Ben Israel, whom I had met several times with Prince Asiel. Zockriel, who served as the play's narrator, explained that this tour was the play's second in two years. Last year, he said, *Sound and the Kidnapped Afrikan* had been performed in more than a dozen cities in just a few weeks. Zockriel boasted that this year's performance was enhanced by a new metallic backdrop on which giant slides were projected and other sets mounted.

The play opened with a lone woman in colored robes performing an elaborate dance. Zockriel, his voice amplified across the theater, explained that the dancer was "Sound," an expression of the God of Zion's love for the African people. While Sound performed, Zockriel declared that God created the world with the African people as his chosen, most beloved subjects. The stage was changed into a court during the golden age of African civilization. Drums heralded the arrival of a king, for whom a troupe of women danced passionately.

Zockriel declared that God had become disappointed with the African people. To punish them, God sent the ships of white slavemasters to take them into exile. The king of the scene entitled "Afrikan Glory" now found himself in the center of the stage, bound by chains. Still surrounding him, the dancers sang a wailing lament. On the backdrop a large image of a slave ship alternated with a portrait of brutal Africans beating the terrified slaves.

The set then transformed into a field on a Southern plantation. The actors who had portrayed the African royal court now took on the roles of slaves. After this portrait of Southern slavery, the play focused exclusively on the lives of African Americans in the urban North. In one scene an unscrupulous minister led an identically dressed choir in a song about Jesus and the salvation of his congregation. The minister's cohorts effected a passing of the hat through the audience. When they had finished with the mock collection, the minister greedily turned his back on the singing choir to count the money.

Later scenes portrayed the depravation of life on the inner-city streets. As pop songs filled the theater, the performers acted out scenes in which they drank themselves into oblivion, shot heroin into their veins, and smoked marijuana. The African king of old, now dressed in a lemon yellow jumpsuit and matching widebrim hat, pimped a beautiful woman and sold drugs on the street until they both collapsed, overcome with debauchery.

In the opening sequence of the final scene, three African American men took the stage in a procession. An economically successful African American man, with the shadow of the Capitol building to his back, posed with his briefcase and informed the audience about his concern for his personal success—to the detriment of his community. A minister and a street hustler emerged next, proclaiming their efforts to corrupt and exploit the poor neighborhoods where they dwelled. Suddenly the desperation of these figures was interrupted by the arrival of a different type of man. Young, healthy, and handsome, this figure walked onto the stage dressed in white robes with a white cap. The personification of Hebrew Israelite manhood, he offered the audience an alternative to the triple vision of corrupted masculinity. The Hebrew Israelite spokesman exhorted the audience, rather than continuing to live a defiling life in America, to relocate to "Northeast Africa" (i.e., Israel), the original home of the African exiles. Before a painted backdrop of a black family dressed in African-style clothing boarding a jetliner, the performers shed their American street clothes in favor of Hebrew Israelite dress and began a triumphant dance as "Sound" joined them on the stage. This final scene recalls a classical Zionist image: the various diasporic Jewish populations—Yemenite, Ethiopean, Soviet—which arrived in Israel on the "wings of an eagle,"—that is, a jet plane.

Conclusion

The Hebrew Israelites travel on the same currents in African American thought that have made Malcolm X and Louis Farrakhan leaders for many African Americans. They float on the same river that carried Jamaican-cum-New Yorker Marcus Garvey and the members of the United Negro Improvement Association. The Hebrew Israelites also find kinship, common rhetoric, and musical solidarity with Rastafarians, who draw on many of the same biblical associations and traditions. But Ben Ammi took the Hebrew Israelites in a unique direction when he brought his followers to the modern state of Israel in the 1960s. The Hebrew Israelites' resolve to establish a thriving community in Israel has inexorably altered their philosophy and practice.

In several interviews Ben Ammi explained to me that the Hebrew Israelites came to Israel with deep suspicions about the nature and birthright of Jews. These views complicated and sometimes inflamed relations with their new Israeli neighbors, and particularly with the Israeli government. Today, with their status in Israel at least temporarily resolved, Ben Ammi preaches a common heritage for African Americans and Jews. Indeed, he sees a special role for himself and the Hebrew Israelites in unifying Jews and African Americans in Israel and the United States. To that end, the Hebrew Israelites currently seek out allies in American Jewish groups and Israeli political organizations. The Hebrew Israelites' aspirations also depend on a continued presence in African American communities. Branches in Chicago and other American cities operate businesses, recruit new members, and actively work to improve conditions in inner-city neighborhoods.

By establishing their home in Dimona, Ben Ammi's Hebrew Israelites have sailed into uncharted waters. They have developed an international organization with roots in both Israeli and African American soil. Overall, the Hebrew Israelites appear to be successfully navigating between African American groups such as the Nation of Islam, American Jewish organizations, and the Israeli government—groups that are often embroiled in conflict with one another. Moreover, the Hebrew Israelites have demonstrated that all borders are porous by adding Israeli political and cultural views to their core of African American religious beliefs.

As I was leaving the compound in Dimona during my 1996 visit, I noticed three young men walking together in an alley. Two premilitary Israeli youths, with the short cropped hair typical of their age group, walked next to a young Hebrew Israelite wearing a traditional knit skullcap and print tunic—but also a pair of blue jeans. The Hebrew Israelite community will continue to be influenced by Israeli society, even as the Hebrew Israelites make their own contributions to the broader Israeli community.

PART II

African American Muslims and Judaism

ISLAM HAS BEEN part of the African American religious experience since the arrival of the first Muslim slaves in the New World from Africa. Despite this enduring history, the significance of Islam in black life and culture has been generally unappreciated and misunderstood. Although the Nation of Islam perhaps represents the most visible contemporary example of the Islamic presence in black America, African Americans belong to a host of other Muslim-identified groups. Furthermore, although most Americans know of the Nation of Islam, they are more aware of the group's political beliefs than they are of its religious doctrines and practice. The first essay in this section treats the Nation of Islam first and foremost as a religious movement, thereby functioning as a corrective to popular tendencies to consider the Nation of Islam (and indeed, Islam more generally) in political rather than religious terms. Nathaniel Deutsch considers two critical figures, Elijah Muhammad, the NOI's longtime leader and prophet; and Louis Farrakhan, the group's current leader. While in his writings and speeches Muhammad demonizes Jews along with other whites, he also praises Orthodox Jews for their righteousness in attempting to follow proper dietary laws, and he exhorts his followers to emulate the same. Likewise, Louis Farrakhan frequently excoriates Jews but applauds them as a nation that has historically received divine favor. Indeed, as Deutsch suggests, both men hold Jews to a higher spiritual standard than other whites, a view with both positive and negative implications.

The second essay expands our perspective of black Islam in the United States by examining a group of African American Muslims that has received scant attention: the Holy Tabernacle Ministries, also known as the Nubian

Islaamic Hebrews or the Ansaaru Allah Community. Kathleen Malone O'Connor places the Holy Tabernacle Ministries within a multifaceted historical context that includes the advent of African American Muslim groups such as the Nation of Islam and the Five Percent Nation of Gods and Earths, and black Jewish organizations such as the Commandment Keepers and the Hebrew Israelites. O'Connor also examines the midrashic style of exegetical analysis and scriptural interpretation of the Holy Tabernacle Ministries, as well as their holiday rituals and traditional clothing, and she provides other evidence of the alliance of Muslim, Jewish, and Christian elements in the formation of the group's religious and ethnic identity.

5

The Proximate Other

The Nation of Islam and Judaism

Nathaniel Deutsch

The radically "other" is merely "other"; the proximate "other" is problematic, and hence, of supreme interest.

Jonathan Z. Smith, "What a Difference a Difference Makes"

IN HIS ESSAY "What a Difference a Difference Makes," historian of religions Jonathan Z. Smith has argued that the most provocative challenge to an individual or group is always posed by what he calls the "proximate other," or as he puts it, "The problem is not alterity, but similarity—at times, even identity."[1] Only when the other appears like us or even claims to be us is our sense of self truly threatened and our interest captured. Smith's theory provides an entrée into the Nation of Islam's complex views on Jews and Judaism. These views range from classical anti-Semitic stereotypes of Jewish economic conspiracies to profound religious identification.

As in the case of many African American religious groups, the biblical narrative of Israel's enslavement and liberation serves as a type or model for the Nation of Islam's own self-understanding. According to the Nation of Islam, African Americans have forgotten their chosen status and must be reminded of their noble origins and identity. The fact that another group—contemporary Jews—already calls itself the "Chosen People" poses a direct challenge to the identity claimed by the Nation of Islam for African Americans. Whereas black Christians may be converted or, more precisely, "reverted" to their original identity as members of the Nation of Islam, Jews, if they are white, cannot be assimilated.[2] Yet, unlike white Christians, who are beyond the pale, Jews are close enough to the Nation of Islam's own self-definition to inspire a highly ambivalent relationship, being alternately embraced and rejected in the group's teachings.[3] In the following pages I will examine this relationship in the speeches and writings of Elijah Muhammad, the prophet and previous leader of the Nation of Islam, and of Louis Farrakhan, the group's current leader.

A chief goal of this chapter will be to illuminate the religious character of the Nation of Islam. The mainstream media consistently depict the Nation as primarily a political or social organization. By contrast, this work treats the Nation of Islam as first and foremost a religion, one that also takes a keen interest in political, social, and economic issues. Indeed, the Nation of Islam is one of the most interesting and complex indigenous American religious movements of the twentieth century. There are a number of reasons for the popular downplaying of the religious character of the Nation of Islam in favor of its political and social dimensions. Traditionally there has been a tendency to characterize African American religious leaders by their political activities. While the religious background of figures like Martin Luther King, Jr., and Malcolm X could never be completely ignored, the media have typically focused on political implications to the exclusion of religious inspirations. Finally, when the media have addressed African American religiosity, they have tended to define it narrowly, concentrating on Protestant Christianity.

Another reason why the religious dimension of the Nation of Islam has been virtually ignored is the dismissal or outright condemnation of the Nation as a hate group because of its negative attitudes toward whites and Jews. Before addressing the views of the Nation of Islam, it is important to point out that a particular group's demonization of others does not invalidate its character as a religious movement. In fact, many religions' etiological myths demonize another group (or groups) as a means of self-differentiation and self-definition.

To illustrate this point let me quote from two religious documents:

> 1. The white race is not, and never will be, the chosen people of Allah [God]. They are the chosen people of their father Yakub, the devil.[4]
>
> 2. They [the Jews] said to him, "We are not illegitimate children; we have one father, God himself." . . . [He said to them] "You are from your father the devil, and you choose to do your father's desires."[5]

These remarkably similar quotations come from two very different contexts. The first is from *Message to the Blackman in America*, probably the most important work of Elijah Muhammad. The writings of Elijah Muhammad constitute what may be called the scriptures or canon of the Nation of Islam and are therefore an indispensable source for understanding the Nation of Islam's relationship to Jews and Judaism. A complete understanding of the above quotation requires a firm grounding in the mythology of the Nation of Islam, which I will examine in detail below. What is clear, however, is that the text demonizes whites in a literal sense. Understandably, this stance has given rise to charges of racism. The second quotation is from the Gospel of John. In this work the Jews reply to an accuser that they are the legitimate children of God. Their accuser responds that not only is God *not* their father, but their true father is actually the devil, a declaration that greatly resembles Elijah Muhammad's charge against whites. The identity of the figure who so condemns the Jews? Jesus.

Both texts literally demonize a particular group of people: whites, and Jews who refuse to accept Jesus, respectively. And yet no one would deny that the Gospel of John is a religious document and many people would take umbrage with the description of Christianity as primarily a hate group rather than a religion. It is possible to understand the Gospel of John as anti-Jewish and the *Message to the Blackman in America* as racist and yet still acknowledge that both are religious works, indeed, even similar works in a number of ways. Both contain mythological narratives concerning the incarnation of God in human form (Jesus and Fard Muhammad, respectively), and both have a dualistic, apocalyptic worldview, splitting humanity into two camps, the righteous who will be redeemed and the wicked who will be damned. I write this not to apologize for the views espoused in the Gospel of John or the *Message to the Blackman*, nor to equate the two works, but rather to argue against a simple calculus in which a dualistic worldview and the demonization of others that frequently accompanies it prevent a work or movement from being accurately described as religious. Indeed, it is unfortunate that many if not most religious movements have produced such intolerant views at some point in their history.

Elijah Muhammad

In October 1897 a boy named Elijah was born to Mariah and William Poole in the small Georgia town of Sandersville. Elijah Poole's childhood was marked by a loving home life and a father whose fire-and-brimstone sermons he admired, as well by the hard physical labor he and his siblings performed in order to help their family. The extremely racist climate of rural Georgia profoundly affected the young Elijah Poole, and by the time he was ten he had already witnessed the lynching of a black youth. Eventually, racism, economic hardship, and the promise of greener pastures led Elijah Poole, his wife Clara, and their two children to migrate to Detroit in 1923.

In 1931 Elijah Poole had the fateful meeting that would transform him forever and herald the genesis of the Nation of Islam. The man who would have such a powerful impact on Poole was called by a variety of names, including W. D. Fard and Fard Muhammad.[6] With a light complexion and straight black hair, Fard resembled a white man, and FBI files suggest that he was a half-Polynesian and half-white ex-convict, although the veracity of the FBI documents is in question. According to the Nation of Islam, Fard's father was a black man named Alphonso from the Meccan Tribe of Shabazz and his mother was a white woman named Baby Gee from the Caucasus.[7] Later Nation literature declared that Fard's white appearance enabled him to navigate between blacks and whites. To Elijah Poole, Fard Muhammad identified himself as God incarnate, a belief that became one of the cornerstones of the future Nation of Islam.[8]

Over the next few years, until he mysteriously disappeared in 1934, Fard instructed his chief disciple, whom he renamed Elijah Muhammad, in his teachings. After Fard's disappearance, a power struggle ensued among his disciples during which Elijah Muhammad feared for his life. Ultimately, however, Elijah Muhammad withstood this baptism in fire and emerged as the leader of what came to be called the Nation of Islam. For the better part of four decades until he died in 1975, Elijah Muhammad was the prophet and leader of the Nation of Islam, nurturing the movement from its humble beginnings into a religious organization with its own complex theological and social structures.

Throughout his many writings and speeches, Muhammad called upon the "so-called Negro" to throw off the physical and mental chains of racist America and recover his original divine nature. The liberatory knowledge of self promoted by Muhammad recalls the late antique religion known as Gnosticism (after the Greek word for knowledge, *gnosis*). As we will see, like the ancient Gnostics, Muhammad anchored his gnosis in an elaborate myth of creation based on the biblical book of Genesis. Also like the Gnostics, Muhammad argued that the world was ruled by evil beings who sought to prevent the truly divine from achieving salvific knowledge of self. In the mythology of the Nation of Islam these evil rulers were the white race, and the chief means for keeping the minds of black people in shackles was Christianity, as Muhammad writes:

> The only thing that will hold the Negro is his belief in whites as a people of divinity. They hold to his religion (Christianity), which they use to deceive everyone they possibly can. It was through Christianity that they got their authority over the black, brown, yellow and red races.[9]

During his lifetime Muhammad produced a number of written works and delivered hundreds of speeches to his followers. If one could speak of a canon for the Nation of Islam, then Muhammad's book *Message to the Blackman in America* would be at its center. This work, one of the most interesting in the history of American religions, contains an elaborate mythology, theology, and eschatology. As in his other works, the chief focus of Muhammad's invective in *Message to the Blackman* is against white people and Christianity. Not only did he view Christianity as the means by which whites historically enslaved blacks, he also viewed it as theologically heretical (how could God impregnate a virgin, for example?). Just as important, Muhammad correctly perceived Christianity to be the main religious competition for the Nation of Islam. If the Nation were to appeal to black people in America, it would first have to radically undermine the position of Christianity within the black community.[10]

This is the broader context for understanding many of Elijah Muhammad's comments concerning Jews and Judaism. Indeed, Muhammad generally treats Judaism as part of his more central polemic against Christianity and the white race. According to Muhammad, Jews are whites and therefore devils, implicated in the history of racism against blacks.[11] They are not, however, any more corrupt or oppressive than other whites, indeed, as we will see, at least one group of Jews are actually more righteous than other whites.

In a number of places Muhammad lumps Jews together with Christians for criticism. For example, he writes, "Both Jews and Christians are guilty of setting up rivals to Allah (God)," and "He [Muhammad] and his followers obey the law of (the one God) Allah, while the Jews and the Christians preach it and do otherwise."[12] Elsewhere Muhammad specifically condemns Jewish and Christian biblical exegetes for perverting the meaning of the Bible: "The original scripture called 'The Torah'—revealed to Musa (Moses)—was Holy until the Jews and the Christian scholars started tampering with it."[13] Far more common than statements that criticize both Jews and Christians, however, are those that demonize Christianity: "The old Christian religion has been the white man's whip to lash the black man ever since it was organized. My people here in America are fast awakening to the slavery teachings of Christianity to the dislike of their enemies."[14] Muhammad even goes so far as to equate Christianity with slavery: "Once the so-called Negroes drop slavery (Christianity), and accept Allah for their God, and His religion (Islam) Allah will remove their fear and grief, and they will not fear nor grieve any more."[15]

If Muhammad considered contemporary Jews to be a subset of whites, he understood the biblical Israel as a model for American blacks. In this regard, Muhammad inherited the typological method of biblical exegesis practiced by African American Christianity, wherein the black experience in the United States was read through the lens of the biblical story of Israel. Thus, Muhammad writes:

> Our enemies, the devils, know and now seek to prevent us from being a nation through our women, as Pharaoh attempted to destroy Israel by killing off the male babies of Israel at birth. . . .
>
> Pharaoh was envious of Israel's future of becoming a great nation, beloved of Allah which would overcome Egypt and her future as a world power.
>
> The same goes for the so-called Negroes and the slave-masters' children. The slave-masters envy their once-slaves' future and want to destroy it.[16]

How to Eat to Live

Judaism does not even warrant a separate index entry in *Message to the Blackman in America*. This is not the case, however, in another of Muhammad's most important religious treatises, the two-volume *How to Eat to Live*, which reads like a cross between a contemporary book on healthy eating and a dietary law code akin to that in the biblical book of Leviticus. Muhammad emphasizes that the dietary principles he espouses were revealed to him by Fard Muhammad. These include the oft-repeated recommendation that people eat only one meal a day, a practice that will lead to extraordinarily long life:[17]

> How to Eat to Live? Allah (God) said to me, in the Person of Master Fard Muhammad (to Whom praise is due forever) that we who believe in Him as our God and Saviour should eat but one meal a day (once every 24 hours). Eat nothing between meals, not even candy, fruit, or anything which would start the stomach, digestive processes. In this way, our eating of the proper foods and drinks—at the proper time—would extend our life to 140 years.[18]

The eating of only one meal a day reflects the ascetic tendency of *How to Eat to Live*, as well as a nod to scientific theories concerning the beneficial long-term effects of decreased caloric intake. Other points that suggest knowledge of contemporary health care issues include Muhammad's exhortation that his followers eat raw rather than cooked fruit in order to retain more vitamins and that they decrease the amount of meat, sugar, and starch in their diets: "Since the American citizens eat more meat, sugar and starchy foods than they should, there is almost an epidemic of too much sugar accumulating in the blood."[19] Indeed, Muhammad recommends a vegetarian diet but concedes that his followers may eat meat, though it must be properly slaughtered.

Many of the foods prohibited by Muhammad are precisely those traditionally associated with African American cooking. In a section entitled "A List of Foods We Must Not Eat," Muhammad decries the consumption of swine, black-eyed peas, cornbread, kale, and sweet potatoes.[20] Although Muhammad justifies the prohibition of swine on Islamic grounds and of cornbread for digestive reasons—"because it is very hard on the stomach, and not easily digested"—the underlying principle is that these foods are staples of traditional African American cuisine, which Elijah Muhammad associates with a slave mentality. An important part of recovery for blacks in America is a return to an original diet, one untainted by the pernicious influence of racism and Christianity. In some cases this principle may override popular wisdom on what is healthy to eat, for example, when Muhammad writes, "Do not eat neat leaf vegetable, such as collard greens."[21]

In line with his overall polemic against Christianity, Muhammad reserves his harshest critique in *How to Eat to Live* for Christian eating habits. Thus he writes, "Stay away from the poison food that dresses the Christian's table"[22] and "The Christians—white and black—try to force or deceive my followers into eating foods they know we, the Muslims, do not approve."[23] Christianity's liberal attitude toward diet—exemplified by Peter's vision in Acts 10:11–13, in which he sees a sheet filled with "all kinds of four-footed creatures, and reptiles and birds of the air," and hears "a voice saying, 'Get up, Peter; kill and eat' "—is anathema to Muhammad's view of the innate impurity of certain foods, most notably swine.

Many of Muhammad's prescriptions for healthy eating do not appear to be drawn from Orthodox Muslim sources, although he consistently emphasizes the quranic basis for some of his restrictions. Muhammad identifies only one food appreciated by Orthodox Muslims which followers of the Nation are prohibited from eating: "Orthodox Muslims are very careful of what they eat. The only food we shun that they love are nuts."[24]

Although many of its recommendations are consonant with contemporary scientific theories, *How to Eat to Live* is clearly a religious document. The references to divine revelation and to Scripture (both the Quran and the Hebrew Bible), the listing of prescribed and proscribed foods, and the polemical content are all typical features of religious codes. It is within this context that Muhammad makes what are probably his most signficant remarks concerning Judaism as a religion rather than as an ethnic or racial group.

Muhammad's comments on Jews and Judaism in *How to Eat to Live* are both extensive (they begin on page 1 of volume 1) and generally very positive. Rather than classifying Jews as just another group of whites and therefore devils, Muhammad singles out Jews for their righteousness. Although Jews are white, according to *How to Eat to Live*, their racial designation does not overdetermine their character as it does in other writings. Instead, Muhammad depicts Jews as being the only whites, save for white Muslims, who attempt to live according to the will of Allah. The superior spiritual character of Jews is most evident in their dietary practices, that is, *kashrut*.

In *How to Eat to Live* Muhammad grounds his attitudes toward Jews in the Hebrew Bible, Muslim tradition, and contemporary practice. Muhammad cites the biblical book of Leviticus as a prooftext for both Jewish and Nation of Islam dietary laws:

> Leviticus 11:7–8 "And the swine, though he divide the hoof, and be clovenfooted, yet he cheweth not the cud; he is unclean to you. Of their flesh shall ye not eat, and their carcass shall ye not touch; they are unclean to you."
>
> The dietary law given to Israel by Moses is true today. Israel was given the proper food to eat which Jehovah approved for them, and that which was forbidden to eat we should not eat today.[25]

This quotation is only one example of how Muhammad consistently links Judaism and the Nation of Islam in *How to Eat to Live*. The following quotation elaborates on the affinity between the two groups by declaring that the Orthodox Jews lived among the original Muslims in Asia and continue to follow the prophet Moses' teachings. Moreover, in a refrain repeated throughout the work, Muhammad refers to a quranic teaching that Muslims may eat food prepared by Jews and vice versa. In line with his writings and speeches in general, Muhammad does not cite the quranic verse he has in mind,[26] a striking difference from his explicit citation of biblical texts such as Leviticus, as we saw above:

> The Orthodox Jews are a people who have lived among us in Asia, and they still try to follow Moses' teachings on how to eat to live. The Holy Quran teaches us that we can eat their food and they can eat our (the Muslims')

> food, because the two people (Jews and Muslims) try to eat the right food to live.[27]

Muhammad's assertion that Orthodox Jews and Muslims may share food is not insignificant. Historically, the ability or inability to eat with members of another group has been one of the chief ways of establishing intergroup likeness or difference. Thus early Christianity rejected the laws of *kashrut*, which functioned as a symbolic and, if followed, practical limitation on contact between Jews and non-Jews, in order to appeal to a broader gentile audience. By declaring that Orthodox Jews and Muslims are allowed to eat together while demonizing the eating habits of Christians, Muhammad suggests that the former groups are alike in a profound way while placing the latter group outside the pale.

These interrelated themes—the likeness of Orthodox Jews and members of the Nation of Islam and their shared difference from Christians—appear throughout *How to Eat to Live.*

> If you would like to find good food, such as lamb, beef or even chicken—if you are a Muslim—buy it from the strictly Orthodox Jew. Be certain it is an Orthodox kosher market, because some Jews eat the pig. Orthodox Jews are excellent in protecting their health, even spiritually trying to do and eat like their prophet Mossa (Moses) taught them through the Divine teachings of Allah. *If you respect yourselves as Muslims, the spiritual Orthodox Jew will respect you.* Of course, no one will respect you unless you respect yourself. . . .
>
> *Do not buy the Christians' ready-prepared ground meats, or any ready-ground meat.* Buy the quality meats that you like, and have them ground by *the Orthodox kosher butchers*, through their meat grinders, because they do not have the pig near their shops. *They are like us—they hate the divinely prohibited flesh.* [emphasis added][28]

This passage not only implies that the respect of "the spiritual Orthodox Jew" is something desirable, but also describes Orthodox Jews as "like us [the Nation of Islam]." Muhammad consistently differentiates between Orthodox Jews, whom he praises for following the will of Allah as revealed by Moses, and non-Orthodox Jews, whom he condemns for being Christianized:

> Some of you buy meats from the Jewish stores and some of you believe that all the Jewish people are religious Orthodox Jews and will not eat or sell bad meats, but you are wrong. *There are "Christian" Jews who will eat everything and drink almost everything. The merchandise of these Jews must be shunned, if you desire to live.* [emphasis added][29]

The very different evaluations of Orthodox and non-Orthodox Jews indicates that Muhammad's positive view of Orthodox Judaism is based not on race but on belief and practice. This is quite remarkable given Muhammad's overwhelming tendency toward racial determinism. In Muhammad's view, Orthodox Jews have managed to raise themselves to a higher spiritual level than other whites (including other Jews) by following the laws given by Moses. As he puts it:

> There is a sect among them [the whites] whose members call themselves Orthodox Jews (a few still try to follow the Ten Commandments given to them through Moses). *These are wiser, more skillful, than the Christians.* [emphasis added][30]

Significantly, Muhammad's praise for the righteous behavior of Orthodox Jews resembles his comments concerning white Muslims. In a chapter of his book *Our Saviour Has Arrived,* entitled "A Few White People Are Muslims by Faith," Elijah Muhammad commends white Muslims for attempting to follow the will of Allah, despite their origins. Yet, because they are "Muslim by faith and not by nature," white Muslims will not attain the spiritual heights of black Muslims, as Muhammad writes:

> There are white people in Europe who believe in Islam. They are Muslim by faith and not by nature. They believe in righteousness and have tried, and are still trying, to practice the life of a righteous Muslim. Because of their faith in Islam, Allah (God) Blesses them and they will see the Hereafter.
>
> There are quite a few white people in America who are Muslim by faith. Good done by any person is rewarded and these white people who believe in Islam will receive the Blessing of entering into the Hereafter.
>
> The white people who believe in Islam will not enter the Hereafter that is Promised to the Lost-Found Black People. The Lost-Found People will take on a new birth.
>
> But the white people who believe in Islam will not take on a new birth because they will not be the people to live forever. Because of their belief in Islam, they will escape the great world destruction that we now face.[31]

A few lines later Muhammad adds:

> The white race is not equal with darker people because the white race was not created by the God of Righteousness. . . . Yakub, the father of the devil, made the white race, a race of devils. . . . The white race is not made by nature to accept righteousness. They know righteousness, but they cannot be righteous.[32]

Both Orthodox Jews and white Muslims pose a taxonomic challenge for Elijah Muhammad. They are not righteous by nature, indeed as whites they "cannot be righteous," according to Muhammad, a statement suggesting that righteousness as an ontological quality is limited to black people. Yet Orthodox Jews and white Muslims "know righteousness" and, in sharp contrast to white Christians and non-

Orthodox Jews, attempt to live according to the will of God. Because of their efforts to live righteously, Orthodox Jews and white Muslims will be rewarded, though they will not achieve the new birth and immortality promised to black Muslims.

Because of their dietary practices, Orthodox Jews and Muslims share a common bond which makes them more righteous than Christians. Nevertheless, according to Muhammad, Christians have a "holier than thou" attitude:

> Christians are among the largest consumers of pork in America, and they deliver this rat throughout the world to other people. . . .
>
> And yet, they will tell all the Muslims and Orthodox Jews that they are holier than we who don't dare even to touch the swine's carcass.[33]

In Muhammad's opinion, not only do Orthodox Jews "live more closely to the Muslim way of eating" than other whites, but they have historically gotten along better with Muslims than have Christians. Indeed, the similar practices of Muslims and Jews and their history of being able to "settle their differences," even inspires Muhammad to suggest that "the American Jews and the American Black Man may yet find some way" to establish a better relationship:

> The Jews and Muslims have always been able to settle their differences between each other better than Christians and Muslims. . . . the American Jew and the American Black Man may yet find some way of making a separate relationship out of the other world.[34]

Elijah Muhammad's comments regarding Orthodox Jews in *How to Eat to Live* add an interesting dimension to his demonization of whites in general. Why would Muhammad introduce this element into his system? A number of factors probably contributed to his more positive evaluation of Orthodox Jews vis-à-vis other whites. First, there is the widespread Muslim tradition, rooted in the Quran, that it is permissible for Muslims to eat food prepared by Jews and vice versa. The rigor of *How to Eat to Live* clearly indicates the importance Muhammad placed on diet and eating. Given this intense interest, the Muslim tradition's generally positive evaluation of Jewish eating habits would have had a particularly strong impact on Elijah Muhammad's overall perspective on Orthodox Jews. Muhammad's position was also informed by his understanding of history and what he perceived to be the better relations that Jews and Muslims enjoyed compared with Muslims and Christians. Indeed, this historical analysis only confirmed Muhammad's negative attitude toward Christianity. It may be argued that Muhammad viewed Orthodox Jews favorably precisely because they were not Christians. Thus Muhammad had only scorn for what he considered "Christian" (i.e. non-Orthodox) Jews.

Finally, Muhammad's position may have been influenced by practical considerations. In the late 1960s and early 1970s, when the two volumes of *How to Eat to Live* were first published, finding meat that satisfied Muslim dietary considerations was not easy in many of America's communities; this is still the case to some degree. Far more common than stores selling *hallal* meat (i.e., that properly slaughtered according to Muslim law) were kosher butchers. The necessity of buying food from Orthodox Jews may have influenced Muhammad to adopt a positive attitude concerning their religious observance and character. Perhaps actual experiences with Orthodox Jews by members of the Nation of Islam within this context also positively impacted Muhammad's opinion. As he writes, "If you respect yourselves as Muslims, the spiritual Orthodox Jew will respect you."

Muhammad's "Midrash"

In *How To Eat to Live*, Elijah Muhammad explicitly draws parallels between his own views on proper diet and the beliefs and practices of Orthodox Jews. This provides the context for Muhammad's most extensive and significant comments on the religious character of Jews. In addition to the dietary affinities emphasized by Muhammad himself, there are other, structural similarities between Muhammad's religious expression and Jewish traditions. This section will focus on one of these structural parallels, namely the remarkable resemblance between Elijah Muhammad's biblical interpretation or exegesis and the Jewish form of biblical interpretation known as "Midrash."[35]

Midrash is a notoriously difficult phenomenon to define, although scholars generally agree that it is both a specific literary genre, which includes classical midrashic works such as *Genesis Rabbah* and the *Mekhilta of Rabbi Ishmael*, and a hermeneutical method developed by rabbinic exegetes. Midrashic exegesis is at once wildly imaginative and almost obsessively precise. It freely interprets biblical verses in light of verses from other parts of the Bible, establishes parallels between words on the basis of "false" etymologies and similar sounds, and finds meaning in the numerical value of letters and even their shapes. Midrash is particulary interested in surface irregularities in the biblical text, such as an awkward transition between verses, an unusual word, or a grammatical peculiarity. These "problems" are solved by means of ingenious interpretations, which often involve the "narrative expansion" of the biblical text. As James Kugel, a noted scholar of Midrash, explains: "The distinguishing characteristic of the narrative expansion is that it proceeds by actually *expanding the narrative content* of the biblical text, boldly asserting that, in addition to what is explicitly related in the Bible, other words or actions not specified in the text actually accompanied what is specified."[36] Phrased differently, the Bible is a work which contains many "gaps"[37] which must be filled by creative and meaningful readings. Midrash fills these gaps.

In the following pages I will trace the exegesis of a single biblical verse in three religious traditions: rabbinic Judaism, Gnosticism, and the Nation of Islam. All three traditions identify the same textual gap and attempt to fill this gap via highly mythological narrative expansions of the biblical text. While Elijah Muhammad's bibical interpretation often resembles rabbinic Midrash in style and structure, it resembles Gnostic exegesis (particularly of the biblical book of Genesis) in style, structure, and *content.*

Indeed, Elijah Muhammad's exegesis of the first few chapters of Genesis may best be described as both midrashic and Gnostic in style.[38] Like the rabbis who created Midrash (and the Gnostics as well), Muhammad frequently filled in the gaps of the biblical text with his own narrative expansions. Like the Gnostics, Muhammad also employed what scholars of Gnosticism have termed *Protestexegese* or "Inverse Exegesis."[39] As Ioan Couliano writes, "[T]his exegesis *reverses*, constantly and systematically, the received and accepted interpretations of the Bible. . . . It appears to us as reversed. In reality, Gnostics would see it as 'restored.' "[40]

Echoing his Gnostic predecessors, Elijah Muhammad argued that when he inverted traditional interpretations, he was actually restoring the biblical text to its original meaning, hitherto obscured by deceptive white interpreters. As a result of white exegetes' misinterpretation and manipulation, the Bible had been transformed into what Muhammad called a "Poison Book" and "the graveyard of my poor people."[41] Only Muhammad's own exegesis could restore the holiness to the "Holy Book." Thus, in *Message to the Blackman in America*, Muhammad writes:

> The original scripture called "The Torah"—revealed to Musa (Moses)—was Holy until the Jews and the Christian scholars started tampering with it. . . . The Bible means good if you can rightly understand it. My interpretation of it is given to me from the Lord of the Worlds. Yours is your own and from the enemies of the truth [i.e., white biblical interpreters].[42]

When a biblical verse particularly intrigued the exegetical imagination of the Rabbis, they declared, "This verse cries out, 'interpret me!' " One of the biblical verses that cried out the loudest to rabbinic ears was Genesis 1:26: "And God said, 'Let us make man in our image, after our likeness." The problem posed by the verse was the use of plurals ("Let *us* make," etc.) when referring to God's creative activity. If God alone created humankind, why did the Bible employ plural instead of singular language? Phrased differently, the question becomes "Who was God talking to in Genesis 1:26?"

The Rabbis solved this problem in a number of ways. Among their interpretations for God's exhoration were that God was speaking to the "works of heaven and earth," the "works of each day," or his own "heart" (i.e., God was talking to himself).[43] By the middle of the third century C.E., however, the most common narrative expansion of Genesis 1:26 was that God was speaking to the angels. Thus in about 240 C.E. Rabbi Hannina taught the following midrashic tradition:

> When He [God] came to the creation of Adam, He took counsel with the ministering angels, saying to them: "Let us make man. . . ."[44]

By asserting that God spoke with his ministering angels in Genesis 1:26, the Rabbis hoped to solve the problem of plural language while still preserving the unique authority and divinity of the biblical God—after all, the ministering angels were essentially servants of God rather than partners in creation. Nevertheless, Genesis 1:26 did inspire the kind of heretical interpretation the Rabbis sought to prevent or preempt with their own midrashic exegesis. The existence of such nonorthodox interpretations is alluded to by Rabbi Jonathan, a third-century CE figure from Sepphoris, who authored the following midrashic tradition to explain how the verse was included in the Bible despite its potential for inspiring heresy:

> When Moses was engaged in the writing of the Law [the Bible], he had to write the works of each day [of creation]. When he came to the verse, "And God said: 'Let us make man,'" he said: "Sovereign of all, why do You provide the heretics with an argument?" God replied: "Write! Whoever wishes to err, let him err!"[45]

Among the "heretics" referred to by R. Jonathan, were undoubtedly the various groups known as Gnostics in Late Antiquity. According to Gnostic mythology, the physical world was created by an evil or ignorant Demiurge rather than the true, good God who inhabited a world of light (the Pleroma) above the physical cosmos. The Demiurge, called by a variety of names including Jaldabaoth, Saklas, and Samael, was aided in his creation by a host of demonic beings known as "archons." The Gnostics interpreted the Bible, and in particular the book of Genesis, as a written record of the malevolent activity of the Demiurge, who was identified as the God of the Bible. Thus the Gnostics transformed the biblical God into an inferior deity, at odds with the true God of the Pleroma.

Like their Jewish (and Christian) counterparts, Gnostic exegetes were fascinated by the opening verses of Genesis, including Genesis 1:26. Gnostic interpretations of this verse read very much like Jewish midrashic traditions save for one crucial difference: rather than the true, good God and his ministering angels, the actors in Genesis 1:26 are identified as the evil Demiurge and his archons. For example, in the long recension of the Gnostic work known as the *Apocryphon of John*, the Demiurge and his archons create the first man (Adam) in the image of the true God but in their own likeness:

> And he [the Demiurge] said to the authorities [the archons] which attend him, "Come, let us create a man according to the image of God and according to our likeness, that his image may become a light for us."[46]

Thus the Gnostics inverted the traditional understanding of the biblical text by transforming the good God of Genesis into a malevolent Demiurge and revalorizing the creation of Adam into an act of rebellion.

The Gnostics were not the only group to adopt midrashic techniques. Other hermeneuts influenced by rabbinic Midrash include late antique Christians and medieval Muslims. Unlike many of these exegetes, however, Elijah Muhammad was almost certainly unacquainted with, and indeed was probably unaware of, midrashic sources. If he was exposed to the Christian or Muslim literary traditions influenced by rabbinic Midrash, he did not acknowledge that he was. Indeed, as Malcom X recalled, Elijah Muhammad was not ashamed to admit his lack of formal education:

> "I am not ashamed to say how little learning I have had," Mr. Muhammad told me. "My going to school no further than the fourth grade proved that I can know nothing except the truth I have been taught by Allah. Allah taught me mathematics. He found me with a sluggish tongue, and taught me how to pronounce words."[47]

Nevertheless, some of Muhammad's exegetical style undoubtedly derived from the rich oral tradition of African American preaching; Muhammad was the son of a Christian minister and almost became one himself. This influence probably accounts for the frequently typological[48] exegesis of Muhammad, particularly his identification of the "so-called Negroes" with the Israelites under Pharaoh.[49] It is also possible that Muhammad received some or all of his biblical interpretations directly from the mysterious founder of the Nation of Islam, Fard Muhammad (aka W. D. Fard), who may have been acquainted with midrashic-type exegesis from Muslim sources such as the Ahmadiyyah movement, an originally Pakistani group whose teachings became popular among African Americans in the early twentieth century.

Elijah Muhammad himself frequently described his biblical interpretations as revelations received from Allah, manifested in the form of Fard Muhammad. Not surprisingly, certain groups of rabbis also attributed revealed status to their biblical exegesis,[50] a phenomenon Michael Fishbane has described as the "divinization of the content of exegetical traditions."[51] Fishbane rightly explains this development as an outgrowth of "rival systems of exegesis," which sought divine justification for their interpretations, as well as "the natural theological consequence of the notion that the contents of the interpretation *are part of* the written divine revelation (implicitly or explicitly)."[52] Both criteria are clearly operative in Elijah Muhammad's case as well. Muhammad not only set his own biblical exegesis in opposition to "rival systems" of white Jewish and Christian interpreters, he also viewed his exegesis as a restoration of the *original*, but subsequently obscured, meaning of the written text.

A final explanation for the many parallels between Muhammad's biblical exegesis and rabbinic Midrash is that Elijah Muhammad may have basically "reinvented" certain features of the midrashic literary form. Despite his sometimes sharp invective against the Bible (at least as interpreted by whites), Elijah Muhammad both knew and appreciated the biblical text. The great degree of his knowledge and love of the Bible is attested to by his son's observation that "Elijah Muhammad was a student of the Bible: his father was a Baptist minister. That's why Fard Muhammad chose him, because he was so learned in the Bible";[53] by his own mother's testimony that the young "Elijah spent hours poring through the Bible, with tears shining in his eyes"; and by Malcom X's recollection that "Mr Muhammad told me himself later that as a boy he felt that the Bible's words were a locked door, that could be unlocked, if only he knew how, and he cried because of his frustrated anxiety to receive understanding."[54] Although the young Elijah Muhammad's devotion to the Bible is striking by twentieth-century American standards, it resembles the intimate knowledge of the Bible possessed by the rabbinic authors of Midrash. Muhammad's early view that "the Bible's words were a locked door, that could be unlocked," combined with his extensive knowledge of Scripture and his mytho-poetic imagination, could have generated the midrashic-type exegesis we find in Muhammad's writings.

We have seen that the Rabbis identified the plural subject of Genesis 1:26 as God and the ministering angels, while their Gnostic competitors transformed these righteous beings into the malevolent Demiurge and his archons. In the following pages we will discover how Elijah Muhammad solved the exegetical problem posed by the plural subject of this verse. The most complete version of his midrashic transformation of Genesis 1:26 appears in a section of *Message to the Blackman in America* entitled "The Making of Devil." If any work may be called the "gospels" of the Nation of Islam, it is the *Message to the Blackman in America.* The central myth of this work, and indeed of the Nation of Islam, is the myth of Yakub and his creation of the white race.[55] In his book *The American Religion*, Harold Bloom describes the Yakub myth as "rancid in itself,"[56] and indeed it is extremely racist. Yet, as we are about to see, the myth also reflects a highly crafted exegesis of the first few chapters of Genesis.

According to "The Making of Devil," the first inhabitants of the earth were members of the "original black nation" and lived in Mecca, Arabia, and its environs. Then, Muhammad writes, "Six thousand years ago, or to be more exact 6,600 years ago, as Allah taught me, our nation gave birth to another God whose name was Yakub." Yakub, known as "big head scientist" because of his "unusual size head," was a child prodigy who quickly graduated from "all the colleges and universites of his nation" and began preaching on the streets of Mecca.

Yakub spent his time gathering followers and developing his own genetic theories. As Muhammad writes:

> He [Yakub] learned, from studying the germ of the black man, under the microscope, that there were two people in him, and that one was black, the other brown.
>
> He said if he could successfully separate the one from the other he could graft the brown germ into its last stage, which would be white. With his wisdom, he could make the white, which he discovered was the weaker of the black germ (which would be unalike) rule the black nation for a time (until a greater one than Yakub was born).
>
> This new idea put him to work finding the necessary converts to begin grafting his new race of people.[57]

Not surprisingly, Yakub's activities disturbed the king of Mecca, who allowed Yakub and 59,999 of his followers to leave Mecca and settle on "an Isle in the Aegean Sea called 'Pelan' (Bible 'Patmos')." Once they arrived on Pelan, Yakub instituted a strict eugenics program whose ultimate goal was the creation of the white race: "After the first 200 years, Mr. Yakub had done away with the black babies, and all were brown. After another 200 years, he had all yellow or red, which was 400 years after being on 'Pelan.' Another 200 years, which brings us to the six hundredth year, Mr. Yakub had an all-pale white race of people on this Isle."[58]

According to Muhammad, the malevolent nature of the white race was determined by the genetic experiment that produced it:

> There was no good taught to them [the white race] while on the Isle. By teaching the nurses to kill the black baby and save the brown baby, so as to graft the white out of it; by lying to the black mother of the baby, this lie was born into the very nature of the white baby; and, murder for the black people was also born in them—or made by nature a liar and murderer.[59]

Yakub instructed his "made devils on Pelan" to return to Mecca and sow dissent among the "Holy people of Islam (the black nation)." The white devils succeeded in causing so much trouble in Mecca that:

> Yakub's made devils were driven out of Paradise [Mecca], into the hills of West Asia (Europe), and stripped of everything but the language. . . . Once there, they were roped in, to keep them out of Paradise. . . . The soldiers patrolled the border armed with swords, to prevent the devils from crossing.[60]

In another section of *Message to the Blackman in America*, entitled "The White Race's False Claim to Be Divine, Chosen People," Muhammad makes it explicitly clear that the myth of Yakub is actually an exegetical reading and expansion of the first few chapters of Genesis:

> According to the Bible (Gen. 3:20–24), Adam and his wife were the first parents of all people (white race only) and the first sinners. According to the Word of Allah, he was driven from the Garden of Paradise into the hills and caves of West Asia, or as they now call it, "Europe," to live his evil life in the West and not in the Holy Land of the East. "Therefore, the Lord God sent him (Adam) forth from the Garden of Eden, to till the ground from whence he was taken. So he drove out the man; and He placed at the east of the Garden cherubims[61] (Muslim guards) and a flaming sword which turned every way to keep the devils out of the way of the tree of life (the nation of Islam)." [Gen. 3:23–24] The sword of Islam prevented the Adamic race from crossing the border of Europe and Asia to make trouble among the Muslims for 2,000 years after they were driven out of the Holy Land and away from the people, for their mischief-making, lying and disturbing the peace of the righteous nation of Islam.[62]

In this paragraph Muhammad provides a key to understanding the biblical story of Adam's exile from the Garden of Eden. Muhammad frequently indicates the proper interpretation of key biblical words and phrases by placing the "real" meanings in parentheses. This literary device is similar to the rabbinic use of expressions such as "*'al tiqre . . . 'ela . . .*," which means "do not read. . . but, rather . . .," in other words, do not read the biblical text as is, but replace the standard masoretic text with an alternate reading; and *ve-'ayn . . . 'ela . . .*," as in the phrase, "*ve-'ayn tov 'ela zadik*,"[63] which indicates that the words *tov* ("good") and *zadik* ("righteous one") are being equated with one another or, put differently, the word *tov* means *zadik*.[64] Thus, according to Muhammad, when the Bible refers to Adam and Eve as the parents of all people, it is really referring to the "white race only." Similarly, the cherubim mentioned by the biblical text are to be understood as the Muslim guards of the Yakub myth who patrol the borders of Europe, while the tree of life actually signifies the Nation of Islam.

In the middle of the paragraph cited above, Muhammad quotes Genesis 3:23–24. This biblical text is sandwiched between elements of the Yakub myth: the exile of the white race from Mecca to Europe and the installation of Muslim guards to guard the border. Essentially, Muhammad has created a new narrative context (the Yakub myth) for the biblical verses. Instead of serving as biblical prooftexts for the Yakub myth, however, the verses are actually transformed into what Daniel Boyarin has called "intertexts." As Boyarin writes in his work *Intertextuality and the Reading of Midrash*, the biblical verses are "made *part* of the story itself."[65] In this case, the "story" is Yakub's creation of the white race and their subsequent exile from Mecca.

The biblical verses cited by Muhammad are not so much employed as scriptural justification or proof of the Yakub myth, but rather are transformed into elements within the new narrative framework. The degree to which Genesis 3:23–24 has become part of Muhammad's own discourse may be gauged by his quotation of the verses. Muhammad indicates that he is citing the Bible by placing the text of Genesis 3:23–24 in quotes, and in fact he cites the two verses *almost* verbatim—"almost" because Muhammad has added one feature that does not appear in the biblical text. While the end of Genesis 3:24 refers to a "flaming sword which turned every way to guard the way to the tree of life," Muhammad's version refers to a "flaming sword which turned every way to *keep the devils* out of the way of the tree of life" [emphasis added]. Remarkably, Muhammad has incorporated the detail of Yakub's white "devils" directly into the biblical text. Even more remarkably, perhaps, Muhammad gives no indication that he is making such an addition. His rewriting of Genesis 3:24 blurs what is already a fine line between the myth of Yakub and the biblical text.

Biblical verses are liberally and systematically quoted throughout *Message to the Blackman in America*. Like the sentences authored by Muhammad, the biblical verses form an organic part of the work. Muhammad's frequently seamless integration of quotations and self-authored text reflects what Boyarin has called "the poetics of quotation," a literary practice employed by rabbinic Midrash, modern poets such as Osip Mandelstam and Anna Akhmatova, and the literary critic Walter Benjamin, wherein quotations are woven into the narrative fabric of a new text.[66]

After recounting the Yakub myth in *Message to the Blackman in America*, Muhammad asks his readers the following question: "Just what have we learned, or rather are learning from this divine revelation of our enemies, the devils?" Muhammad answers his own question by referring to Genesis 1:26:

> we learn who the Bible (Genesis 1:16 [sic]) is referring to in the saying: "Let us make man." This "US" was fifty-nine thousand, nine hundred, and ninety-nine (59,999) black men and women; making or grafting them into the likeness or image of the original man.[67]

In Muhammad's exegesis of Genesis 1:26, Yakub and his 59,999 followers take the place of God and the ministering angels of the Jewish tradition and the Demiurge and the archons of Gnostic sources. Like the Gnostic Demiurge, Yakub is conflated with the biblical God, who is thereby transformed into a renegade rather than a righteous deity. Thus, according to Muhammad, the plural language of Genesis 1:26 signifies Yakub's declaration to his 59,999 followers: "Let us make man [i.e. the white race]. . . ."

One of the most remarkable elements of Elijah Muhammad's exegesis of Genesis is the degree to which it reflects and reinforces his dualistic view of the world. As we have seen, Muhammad transformed the first few chapters of Genesis into an etiology for the inherently evil nature of the white race. The depths to which Muhammad relegated whites in *Message to the Blackman in America* and the degree to which he inverted classic racist discourse may be seen in the following quotation, in which Muhammad argues that gorillas and other apes are actually an intermediary stage of development between demonic whites and divine blacks:

> "Yakub's race of devils were exiled in the hills and caves of West Asia (now called Europe). . . . They lost all knowledge of civilization. The Lord, God of Islam, taught me that some of them tried to graft themselves back into the black nation, but they had nothing to go by. A few were lucky enough to make a start, and got as far as what you call the gorilla. In fact, all of the monkey family are from this 2,000 year history of the white race in Europe."[68]

If readers of *Message to the Blackman in America* had any doubts concerning the negative nature of Yakub's creation, Muhammad made it explicit in his later book *Our Saviour Has Arrived*, where he wrote: "The Father (Yakub) of the world created a world of evil, discord, and hate."[69] Muhammad's oppressive upbringing in the extremely racist climate of rural, turn-of-the-century Georgia must have encouraged this highly ironic reading of biblical verses such as Genesis 1:31, where "God saw all that He had made, and found it very good." In Muhammad's mind, things *were* "very good," but only for the white race.

For Elijah Muhammad, the act of interpreting the Bible was liberating, particularly when his interpretations contradicted those of what he called the "white slave masters.... your translators and teachers of the Bible."[70] By establishing exegetical links between Genesis and the Yakub myth, moreover, Muhammad anchored his radical doctrine within the context of an established scriptural tradition.[71] Elijah Muhammad's exegesis was therefore a sophisticated form of resistance to white racism. I would argue that the Rabbis also viewed their biblical exegesis as a way to oppose false interpretations as well as oppressive conditions; a way for the "voice of Jacob"—the study of Torah by the Jewish people—to overcome the "hands of Esau"—the might of the gentile nations.[72]

Louis Farrakhan

When Elijah Muhammad died in 1974 his second youngest son, Warith Muhammad, succeeded him as leader of the Nation of Islam. Warith Muhammad shifted the movement away from his father's teachings and toward those of Sunni Islam, eventually dropping the name Nation of Islam. Louis Farrkahan, who had played an important role in the movement since the 1950s, rejected the changes introduced by Warith Muhammad. At the end of the 1970s, Farrakhan reconstituted the Nation of Islam under Elijah Muhammad's teachings, including the Yakub myth of racial origins. Like his mentor, Farrakhan has also adopted an ambivalent attitude toward Jews and Judaism.

Louis Farrakhan has danced a kind of pas de deux with American Jewish groups since the 1980s. While he has consistently denied charges of anti-Semitism and even called for a rapprochement with Jewish groups, he has also continued to make anti-Semitic remarks.[73] In an interview with Tony Snow published in the online edition of the Nation of Islam's publication, *The Final Call*, Farrakhan reiterated his desire to mend fences with American Jews:

> I would like to have reconciliation with American Jews today, not to wait until the end of my life. But reconciliation can only come based on dialogue, and dialogue has to be between the persons who are ill-effected. If one person is ready to dialogue and the other says we're not going to dialogue with you unless you apologize.... preconditions never will be acceptable to me. But I'm ready at any time to dialogue with the Jewish community and put an end to the controversy that is between us.[74]

The sticking point for Farrakhan's Jewish critics is that he has not acknowledged or apologized for his own anti-Semitic statements or for those in Nation of Islam publications such as *The Secret Relationship Between Blacks and Jews*, a spurious history which seeks to pin the lion's share of the slave trade on Jews.[75] One of Farrakhan's most vocal Jewish critics has been Abraham Foxman, the head of the Anti-Defamation League (ADL).[76] In a 1998 letter published in the *Forward*, a newspaper that focuses on Jewish issues, Foxman criticized those willing to sit down with Farrakhan before he rejects his anti-Semitic past: "Rev. Farrakhan's hollow calls for dialogue are entangled in his decades-long record of hatred that he makes no authentic effort to rectify."[77] Since Farrakhan believes neither that he is anti-Semitic nor that he should repudiate any statements taken by others to be anti-Semitic as a precondition for dialogue, it is unclear when or even if his struggle with Jewish groups such as the ADL will be resolved.

It is not accurate, as some critics have done, to characterize Farrakhan's highly publicized anti-Semitic statements as the only or even the chief reason for his appeal within the African American community. Remarks such as Christopher Hitchens's in *The Spectator* that "[i]t is anti-Semitism that supplies the emotional energy of his entire crusade. Without it, he [Farrakhan] would have nothing to say,"[78] fail to account for the widespread respect that Farrakhan enjoys among blacks of different socioeconomic and religious backgrounds, not to mention a cross section of whites as well. While anti-Semitic statements and publications have certainly drawn the media spotlight, Farrakhan's social and economic positions (many of which are quite conservative) have transformed him into a leader of national stature. Within the Nation of Islam itself, most members are compelled by the movement's religious doctrines and rituals rather than by the anti-Semitic pronouncements of some of its leaders. This is not to downplay the seriousness of the anti-Semitic rhetoric employed by Farrakhan and other prominant members of the Nation. Indeed, it is all the more disturbing and disappointing within the context of Farrakhan's critique of racism in America.

Farrakhan's relationship with Judaism is complex and should not be reduced to blind hatred. Rather than simply rehashing his well-known anti-Semitic statements, I would like to provide some sense of his more nuanced relationship with Jews and Judaism. First it should be noted that Farrakhan's remarks address both the ethnic aspect of Judaism and its religious dimension. On the one hand, Farrakhan has praised Jews for what he perceives to be their unity and their cultural achievements, particularly in the area of classical music (Farrakhan is an accomplished violinist himself). Farrakhan has even speculated that one of his own grandparents was Jewish, suggesting a highly personal sense of identification with Jews that appears in other comments as well.[79] On the other hand, Farrakhan has reiterated the standard anti-Semitic trope about a Jewish cabal which has for centuries conspired to control the government and international banking system and, more recently, the American Medical Association, universities, and Hollywood.[80]

Farrakhan's most infamous reference to Judaism occurred in a 1984 radio broadcast in which he referred to Israelis' "using God's name to shield your dirty religion." This remark was reported in the press as "Farrakhan calls Judaism a gutter religion." For his part, Farrakhan denies that he intended to condemn Judaism but admits that one could easily interpret his comments that way: "'I had no reference whatsoever in my mind to Judaism. However, anybody who distilled that could say, and rightly so, that I was talking about Judaism.' "[81]

Perhaps the most revealing comment Farrakhan has made concerning Jewish religious identity was in a 1985 speech to an audience in Los Angeles:

> I have a problem with Jews and it is not because I am hateful of Jewish people, not at all. But I have a problem because I am declaring to the world that they are not the chosen people of God. I am declaring to the world that you, the black people of America and the Western hemisphere [are the chosen people].[82]

Farrakhan is aware of the impact such statements may have: "The Jews don't like me 'cause I'm saying they're not the chosen people of God," he declared in a 1985 speech in Washington, D.C.[83] Like a number of other African American religious thinkers, Farrakhan has argued that "white" Jews are not the true descendants of the biblical Israel. Instead they are imposters who have attempted to supplant the true Jews, who are of African descent. As one scholar of the movement puts it: "The main point is that the blacks are the original people of the covenant and the principal actors of the Holy Scriptures. . . . The white Jew is a European devil, 'a Johnny-come lately Jew,' a bold imposter."[84] This view seeks to invalidate Jews' claims to their own history and identity, asserting that it is African Americans who are the "real" Jews.

On other occasions, however, Farrakhan has implied that contemporary Jews are in fact physical descendants of biblical Israel. Thus he has asserted that the Jews' rich history of prophecy and revelation has given them an advantage over other people, what Henry Louis Gates, Jr., has called Farrakhan's "theological explanation for Jewish preëminance." As Farrakhan puts it, " 'When you have a people [the Jews] who receive revelation. . . . they can do very good things or they can become very base, evil and use the revelation for wicked purposes.' "[85] The profound ambivalence of this statement reflects Farrakhan's love–hate relationship with Jews and Judaism. It also recalls the apostle Paul's remarks in Romans 11:28–29: "As regards the gospel they [the Jews] are enemies of God for your sake; but as regards election they are beloved, for the sake of their ancestors; for the gifts and the calling of God are irrevocable." Indeed, Jabril Muhammad, one of the Nation's chief theologians, has actually identified Farrakhan with Paul: "As Paul was to Jesus, according to Christian theology, so is Min. Louis Farrakhan to the real Christ [i.e., Elijah Muhammad]."[86] Farrakhan himself has accused contemporary Jews of treating him as their ancestors treated Jesus, "You didn't like Jesus and you don't like Farrakhan,"[87] a statement that equates today's Jews—albeit critically—with biblical Israel. Such remarks also indicate that Farrakhan's negative attitudes toward Jews are influenced by traditional Christian views as well as by more recent conspiracy theories.

Notwithstanding Farrakhan's condemnatory remarks concerning Jews, there is evidence that he appreciates Jewish religious traditions. This tendency may be seen most graphically in the "World's Day of Atonement," or "Holy Day of Atonement" an annual religious event developed by the Nation of Islam in the aftermath of the Million Man March of 1995.[88] There are a number of striking parallels between this day and the Jewish holiday of Yom Kippur, the "Day of Atonement." A list of "Holy Day of Atonement" activities published by the Nation exhorts people to fast from sunrise on October 15 to sunset on October 16.[89] Members are expected to read Scriptures, attend a house of worship, pray, and reconcile differences. The list of prohibitions declares, "No School, No Work, No Sport, No Play, No Spending." While many of these elements resemble Jewish, Muslim, and Christian holy day traditions, they are most similar to the rituals of Yom Kippur, which tends to fall some time around October or late September (depending on the Jewish lunar calendar).

Jesse Jackson, who delivered an address at the original "Million Man March and World's Day of Atonement" in 1995, has since commented that because the event had "essentially a religious theme—atonement—disconnected from public policy," it failed to have a positive impact on legislation and specifically the welfare bill that was being debated in Congress at the time.[90] Jackson contrasted this result with the March on Washington of 1963, which helped produce the Civil Rights Act. Although he was critical of its lack of connection to public policy, it is significant that Jackson should appreciate the event's primarily religious character, something that many observers failed to acknowledge or examine.

Farrakhan's views on Jews and Judaism run the gamut from genuine admiration to condemnation, from a desire to emulate to a desire to displace. They reveal the influence of modern anti-Semitic conspiracy theories as well as traditional Christian and Muslim views toward Jews. Perhaps the most significant factor, however, is a profound sense of identification, one inspired by both personal history and the rich tradition of African American identification with biblical Israel. In an essay on Farrakhan, Henry Louis Gates, Jr., eloquently expresses the ambivalence that results from this identification:

> What is one to make of all this? Farrakhan isn't feigning admiration for Jews as a distraction from his hate-mongering. Rather, his love and his loathing flow from the same ideas. There's a sense in which Farrakhan doesn't want his followers to battle Jews, but, rather, wants them to *be* Jews. Yet when he describes Jews as "world leaders" it is a double-edged compliment.[91]

Conclusion

The relationship of the Nation of Islam to Jews and Judaism cannot be reduced to the well-publicized anti-Semitic statements of recent years. Like Elijah Muhammad, his predecessor and mentor, Louis Farrakhan has a complicated view of Jews. Both men condemn Jews as whites, yet they also explicitly and implicitly regard Jews as different from other whites—for good and for bad. Because of their history of revelation, Jews have the potential for greater righteousness than other whites. According to Elijah Muhammad, this capacity for righteousness bears fruit among Orthodox Jews, whose ancestors "lived among us in Asia" and who scrupulously follow the laws of *kashrut* and are "wiser, more skillful, than the Christians." The negative side of such higher expectations is more apparent in the remarks of Louis Farrakhan. Although Farrakhan also acknowledges the spiritual potential of Jews—"they can do very good things"—he frequently focuses on the perceived failure of Jews to live up to their spiritual potential, or as Farrakhan puts it, they "use the revelation for wicked purposes." Only time will tell whether Farrakhan's recently expressed desire "to have reconciliation with American Jews today" heralds a new chapter in the history of relations between the two groups.

Notes

An earlier version of one section of this essay appeared in Nathaniel Deutsch, "Muhammad's Midrash: Elijah Muhammad's Biblical Interpretation in Light of Rabbinic Midrash," *Prospects: An Annual of American Cultural Studies*, 1995. I Thank Cambridge University Press for allowing me to reprint it here in a revised version.

1. Jonathan Z. Smith, "What a Difference a Difference Makes," in Jacob Neusner and Ernest Frerichs, eds., "*To See Ourselves as Others See Us" Christians, Jews, "Others" in Late Antiquity* (Chico, Calif., 1985), p. 47.

2. On the issue of whether Jews are white according to the Nation of Islam and an explanation of the minority position within the Nation that Jews are not white but "Semites," see C. Eric Lincoln, *The Black Muslims in America*, rev. ed. (Boston, 1973), pp. 175–82.

3. As I will show below, the Nation of Islam's attitudes toward white Muslims—like their attitudes toward Jews—have traditionally been ambivalent. On the one hand, Nation of Islam writings indicate respect for the efforts of white Muslims to live righteously, on the other, they suggest that because of their base origin in Yakub's experiment, white Muslims can never achieve the spiritual heights of African Americans. Recently, however, Louis Farrakhan has indicated that he is moving toward a more racially inclusive attitude concerning membership in the Nation of Islam; see, for example, Farrakhan's comments to interviewer Tony Snow in *The Final Call On-Line Edition*, Dec. 9, 1997, online March 30, 1998 (the interview originally appeared on Fox TV's *Tony Snow Show.*)

4. Elijah Muhammad, *Message to the Blackman in America* (Newport News, Va., 1992, reprint), p. 134.

5. John 8:41–44.

6. On Fard, see E. U. Essien-Udom, *Black Nationalism: A Search for an Identity in America* (New York, 1962), pp. 55ff.; and Lincoln, *The Black Muslims in America* (Boston, 1961), pp. 10ff. And more recently, Claude Andrew Clegg, *An Original Man: The Life and Times of Elijah Muhammad* (New York, 1997), esp. pp. 20–37; Mattias Gardell, *In the Name of Elijah Muhammad: Louis Farrakhan and the Nation of Islam* (Durham N.C., 1996), pp. 50–58.

7. Clegg, *An Original Man*, p. 60.

8. Muhammad, *Message to the Blackman in America*, p. 164. Number 12 in the list of beliefs of the Nation is the following: "We believe that Allah (God) appeared in the Person of Mas-

ter W. Fard Muhammad, July, 1930—the long awaited 'Messiah' of the Christians and the 'Mahdi' of the Muslims."

9. Ibid., p. 47.

10. Gayraud Wilmore, in *Black Religion and Black Radicalism* (Garden City, NY, 1972), p. 253, writes, "The long-range goal of the Muslim movement was to entice Blacks away from the churches and to bring the entire race into the Nation of Islam."

11. Although he did not include a separate discussion of Jews and the Nation of Islam in his first edition, Lincoln did include a section in his 1973 edition of *The Black Muslims in America* (pp. 175–82). Lincoln argues on p. 178 that "none of the beliefs [concerning Jews] are more virulent than those held by the Mulsims about the white man in general. The Jews have not been singled out, so far, as a special target of a concentrated attack." Note that this was written before the ascendency of Louis Farrakhan and that Lincoln writes "have not been singled out, *so far*. . . ." [emphasis added]

12. Muhammad, *Message to the Blackman*, pp. 74-75.

13. Ibid., p. 87.

14. Ibid., p. 79.

15. Ibid., p. 99.

16. Ibid., p. 65.

17. Elijah Muhammad, *How to Eat to Live*, Book One (Newport News, Va., 1967), p.2. "Thanks to the coming of Allah in the Person of Master Fard Muhammad, if we obey what He has given to us in the way of proper foods and the proper time to partake of these foods, we will never be sick, or have to pay hundreds, thousands and millions of dollars for doctor bills and hospitalization."

18. Ibid., p. 53.

19. Ibid., p. 24.

20. Ibid., p. 63.

21. *How to Eat to Live*, Book Two (Newport News, Va., 1972), p. 176.

22. Ibid., p. 101.

23. *How to Eat to Live*, Book One, p. 2.

24. Ibid., p. 67.

25. Ibid., p. 95.

26. Elijah Muhammad apparently has in mind Sura 5:5 of the Quran "On this day all things that are clean have been made lawful for you; and made lawful for you is the food of the people of the Book, as your food is made lawful for them."

27. *How to Eat to Live*, Book One, p. 24. The food of Jews is not permissable according to all Muslims (the Shi'ites, for example), and Jews who follow the laws of *kashrut* are not allowed to eat meat slaughtered by Muslims. For other references to Judaism and Jews, see *How to Eat to Live*, Book One, pp. 1, 68; Book Two, pp. 105, 128.

28. *How to Eat to Live*, Book One, pp. 11-12.

29. Ibid., p. 109.

30. Ibid., pp. 52–53.

31. Elijah Muhammad, *Our Saviour Has Arrived* (Chicago, 1974), p. 89. Muhammad continues by emphasizing that "The white race is not equal."

32. Ibid., p. 90.

33. *How to Eat to Live*, Book One, p. 13.

34. *How to Eat to Live*, Book Two, pp. 88–89. It is unclear what Muhammad means when he writes, "out of the other world."

35. The body of literature on midrash is enormous. Some of the most important works include Yitzhak Heinemann, *Darkhe Ha-Aggadah*, 3rd ed. (Jerusalem, 1974); H. Strack and G. Stemberger, *Introduction to the Talmud and Midrash* (Edinburgh, 1991, reprint); Michael Fishbane, *The Garments of Torah: Essays in Biblical Hermeneutics* (Bloomington, Ind., 1989); James Kugel, *In Potiphar's House: The Interpretive Life of Biblical Texts* (Cambridge, 1990); Daniel Boyarin, *Intertextuality and the Reading of Midrash* (Bloomington, Ind., 1990).

36. Kugel, *In Potiphar's House*, pp. 6–7.

37. Here I borrow the terminology of Boyarin, *Intertextuality and the Reading of Midrash*, pp. 41ff. Boyarin defines such textual "gaps" as "those silences in the text which call for interpretation if the reader is to 'make sense' of what happened, to fill out the plot and the characters in a meaningful way."

38. Harold Bloom has already noted a general resemblence between the Nation of Islam's doctrine and Gnosticism in *The American Religion: The Emergence of the Post-Christian Nation* (New York, 1992), p. 250.

39. For the German term "Protestexegese," see K. Rudolph, "Randerscheinungen des Judentums und das Problem der Entstehung des Gnostizismus," *Kairos* 9 (1967), 117. For the expression "Inverse Exegesis," see, I. Couliano, *The Tree of Gnosis: Gnostic Mythology from Early Christianity to Modern Nihilism* (San Francisco, 1992), p. 121.

40. Couliano, *The Tree of Gnosis*, p. 121.

41. Muhammad, *Message to the Blackman in America*, p. 95. See, also, Malcom X's statement in *The Autobiography of Malcom X* (London, 1965), p. 343: "The Holy Bible in the white man's hands and his interpretations of it have been the greatest single ideological weapon for enslaving millions of non-white human beings."

42. Muhammad, *Message to the Blackman*, pp. 87–88.

43. See *Genesis Rabbah* 8:3.

44. Ibid., 8:4.

45. Ibid., 8:8.

46. See the *Apocryphon of John* 15:1–4 in James Robinson, ed., *The Nag Hammadi Library in English* (San Francisco, 1988), p. 113.

47. *The Autobiography of Malcolm X*, p. 304.

48. For a discussion of the typological exegesis frequently employed in African American religious movements, see Theophus Smith, *Conjuring Culture: Biblical Formations of Black America* (Oxford: 994), pp. 55ff. Smith defines typology as "the hermeneutic (interpretive) tradition that links biblical types or figures to postbiblical persons, places, and events."

49. See, for example, E. Muhammad, *Our Saviour Has Arrived*, pp. 8–9.

50. See, for example, *Mishnah 'Abot* i. 1 and parallels, which are ably discussed by M. Herr, "Continuum in the Chain of Transmission, *Zion* 44 (1979), 43–56 (Hebrew).

51. Michael Fishbane, *Biblical Interpretation in Ancient Israel* (Oxford, 1985), p. 4.

52. Ibid.

53. From an interview with Elijah Muhammad's son, Imam W. D. Muhammad, in Clifton Marsh, *From Black Muslims to Muslims: The Transition from Separatism to Islam, 1930–1980*, Metuchen, N.J., 1984), p. 116.

54. Both quotes are from *The Autobiography of Malcom X*, p. 304.

55. The Yakub myth has been reaffirmed by Louis Farrakhan, current leader of the Nation of Islam, but rejected by Elijah Muhammad's son Imam Warith Deen Muhammad, leader of the American Muslim Mission. Yakub, it should be noted, is a highly complex figure, combining elements of the biblical God; the Gnostic Demiurge (Bloom, *The American Religion*, p.

252, has already written that "Yakub has an irksome memorability as a crude but pungent Gnostic Demiurge"); the biblical patriarch Jacob [Heb. Ya'akov/Arab. Yakub, see *Message to the Blackman in America*, p. 126, where Muhammed writes, "the father of the white race (Mr. Yakub or Jacob)"]; the leader of the fallen angels; John of Patmos (who received the New Testament's book of Revelation, see, for example, Muhammad's comments in *Message to the Blackman*, pp. 124–26); and a traditional trickster figure (Smith, *Conjuring Culture*, p. 248, n. 49, notes the tricksterlike quality of Yakub).

56. Bloom, *The American Religion*, p. 251.

57. *Message to the Blackman in America*, pp. 112–13.

58. Ibid., pp. 115–16.

59. Ibid., p. 116.

60. Ibid., pp. 117–18.

61. Muhammad apparently understands the term "cherubim" to be singular and adds an "s" to make it plural. The form is, however, already a plural of the singular "cherub" or *keruv* (Heb.).

62. *Message to the Blackman in American*, p. 133. Henceforth, all parentheses are in the original.

63. See, for example, Babylonian Talmud Hagigah 12a.

64. I am indebted to Michael Fishbane for this understanding of the rabbinic phrase.

65. Boyarin, *Intertextuality and the Reading of Midrash*, p. 40. Boyarin examines the use of intertexts in midrashic literature.

66. Ibid., p. 37.

67. *Message to the Blackman in America*, p. 118.

68. Ibid., p. 119.

69. Muhammad, *Our Saviour Has Arrived*, p. 75. See also p. 116.

70. *Message to the Blackman in America*, p. 109.

71. See Boyarin, *Intertextuality and the Reading of Midrash*, p. 37, "Midrash seems to have great appeal to many people in our culture. To some, midrash is perceived as a liberating force from the tyranny of the "correct interpretation." . . . Our study of midrash suggests that another reason that it may appeal to the postmodern sensibility is not so much for the way it liberates from cultural examplars (that work really needs no buttressing in our culture!), but for the way that it preserves contact and context with the tradition while it is liberating."

72. For an explicit example of this view see *Genesis Rabbah* on Genesis 27:22. In rabbinic writings, the "voice of Jacob" signifies the study of Torah, while the "hands of Esau" signify the military might of the gentile nations, and in particular the Roman Empire, as Esau was considered the ancestor of Rome.

73. The denials of anti-Semitism by Farrakhan and other members of the Nation of Islam are many. One of the more interesting and ambitious appears in Jabril Muhammad, "Torah Exposes Jewish Lies on Farrakhan," January 25, 1994. Farrakhan himself has responded frequently, including in "Farrakhan on Anti-Semitism," *The Final Call*, February 16, 1994. For a biographical examination of Farrakhan with significant discussion of his attitudes toward Judaism, see Arthur Magida, *Prophet of Rage: A Life of Louis Farrakhan and His Nation* (New York, 1996).

74. *The Final Call On-Line Edition*, Dec. 9, 1997, online March 30, 1998.

75. *The Secret Relationship Between Blacks and Jews*, NOI Research Department, 1991, has been thoroughly refuted by a number of historians including Eugene Genovese and Harold

Brackman. See Harold Brackman, *Ministry of Lies: The Truth Behind the Nation of Islam's "The Secret Relationship Between Blacks and Jews"* (New York, 1994).

76. The ADL has published a number of reports on Louis Farrakhan, many of which quote from his own speeches. For a partial list of these reports, see *In the Name of Elijah Muhammad*, p. 407, n. 134; pp. 453–54.

77. Abraham Foxman, "Farrakhan's True Colors Always Emerge," letter to the editor in *Forward*, February 13, 1998.

78. C. Hitchens, "The False Messiah Who Hates Jews," *The Spectator*, January 25, 1986, p. 13.

79. Henry Louis Gates, Jr., "The Charmer," *The New Yorker*, April 29 and May 6, 1996, p. 125. Formerly known as Gene Walcott, Farrakhan was a Calypso singer called the Charmer before joining the Nation.

80. See *In the Name of Elijah Muhammad*, p. 260, referring to a Farrakhan speech, "The Crucifixion of Jesus: The Destruction of Black Leadership," delivered at Mosque Maryam, Chicago, March 26, 1989; also Gates, "The Charmer," p. 126.

81. "The Charmer," p. 125. For a somewhat apologetic analysis of this remark, see *In the Name of Elijah Muhammad*, pp. 245-46; 254–55.

82. As reported in Judith Cummings, "Diverse Crowd Hears Farrakhan in Los Angeles," *New York Times*, Sept. 16, 1985, p. 10. See, also Hans Baer and Merrill Singer, *African-American Religion in the Twentieth Century: Varieties of Protest and Accommodation* (Knoxville, 1992), p. 123.

83. Farrakhan speech, "Power at Last . . . Forever!" delivered at the John F. Kennedy Center, Washington, D.C., July 22, 1985.

84. *In the Name of Elijah Muhammad*, p. 258.

85. Gates, "The Charmer," p. 125.

86. Jabril Muhammad [Bernard Cushmeer], *Farrakhan, the Traveler* (Phoenix, 1985), p. 4.

87. Farrakhan speech, "By the Time Surely Man Is at Loss," delivered at Michigan State University, February 18, 1990.

88. For a description of the 1996 event see Charisse Jones, "Thousands Rally at United Nations on 'Day of Atonement,'" *The New York Times*, October 17, 1996.

89. From "Young Gifted and Atoning," on the Nation of Islam web page, March 30, 1998.

90. See Gates, "The Charmer," p. 129.

91. Ibid., p. 126.

6

The Nubian Islaamic Hebrews, Ansaaru Allah Community

Jewish Teachings of an African American Muslim Community

Kathleen Malone O'Connor

THE NUBIAN ISLAAMIC Hebrews (NIH), also known as the Ansaaru Allah (Ansarullah) Community and currently as the Holy Tabernacle Ministries (HTM), is one of a number of African American Muslim movements that have generated new and indigenous forms of Islam in America. This community can best be understood within the black prophetic, millennial, and messianic traditions of the Moorish Science Temple (begun in 1915), the Nation of Islam (arising in the 1930s), and the Five Percent Nation of Gods and Earths (a youth group branching off from the Nation of Islam in the late 1960s). The NIH also parallels the black nationalist and civil rights movements and contributes strongly to the current trend of Afrocentrism in African American social and cultural discourse.[1] These communities remain relatively unknown in the study of contemporary African American religion and are unacknowledged contributors to the spectrum of religious identity in the larger pluralistic environment of American society. Even the Nation of Islam, which has received perhaps the greatest scholarly and popular attention, has been seen primarily as a sociopolitical movement, with its full religious dimensions and connections to the larger Judaic-Christian-Islamic tradition[2] still inadequately explored.

The nature of engagement with Judaism by these African American Muslim groups must be seen within the context of the ongoing development of African American Jewish groups in their own right, their joint relationship to the Falashas, or black Jews of Ethiopia, as well as their problematic relationship to the larger Ashkenazic and Sephardic communities of the Jewish Diaspora and the creation of the Jewish state and society of Israel in the mid-twentieth century.[3] Indigenous African American Jewish communities have an even longer history in this country than African American Muslim communities. This history begins with the Moorish Zionist Temple in 1899, followed by the Temple of the Gospel of the Kingdom, or the

Black Jews, founded by the messianic figure, Roberson in 1917. The Moorish Zionist Temple was reorganized in 1921 under the leadership of Mordecai Herman and developed an offshoot, Beth B'nai Abraham, led by Arnold Ford in 1925 until its decline in 1930. In the 1930s the Commandment Keepers Congregation of the Living God, or the Black Jews of Harlem, were established under the leadership of Rabbi Wentworth A. Matthew, and the Church of God was founded in Philadelphia by Prophet F. S. Cherry. Such early black Jewish communities, clearly paralleled by the early development of indigenous African American Muslim communities, were followed by later groups such as the Hebrew Israelites, often known as the Black Hebrews, founded in the 1950s by Nasi Shaliach Ben Yehuda (Louis Bryant), advocating emigration to Liberia and later to Israel (currently under the leadership of Ben Ammi Carter). Other groups that remain exclusively within the African American context such as the Israeli Church, or Sons of Yahawah, and the Black Israelite Hebrews led by Yahweh Ben Yahweh, who is believed to be the son of Yahweh the Messiah,[4] are characterized as black Jewish nationalist organizations that draw in various ways upon the core concept of "Black Zion," or the "chosenness" of black people as the true descendants of Abraham, who form a unified messianic Nation.

The Nubian Islaamic Hebrews, Ansaaru Allah Community: An Introduction

The differing engagements of African American Muslim groups with Jewish and Christian prophecy and scripture, iconography and dress, sacred calendar and ritual observance are demonstrable examples of religious pluralism, not only between different religious communities but as intersecting allegiances within single communities. Historical and phenomenological kinship with Islamic mysticism and sectarianism[5] provides these communities with Islamic prototypes for the African American Muslim realities of human divinity, cyclic prophecy, and ongoing revelation, and establishes the Islamic stage upon which Jewish (and Christian) themes are enacted. In this group, one of whose early names was the Nubian Islaamic Hebrews, later the Ansaaru Allah (the Helpers of God) Community,[6] and currently the Holy Tabernacle Ministries, it is possible to chart the convergence of these three prophetic traditions, Judaism, Christianity, and Islam.[7] Each "school" of teaching throughout its 30-year history is distinguished among other contemporary African American Muslim groups by its emphasis on the equal primacy of Hebrew as well as Arabic prophets and scriptures, and extensive use of exegetical techniques with strong Jewish and Islamic precedents such as mystical numerology and the manipulation of esoteric alphabets.[8] A summary history of their shifts in self-naming as an ongoing process of doctrinal and social evolution, and an analysis of the significance of the earlier designations in relation to the later, will show this community's claim to a share in the larger heritage of Jewish prophecy and revelation. The focus of attention will be their period of Jewish teachings (circa 1992–1993) generated under the founder's Jewish persona, Rabboni: Y'shua, as well as earlier and later reflections or revisions of Jewish themes and motifs in the extended corpus of the community's sacred writings, religious material culture, and iconography.[9]

This community, most frequently known as the Ansaaru Allah, or Ansarullah, Community and currently known as the Holy Tabernacle Ministries, began in the mid 1960's under the name Ansar Pure Sufi, claiming a connection to the mystical teachings of Islam and organizing itself as an African American variant on the traditional Sufi brotherhoods of the larger Muslim world.[10] In 1969 the name Nubian Islaamic Hebrews came into use, emphasizing African heritage and ancient Egyptian (Nubian) origins; dress and symbols of Africa were also adopted. In 1970 the community established itself formally with headquarters in Bushwick Ave, Brooklyn, instituting segregated dormitories for communal living, and it began to publish teaching texts and a newspaper. In the mid- to late seventies the name Ansaaru Allah ("Helpers of God") Community was adopted, reflecting a commitment to Islam as the "natural" religion of black people. The founder, Dwight York, also known as Isa Muhammad (or "As Sayyid Isa Al Haadi Al Mahdi," "the Lord Jesus Guide and Savior"), claimed both genealogical and spiritual descent from the Sudanese Mahdi, the messianic leader of the late nineteenth-century Islamic revivalist/millenarian movement against British and Turkish colonial rule in the Sudan. Throughout the 1970s and 1980s, the Islamicization of the community was in full swing, and the study of Quran and its *tafsir* and *ta'wil* (mystical and esoteric interpretation) generated an enormous body of devotional literature by the founder. At the same time as the community was fully committed to an Islamic worldview and an Islamic way of life (including changes in social patterns, dress, and food customs), the interpretive tradition of the founder continued to engage with the legacy of Jewish and Christian prophecy and scripture through the filter of Islam.

Each stage of the community's growth was signaled by a change in name, dress, and outward symbols.[11] In 1992, for example, Islamic dress for men and women was abandoned, indicating a major shift in teachings which was structurally manifested as a reorganization of the existing mystical teaching order of al-Khidr[12] and the establishment of the Ancient Mystic Order of Melchisedek.[13] For a two year period, 1992–1993, interpretive literature in journal, pamphlet, and book form bore the mark of the founder's shift in teachings to engage Judaism centrally as part of the Nubian spiritual legacy.[14] Called "The Doctrine of the New Covenant," the change in teachings was reflected in a corresponding change in male and female dress and symbols. Since 1994 the community has moved on to its current self-identification as the Holy Tabernacle Ministries, whose doctrines have evolved into a growing concern with extraterrestrial origins and apocalyptic agency.[15]

The founder, therefore, is the litmus paper for the permeability of Jewish, Christian, and Islamic frames of reference: as his teachings evolved, so too did his many titles and spiritual designations. From ancient Egyptian inspiration and the period of Egyptian teaching comes "Amunnubi Rooakhptah" ("Faithful Informer, Soul of the

Ptahites," "supreme being for the renewal of your forgotten history").[16] From the book of Revelation and the Gospels of the New Testament in the period of Christian teaching comes the motif of the Lamb on Mount Zion (Rev. 14:1), understood as the Islamic Jesus, prophet and savior.[17] From the period of Jewish teaching comes his designation "Rabboni: Y'shua," indicating his status as teacher and rabbi who is the forerunner and herald of the messiah (Y'shua Bar Dawiyd, Jesus son of David), who will come at the end of time and bring the Judgment Day. From the several eras of Islamic incarnation and mahdist teachings comes his most common title, "As Sayyid Al Imaam Isa Al Haadi Al Mahdi," with its short forms of Isa Muhammad (an Arabic name which draws upon the prophetic legitimization and authority of both Jesus and Muhammad), or Imaam Isa (Imaam in the Shi'i sense of charismatic, semi-divine descendants of the Prophet Muhammad through his daughter Fatima and son-in-law Ali). Finally, all titles and persona have been absorbed, revised and reordered by the current teachings of Dr. Malachi Z. York (Malachi Zodok or Melchizedek), devoted to the "science" and "facts" of Nuwaubu.[18] In the current era, Dr. York is generating ongoing and expanding narratives regarding Nubian extraterrestrial origins from the procreative activities of angelic and celestial visitors, the ELoheem, who seeded their "children" here on earth,[19] and the millennial expectations of their starship, the Motherplane, the crystal city, Nibiru, associated with Ezekiel's vision of the divine chariot or Merkavah,[20] which will return at the endtimes to carry off the righteous remnant.[21]

Among the most significant social parameters of these changes in doctrine have been the periodic transformations in self-naming and dress within the community. Dr. York explains one of the most recent shifts, circa 1992, away from Islamic dress—particularly abandoning veiling for women—to adopting a mode of dress identified as Jewish, and after 1994 a return to secular American dress. He interprets these shifts in the context of (1) events he had foretold from the very beginning, that is that such dress and forms were never intended to be permanent, and (2) events that were dictated by social and political necessity, the increasing hostility toward Muslims in the West and identification of Islam worldwide with terrorism, which became a danger to the Ansarullah Community.[22] From a 1995 issue of the *HTM* journal, "The Savior," in an article entitled, "Whatever Happened to the Name Abdullah Muhammad?" comes the following discussion of this disassociation from the larger Muslim and Jewish worlds.

> The importance of the meaning of a good name has been established since the beginning of time and can be traced all the way through the Scriptures. Even Yahuwa Eloh (He Who is the Source) has changed names for particular reasons such as Abram being changed to Abraham in Genesis 17:5. . . . In this day and time, we, of the Holy Tabernacle Ministries, use American names, because it could be very dangerous just as the Lamb had warned us years ago. With all the killing and terrorism going on in the so-called Muslim world, we do not wear Islaamic clothing, the veil, and we will not use Islaamic names.

> We do not want in any shape, form or fashion to be associated with any anti-government or terrorist groups of Muslims, Moslems, Hebrews or the like, not even with our own brothers of Sudan. We are only Islaamic in the sense that we are in a state of peace ["Islam" comes from an Arabic root word meaning peace] when practicing our cultural observances passed down to us by Abraham, which makes us true Hebrews. Therefore, we refer to Arabic or Hebrew names [only] as our spiritual names.[23]

Within the context of such evolutionary change, therefore, we can explore the adoption, elaboration, and transformation of Jewish themes, motifs, and exegetical methods by examining four basic contexts of Nubian Islaamic Hebrew discourse: the covenant of the chosen people; scripture and its interpretation; sacred calendar and ritual observance; and religious material culture, dress, and iconography.

Covenant: Abraham and the Descendants of Ishmael

In contrast to traditional black Christian interpretation which tends to emphasize the relationship between the African American experience of slavery in the New World and the experience of Hebrew bondage in Egypt through the prophethood of Moses and the Exodus, Nubian Islaamic Hebrew discourse returns even further back into prophetic and genealogical origins to the figure of Abraham and his promise from God that his descendants would form a great nation (*goy gadol*)[24] and would be his chosen people above all others.[25] All Nubians (originally meaning black Americans, then all people of color, and now the black origin of all humanity) claim tribal origins and spiritual investiture as the true descendants of Abraham. His designation as the first "Hebrew" (*Avram ha-'ivri*, or he who "crossed over"; Gen. 14:13) is conflated with the African slaves who also "crossed over" in the Middle Passage.[26] The Nubian Islaamic Hebrews trace their lineage in Islamic fashion through Abraham and his son Ishmael, and grandson, Kedar, rather than through the traditional Jewish patriarchal lineage of Abraham, Isaac, and Jacob or Israel. Thus they are linked to Israel genealogically but view the Ishmaelite branch as the true inheritors of God's promise of salvation: "The tribe of Israel are in us and we in them because we are the seed of Abraham. But they went bad real bad."[27] Paradoxically, The Nubian Islaamic Hebrews/Holy Tabernacle Ministries disavow any kinship with world Jewry, whether Ashkenazic or Sephardic in cultural origin, as racially alien and spiritually disconnected from the Nubian Abrahamic legacy. "The Jews of today are not from the time of Abraham,"[28] according to Dr. York, and by this is meant that "Israel" is the seed of "Canaan" and therefore can only be "false" or "fake" Jews because of their contaminated and demonic European (white) lineage:

> The name "Jew" is really a Yiddish word. This name was created by two groups of Jews: The Sephardim and Ashkenazim . . . who converted . . . and

> used it as their own when in fact they were from the seed of Canaan. . . . Now-a-days the name is falsely applied. . . . The fake Ashkenazim have developed a set of distinctive customs and rituals, different from those of the Sephardim, the fake Jews from Spain, Portugal, the Mediterranean countries and North Africa. . . . All of the sons of Shem (Gen. 10:21–32), the original Shemite (Semitic, [Shem] one of the triplet sons of Noah), had very dark brown skin with woolly hair [i.e., he was Nubian]. . . . The real Sephardim are in Yemen, Morocco, Sudan, Ethiopia, and America as American Negroes and the real Ashkenazim are in Ethiopia and mixed with the Nigerians (Ebo), and the Ashanti, and also in America as American Negroes, as well as all over the Caribbean.[29]

So if world Jewry are the fake Jews, how do the Nubian Islaamic Hebrews stake a claim to a genuine Jewish identity? In a cosmological and eschatological sense, Nubians owe their "Jewishness" not to Judaism, but to their genealogical descent and divine spiritual investiture which they distinguish as "Hebrew."[30] Dr. York defines the unity of the Nubian Nation and the Abrahamic Nation in Islamic fashion as those who inherit and follow the "rites" of Abraham, meaning the rites of circumcision, but in a larger Islamic sense the rites of monotheism.

> The Jews are another group of people who's thinking that we (Nubians) are following what they call "their religion." Them Jebusites [Jews] got a lot of nerve to even think that way, when it proves to you right in the Scriptures that "Judaism" is part of our culture. Judaism is part of our culture by way of Abraham, son of Terakh and Nuwna. Abraham was of the dark brown race, and was said to be the father of all nations (Gen. 17:4). . . . So if you are not following "*Millath* Abraham" (rites of Abraham) you are not a real Hebrew or Israelite or Muslim or Christian.[31]

This claim via genealogical descent through Abraham and the line of Ishmael is constructed upon a concept of the pre-Judaic-Christian-Islamic religion of Abraham, described in the Quran (2:130, 3:95, 16:123) as "*millat* Ibrahim," "the creed, or way of Abraham," a more inclusive meaning than the Hebrew *millah*, meaning literally "circumcision."[32] All Nubians whose natural religion is Islam are "descendent of Abraham through Hagar's son Ishmael, and Ishmael's son Kedar." Nubians follow in an immediate sense the prophet of Islam, Muhammad, whose purpose, they believe, "was to testify of Jesus; meaning not to teach anything other than what Jesus, Moses and Abraham taught before him."[33]

Thus, in Nubian Islaamic Hebrew perspective, "The only pure Hebrews remaining [are] that of the Tribe of Kedar, House of Ishmael."[34] Islam acknowledges its inheritance of Jewish and Christian revelation/scripture and the long line of divinely inspired prophets sent by God, going back to Adam. The mantle of prophethood in Islam passes on in a natural progression from the earliest individuals whom God approaches in covenant before the establishment of Judaism, Christianity, or Islam.[35] The notion of prophecy passing from one community or people to another in a divinely appointed chronology of revelation undergirds the direct claim by the Nubian Islaamic Hebrews to Abrahamic authority and the lineage of Ishmael (Muslim kinship) and Kedar, which attests to Nubian kinship, as in Song of Songs 1:5: "I am black, but comely, as the tents of Kedar."[36] In the course of spiritual evolution, the Islamic and Jewish identity of this community passes into another dispensation, the extraterrestrial teachings of Nuwaubu. In this context, Nuwaubu means a whole new dispensation to teach, manifested in (1) "Supreme Mathematics," a new science of mystical and apocalyptic numerology; (2) Nuwaubian, the new language created for the New Being/Nubian; and (3) *The Holy Tablets*, the new scriptures "revised" to incorporate/interpret previous revelations/scriptures (Mesopotamian, Egyptian, Jewish, Christian, Islamic) to the new millenarian community, linking the old prophecy to the new through the teachings of the founder. "In the new *du'a* [Muslim mission to teach] as found in the beginning of *The Holy Tablets* [Chap. 13, 1:25–30] [it] is because we were Ansaars [Ansaaru Allah, "aiders of Allah," i.e., Nubian Muslims] then and we said to follow the *Millat* 'Rites or Rituals' of Abraham [Q. 2:130]. And now the *Millat* Ibrahiym led us to Nuwaubu."[37]

Scripture and Interpretation: Torah, Targum, and Midrash

The earlier embodiments of the community, whether Islamic in primary identification (Ansarullah Community) or Jewish in primary identification (Nubian Islaamic Hebrews), conceived of the Judaic-Christian-Islamic tradition to which they were heirs as the repository of diverse scriptural legacies: the Hebrew Torah, the Christian Gospels, and the Islamic Quran.[38]

Although the exegesis of the founder does not categorize scripture in traditionally Jewish ways, it does use methods of interpretation that follow rabbinic exegetical pathways, specifically in two areas. The first are the traditions of *targum*,[39] which is the Aramaic "translation" and paraphrase of written Torah (the Torah read at synagogue services) such as Targum Onqelos, Targum Jonathan, and others; the second is the larger discourse of *midrash*, which is the interpretive elaboration of Torah, including ethical teachings, folklore and legendary material, characterized as "oral Torah" in contrast to written Torah. In the sense in which both these activities are practiced by the founder as a form of divinely inspired teaching, his interpretive and comparative analysis of Scripture combines the two types of rabbinic discourse. The first is *peshat*, which is the "plain sense of things," the authoritative interpretation; the other is *derash*, the discursive elaboration or application of historical/contextual meaning.[40] However, as Boyarin's study of intertextuality in biblical literature suggests, the opposition between objective and subjective readings of scripture obscures the interpretive dynamics within all texts. "If the term 'intertextuality' has any value at all, it is precisely in the way that it claims that . . . every text is constrained by the literary system of which it is a part and that every text is ultimately dialogical in that it cannot but record the traces of its contentions and doubling of earlier discourses."[41]

The way in which Malachi Z. York interprets Hebrew scripture has as much to do with his unique and idiosyncratic understanding (or "over"standing, as he would say) of philology and comparative linguistics as it does to his re-creation of scripture according to a new mythological ground. This linguistic and mythological interpretation partakes of both "translation" of language and "interpretation" of the meaning of Hebrew, Arabic, Greek, Ancient Egyptian, and Mesopotamian "scriptures." His transformative and intertextual "reading" is a *midrash* in the same sense that Jewish *midrash* is a "reading" of Torah:

> "This perspective comprehends how later texts interpret and rewrite the earlier ones to change the meaning of the entire canon, and how recognizing the presence of the earlier texts in the later changes our understanding of these later texts as well . . . an almost classic intertextuality, defined as 'the transformation of a signifying system.' This is what the *midrash* itself refers to as 'stringing [like beads or pearls] the words of Torah together . . . from the Torah to the Prophets and from the Prophets to the Writings' [*Song of Songs Rabbah*]."[42]

York's voluminous teaching texts include intensive scriptural interpretation, both translation and commentary, which are the transformation of the signifying system of Hebrew scripture according to the internal and evolving cosmological and eschatological narrative of the community, and form an extensive body of *midrashim.*

A brief sample of the Nubian Islaamic Hebrew equivalent of *Bereshit Rabbah*, or *Midrash on Genesis* (woven throughout various exegetical works), will demonstrate both the founder's engagement with but also transformation through "translation" of Hebrew philology and the scripture of which it is a part.[43] Like midrashic activity as a whole, "which claims that the new context is implied by the old one, that the new meaning (Oral Torah) revealed by recontextualizing pieces of the authoritative text are a legitimate interpretation of the Written Torah itself . . . given with its very revelation,"[44] Malachi Z. York's midrashic analysis of Hebrew scripture "reads" a radically different narrative as inherently present or as a subtext of the written Torah, requiring only the decoding of "right knowledge, right wisdom, and right overstanding," or knowledge of true Nubian origins. In the 1993 issue of *Nubian Bulletin: The Truth*, "The True Story of the Beginning," the narratives of black human origins are woven from a *targum* and *midrash* of various threads of the Genesis text. It points out that the traditional Bible still most commonly used in the black community is the King James Bible, a "mistranslation" which the founder seeks to correct by a directly engaging with the original Hebrew text, what he calls "Barashith of Mosheh [Moses]," implicitly acknowledging the rabbinic belief that the five books of

Torah (and implicitly all of the law, whether written or oral) were given to Moses by God on Sinai.[45] In retranslating the opening line of Genesis while simultaneously offering the original Hebrew text and phonetic transcriptions of key Hebrew terms in his translations, York renders visible three important Nubian Islaamic Hebrew doctrines: (1) that creation as described in Genesis is not original but a "re-construction," (2) that God or *Elohim* is not one divine creative power but a grammatical plurality of powers, and (3) that heaven is not a single immaterial realm above the earth, but grammatically dual, that is, "*shamayim*, or "two skies," implying our sky above the earth and another sky, the heavens of outer space.

> Barashith of Mosheh (Moses) Genesis 1:1[46]
> In the period of the BARA (pro-creation/re-construction), ELOHIM (the angelic beings of EL) BARA (reconstructed) the SHAW-MAH-YEEM (two skies) and EH-RETS (the planet Earth).
> —Right Translation in Aramic (Hebrew) by: Rabboni: Y'shua[47]

In the year following the period of the Jewish "school," he continues to amplify on this engagement with Genesis 1:1, explaining the meaning of BARA (reconstruction):

> The title of the *Scroll of Barashith* in itself confirms the fact that Genesis is a recording of the reconstruction of the planet earth, and man, and not the original creation. It is obviously clear that by the definition of these [Hebrew] words, and the very meanings have been misinterpreted and translated to misguide you and cover up the truth. Barashith, so far as meaning reconstruction, is rather a *rereplenishing* and repopulating of a selected part of the planet earth by a selected and bred stock or tribe of people. . . . It is about their story and their generation, who they descended from (the *Angelic Beings*, the *Eloheem*, the *Anunnaqi—those who came from Anu in 50's*), and who descended from them (the Enos [Mortal Man]).[48]

The full doctrine of the divine name, ELoheem, understood as the divine plurality of "angelic beings," who visited earth to "seed" it with their "children," is used to explain the significance of the term wherever it appears but particularly in the Genesis narratives. The first creation/evolution of life is described as evolving from water, or "marine life": "The tablet of the ancients were given to Adam and Eve by the Elders (Eloheem), APSU and TIAMAT. They were known as marine life. Apsu–Fresh Water, and Tiamat–Salt Water, from which all life came and that is why, it's said that man comes 'from the sea' [Gen. 1:20]."[49] The cosmological-biological nature of plural creations or terrestrial evolutions is explained via the meteor impact theory of dinosaur extinction (favored by many paleontologists), after which "the ELohim drew up water in the forms of clouds and started life in vegetation and re-animation of life on the planet earth. Then 49,000 years ago the ELohim (Angelic Beings of EL) were ordered to procreate a human being in their image and after their likeness and called them Adama."[50]

> Barashith of Mosheh (Moses) Genesis 5:2:
> Zakar and Nekaybaw BAW-RAW (procreated) He (Israa'EL) them (Zakar and Nekaybaw); and gave them BAW-RA-QAW (his blessings) and QAW-RAW (called) their SHAME (name) AW-DAWM (Adamite tribes, those of the ground, Earth). In the YOME (day of 7,000 years) when they were BAW-RAW (procreated at the 42,000 years, the sixth day).
> —Right Translation in Aramic (Hebrew) by: Rabboni: Y'shua[51]

He continues to specify the "pro-creative" process between these Angelic Beings and the process of human evolution:

> El Yahuwa [YHVH] sent three of the Agreeable ELohim to fashion Zakar [male] and Nekaybaw [female] (the superior beings). This is the re-creation of Zakar (Adam) and Nekaybaw (Eve). . . . The Elders amongst them [the ELohim] called Kohane were under beings called Zodok [a current identification of the founder, Malachi-Zodok], later mythology called them Angels, and turned them from spiritual beings into spooks."[52]

Cosmological narratives and social and moral applications of these creation narratives to the Nubian community form the midrashic substrate of Dr. York's Genesis *targum* or interpretive translation. The founder links Genesis 1:27–28, "being fruitful and multiplying," with Genesis 2:8, the "garden enclosed," a metaphor for the biological context of human conception and embryology within the womb. He embeds his translations of both texts within an extended and biting pro-life midrash on the evils of environmental racism embodied in the self-destructive traffic in drugs, which creates "crack babies," and in the physical assault on the black community of modern fertility, contraceptive, and abortifacient technologies, as well as the hazards to conception and gestation of electrical field exposure, ionizing radiation, and other environmental contaminants. "The True Story of the Beginning" becomes a cautionary tale for the community, contextualizing birth control, planned parenthood, and pro-choice perspectives as a concerted and demonic conspiracy of white medicine and government to commit genocide on black people. "Nubian genocide is already in the making; Sama'EL (Poison those of EL), will not be satisfied with merely suppressing us, he's trying to completely annihilate us [as] a race, to make us extinct."[53] Through his apocalyptic analysis, the founder's midrash on Genesis is a retelling, a "re-construction" of the creation narrative with special focus on human creation as it is applied to the social context of black society in America. Oral Torah and its written embodiment in the literature of Midrash is "a spiritual vehicle for the reliving of these great events [the theophanic moments in biblical history], for making them present."[54] Nubian fertility is viewed in this context as the contemporary challenge of remaining faithful to the theophanic moment of human/divine procreation and evolution in Genesis 1:27, whereby Nubians are born as the children of EL Elohim.

Sacred Calendar: Holy Days and Ritual Observance

The "Nubic Calendar" of the Ansarullah incorporates such Jewish markers of sacred time as Shabbat, the Fast of Gedaliah, Pesach, Sukkot, Rosh Hashanah, Yom Kippur and "Hanaka."[55] These reflections of the teachings of the Jewish school are blended with their adoption of American national holidays, Islamic ritual celebrations and feasts, Christian holidays, and finally "Nubian" or Mahdist holidays. The Nubian Islaamic Hebrew's sense of sacred time was marked by public/communal observances as well as private/familial ones. "Then We moved on to a School of the Judaism. I dissected the Old Testament and translated the Torah in Hebrew, Aramic as well as Amhoric, translating it word for word," writes York. "We observed the Sabbath, the Bar and Bat Mitzvah, Passover, Rosh Hashana, Yom Kippur, and Hanaka, etc."[56] The Nubian calendrical system is neither solar (Christian) nor lunar (Jewish/Islamic) and shows a strong numerological structure emphasizing the number 19.[57] Just as in Christian and Muslim dating, the founding of the new faith community marks a break in time between the old order and the new spiritual and social dispensation. Islamic dating, or *Hijri* dating, is marked by such an event, known as the *hijra*, or emigration, of the Prophet Muhammad and his early followers from Mecca to their first political and social settlement as a nascent community in Medina. The Nubian calendar begins officially with the year 1970, the year of the official establishment of their new Umma or religious community, described eschatologically as the "opening of the Seventh Seal," in reference to Revelation 8:1. The advent of this new teaching marks the "opening the seal" of millenarian awareness and heralds the coming of judgment day for the evildoers/oppressors and salvation/liberation for the oppressed. Thus 1970 is the beginning of Nubian time, the year 1 A.T., short for "*A*fter the *T*ruth" (*Ba'dal Haqq*), meaning after awakening to the truth of black origins and resurrection from the mental death and social slavery of "Negro" identity in America.[58]

Beginning with the weekly observance of sacred time, the Sabbath is begun and concluded in the Jewish manner, from shortly before sunset Friday to just after sunset Saturday.[59] As in postmedieval Judaism, the role of the mother of the Nubian household in "welcoming" the Sabbath is ritually highlighted. She conducts Sabbath into the house by lighting the Sabbath candles, which are placed in special candlesticks used only for Shabbat and displayed on a white tablecloth. She recites the "Prayer of Light" while cupping her hands over the candles and then bringing her hands and the light up to her face and eyes. If there is no woman of the house, the father or oldest son recites the prayer. As on the traditional Jewish Sabbath, a small cup of wine or grape juice is set on the Nubian table, along with two loaves of bread for the double portion of manna that the Israelites received on the sixth day for the Sabbath (Exod. 16:22–26). Although Shabbat is described as a festive or joyous day of rest, the Jewish halakhic restrictions on work, travel, and transportation seem not to be noted or observed. Similarly, although the welcoming of the Sabbath is done, the traditional Kiddush, or sanctification of the outgoing Sabbath, is not mentioned here.[60]

The Nubic Passover festival (*Idul Fasih*) is both innovative (placed within an Islamic/quranic context while still) consistant with the symbolic meaning and many of the practices of Jewish Passover tradition. The Nubic rite begins with a day of fasting after which the Nubians stay in their houses until morning,[61] commemorating the "Sustainer" (a name of God in the Quran) who "passed over (or protected) the firstborn of the houses of the Israelites (Exod. 12:23). . . . This 'passing over' occurred when the Prophet/Apostle Moses told the Israelites to slaughter their lambs and dip a leafy branch in the lamb's blood and smear it on their doorposts . . . the Angelic Being of Death, Izraa'il, . . . when he saw the blood on the door, would pass over the door." Passover is also known as the "Feast of the Unleavened Bread" because of "the hasty manner in which the Israelites carried the unleavened bread when they were driven out of Egypt."[62] Both a public communal worship service in the Manzil al-Rabb ("House of the Lord") and a home seder (Passover meal and home liturgy) are celebrated in order to commemorate how the Israelites were sustained and delivered from bondage in Egypt, transposed into the key of African slavery in the New World, the land of the Amorites. "The head of the house answers [the question: 'Why do we eat unleavened bread and why do we observe the ceremony?'] by relating the story of our descendants, the Israelites, and of the Exodus when the Israelites' 430 year bondage under the Egyptians was over (Exod. 12:40). He also relates how our freedom is coming soon when we will be free of the 400 year bondage under the Amorite (Gen. 15:13)."[63]

Although the occasion is commemorated with a home feast, the scriptural criteria of the Nubian Islaamic Hebrew for what is legally and ritually binding reject the traditional Jewish "symbolic" foods of the seder, which are Islamically coded as heretical "innovation" (*bid'a*).[64]

The Jewish High Holy Days are represented in the Nubic calendar by the cycle of Rosh Hashanah and Yom Kippur. It begins with "*Ra'sus Sanah*, literally 'Head of the Year' thus 'New Year.' The Hebraic New Year autumn festival celebrated on the first day of Tishri. . . . This holy day season is in memory of the covenant the Prophet/Apostle Abraham received." Blowing the *shofar*, the ram's horn (Lev. 23:23–25, Exod. 19:19), occurs every day for the ten days of the penitential season. Home rituals to "sweeten" the year are customary, with honeyed foods and an Arabic verbal greeting which translates, "May you be inscribed in the book of life for a good year."[65] The end of the ten-day cycle of penitence is the culmination and ritual peak of the Jewish calendar, Yom Kippur, the Day of Atonement, with its focus of personal, communal, and cosmic cleansing of sin, purification, and restoration to a state of holiness by reflection or prayer, confession, and atonement.[66] "It is a solemn day of absolute abstinence from food and drink until after sunset worship. Man must cleanse himself of all sins (Lev. 16:30). . . . The Day of Atonement is also in commemoration of the day in which the Prophet/Apostle Abraham was circumcised by the Angelic Being Gabriel. *Yawmul Kafaarah* (Lev. 23:27–32) is also the day that the Prophet/Apostle Moses came down from Mount Sinai with the second set of tablets and announced the Sustainer had pardoned our descendants, the Israelites, for the sin of the golden calf."[67] In contrast to the Islamic rite of "atonement," or collective animal sacrifice during the canonical feast of *Id al-Adha* ("Feast of Sacrifice," commemorating Abraham's sacrifice of a ram instead of his son Isaac, Q. 37:102–13), the Nubian analysis of Yom Kippur rejects this Islamic practice as "a made up holiday not found in any of the Scriptures of the Sustainer, Allah." The Jewish school teaches the primacy or channeling of Islam through Judaism, or at least "Abraham's religion." "We only obey the Prophet/Apostle Muhammad insofar as he was commanded to follow Abraham's religion: 'Then we (Allah and the Angelic Beings) inspired you (Muhammad), that you are to follow the religion of Abraham (*millatu Ibraahim*) the upright (*hanifan*) and he (Abraham) was not one of the idol worshippers (the Babylonians of Nimrod's time)' (Q.16:123)."[68] Islam teaches that Abraham and the other Jewish and Christian prophets, as well as Muhammad before his first revelation of the Quran from God, were *hanif*, that is, upright, righteous, God-fearing folk rather than polytheists or pagans. They were pre-Judaic-Christian-Islamic monotheists. This teaching is recast in the Jewish school of the Nubian *Islaamic* Hebrews to emphasize the primacy of the *Abrahamic* legacy, through which Islamic revelation and prophecy are filtered, rather than the reverse tendency in traditional Islamic perspective of Jewish and Christian revelation filtered through the "final" revelation of Islam.

The final Jewish festival in the Nubian annual cycle is *Hanuka*, or the festival of lights, observed on December 20, which "commemorates a victory of the Children of Israel," the Maccabean revolt against Antiochus Epiphanes and the week-long purification and rededication of the Temple sanctuary in 165 B.C.E. This purification rite is symbolized by the consecutive lighting each evening of the eight-branched candlestick, the Nubian *hanukiyya*. The lighting is accompanied in this Nubian Islaamic Hebrew context by Islamic prayers in Arabic, witnessing the central doctrine of both Judaism and Islam, God's absolute Oneness (*Tawhid*): "*Ash Shadu An La Ilaha Illa ALLAH, Wahdahu La Sharika Lahu*" (interpreted as "I bear witness that nothing would exist if ALLAH didn't create it, he is alone and has no partners"). There is also a cycle of Nubian prayers (from Isa Muhammad's *The Book of Light*) which express the number of day on which they are to be recited (day 1: *tawhid*, or divine oneness; day 2: knowledge of good and evil; day 3: the three abodes—human/*nasut*, angelic/*malakut*, and divine/*lahut*; day 4: Allah, humanity, angels, and devils; day 5: the five pillars of Muslim ritual practice—*tawhid*/oneness, *salat*/worship, *zakat*/charity, *sawm*/fasting, and *hajj*/pilgrimage; day 6: Adam created on the sixth day; day 7: seven days of creation, the Sabbath as the seventh day, and seven Holy Scriptures; and day 8: circumcision to be performed on the eighth day of life, and eight prophetic messengers—Adam, Noah, Abraham, Moses, Jesus, Muhammad, Muhammad Ahmad ibn Abdullah (the nineteenth-century Sudanese Mahdi), and As Sayyid Issa Al Haadi Al Mahdi (the "reviver of Islam" and founder of the Ansarullah Community).[69]

Ritual aspects of Jewish life have also been reflected in this community's exegetical literature and ritual practice, including some basic tools and contents of Jewish prayer. The fundamental Jewish prayer or credo, the Shema ("Hear, O Israel, the Lord is Our God the Lord is One," Deut. 6:4) is printed in Arabic in its Nubian form on the back of each of the 19 *Nubian Bulletins: The Truth*: "LISTEN, O ISRAEL (Abraham's seed is for Abraham's whole house—Yisrael, Yishmael, Midian) HE WHO IS, YAHUWA ELOH, HE IS ALONE (has no partners) AND YOU ARE TO LOVE YAHUWA ELOH USING YOUR WHOLE HEART, AND BY USING YOUR WHOLE SPIRIT (being [i.e., Nubians are "new beings"]) AND BY USING ALL OF YOUR POSSESSIONS (strength and power)."[70] There is also discussion and illustration of *tefillin* (phylacteries) and the *tallit* (prayer shawl with tassels and edged with two wide bands of dark blue stripes, according to Numbers 15:38–41) for male ritual prayer in the morning service.[71] The tefillin hold Scripture passages (Exod. 13:1, 11; Deut. 6:4–9 and 11:13–21) on parchment, contained in a black leather box worn on the forehead; these verses in Nubian exegesis, are associated with the box-like shape of God's sanctuary, the tabernacle (Exod. 25:8–9), and the house of God that Abraham built, the Kaaba in Mecca (Q. 2:125).

The physical signs of Abrahamic covenant are coded by gender, including male circumcision (associated with Yom Kippur, the Day of Atonement)[72] and the female marking of Bat Mitzvah through piercing in the nose ring ceremony at the onset of menses.[73] The marking of male adulthood in the Bar Mitzvah ("The Son of Commandments Ceremony") is symbolized by adopting the "Tools of Manhood," the tefillin and tallit, as well as a walking staff, or *shoba*.[74] Religious domestic space is marked in Judaism with, among other things, the *mezuzah* mounted on the doorpost (it is carved or engraved with the Hebrew letters *shin*, *dalet* and *yod* of the divine name *Shaddai*, the "Mighty One," Exod 6:3), which is kissed with two fingers on entering, a symbol associated with the Passover[75]; with the *menorah* (seven-branched candlestick associated with the seventh day, keeping the Sabbath holy, and with the Opening of the Seventh Seal, Rev. 8:1), which is displayed at home for "Children's Day" (i.e., Christmas); and with the Shabbat candlesticks mentioned earlier.[76]

Finally, for the Nubian Islaamic Hebrews, particularly their later incarnation, the Holy Tabernacle Ministries, the physical definition of public and communal ritual space is based on the re-creation of the forms of the ancient "Hebrew" Temple cult, the ark and tabernacle, and altars for ritual sacrifice. A four-page color insert into the 1996 Savior's Day journal documents with lavish illustrations and exegetical text the various features and significance of their Temple sanctuary, which is intended to evoke "The Mystery of Solomon's Temple."

> "The Temple of Solomon, also known as *Haiykal Qodesh*, meaning "The Tabernacle," has been re-erected on our own land called Mount Paran where we have our own language[77] and our own culture, which makes us our own people called Nuwaubians. . . . The first temple built by the Nubians and ancestors is built in America. A replica of the first temple of kings, Solomon's, with all the artifacts, including the twin pillars, the golden ark of the covenant, the two-edged sword, the golden menorah, the pool of Solomon, the Lazer, the basin sea, the altar of incense and the Cleopatra Needle called the Banban of the Obelisk."

The rebuilding of an idealization of Solomon's Temple has been accomplished in upstate New York (referred to here as Mount Paran), based upon ancient Egyptian/Nubian artifacts (Cleopatra's Needle, sphinxes, pyramids, scarab beetles, a ceiling mural of the Zodiac of the Temple of Dendera) along with the artifacts and structures described in the Torah for the ark of the covenant (golden winged cherubim, Exod 25:10–22, 1 Samuel. 3:3, 4:11, 1 Kings 8:9; an altar of sacrifice and its accouterments, 2 Chronicles. 4:19–22; the seven-branched menorah, Revelation. 1:20; and the Temple's overall cubelike dimensions).[78] Adjacent to this sanctuary compound, the elect membership of the A.M.O.M. also have a miniature realization of their Egyptian/Nubian heritage: "It was a sight to see the family gazing at the temple, to see a long golden term finish, and turn to a little Egyptian village, the entrance as only allowed to the Members of the Ancient Mystic Order of Melchizedek, who have reached the degree of temple initiation." This juxtaposition of ancient Israelite and ancient Egyptian symbolic orientation leads to the final category of engagement with Judaism, or at least Jewish motifs: the various prophetic and communal representations of spiritual authority found in domestic religious material culture, which includes dress, jewelry, and religious "goods" (statues, plaques, and poster art), the subject of the next section.

Religious Material Culture: Dress and Iconography

The Ansarullah Community, since its earliest days and throughout its evolutionary forms of teaching, has represented spiritual awakening and faith commitment via outward material signs: changes in dress, symbols, and icons. In fact, dress and its accompanying use of symbols has operated for this community as an icon, a visual representation of new identity and destiny. As a consequence there has always been a lively trade not only in the latest teaching texts, tapes, and videos, but also in the current doctrinally oriented clothing, jewelry, ritual objects, and visually/symbolically coded household items.[79]

Dress has been one of the most consistent and visible markers of teaching. The

"Clothing of the New Covenant,"[80] the everyday and ritual clothing of the Jewish school, was marked by the use of specific Jewish symbols [81]: the six-pointed star or shield, the menorah, the crown, and jeweled breastplate.

The clothing of the new covenant made distinctions between the founder, who wore the garb of the "Kohane and Levitical priests,"[82] with its crown and jeweled breastplate of the high priest of the ancient Israelite Temple sanctuary, and the followers, who wore simply the "attire of the Israelites" (Num. 15:38–40; Deut. 22:11; Rev. 1:13; Exod. 39:30, 28:6, 25; Lev. 16:4). This regular dress included for men, loose trousers drawn tight at the ankles, over a long-sleeved split tunic with mandarin collar (with the male addition of *tzitzit* or tassels and fringe with blue thread at the four corners to remember the *mitzvot* or commandments, Num. 15:38–40, Deut. 22:12), a skullcap (*kupa*), and a golden girdle or sash (Rev. 1:13); and for women, a light veil covering the hair and shoulders, and nose ring.[83]

Three Jewish symbols have characterized this community are united both leader and followers throughout its entire history, even before its brief period of specifically Jewish teachings: the shield, the crown, and the breastplate. The six-pointed star, or shield, is associated with the martial quality of ancient Israelites as a powerful people/nation.[84] This symbol has been incorporated in all the major "schools" of teaching, from the original symbol of the Ansar Pure Sufi and Ansarullah Community—an ankh embossed on a six-pointed shield poised above the recumbent Islamic crescent—to the symbol above the crescent (excluding the ankh) for the Nubian Islaamic Hebrews, to its use by itself in the era of Jewish teachings, and to its return in amalgamated form (ankh/star/crescent) in the Holy Tabernacle Ministries as the finial on the "dome" of the crown.[85]

Wearing the priestly "crown," in whatever form, is a sign of retrieving one's spiritual lineage as a descendant of Abraham.[86] In its special function as the garb of the high priest, who is "responsible for making contact between the people, . . . the Elohim, and EL Yahuwa," according to the group it is associated in both ancient Israelite Temple practice and contemporary Holy Tabernacle Ministries practice with the person of Malachi Z. York (Melchizedek), who transects both moments in time.[87] York's transhistorical reality and the crown which is his symbol are the seal of divine blessing and the ongoing covenant[88] (fig. 6.1).

The third physical symbol of priestly and prophetic authority worn by the founder is the breastplate (*hashen*) containing twelve precious stones, originally one for each of the twelve tribes of Israel, whose names the priest "carried . . . upon his heart."[89] The ritual role of this item of garb was to protect the priests when they entered the Holy of Holies, where the Ark of the Covenant was kept. In modern usage by the Nubian Islaamic Hebrews and Holy Tabernacle Ministries, the breastplate and the Ark which it evokes function as a spiritual "conductor. . . a communicator between the Eloheem and the Priest."[90] In addition to its ritual use by the founder in his role as Rabboni: Y'shua, the breastplate was also designed and marketed as jewelry, "breast plate pendants, Shimut [Exod.] 28:15," for the Nubian Islaamic He-

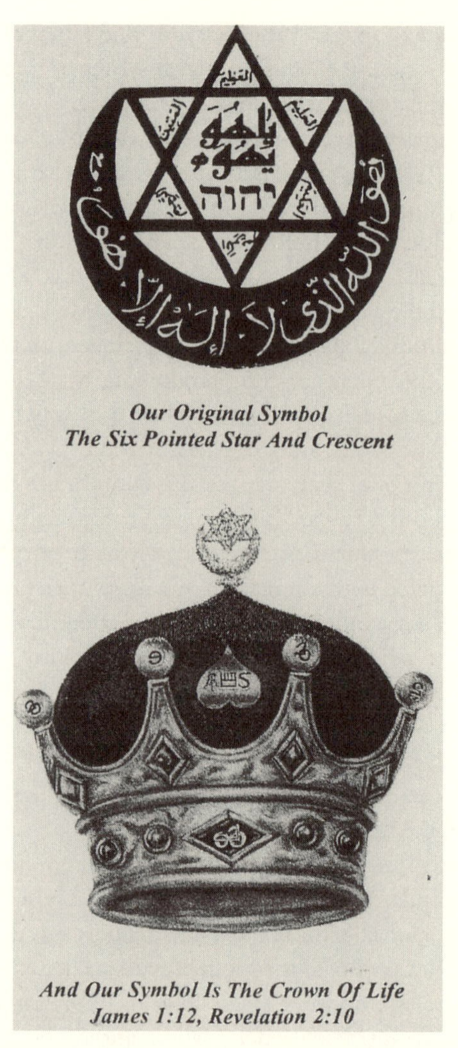

FIGURE 6.1. *Six-pointed star and crescent of the Nubian Islaamic Hebrews. From Malachi Z. York,* Questions and Answers, Debates and Discussions, Book Seven, *Scroll 140, Holy Tabernacle Ministries, n.d.*

brew followers. Advertised as the "same breastplate as worn by The Lamb of El Eloh," it is promoted as "a talisman against evil."[91] This idea of "talisman" conveys that symbolically appropriate and intrinsically powerful objects can transfer to the believer a trace of physical holiness and protection which in Islam would be coded as *baraka*, the divine blessing or grace transmissible via contact with those who are intimate with God, such as prophets and saints, as well as holy places or objects, particularly the physical Quran as an embodiment of divine speech. Thus the spiritually conductive powers of the breastplate are embodied in its physical/ritual form as a channel for messages between earth and heaven, humanity and the Eloheem, and ultimately EL Eloh.

It is, finally, in the founder's visual and symbolic representation in Nubian Islaamic Hebrew/Ansarullah iconography[92] where the successive periods of revealed teaching and the multiple personae of the founder meet. This is where the Jewish Jesus as Rabbi, or Rabboni: Y'shua, meets the Islamic Jesus, or Imaam Issa, and currently where both are absorbed and transmitted through the figure of Malachi Z. York, or Malchi-Zodok/Melchizedek, the extraterrestrial visitor, prophetic messenger, and herald of the returning messiah, Y'shua Bar Dawiyd. Two related iconographic representations of the founder express the Jewish school particularly. They both show him as "The Lamb" inspired by the book of Revelation. This is not, however, the Christian sacrificial Lamb, but rather (1) the Lamb as teacher and leader, Rabboni: Y'shua, who awakens the flock, the Lamb who goes out among wolves and who is also the Lion of Judah; and (2) the apocalyptic Lamb, Rabboni: Y'shua Bar El Haady, bringer of the Day of Judgment, Opener of the Seven Seals, bearing seven stars and the seven-branched menorah.

These messianic images are framed by an exegetical discourse regarding the authority to teach and lead embodied by the crook or scepter of prophethood shown in iconography from every stage of the community's development. The shepherd's crook, shaped like the Arabic letter *Laam* (L), becomes a visual and phonic reminder of the Lamb (*Laam* = Lamb) who is the shepherd of the flock. A Sufi-style exegesis using the Islamic number and letter mysticism called *abjad*, paralleling kabbalistic *gematriya* within Jewish mysticism, interprets the messianic and apocalyptic meaning of the letter *Laam* and visually links the function of the Lamb as shepherd and his crook to his role as bringer of the apocalypse.[93] The crook or staff is exegetically linked with the color green, in Islam the color of prophetic authority and divine illumination, and in Nubian exegesis the color of the "melanin-ite" children and immortal life.[94] The staff of authority is passed down from Hebrew prophets, to Christian, to Muslim, and finally to the Holy Tabernacle Ministries.[95]

The two icons of the Lamb visually embody this community's claim to Jewish heritage, in essence their appropriation of the heritage of Jewish covenant and their claim to the promise of Jewish messianism to restore the glory of the people of Israel via the Nubian tents of Kedar. The first Lamb is the Lamb among wolves, the Lamb that lies down with the Lion, the Lamb who is also the Lion of Judah. During the period of Jewish teaching this iconic variant was published in at least two bulletins as well as in poster form. "The Lamb: Rabboni: Y'shua" is shown as the Rabbi Jesus dressed in simple white robes teaching his Nubian flock (the 144,000 righteous who will be redeemed, Revelation 7:4 and 14:1). He is holding a lamb, with a lioness lying at rest beside him. His name, Yashu'a, is inscribed in large Hebrew script below him, a replica of a first-century Aramaic inscription.[96] This image/trope of the Lamb who is also the Lion is defined in teachings during and after the Jewish school: "We have learned from the Master . . . Melchizedek himself, Dr. Malachi Z. York, He is like a Lamb and can be a Lion" and "Gather on the Holy Mountain of Qodesh, and sit at the feet of his son, the Lamb, that has been transformed into the Lion!"[97] Thus the visual promise to the community is that it will be led from weakness (the lamb) to strength (the lion).[98]

The second Lamb, Opener of the Seven Seals, Bringer of the Apocalypse, "Rabboni: Y'shua Bar El Haady,"[99] is perhaps the ultimate visual expression of the period of Jewish teaching. He is robed in white and gold, carrying the menorah of illumination and wearing the priestly breastplate of prophecy and leadership.[100] The image connecting the Lamb with the Messiah (conceived in Islamic terms as the Mahdi and in Jewish terms as Haady [guide,] and Mashiach [messiah]) is accompanied by exegetical text explaining his messianic role.[101] The Lamb as "Rabboni: Y'shua Bar El Haady" joins rabbi and teacher with apocalyptic, messianic, and ultimately extraterrestrial messenger and herald of deliverance (fig. 6.2).[102]

Conclusion

The founder's many images and teachings link all "schools" in preparation for the fulfillment of the Abrahamic covenant between EL Eloh and the children of the Eloheem. Whether in his guise as Rabboni: Y'shua Bar EL Haady, or as Malachi Z. York, the Angelic Being Melchizedek, he is a constant link between Abraham, the original founder of the covenant, and the awaited Mashiach (messiah), bringing redemption and deliverance from this earthbound existence and elevation to the glory of divine/extraterrestrial reality. Although current Holy Tabernacle Ministry teachings move beyond the scriptural limits of the Jewish school, the new title still defines the entire community as priests and worshippers serving the Holy Tabernacle of the Temple of Solomon. The Tabernacle of the Temple resonates with the Ark of the Covenant, which guided the wanderings of the ancient Israelite tribes in the desert of Sinai before they entered their Promised Land, as it does the Nubian (or Nuwaubian, i.e., speakers of Newaubic) wanderers in the "wilderness of North America." [103] The current symbolic and iconographic landscape of the community bears little resemblance to that of the Nubian Islaamic Hebrews, but the Jewish framework of covenant and its messianic fulfillment continue to validate the new teachings as they did the old. At the appointed time, "small passenger ships called Sham, will be released to transport those chosen few, who are worthy, back to Nibiru to be with their deity (Rev. 21:3). . . . In 2030 A.D. Nibiru will leave. . . . Like the children of Yisrael who were spared to pass on the covenant (2 Kings 17:18 and Isaiah 1:25–27), we hope that we can be that remnant and have that same mercy showered on us. . . . Only El Eloh, The Heavenly One, ANU, will judge if we will regain the right to that seat and covenant (Isaiah 1:19, 2:2,3)."[104]

FIGURE 6.2. *Rabboni Y'shua Bar El Haady. From "The Savior,"* HTM, the Holy Tabernacle Ministries of the World, *1995*.

Notes

I would like to acknowledge the Michigan Society of Fellows, under whose aegis the research and writing of this article were completed, and the additional financial support of the University of Michigan's Office of Academic and Multicultual Affairs, whose research grant made possible acquisition of primary devotional materials crucial to the study of this religious community. I would also like to thank my informants in the HTM for their help in acquiring out-of-print sources for the Nubian Islaamic Hebrews and the Jewish school. Final thanks to Brian Schmidt for sources on *targum* as a genre of "translation" that is also exegesis of the Hebrew Bible.

1. For recent statements of Afrocentrism as a mode and approach to African American religion and culture, see Molefe Kete Asante, *Kemet, Afrocentricity and Knowledge* (Trenton, N.J.: Africa World Press, 1990) and Na'im Akbar, *Light from Ancient Africa* (Tallahassee, Fla.: Mind Productions & Associates, 1994).

2. This term refers to the common legacy of monotheism, revelation, prophecy, and scripture that binds these three sister traditions. The more common term, Judeo-Christian, has been used primarily in modern Christian discourse to refer to Christianity's incorporation of the legacy of Hebrew prophecy and Scripture. Modern Jewish studies, and particularly Jewish feminism, have rejected this term as an erasure of Judaism within the embrace of Christianity, and in the belief that its use has been accompanied by subtle and not-so-subtle Christian and feminist expressions of anti-Judaism. My term is a nod to that criticism, with each element standing equal (and not prefixed) to the other. It purposely includes a reference to Islam as a reminder of the third inheritor of this legacy, one that has been excluded altogether by the more commonly accepted term, Judeo-Christian.

3. Yosef A. A. ben-Jochannan, *We the Black Jews: Witness to the "White Jewish Race" Myth*, 2 Vols. (Baltimore, Md.: Black Classic Press, 1993) offers an emic perspective on the kinship of the black Jews of America with the Falashas, their joint interactions with world Jewry, and their perception/experience of racism in the dominant Ashkenazic cultural climate of Israel.

4. For a historical and doctrinal survey and sociological approach, see Morris Lounds, Jr., *Black Hebrews: Black Americans in Search of Identity* (Washington, D.C.: University Press of America, 1981). This work compares the Nation of Islam as a prototype of African American Muslim groups with its African American Jewish contemporary, the black Jews, and both with the later Jewish group, the Hebrew Israelites, who have advocated emigration to Israel. Devotional works by the founder of the Nubian Islaamic Hebrews or Ansarullah Community, Dr. Malachi Z. York, also contribute reactions to and reflections of the engagement with Judaism by these later communities and contemporary African American Jewish leadership in such recent works as *360 Questions to Ask a Hebrew Israelite*, parts 1–4 (1994–1995) and *360 Questions to Ask the Israeli Church*, part 1 (1995–1996). See discussion of the leadership of Ben Ammi Carter and Yahweh Ben Yahweh in *360 Questions to Ask a Hebrew Israelite*, part 1, pp. xiv–xv, and the annotated chart found in many devotional publications (for example, in their devotional journal, *Nubian Bulletin: The Truth*, "Who Do People Say I Am?" special edition, 1992, pp. 1–2) listing the main prophetic/inspired leaders of black Christian, Jewish, and Muslim communities as well as the Rastafari.

5. Islamic mysticism and sectarianism would include Sufism, Sevener and Twelver Shi'ism, and the Druze, as well as such "revivalist" movements as Ahmadiyya and Mahdiyya.

6. The name Ansaaru Allah, or Ansarullah, resonates both with Jesus' disciples and with

those who aided the Prophet Muhammad to establish the first Muslim community in Medina. Quran. 61:14: "O You who believe, be helpers of God [*ansarullah]*, as Jesus, son of Mary, had said to the disciples: 'Who will help me in the way of God?' and they had answered: 'We are the helpers of God.' "

7. This historical progression of naming and teachings is framed by apocalyptic signs, the coming of a comet as the herald of the opening of the seventh seal in the book of Revelation, explained in the 1996 Savior's Day journal, "Man of Many Faces Brings Us One Message from Mount Paran," p. 23:

> In 1970, the sighting of a comet called Bennet was sighted signaling the opening of the Seventh Seal [Rev. 8:1] and the official establishment of the Ansaar Allah Community in the West. This was the first school of learning, Islaam, a flourishing religion at this time needed for the discipline. We mastered this school and its teachings and after going through much slander and back biting we still continued to grow and moved on with a new name, The Nubian Islaamic Hebrews. Under this school we master the Hebraic Commandments and Laws from Abraham, and our sacraments. As we progressed and expanded, we moved on with the same teachings. We continued to build and progress the many opposing that were against us. [We] are in 1996 A.D. 26 [years] later on Mount Paran, known throughout the world as The Tabernacle Ministries, still spreading a profound [truth] that no one has been able to [with]stand even with all of the attempts made [against] us.

8. In Judaism, the kabbalistic and hasidic manipulation of Hebrew letters and numbers that stand for those letters was an exegetical technique known as *gematriya*. In Islam, similar manipulation and interchangeability of numbers and letters of the Arabic alphabet was known as *abjad* (an acronym for the first five letters of the alphabet) or *ilm al-huruf* ("the science of letters"). These exegetical techniques regarded the letters of each alphabet as the physical and symbolic representation and embodiment of divine speech in the Torah and the Quran. These mystical and esoteric discourses in medieval and early modern Judaism and Islam particularly elaborated upon the letters of the divine names and names of divine attribution, as well as other scriptural words and formulaes which were exegetically combined, recombined, and encoded as systems of divination, magical talismanry, and mystical prayer.

9. Sources for this article draw from primary exegetical works of the community's founder, Dr. Malachi Z. York (Dwight York), including paperback teaching texts and pamphlets; a Nubian calendar and book of days; a guide for family practice; the Nubian bulletin, *The Truth*; special-issue newspapers documenting the festivities in annual commemoration of Savior's Day; and culminating in York's most recent "recension" of the sacred scriptures of Judaism, Christianity, and Islam.

10. A scholarly version of the historical chronology of the community is offered in "The Ansaaru Allah Community," in *Mission to America: Five Islamic Sectarian Communities in North America*, ed. Yvonne Y. Haddad and Jane I. Smith (Gainesville: University of Florida Press, 1993), pp. 105–136. Although the early stages of the community's development are reliable, the more recent shifts postdate the publication of this article. For the transition through the Jewish school of teaching and beyond (1993 onward), various accounts are given with minor variations in sequencing and periodization in Dr. York's recent works (*Does Dr. Malachi Z. York Try to Hide the Fact that He Was Imaam Issa?* 1996, pp. 56–89; *The Holy Tablets*, chat. 19, tablet 6:185–327). Exact chronology of naming and social practices is difficult, however, because of lack of publication dates in some volumes and the tendency, as

the teachings shift, for the previous periods to undergo doctrinal and historical "revision" according to the interpretive filter of the newer teachings.

11. Such changes in persona and teaching are explained by the founder and made not only acceptable but desirable as forms of communal and individual self-identification. Dr. York explains why such cosmological and eschatological "change" is so important: "Because anything that does not undergo any changes during its life is not progressing or, for lack of a better word, [is] DEAD. Sometimes environments, modernization, or current world situations cause for a change in order to survive. In all of my years of teaching, one of the things that I have always taught my followers was that 'There is only one real thing in existence and that is change.' . . . All of the stages that we went through as a community is not a mistake. I am not some confused man who changed just because I wanted to. . . . When you finish with one course you advance to the next class. And that's what we did when we finished one school we advanced to the next class" (*Does Dr. Malachi Z. York Try to Hide?* pp. 89, 112).

12. Al-Khidr, "the green one," associated in Islam with the antediluvian prophet Enoch (Gen. 5:21–24), known as Idris in Islam (mentioned twice in the Quran, 19:56–57 and 21:85). The persona of Idris in the Islamic tradition also absorbed and conflated associations derived from late rabbinic, apocryphal, and romance legends circulating about a prophetic or immortal figure who transmitted secret wisdom to humankind (similar to the persona of Hermes Trismegistus in the Greek Hermetica and the Arabic Occult Sciences). This legendary character had a long and checkered career in both oral and written forms: Utnapishtim in the Gilgamesh epic, Andreas in the Alexandrian Romance cycle, Elijah in the midrashic version of Elijah and Rabbi Joshua ben Levi, and al-Khidr in Islamic folklore (alluded to in Quran. 18:60–82 and Hadith, and elaborated in the oral/written narratives, the Qisas al-anbiya', or Stories of the Prophets).

13. Malachi Z. York, *The Scroll of Malachi*, (Eatonton, Ga: The Holy Tabernacle Ministries; 1994), pp. 10–11. In HTM exegetical tradition, Melchisedek is one of the names/titles for the founder representing his current era of teaching. The inner meaning of this title includes the name of the last Hebrew prophet, Malachi, plus the Hebrew term *zedek*, or "righteousness." Thus, Melchisedek means "Malachi, the Righteous." The name Malachi is also linked with the name and color of the green mineral malachite. All of these meanings are joined in the founder's current name, Malachi Z. York. York, *Scroll of Malachi*, pp. 4, 10-11.

14. My dating of these shifts is approximate and based upon the title currently in use by the founder in the annual journals for these years. When, for example, the translator and exegete of Scripture shifts from al-Sayyid Issa al-Haadi al-Mahdi or Imaam Issa to Rabboni: Y'shua, this is a prime indicator of a shift in teaching from the Islamic to the Jewish "school." The 1992–1993 time frame for the period of "Jewish" teachings is indicated internally in various issues of the *Nubian Bulletin*, *The Truth*, and in other works rebutting black Jewish groups, such as the *360 Questions* series, and in the newest recension of Scripture, *The Holy Tablets*, chapter 19 of al-Khidr/Murdoq. See the most current narrative chronology at the end of *The Holy Tablets*, Chapter. 19, 6:185–380.

15. Although change is frequent, and in some cases radical, the scholarly approach to doctrine and practice that suits this community best is one that sees these changes in a biological and evolutionary way. Dr. York himself acknowledges these "changes" and places them firmly within a doctrinal context (*Does Malachi Z. York Try to Hide?*, pp. 89, 112). The periods or "schools" of Dr. York's teaching (Egyptian, Christian, Jewish, and now extraterrestrial, or Nuwaubu) are part of a collective whole filtered through the consistent framework of African American Muslim millennialism and messianism: "My name changes are forms of schools.

Schools that I take the followers of Nuwaubu through.... I came giving you what you want so that you would learn to want what I have to give" (*Does Malachi Z. York Try to Hide?* pp. 58–59).

16. Malachi Z. York, *Nuwaubu and Amunnubi Rooakhptah: Fact or Fiction?* (n.d.), pp. 4, 114–115, 118.

17. The Islamic Jesus, although not the son of God, is revered within the long line of prophets sent by God, and also is frequently conflated in Islamic millennial and messianic discourse with the Mahdi, the savior who will return at the end of time to bring about Judgment Day. Dr. York uses the New Testament to suggest that there are many embodiments of the Lamb as teacher and leader, not just the historical Jesus: "I send you forth as Lamb*s* among wolves" (Luke 10:3, cited in *Does Malachi Z. York Try to Hide?* pp. 52–53, emphasis mine). See also *360 Questions . . . /Israeli Church*, part 1, pp. xxiv, and p. xxii associating Lamb with Ram as a symbol of mature power and aggressive defense rather than passivity and vulnerability to attack.

18. Nuwaubu, from the Arabic root word *nuwb*, "of color inclining to black," means "the science of sound right reasoning. . . Right Knowledge, Right Wisdom, and a Right Overstanding," which are the "forces and powers [of] liberty, equality, justice, rightness and proper survival for new being—Nubians everywhere" (York, *Nuwaubu and Amunnubi Rooakhptah*, pp. 4, 114–115, 118).

19. This resonates with Genesis. 6:1–4, which describes the multiplication of humanity in the procreation of the "sons of God" with the "daughters of men." See the Genesis narrative reinterpreted in *Nubian Bulletin: The Truth*, "The True Story of the Beginning," edition 10, 1993, 1–2. Here one of the Hebrew names or titles for God, *Elohim*, is defined according to its grammatical plurality as "gods" ("Thus the 'God' of the Bible is a part of a group of gods," *360 Questions . . . /Hebrew Israelite*, part 1, pp. 16–17), making man in "our" image, etc.

20. The theophanous vision of the throne chariot, or Merkavah, is described in Ezekiel. 1:4–28 and elaborated in York, *Man from Planet Rizq* (n.d.), pp. 9, 23.

21. The "144,000 sons of Israel," Revelation 7:4, who await their deliverance at the endtimes symbolize completeness, that is, that all of the righteous community will be redeemed. Later, in Revelation. 14:1, the Lamb (coded as Rabboni: Yeshua/Dr. York) stands on Mount. Zion with "the 144,000 who had his name and his Father's name written on their foreheads," represented graphically in the ritual crown of the high priest which bears God's name, *qodesh le YHVH*, "Holy to Yahuwa," on its brow.

22. *Does Malachi Z. York Try to Hide?* pp. 103, 107–8.

23. *HTM* journal, "The Savior," edition 1, 1995, p. 18.

24. Genesis. 12:2: "They will be a 'great nation' whose name will be made great."

25. The Lord's "chosen people" are chosen not because they were great in number, rather they were few (Deut. 7:6–7). This idea resonates with the self-perception by this and other African American Muslim communities that they are an embattled minority even within the larger Muslim world, but one selected by God for a special destiny and role in salvation history. See elaborations of the "chosen people" theme in *360 Questions . . . /Hebrew Israelite*, part 3, pp. 18–19, 21–22.

26. *360 Questions . . . /Israeli Church*, part 1, pp. 107–9.

27. *360 Questions . . . /Israeli Church*, part 1, p. 172. The full implications of this "bad" character of world Jewry is manifested as a series of interconnected anti-Semitic themes such as casting Jews, or "Jebusites," in the role of slavers spelled out in recent Holy Tabernacle Ministry narratives as well as in earlier and ongoing African American Muslim and African Amer-

ican Jewish sacred histories (Nation of Islam, Five Percent Nation, black Jews, Hebrew Israelites, etc). In HTM teaching, the Jewish patriarch Noah cursed Canaan with slavery and Joseph's Jewish brothers sold him into Egyptian slavery (*360 Questions . . . /Israeli Church*, part 1, p. 135). Like Nation of Islam narratives which claim Jewish participation in the "Black African Holocaust" of the Middle Passage via Jewish slave trading in Africa and the Americas (see Nation of Islam text, *The Secret Relationship Between Blacks and Jews*, vol. 1 [Boston: The Nation of Islam, 1991], vii *The Secret*, passim), Jews are implicated in HTM narratives on the African slave trade to the New World: "The [European/white] Jews of Spanish and Portuguese origin [are] responsible for the slave trade" (*360 Questions . . . /Hebrew Israelite*, part 1, p. 15). See also *The Melanin-ite Children* (1994), pp. 55–57, on Jews as slavers, slave owners, and financiers of the slaving ships/voyages of the Middle Passage, as well as on black appropriation of Holocaust imagery while simultaneously dismissing the Jewish Holocaust: "6,000,000 Jews in gas chambers is next to nothing in comparison with what they have done to innocent blacks" (p. 88).

28. *360 Questions . . . /Israeli Church*, p. 147.

29. *360 Questions . . . /Hebrew Israelite*, part 1, pp. 13–14, 16.

30. *Melanin-ite Children*, pp. 90, 94–95: "Jews are not Hebrews, nor are they of the Pure Seed of Abraham."

31. *Nubian Bulletin: The Truth*, "The 7 Heads and the 10 Horns," edition 14, 1993, pp. 8–9.

32. The concept of Melchizedek teaching Abraham his *millath* gives a transcendental and transhistorical quality to the prophetic persona of the founder moving backward and forward in time. "We also get *Milla* 'A Righteous Way of Life' taught to Abraham by this Melchizedek (Gen. 14:18) [referring to the founder's most recent name, Malachi Z. York = Malchi-Zodok = Melchizedek]. It became *Milla* Ibrahim. I tried to teach you (Quran 2:130)" (*Scroll of Malachi*, p. 35). See also *The Holy Tabernacle Family Guide*, 1994, p. 45.

33. *Scroll of Malachi*, p. 28. The text refers to the Islamic concept (Quran. 2:4) that Muhammad's prophecy was a fulfillment and essentially a continuation of the prophecy of Jesus, Moses, Abraham, and the other prophets mentioned in Jewish and Christian revelation/scripture.

34. *Melanin-ite Children*, p. 100.

35. The mantle of prophecy is based upon a much earlier covenant, that of the pure "natural" monotheism of the *hanif*, or "upright" man. Abraham is the prototype in Islam of the *hanif*: "We follow the way (*millat*) of Abraham the upright (*hanif*), who was not an idolater. . . . We believe in God and what has been sent down to us, and what had been revealed to Abraham and Ishmael and Isaac and Jacob and their progeny, and that which was given to Moses and Christ, and to all other prophets by the Lord. We make no distinction among them, and we submit to Him" (Quran 2:135–6).

36. This rendering of the verse is given by Malachi Z. York in *360 Questions. . . . /Hebrew Isrealite*, part 3, p. 26. The "Tents of Kedar" refers to the inclusion of all Nubians within the fold of Islam among the true descendants of Prophet Ishmael (identified in Islam as the symbolic progenitor of the Arab/Muslim people) and original speakers of Arabic. "Kedar was the Prophet/Apostle Ishmael's second son, who because he stayed true to the traditions of his father, the Prophet/Apostle Ishmael, he was also considered 'a wanderer of the desert,' 'Bedouin,' or 'an Arab,'" (Isa Muhammad, *Book of Revelation*, vol. 1, chaps. 1–8, [1991/1979], p. 16). Thus the Ansarullah Community in its Muslim incarnation, like the Nation of Islam and other African American Muslim groups, saw themselves as the spiritual and tribal descendants of Ishmael and inheritors of Judaic-Christian-Islamic scriptures, dwelling in the "tents of

Kedar." Dr. York distinguishes Nubian Islaamic Hebrew/Ansarullah spiritual lineage from those of other "inheritors": "The descendants of the Tribe of Judah passed the scepter of prophethood to their brethren, the descendants from the tribe of Kedar, the Ishmaelites. Many so-called Muslims claim they follow the *sunnah* [custom/practice] of Muhammad. If they did, they would adhere to the commandments of the Torah, which came before the Koran, and follow *Millatu Ibraahiym* (the Rites of Abraham) as their way of life." Malachi Z. York, *The Wisemen*, (Eatonton, Ga: The Holy Tabernacle Ministries, 1995/1989), p. 90.

37. *Does Malachi Z. York Try to Hide?* p. 16.

38. For York, Hebrew scripture includes the Torah, or five "Books of Moses"; Prophets, particularly Elijah, Ezekiel, and Malachi; and Writings, but excludes the Oral Torah encoded in talmudic and midrashic literature. Christian scripture, or what Dr. York, in Islamic mode, calls *injiyl*, or Gospels, includes special emphasis on apocalyptic texts such as the *book of Revelation*, but excludes Acts and the Pauline and other "letters." The Quran constitutes Islamic scripture from which York rigorously excludes the authority of the prophetic Hadith corpus. York's exclusions are based on these texts' being products of human invention and therefore neither divinely revealed in origin or authorship nor binding upon practice.

39. See "Targum" in *Anchor Bible Dictionary*, 1st ed. (New York: Doubleday, 1992), and *targumim* or "ancient translations" of Torah in Emanuel Tov's *Textual Criticism of the Hebrew Bible* (Minneapolis: Fortress Press, 1992), pp. 148–51.

40. Daniel Boyarin, *Intertextuality and the Reading of Midrash* (Bloomington: Indiana University Press, 1990), pp. 11–12 and note 34.

41. Boyarin, *Intertextuality and the Reading of Midrash*, p. 14.

42. Boyarin, *Intertextuality and the Reading of Midrash*, p. 16.

43. For a traditional reading of the relationship between Hebrew scripture and its rabbinic exegesis, see "How the Sages of Judaism Read the Book of Genesis as a Parable for Their Own time," in Jacob Neusner, *The Way of Torah*, 5th ed. (Belmont, Cal.: Wadsworth, 1993), pp. 57–63.

44. Boyarin, *Intertextuality and the Reading of Midrash*, p. 23.

45. In his recent rebuttal of Hebrew Israelite teachings (*360 Questions... /Hebrew Israelite*, part 3, pp. 48–49), York has amended this to say that only the two books of Torah that deal specifically with divine laws (Leviticus and Numbers) are revealed books received by Moses on Sinai, the rest of the Pentateuch being lesser and purely human products of the community (and therefore both less authoritative and less binding on practice).

46. Samples of Dr. York's use of capitalization are included to give the "flavor" of his exegetical text. In lieu of italics or underlining, he uses capitals to indicate foreign language terms (including Hebrew, Arabic, Latin, Greek, Egyptian, and Sumerian/Akkadian) as well as to parse a given term in context, give an English pronunciation guide, and define it according to his own unique understanding for his English-speaking audience. He also frequently engages in etymological exegesis using capitals.

47. *Nubian Bulletin: The Truth*, "The True Story of the Beginning," June 22, 1993, p. 1. See also later doctrinal reflections and evolutions of these teachings in *360 Questions... /Hebrew Isralelite*, part 1, pp. 82–83, and part 2, pp. 4, 23–24. It is unclear what ancient Semitic language York intends when he employs the term Aramic, but it does not appear to be Aramaic.

48. *360 Questions.../Hebrew Isrealite*, part 1, p. xvi.

49. *360 Questions . . ./Hebrew. Israelite*, part 1, p. xvii. Apsu and Tiamat are from the *Enuma Elish*. For reference to Tiamat as the "maiden of life," see *360 Questions.../Hebrew Israelite*, part I2, p. vii, and part 3, p. 46. *Nubian Bulletin: The Truth*, "The True Story of the Be-

ginning," p. 12, constructs the biological metaphor of sperm (tadpole) and nutritive egg swimming the primordial waters which bred "swarming creatures that live, and birds that may fly" as example of Genesis 1:20.

50. *Nubian Bulletin: The Truth,* "The True Story of the Beginning," p. 2.

51. Zakar and Nekaybaw are defined in this narrative as "the personal names that the ELohim who blessed and pro-created them, named them, and their tribal name they called Adamites; at the beginning of the 7,000 year period of their pro-creation." Ibid.

52. Ibid. "Spooks" in NOI and Ansarullah/HTM doctrine represent the illusory belief in nonmaterial beings associated in the "mystery" religions, that is, Judaism, Christianity, and Islam, with the figures of God, the angels, ghosts, and other spirits. NOI and HTM teachings affirm that all of those positions are occupied by human beings; this is based primarily on the biblical/quranic statements that God created humanity in his image and likeness, and therefore the Nubian image is like God and God is the "blackman." *Nubian Bulletin: The Truth,* "The True Story of the Beginning," p. 18.

53. *Nubian Bulletin: The Truth,* "The True Story of the Beginning," pp. 16, 18.

54. Boyarin, *Intertextuality and the Reading of Midrash,* p. 128.

55. For a general introduction to Jewish festivals, fast days, and holy days, see Theodor H. Gaster, *Festivals of the Jewish Year* (New York: Morrow Quill, 1978/1952).

56. Does *Malachi Z. York Try to Hide?* p. 77.

57. The *Nubic Calendar: A Daily Word from the Lamb, the Light of Your Life* (1992) reflects a dating system strongly grounded in the numerology pattern of the number 19, showing the strong influence of the teachings of another American Muslim millenarian group, the United Submitters International, or 19ers, founded by Muslim scientist Rashad Khalifa, in accordance with his computer analysis and apocalyptic interpretation of the patterns of the number 19 in the Quran. For the teachings of this community, see "United Submitters International" in *Mission to America: Five Islamic Sectarian Communities in North America,* ed Yvonne Y. Haddad and Jane I. Smith (Gainesville: University Press of Florida, 1993), pp. 137–68.

58. *Nubic Calendar,* p. 15. Nubian perspective rejects conventional solar reckoning and the Christian framework of the Gregorian calendar using B.C. (Before Christ), and A.D. (Anno Domini, "Year of Our Lord")—or even scholarly versions based on that system, B.C.E./C.E. (Before the/Common Era)—as pagan and demonic. Similarly rejected are the parallel lunar dating systems in Judaism and Islam. As feminists have done to white patriarchy, Dr. York deconstructs white cultural hegemony, shifting the moral center and determining event of sacred history to the European slavery of peoples of color (i.e., Nubians) in Africa and the New World: "A.D.—Does not mean After the Death of Christ. It means After the Death of the Nubian, which made them Negroes—or dead blacks." *Nubic Calendar,* 1994, p. 14.

59. Deuteronomy 5:12 for the "Prophet/Apostle" Moses and Quran 16:123–24 for the "Prophet Apostle" Muhammad are cited as divine commandments binding upon the Nubian community to observe Sabbath. *Nubic Calendar,* p. 18.

60. *Nubic Calendar,* pp. 18–19.

61. Another Jewish fast day observed, that of Gedaliah, is listed under the Islamic category of al-Sawm ("fasting") but divided into two types: "Fasts observed by the Sons of the Prophet/Apostle Abraham," that is, both the Israelites and the Ishmaelites. The Israelites commemorate the events that culminated in the destruction of the Temple of Jerusalem. "This fast is called Sawm Gedaliah (II Kings 25:25) and the ten days of repentance . . . practiced between the first of Tishri which is Ra'sus Sanah [Rosh Hashanah], the New Year, and lasts until

Yawm Kafaarah [Yom Kippur], Day of Atonement." The Ishmaelites, in their turn, commemorate the traditional month-long Islamic fast of Ramadan (al-Qur'an 2:189). *Nubic Calendar*, pp. 61–63.

62. *Nubic Calendar*, pp. 90–91.

63. *Nubic Calendar*, p. 95.

64. *360 Questions . . ./Hebrew Israelite*, part 1, pp. 56–58.

65. *Nubic Calendar*, pp. 201–202.

66. Gaster, *Festivals of the Jewish Year*, pp. 138, 154, 166–70. The evolution of rabbinic interpretation of this holy day since the destruction of the Temple (and its cult) has increasingly emphasized interior/individual rather than exterior/collective actions.

67. *Nubic Calendar*, pp. 208–9.

68. *Nubic Calendar*, p. 210.

69. *Nubic Calendar*, pp. 258–61, see also parallel discussion of Hanuka in *360 Questions . . ./ Israeli Church*, part 1, p. 58–59, where the seven-branched menorah is conflated with the eight-branched hanukiyya.

70. See *Does Malachi Z. York Try to Hide?* p. 79. For general background on the Shema prayer in Judaism, see Neusner, *The Way of Torah*, Chap. 12, "Hear O Israel."

71. Tefillin is discussed in *360 Questions . . ./Hebrew Israelite*, part 1, p. 31, and the tallit in *360 Questions . . ./Christian*, part 1, p. 10, and in *Nubic Calendar*, pp. 20–21, described as "the Shaal." These ritual items are discussed both in the context of Nubian use at the Bar/Bat Mitzvah and also as a critique regarding what other black Jewish groups *should* wear and what Jesus as a Jewish rabbi would have worn, and therefore what Christians *ought* to wear as his followers.

72. *Nubic Calendar*, pp. 208–9. Male *and female* circumcision (excising male foreskin, or excising the clitoris or other female external genital tissues) are practiced in parts of the Muslim world, particularly in the African Muslim world, under the justification that it is part of the Prophet Muhammad's sunna, or customary practice. The Sudan, which has inspired other doctrinal and ritual aspects of the Ansarullah Community, is known for some of the most severe forms of female circumcision, such as infibulation (the removal of external genitalia and the surgical closure of the vaginal opening, allowing only a small passage for menstrual flow); see Raqiyya H. Abdallah, *Sisters in Affliction* (London: Zed Press, 1982). There is no indication in the community's literature whether female circumcision as well as male circumcision is practiced and, if it is, in what form. The scriptural examples cited refer to the Abrahamic covenant of male foreskin only (Gen. 17:9-14, and *Holy Tablets*, Chap. 13, 5:31–35).

73. Bar/Bat Mitzvah ceremony is described in *Nubic Calendar*, pp. 20–23. See also *HTM*, "The Savior," pp. 5 and 17, for other references to the nose ring as part of the female garb of the Jewish school, based on both African and Abrahamic practice (Gen. 24:22–24, 47, and *The Holy Tablets*, Chap. 13, 9:3, refer to Hagar and the daughter of Rebecca as gifted with a nose ring).

74. The *shoba* is the name given here to a traditional African symbol of male authority, the staff. The ritual and even magical use of such staffs is part of African Islam, both East and West African (see manuscript recipes in Arabic from Ghana for the creation of a *khatim*, or magic "seal," in the form of a staff covered with quranic talisman parchment which gives protection, power, and prestige to the user, David Owusu-Ansah, *Islamic Talismanic Tradition in Nineteenth-Century Asante* (Lewiston, Me.: Edwin Mellen Press, 1991), p. 87. Ansarullah/Holy Tabernacle Ministries iconography has shown various staffs marking the prophetic authority of the founder. See the staffs held by "The Many Faces of the Lamb!" either L-shaped shep-

herd's crook or the Y-shaped staff on the back pages of every full-size teaching text, and both staffs in iconic montages provided in the various annual Savior's Day journals.

75. *Nubic Calendar*, pp. 92–94. See also the sense that the ritual of kissing the mezuzah is "innovation," or *bid'a*; *360 Questions . . ./Hebrew Israelite*, part 1, pp. 36–37.

76. *Nubic Calendar*, p. 262, and the use of the menorah in Children's Day, *HTM*, "The Savior," pp. 7–8. See more in-depth discussion of the menorah in *360 Questions . . ./Israeli Church*, part 1, pp. 58–59.

77. Dr. York's profound engagement with the primary languages of Judaic, Christian, Islamic, and ancient Near Eastern sacred scriptures (Hebrew and Aramaic, Arabic, Syriac, Amharic, Greek and Latin, hieroglyphics and cuneiform) has evolved into his current "recension"/creation of the divine speech and true language of Nubians, or "New Beings": NUWAUBIC. In the cassette teaching "The Nuwaubic Lessons Made Easy for You," which is advertised as "our last chance to learn *our own language!*): "In 'Re-Newing' ourselves with our own culture and our own commitments and our own scripture, called 'The Holy Tablets', we needed our own language. Thus, the master teacher, Dr. Malachi Z. York, has put together our own tongue (NUWAUBIC), out of our original language. NUWAUBIC is a combination of ancient Ashuric [Arabic], Aramic [Hebrew], Cuneiform, Akkadian, Chaldean, Nubian Dialect and whatever else we needed to communicate. It has been made very easy just for you." This teaching tape was advertised in the 1996 Savior's Day journal, "Man of Many Faces Brings Us One Message from Mount Paran," p. 5.

78. *The Holy Tablets*, Chap. 19, 2:28. See also other discussions of the ark, the two inner rooms of the tabernacle (said to reside today with the Falashas of Ethiopia), and ritual altars in *360 Questions . . ./Israeli Church*, part 1, pp. 177–80; *360 Questions . . . /Hebrew Israelite*, part 1, pp. 32–33, 40; and expression of the Tabernacle via the Holy Crown symbol, *The Holy Tabernacle Family Guide*, pp. 3–9.

79. Annual issues and back issues of *Nubian Bulletin: The Truth*; teaching texts, "True Light" cassette tapes, and "Truth Is Truth" videotapes were produced for the Jewish school by The Lamb, Rabboni: Y'shua Bar El-Haady. Each period of teaching generates its own characteristic religious goods. Just as the Jewish period generated texts and tapes under the name of Rabboni: Y'shua, and home and health care products sold with the imprimatur of The Lamb; the Islamic period generated numerous publications by Isa Muhammad, "As Sayyid Al Imaam Issa Teaches the Truth" tapes and videos, as well as music tapes under the label of Mahdi Records and Mahdi consumer products (like incense and shampoo); and now Dr. Malachi Z. York generates teaching texts/tapes, makes available CD music such as "Magic Moments with Dr. York," and produces home/household items (like umbrellas and license plates) under the HTM logo.

80. *HTM*, "The Savior," p. 5.

81. See back-page advertisements in the *Nubian Bulletin: The Truth* for that period (1992–1993) as well as in the Savior's Day journals after that time for Shield or Crown or Menorah patches, decals, buttons, rings, pendants, lapel or stickpins, wristwatches, as well as decal umbrellas, license plates, book bags, and nonritual clothing such as jackets, sweatshirts, and T-shirts, all "originally designed" for either the Nubian Islaamic Hebrews or the Holy Tabernacle Ministries (depending on the teaching era) by Rabboni: Y'shua or Dr. Malachi Z. York.

82. "Mark of the Father," the Dress of the Levitical High Priest, Aaron, includes breastplate, ephod or sleeveless apron, robe ornamented with bells and pomegranates, and katnuth or undertunic. *Nubian Bulletin: The Truth*, "The 7 Heads and the 10 Horns," pp. 15–18.

83. Daily communal dress for the period of the Jewish school is documented and illustrated in a number of sources: *Nubian Bulletin: The Truth*, "The 7 Heads and the 10 Horns," p. 13; *Does Malachi Z. York Try to Hide?* pp. 77–78; *360 Questions . . . /Hebrew Israelite*, part 1, pp. 74–75, 77–78; and *360 Questions . . . /Christian*, part 1, p. 9.

84. "When you exalt your symbol as the Star of David, the word you are using for star is really '*magan*' as found in Genesis 15:1 and translates as 'shield' and this is a physical shield. . . . So when the word *magan* 'shield' is being used as in 'a shield of God' or 'God is my shield' it is not talking about a six-pointed star, it's talking about a block or a protection against an enemy physically or mentally." *360 Questions . . . /Hebrew Israelite*, part 1, pp. 66–68.

85. See early discussion of the star/shield in *360 Questions to Ask the Orthodox Sunni Muslims*, 1989, pp. 182–84, and *The True Star of Al-Islaam*, edition #165, from the era of Imaam Isa, compared with discussion in *Nubian Bulletin: The Truth*, "The True Story of the Beginning," pp. 21–25, from the era of Rabboni: Y'shua and the Lamb; and finally, the six-pointed star in the celestial crown in *The Holy Tabernacle Family Guide*, p. 4.

86. "Return to our rightful state of Elohim and become the Kohen (priests); the pure ones having the name of the father [*qodesh le YHVH*, "Holy to Yahuwa"] in their foreheads, which is found on the miter or 'crown' worn by the priests (Exod. 28:36 and Rev. 1:6)." *Nubian Bulletin: The Truth*, "Who Do People Say I Am?" p. 22.

87. The crown becomes reinterpreted in the later extraterrestrial ministry to represent the celestial crystal city, the Mothership, NIBIRU, Merkavah or divine chariot, which is going to come to take up the righteous and return them to their celestial abode. See HTM extraterrestrial teachings on the crown-shaped headcovering, called *tajj*, being the same shape as the crystal city, and the gems studding the crown as the crystalline lights of NIBIRU, expounded throughout the Supreme Mathematics series (all produced since 1994), for example, *Man from Planet Rizq*, pp. 87–88, 96–97; *Shamballah and Aghaarta: Cities Within the Earth*, pp. 32–37; and *The Wisemen*, pp. 69–71, 88–89.

It is also worn by all men for festival or holy days and called either *tajj* or *'immah* (Exod. 28:4). Outside of a ritual context, it is the most common form of decal accompanied by the abbreviation, HTM, to represent the Holy Tabernacle Ministries, popular in secular clothing, patches, and buttons or jewelry worn by both members and friends of the community.

88. "If such a seal and crown were to be removed, this would have meant [would mean] that the people had transgressed and no longer had the blessings of the Father, EL Yahuwa (Ezek. 21:26)." *Nubian Bulletin: The Truth*, "The 7 Heads and the 10 Horns," pp. 16–17.

89. *The Wisemen*, pp. 88–89. The breastplate of the tribes of Israel is decorated with the following gemstones: sardius/Reuben, topaz/Simeon, red carbuncle/Levi, emerald/Judah, sapphire/Dan, diamond/Naphtali, jacinth/Gad, agate/Asher, amethyst/Issachar, beryl/Zebulun, onyx/Joseph, and jasper/Benjamin, Exod. 28:17–21. Two comparative charts of twelve stones are given, one chart showing the above stones assigned to the twelve tribes of Israel and a second, similar chart of the twelve stones assigned to the twelve tribes of Ishmael. The Nubian Islaamic Hebrew breastplate is based, of course, on the stones appropriate to the twelve tribes of Ishmael, from whom they trace their descent by the tribe of Kedar.

90. Ibid. Its role is defined similarly as an oracle: "When placed all together and in proper position they [the gemstones of the breastplate] were called the *Urim* and the *Thummim*, which means lights (*Urim*) and the guidance or perfections (*Thummim*) . . . and were used as an oracle (a medium by which knowledge is revealed) by the Kohane high priest. It allowed them direct contact to the Elohim . . . to receive guidance for the people (1 Sam. 23:9–12)." *Nubian Bulletin: The Truth*, "The 7 Heads and the 10 Horns," p.17

91. It is pictured and described in the back pages of the 1992 special edition of the *Nubian Bulletin: The Truth*, "Who Do People Say I Am?" in contradistinction to other references in earlier and later texts which decry the talismanic nature of icons, symbols, and jewelry within other religious traditions because their use is superstitious and idolatrous.

92. Displayed and disseminated in their devotional book stores as color posters and postcards, and published as black and white line drawings and color photographs in their exegetical literature.

93. HTM analysis acknowledges its historical and doctrinal debt to the prophetic ministry of Elijah Muhammad and the Nation of Islam: "The Honorable Elijah Muhammad was given a sign of the coming, of the unlocked secrets of the letter *Laam* (L) and the Coming of the Lamb. . . . The true significance of the letter *Laam* (L) stems from *Alif* (A), *Laam* (L), *Miym* (M), which is the first *ayat* (verse) of Surat al-Baqarah (Chapter of the Heifer). . . . The 23rd letter of the Arabic Alphabet is *Laam* (L) and its numerical value is 30, which is the 30 years from 1970 A.D. [the founding of the Ansarullah Community] to the year 2000 A.D., which is the end of the Devil's rule." 1996 Savior's Day, "Man of Many Faces Brings Us One Message from Mount Paran," p. 26.

94. Prophecy, divine light, and life on this planet are all associated with the color green in Nubian analysis. The green stone, emerald, is the traditional stone of the Tribe of Judah and also the Tribe of Kedar. "The color green was the original color of the Eloheem when they came to earth. You can see evidence of this, . . . for instance, the deity Osiris had an olive green skin tone. . . . Your skin was originally green until you began to rust. . . rust is the dark brownish color on metals and has become your natural skin color today." *The Wisemen*, p. 89, and see also *The Melanin-ite Children*, pp. 4–5, 17. Cf. discussion in Quran that God gives us his "hue," or coloration (*sibgha*, Q. 2:138) which is coded in HTM discourse as green, and the color of the founder in his current designation, Malachi (i.e., malachite, or green stone). Green is also the Prophet Muhammad's color and the color associated with the pure light (*nur*) of divine creation in Sufi mysticism.

95. See *The Holy Tablets*, chap. 19, 3:90–100 and the scriptural exegesis of *The Wisemen*, pp. 83, 86–87, 90:

> "The staff of authority will not part from Judah, nor the right to make laws depart from between his feet . . . and to him will be the gathering of the Nation of People" (Gen. 49:10). . . . The one destined to pass the scepter of prophethood to Muhammad, Bilal ibn Rabah, was born into the Mosaic Law . . . and was made aware of the prophecies of the Torah by his father, Rabah ibn Naufal. . . . He passed the scepter to Muhammad in Mecca. The scepter, previously a possession of Abraham, Ishmael, and Moses, was awarded only to those who received teachings from the Ancient Order of the Melchizedek, also known as al-Khidr (the Green One). Bilaal also gave the color green to Muhammad. . . . Green is the color reflected by the Archangel Michael, it represents life and is the color of *Naasuwt*, the realm of man. It is also symbolic of the Tribe of Judah, as mentioned in Exod. 28:18. . . . The descendants of the tribe of Judah passed the scepter of prophethood to their brethren, the descendants from the tribe of Kedar, the Ishmaelites.

96. *Nubian Bulletin: The Truth*, "Who Do People Say I Am?" p. 22, with the inscription of Jesus (Yashu'a) on p. 23; and in the *Nubian Bulletin: The Truth*, "The 7 Heads and the 10 Horns," p. 20, this icon is reprinted without the Hebrew name below, having only the English subtitle.

97. *The Holy Tabernacle Family Guide*, pp. 189–190, and *Does Malachi Z. York Try to Hide?* p. 52.

98. As is already shown above, there have been several versions of the the Lamb and the Lion icon. There have been at least two main forms of this icon in the history of the community. The earlier is Islamic in orientation, showing the Lamb holding a lamb with lioness standing beside him. His audience is clearly (Nubian) Muslims (in that the men are turbaned and the women wearing head veils). The legend of that early image identifies the Lamb as the Islamic Mahdi and both with the founder in its title, "As Sayyid Al Imam Isa Al Haadi Al Mahdi." The image is also bordered with Arabic calligraphy. This Lamb/Lion as Mahdi image is printed as frontispiece/endpiece in Isa Muhammad's text, *You Are Adam's Descendents,* ed. 145 (Brooklyn: Nubian Islaamic Hebrews Ansaaru Allah Publications, 1985). The later, Hebrew-oriented image is also advertised as a poster using the exact same iconography as the Islamic image, the Lamb holding a lamb and a lioness, this time lying at his side, but his audience has been transformed into (Nubian) Hebrews without veils or turbans, but with a small child seated in the foreground wearing the kippa/yarmulka. The legend for this poster reads: "Peace in the Lamb, It's Truly Wonderful." It is advertised in one of the clearly Hebrew-oriented issues, "Are You Still Eating Pork?" of *The Truth: Nubian Bulletin*, 1993, ed. 13, p. 14. This example of the recycling of images shows how the community achieves continuity of belief via a constant visual vocabulary despite successive doctrinal dispensations (Islamic, Christian, Hebrew, Ancient Egyptian, and now Extraterrestrial). The Nubian images remain constant, but the communal/doctrinal referents in them shift as needed.

99. This Jewish designation, "Our Teacher/Master: Jesus Son of God and Guide," is almost an exact translation of his earlier Muslim title, As Sayyid Al Imaam Issa Al Haadi Al Mahdi: "These are really the same two names but in two different dialects." *Man from Planet Rizq*, p. 25.

100. This image was published in miniature and full-page formats in 1992 and 1993 issues of the *Nubian Bulletin: The Truth* and issued in color posters as well.

101. "Rabboni: Y'shua looked down for many years at the many liars who came in the name of the Savior to wax the hearts of his true followers cold, but now the time has come for his coming forth and the whole world knows he is here. No rock will be left unturned (Matt. 24:2). He has uncovered the Truth about Christianity. He has uncovered the Truth about Islaam. And he has uncovered the Truth about Judaism. . . . The Lamb claimed his ancestry from the Mahdi family in Sudan. . . . Now he is being called Y'shua Bar Dawiyd which means Jesus, son of David. . . . It is a known fact that all Nubians are descendants from the lost tribe of Israel. So we know that this man from the descendant of the lost tribe of Israel; Haady as said before comes from Judah . . . [and] if you say he's from the Mahdi, then that's tying it back to Muhammad and back to Abraham." *Bulletin: The Truth,* 1992, "Who Do People Say I Am?" pp. 17–18.

102. "The Lamb has done so many things to raise our minds to a certain awareness to teach us what we were not really to know before. Look at this recent picture of the Elohim (Angelic Being Melchizedek) also known as Malachi Zodok, descending from the clouds as described in Khazown Yowkhanan's (John) 1:12–13 Revelation of Yashu'a (Jesus) of 2,000 years ago, holding the seven candlestick menorah representing the seven churches, girded in his white robe of righteousness. He is one just like the 'son of man' [Rev. 1:13–16] appearing from out of the heavens with seven stars and seven golden candlesticks, (Khazown Yokhanan [Rev.] 1:20)." *Nubian Bulletin: The Truth*, 1992, "Who Do People Say I Am?" p. 17. See iconic

representation of the Lamb/Son of Man within teachings of the Jewish school in *HTM*, "The Savior," p. 11, and *Nubian Bulletin: The Truth*, "Who Do People Say I Am?" pp. 17–18, 21–22.

103. According to Machi Z. York, "*Nuwaubu* is an Ancient Nubian word which is 'Right Knowledge, Right Wisdom, and a Right Overstanding—Finite and Infinite, To Know'. According to Lane's Arabic-English Lexicon, the Ashuric/Syriac (Arabic) root word *nuwb* means 'of color inclining to black.' . . . *Nuwaubu* and the forces and powers thereof are Liberty, Equality, Justice, Rightness and Proper Survival for New Beings [i.e.,] Nubians everywhere." Malachi Z. York, *Nuwaubu & Amunnubi Rooakhptah: Fact or Fiction?* Scroll #152, (Eatonton, Ga: The Holy Tabernacle Ministries, n.d.), pp. 4, 115. On the latest incarnation of the group as the Yamassee Native American Nuwaubians and their settlement in Eatonton, Georgia, see Tom Lasseter, "Tensions Simmer Around a Black Sect in Georgia," *The New York Times*, June 29, 1999.

104. *HTM*, "The Savior," p. 19. Although this text stipulates the apocalypse as the year 2030 and other texts say 2000, the founder's earlier exegesis of the book of Revelation (Chaps. 1–8, pp. 82–83) explains that the devil has been given an extension (beyond the year 2000) to work out the final stage of the divine plan. The book of Revelation mentions the "silence in Heaven for about a half hour" (8:1). In God's time, 30 minutes equals 30 years of silence or a 30-year abeyance of Judgment Day, which is postponed until 2030 A.D.

PART III

African American Christianity and Judaism

African American Christians have long identified with Israel, although they were not the first Christians to do so. The central narratives of Israel in the Hebrew Bible resonated intensely with African American Christians, for they saw in them their own experiences of enslavement, exile, return, and redemption. For black Americans, the Old Testament, and its portrayal of the communal history of the ancient Israelites, powerfully informed their own sacred history.

The essays in this section explore aspects of the relationship between African American Christianity and Judaism, examining how black Christians have interacted with Jewish traditions, spaces, texts, and figures. Allan Callahan examines the meanings of the book of Nehemiah in past and contemporary black theology. Callahan finds that the figure of the prophet Nehemiah, virtually absent in the early African American spiritual imagination, is forcefully recovered in the rhetoric of contemporary African American thinkers. In the religious discourse of present-day black Christian prophets, the themes of reconstruction and restoration emerge as powerful tropes.

Susannah Heschel considers another dimension of black–Jewish encounters in her essay on Martin Luther King, Jr., and Abraham Joshua Heschel, whose theological and spiritual affinities led them to forge lifelong bonds of friendship, mutual respect, and a shared commitment to justice. Heschel examines the striking parallels between King's and Heschel's use of the Bible, their religious language, and the ways that their respective interpretive visions informed their political activities. Her essay recalls a historical context in which African Americans joined with Jews in the civil rights struggle, an experience that spiritually transformed members of both communities.

Yet at the same time that blacks and Jews were marching in the South, many traditionally Jewish neighborhoods in the northern cities were becoming predominately African American. This demographic transition was accompanied by religious transitions as well, such as the establishment of African American churches in buildings formerly occupied by synagogues. Karla Goldman examines this phenomenon in her article on African American congregations on Cincinnati's Reading Road. Goldman draws on interviews as well as her own architectural observations of these sacred spaces, concluding that the reconfiguration of Jewish symbols and architecture by black Christians in these spaces has provided church members with a means to reconnect with their own spiritual roots and to a past to which they have no organic link.

The final essay, by Elizabeth McAlister, focuses on how Haitian Vodou practitioners and Catholics have interpreted the symbol of the Jew in their beliefs and rituals. Until recently Haitians of all social classes erected and burned effigies of Jews during the Easter season, a custom reflecting an older tradition of belief that the Jews crucified Jesus. McAlister reveals that Haitian Vodouisants have embraced the image of the Jew for its empowering and subversive qualities vis-à-vis Catholic hegemony. Like some other practitioners of African diasporic religions, Haitian Vodouisants identify themselves as symbolic and even genealogical descendants of the ancient Jews. Yet whereas others have emphasized their connection to the Israel of the Hebrew Bible, Vodouisants identify with the Israel of the New Testament, whose supposed role in Jesus' crucifixion they not only accept but valorize for its oppositional significance.

McAlister's essay expands the scope of *Black Zion* in several illuminating ways. First, it indicates how some black Catholics, as distinguished from Protestants, have conceived of Jews. Second, by focusing on Vodou, the essay points to the broader issue of African influences in African American religious movements and underscores the ways that these influences have converged with Jewish, Christian, and elements in black American traditions. Finally, by concluding the volume with an essay on Haiti, we seek to argue for a common thread that connects all African American religious traditions—whether found in the United States, the Caribbean, Brazil, or elsewhere—and to expand the conceptual borders of this study beyond the political boundaries of the United States.

7

Remembering Nehemiah

A Note on Biblical Theology

Allen Dwight Callahan

No Negro spirituals sing the praises of Nehemiah. And it is in the spirituals, the *fons et origo* of African American biblical figurations, that we first observe Nehemiah's virtual oblivion in African American life and letters, where biblical topoi have always recrudesced and recombined even in the most secular of times. For black folks, biblical figurations have become over time the topoi not only of theology, but of political philosophy, popular culture, and belles lettres. And in any survey of these genres across the generations, Nehemiah is conspicuous only by his absence. The momentous project of the restoration of Jerusalem that he undertakes has had little influence on the African American biblical imagination. Nehemiah is so thoroughly forgotten by black folks that the recent remembrance of him in the thought and action of African American Christians is itself remarkable. It is Nehemiah's oblivion, and his recent remembrance among some black Christian intellectuals, that I shall explore in this essay.

The book of Nehemiah is a first-person account of a Jewish official in the Persian court in the mid-fifth century B.C.E., Nehemiah son of Hacaliah. Nehemiah turns his high position to historic advantage by petitioning the Persian emperor for a leave of absence to supervise the reconstruction of the ruined capital of his ancestral homeland. Given leave, time, and imperial resources, he makes two trips to Jerusalem to oversee the rebuilding of the walls of Jerusalem and the rebuilding of the troubled, repatriated society torturously taking shape within those walls. Although challenged by the devastation of the city, threatened by the indigenous leadership of the imperial province, and enraged by the laxity of his fellow returnees, Nehemiah perseveres to direct the restoration of the holy city. He institutes reforms to ensure the stability of both the reconstituted Jerusalem cultus and the political economy by which it will be sustained. Pursuing his vocation with a brusque blend of piety and anxiety, the able and occasionally offensive administrator frets about how his noble efforts will be remembered in later ages, and perhaps even in his own. His memoir is punctuated with pleas not to be forgotten.

> Remember for my good, O my God, all that I have done for this people. [5:19]
>
> Remember me, O my God, . . . and do not wipe out my good deeds that I have done for the house of my God and for his service. [13;14]
>
> Remember this also in my favor, O my God, and spare me according to the greatness of your steadfast love. [13:22]
>
> Remember me, O my God, for good. [13:31]

But Nehemiah is in danger of being forgotten in the very place he is first remembered—the Bible. In the Masoretic text of the Hebrew Bible, Nehemiah's apologia is counted among neither the Law nor the Prophets; his book is neither history nor prophecy, but one of the *Ketuvim* or Writings. The stories of the composite book Ezra-Nehemiah, the superscript of Nehemiah 1:1 notwithstanding, are a single narrative moment. Contrary to their different historical moments and missions, Ezra and Nehemiah nevertheless stand together in narrative time (see Neh. 8:9). This single narrative is then followed by Chronicles, a reprise of the history of Israel from Adam to the decree of the Persian emperor Cyrus that ends the captivity of the Jews. At the end of Chronicles, the last historical book of the Hebrew canon recounting the last historical moment of the Hebrew canon, the events of Ezra–Nehemiah are summarily recapitulated in the last verse of the last chapter. "Thus says King Cyrus of Persia: the Lord, the God of Heaven, has given me all the kingdoms of the earth, and he has charged me to build him a house at Jerusalem that is in Judah. Whoever is among you of all his people, may the Lord his God be with him. Let him go up!" (2 Chron. 36:23). "Whoever" indeed: in the last sentence of history in the Hebrew canon, Nehemiah, latter-day architect of Zion's restoration, is effectively effaced by an indefinite pronoun.

In the Septuagint, the canonical Greek translation of the Hebrew Bible, the books of Ezra and Nehemiah follow Chronicles. In the language of the Alexandrian Jewish translators, the Hebrew title of Chronicles, *divrei ha-yomim*, literally, "Account of the Days," becomes *Paraleipomena*, "those things which are left over." The narrative of Nehemiah's administration thus becomes a chronicle left over after the Chronicles that are left over, almost a canonical afterthought. The Septuagint, properly speaking, does not have a book of Nehemiah at all: there the book we now know as Nehemiah is entitled *Esdras gamma*, "Third Ezra," and later, in the Latin of the Vulgate, 2 Esdras. In the Septuagint book of Ezra, that is, *Esdras beta*, the Vulgate's 1 Esdras, the Nehemiah narrative is wholly absent, and a character named Nehemiah has but a cameo role. What Nehemiah feared most has come to pass: the Scriptures themselves are at risk of all but forgetting his ernest labors.

For one Israelite lineage, however, Nehemiah's star shone without eclipse. The descendants of the repatriated Jews who constituted the ruling class of Judea remembered Nehemiah as the repairer of the breach and the restorer of the streets to dwell in. Jesus ben Sirah, writing in Jerusalem sometime at the turn of the second century B.C.E., includes Nehemiah in his praise of famous men: "The memory of Nehemiah also is lasting; he raised our fallen walls, and set up gates and bars, and rebuilt our ruined houses" (Sirah 49:13). Nehemiah is the forerunner of the project of reconstruction pursued in ben Sirah's time by the high priest Simon, extolled at length in Sirah 50. Simon was a scion of the Oniads, inveterate enemies of the Tobiads, with whom they struggled for power in Jerusalem and whose eponymous forebear, Tobiah, was Nehemiah's nemesis (Neh 4:3, 7; 6:1, 17–19). The Oniads and their retainers no doubt saw their own efforts foreshadowed in Nehemiah's violent rejection of Tobiad influence in the holy city (Neh 13:4–9). The partisans of the Hasmoneans, the royal priesthood established in Israel after the successful revolt against Greek imperial rule in the second quarter of the second century B.C.E., remember Nehemiah as the father of the Second Commonwealth. According the Hasmonean propagandist responsible for 2 Maccabees and *pace* the biblical account in the book of Ezra, it is Nehemiah, not Zerubbabel, who rebuilds the altar and the Temple in Jerusalem (2 Macc. 1–2). At the end of the first century of the Common Era, the Jewish historian Josephus retells the story of Nehemiah's restoration of Jerusalem. Josephus identifies himself as a descendant of a Hasmonean priestly family; his glowing account in *Antiquities* 11.159–83 of Nehemiah's efforts to rebuild the fallen Temple and the holy city is free of the angst and conflict of the biblical narrative. According to Josephus, Nehemiah dies full of days and with full honors in Jerusalem.

The collective memory of the Hasmonean heritage was the perspective of those in, and still in qualified control of, the homeland. Their legacy was to fulfill that beautifully grandiose poetry Isaian that summarizes the dream of return from exile: "You shall raise up the foundations of many generations; you shall be called the repairer of the breach, the restorer of streets to dwell in" (Isa. 58:12). But the very grandiosity of the postexilic vision proved to be a burden; there is much in the later biblical witness that testifies to a less than glorious repatriation of the exiles. Isaiah predicted that the wealth of the nations would flow into Jerusalem's coffers (45:14–15); that the restoration of the holy city would be the focus of international attention (49:6); that the exiles would joyously escape captivity and want (51:12–15). But Nehemiah attests that during his administration poverty and the exploitation of the poor continue to be a problem (Neh 5:1–5). He reinstates and oversees the apportionment of the tithe to the priests, who deserted their service in the Temple to find gainful employment elsewhere (Neh 13:10). The reports of Haggai and Zechariah, the prophets of the earlier phase of the restoration under Ezra (Ezra 5:1–5), are even direr. Whereas Isaiah foretold that bread would not fail in Zion (Isa. 51:15), the failure of bread is precisely the problem that the prophecy of Haggai addresses. It is clear from his words that the Jerusalemites were struggling to feed themselves (Hagg. 1:6). Compared with Solomon's Temple, the Second Temple, built under Zerubbabel, is a diminutive anticlimax to the Israelite cultus (Hagg. 2:3). Its completion is not a moment of glory, but the "day of small things" (Zech. 3:10).

The consolation of the returnees, perhaps the sole consolation, was that they were, after all, in their ancestral land, and God was there with them (Zech. 2:11). The seeds planted in the land would eventually bear fruit (Hagg. 2:19). The land of their heritage was charred, barren, desolate, and for all that, contested. The Jews found themselves struggling against their adversaries and against the very elements for a prize of dust and ashe. Even the skies begrudged them rain (Hagg. 1:10–11). But the dust and the ashes were theirs. For these erstwhile exiles and refugees, and perhaps for all such, land was their only peace.

For other Israelites, however, the disappointment of the return was too great to ignore. Mere territory was cold comfort for the diminutive Temple cult and tenuous, imperfect political autonomy. There is a widespread tendency in the intertestamental literature to ignore the entire disappointing project of the return from captivity. Many of the literary works of the Second Commonwealth regard the disaster of exile as lasting beyond the time of the Nehemian regime in Jerusalem. Neither the apocalyptic rehearsal of Israel's fortunes in Daniel 9:24–27, nor in the so-called Apocalypse of Weeks in the book of Enoch (1 Enoch 93:8–10) acknowledges that the exile ended with the decree of Cyrus.[1] The exegetes of Qumran also pass over Nehemiah's administration in silence. For the Dead Sea community, the exile was not over at the end of the sixth century[2]; a "Wicked Priest" presided over the improperly consecrated Temple, and the Jerusalem cultus, which the Qumranites viewed with disgust from their own self-imposed desert exile, was a profaned travesty. Another eschatological movement of the ancient Israelite legacy, whose adherents came to be called Christians, say nothing of Nehemiah or his project. The return from exile is absent from the rehearsals of biblical history in Acts 7 and in Hebrews 11; the latter implies a knowledge of the trials of Daniel and the Maccabees (see Heb. 11:33–35), but knows of nothing and no one in between. We may say the same of other early Christian literature.

Nehemiah emerges from oblivion after the end of the Second Commonwealth in what is at best faint praise but more often mere disparagement of the Rabbis. Nehemiah is but a minor luminary of early Judaism.[3] In the Rabbinic imagination, on the other hand, Ezra becomes another Moses, a second Lawgiver restoring the legacy of the first.[4] The Rabbis continue, without the apocalyptic trappings, what the author of 2 Esdras started in the reinterpretation of Ezra as a prophet of Mosaic stature: Ezra translates the Torah into Aramaic[5] and writes the books of Chronicles as well as the book that bears his name. [6] An alternative rabbinical tradition identifies Nehemiah as the author of the book of Ezra; Nehemiah loses his byline, however, because of his excessive pride and superciliousness toward those who came before him. [7] Ezra is later identified with the compilation of the Mishna and the first generation of Masoretes. [8] The tendency to prefer Ezra the saintly scribe over Nehemiah the pragmatic layman realizes its logical extreme in b. Sanhedrin 38a, where Nehemiah becomes but the Hebrew name for the true hero of the end of the captivity, Zerubbabel. Merely a cipher for someone else, Nehemiah is forgotten for good.

The anonymous authors of the Negro spirituals agree with the tacit judgment of the Old Testament, the scripture of the Second Temple, and the consensus of the Rabbis. The legatees of the traditions of ancient Israel forgot Nehemiah for good. And among these legatees may be numbered African Americans who read their own peculiar experience into and out of Holy Writ. For African American slaves, a new people in the New World, the Bible became the canon of expression and experience. "[Black] culture," as Theophus Smith has observed, "inscribes its experience in the world of Scripture as an extension of that world—as if the Bible were its own literary record of divine encounter."[9] This inscription read the mighty acts of God as moments that had been, were, or would be typologically recapitulated in the life of the slaves. These "Unknown Bards," as James Weldon Johnson called them, saw God's actions in history as transcending history; the Bible bears testimony to a transcendent salvation that extends from the Red Sea to the enslaved singers of the spirituals. Thus the chorus of "Didn't My Lord Deliver Daniel" concludes; "Didn't my Lord deliver Daniel/An' why not-a every man." A variant of the song, "O Daniel," is even more explicit:

> O my Lord delivered Daniel,
> O Daniel, O Daniel,
> O my Lord delivered Daniel,
> O why not deliver me too?

The slaves read deliverance both in the Exodus and in the Exile through their repeated appropriation of Daniel and his companions. In these figures from the book of Daniel, slaves of the Babylonian court, African American slaves read their own story of slavery told with flourishes of drama and heroism. It was the story of the terror of man and trust in God. Recounting Daniel's victorious survival as a prisoner of conscience in the lion's den, the Unknown Bards sang:

> Daniel, faithful to his God, would not bow down to men,
> An' by God's enemy he was hurled into the lion's den,
> God locked the lion's jaw, we read,
> An' robbed him of his prey,
> An' de God dat lived in Daniel's time is jus' the same today.

Daniel's is a story of the loss of ancestry, home, and language.

> Then the king commanded his palace master Ashpenaz to bring some of the Israelites of the royal family and of the nobility, young men . . . competent to serve in the king's palace; they were to be taught the literature and language of the Chaldeans. [Dan. 1:3–4]

Their story was the story of the loss of their own names.

> Among them were Daniel, Hananiah, Mishael, and Azariah, from the tribe of Judah. The palace master gave them other names: Daniel he called Belteshaz-

> zar, Hananiah he called Shadrach, Mishael he called Meshach, and Azariah he called Abednego. [1:6–7]

In the spirituals, Daniel's three associates at court are called "the three Hebrew boys." Yet they are referred to individually only by their Babylonian names, as though Shadrach, Meshach, and Abednego were but the biblical analogs of the slave monikers "Kizzie," "Toby," and "Tom." The three together would always be Hebrews, even as the slaves together would always be Africans, in defiance of their servile names. Their story was the story of the maintenance of collective identity and the loss of cultural patrimony. The Spirituals insist on the last vestige of the three boys' peoplehood. Although their names had been changed, their cultural memory all but erased, the labor of their quick minds expropriated at the pleasure of their oppressor, the spirituals would not suffer them to be stripped of their peoplehood as "Hebrews." The Unknown Bards had learned that peoplehood becomes most urgent in the face of the dissolution of personhood. The stories of Daniel and the three Hebrew boys were stories of the courage to which black Christian slaves aspired in the face of permanent exile.

Ezekiel, another hero remembered in the spirituals, is also a man of exile who never returns to his homeland. The inaugural vision of Ezek 1:15–16, rendered in verse by the Unknown Bards, dramatizes the presence of God with the exiles.

> 'Way up yonder on the mountaintop,
> Wheel in the middle of a wheel,
> My Lord spoke an' de chariot stop,
> Wheel in the middle of a wheel.
> 'Zekiel saw de wheel, 'Way up in the middle of the air,
> 'Zekiel saw the wheel,
> 'Way in the middle of the air.

The "wheel within the wheel" rotates on the axle of the chariot of God. In the spiritual "Dry Bones" the Bards recalled the vision of a dead, disjointed people in Ezekiel 37:1–14: "Them bones, them bones, them dry bones/Now hear the word of the Lord."

Theologian Charles Shelby Rooks proposed that the Exodus typology had outlived its usefulness in black theology and that it might be fruitfully supplanted by the figures of Exile and Diaspora: "It is to the end of the biblical history of Israel that black Americans must look rather than to the beginning."[10] We see here, however, that the "new image . . . of an African Diaspora based on the Biblical story of the Babylonian Exile and the Final Jewish Diaspora" that Rooks recommended is anticipated in the spirituals' celebration of heroic biblical exiles. The favorite figures of African American biblical imagination, like African Americans themselves, go out in Exodus and go into Exile.

But there is no postexilic moment for the slave singers, for they never return home. The glory of the Lord was to be revealed not at the end of the exile but the end of the age. Existence after exile would be realized in the Eschaton, and that day would not be the day of small things but the Day of the Lord. The postexilic oracle of Isaiah 60:1, "Arise, shine, your light has come / And the glory of the Lord has risen upon you," is troped and transformed by the Unknown Bards: "Arise, shine, for thy light is a-coming / My Lord said He is coming by and by." Here the end of exile has become eschatology. Though the rest of the biblical oracle is in the future tense, the composers of the spiritual did not allow the verbs of the opening verse to remain in the perfect tense: "has come" and "has risen" are into the progressive present "a-coming" with its strong accent of futurity.

Ezekiel too is but a prophet of the God of exiles and, as his inaugural vision attests, a prophet of the exile of God: the spirituals recall the wheel within a wheel of God's El Dorado and the valley of dry, exilic bones. Ezekiel's oracles of the new temple and Judean repatriationl, however, are absent. African American preachers developed a homiletic tradition regarding the Valley of Dry Bones that focused on the desiccation of the Spirit's absence and eschewed the destiny of national restoration.

The sermon of Carl J. Anderson is an exemplar of this tradition that shows the implicit refusal of black preachers to turn to the tuning of Israel's captivity.[11] In his sermon, Anderson describes Ezekiel's bizarre division of his hair into three parts as one of his "symbolic actions depicting the siege of Jerusalem." The preacher comments, "by way of parenthesis," on the numerological significance of Ezekiel's prophetic demonstration by explaining that "three is Heaven's complete number." The sun, moon, and planets are three heavenly bodies; land, water, and air the three great elements, in the three different states of solid, liquid, and vapor; land-dwelling, airborne, and seafaring animal life. And the Bible is replete with triads: Noah had three sons; Moses was hidden for three months, and his life was divided neatly into three periods of forty years each; three classes of workmen built Solomon's Temple; three Hebrew boys "Composed heaven's fireproof unit." But after the three Hebrew boys, Anderson skips to the New Testament to cite the remainder of the biblical triads: three gifts are given to the Christ child; three disciples witness the Transfiguration, one of whom, Peter, "got happy there" and suggested building three tabernacles. Of the completeness manifest between Babylon and Bethlehem the preacher says nothing. The oversight cannot be due entirely to ahistorical excess, for toward the middle of the sermon Anderson accurately situates the career of Ezekiel in the history of ancient Israel.

> While in Babylon, Ezekiel was with them in servitude
> He heard their cry as is recorded in the one hundred thirty-seventh
> number of the Psalms
> Judah had lost her political existence as a nation

And the temple was destroyed . . .
And the walls of Jerusalem was torn down
And the gates had been set on fire

The last two lines of this part of the sermon echo the Judean report of the destruction of Jerusalem that so anguished Nehemiah (see Neh. 1:3). But this is as close as the sermon comes to a remembrance of Nehemiah. When Anderson moves to the climax of the sermon in his description of the desiccated bones Ezekiel encountered in the desolate valley, he likens that desiccation to the spiritual dryness he finds in the church.

And these bones were dry
Do you understand me?
They were so dry no footsteps could be heard anywhere
Yeah, it's a sad thing
Yeah, to go to church and find Christians all dry

The preacher concludes with an existential, thoroughly personalized reading of the Spirit's advent in the valley. There is no peace to Jerusalem, but peace for the solitary soul.

I was in the valley of dry bones
Yeah, I had no God on my side
Yeah, I didn't have no spirit
To make me shout
But when I found the Lord
I found joy
Yeah, joy was found
I found joy
Peace to my dying soul

The selectivity of Anderson's allusions suggests the reticence to reach beyond the rivers of Babylon that characterizes the spirituals. The homiletic tradition here has taken the cue of the black and Unknown Bards: neither poet nor preacher suffers the biblical prophets to speak of life after exile.

Much like the biblical literature of the Second Commonwealth, African American biblical figurations stop at the exile and obviate the postexilic moments of the Bible. For the composers of the spirituals, as for the authors of the latter half of Daniel, of the Enochic corpus, and of the Dead Sea Scrolls, exile is "a state that is to be ended only by the intervention of God and the inauguration of the eschatological era." [12] The Daniel of the spirituals is the vizier of Daniel 1–6, and not the visionary of chapters 7–12; there is little of the critique of imperial domination for which the visions of the latter half of the book provide an apocalyptic, postexilic tableau.

It is remarkable that the biblical imagination of black folk did not commemorate the signal, biblical moment as Nehemiah's return to Jerusalem. And so it is remarkable when, in the twentieth century, African Americans do remember Nehemiah for good. Like the Hasmonean intellectuals of the Second Commonwealth, African Americans who were concerned about making policy in the Promised Land turned to Nehemiah as a righteous exemplar of godly political economy. At the death of Radical Reconstruction and the demise of the post-civil rights era liberal consensus, Nehemiah offered an alternative to a grandiose hope of freedom the deferral of which had made black folks heartsick with political disappointment.

At the turn of the century, twenty years before *The Christian Socialist* was to devote significant attention to African Americans in its 1915 issue, African American Christians themselves were discussing the socialist option in the light of their own embattled interests. The "Nadir Period" had begun. In 1883 the Supreme Court declared the Civil Rights Act of 1875 unconstitutional, and Republicans allowed voting rights legislation to languish and perish in the Senate. The 1890s witnessed the disenfranchisement of Southern blacks through the concerted efforts of white industrialists, planters, and proletarians. Throughout the 1890s and well into the first decade of the twentieth century, African American intellectuals debated the merits of socialism as a viable political and economic alternative in the light of Holy Writ. The most influential of these black Christian socialists was the Baptist minister George Washington Woodbey. Born in 1854 in Johnson County, Tennessee, Woodbey was a zealot for the cause of socialism at the ballot box. He strove to reach the black working class with his lucid, homespun translation of Marxism that brought the message of the Socialist Party to the common people in plain language. Woodbey's writings were so successful in communicating the Socialist platform to those on whose behalf it was being put forward that he was nominated as vice-president to run with Eugene Debs on the Socialist Party ticket in 1908.

For Woodbey, the Bible was the fountainhead of the socialist vision. He explained that Karl Marx, far from being the nemesis of biblical religion, "belongs to the race of Hebrew prophets," and Marx agreed with them that rents, interest, and profits were proscribed by the law of Moses. And Woodbey found in Nehemiah an outstanding opponent of these instruments of economic oppression of working people. Woodbey writes of Nehemiah's outrage against the usurious Judean nobles.

> Here is a minister and judge filled with righteous indignation against men for taking mortgages on the land; while, today, we find ministers and judges indignant against the Socialists, who stand where the prophets did and oppose the system built upon robbery of the poor through mortgages. Who, according to the prophet, was to blame for this violation of the Jewish law opposed to mortgages and oppression? "Then I consulted with my-

> self, and I rebuked the nobles and the rulers and said unto them; ye exact usury, every one of his brother. And I sat a great assembly against them" (Nehemiah 5:7). . . . Here, in Nehemiah's day, the usurers are at work skinning the workers, but the prophet places himself on the side of the oppressed. [13]

"Indeed this case, before Nehemiah," writes Woodbey, "is one in which the class struggle is very apparent, and the material interest is uppermost on both sides." [14] Nehemiah modeled socialist positon—in Woodbey's estimation the only truly Christian position—in the contemporary class struggle in the United States and around the world. Biblical justice requires that people of faith form the vanguard against capitalism; indeed, it was Christianity's complicity with capitalism that was running its integrity and tarnishing its reputation.

> What was not good then is no better now; and those mortgage sharks brought the cause of God into reproach, just as the same class in the church has made Christianity a laughing stock among believers today. Today it is not uncommon for preachers and judges to have their pockets full of mortgages. But here is a judge who said: "I, likewise, and my brethren and my servants (officers) might exact of them money and corn; I pray you, let us leave off this usury!" (Nehemiah 5:10). [15]

Woodbey hails Nehemiah as a hero and exemplar because "he takes the socialist position and arrays, on his side, the masses against the classes, for he says: 'I set an assembly against them.' [He] left it to the people. . . . Like Nehemiah, the Socialists believe that the masses of the people will do to rely upon [*sic*] to perform their promises, when they understand the economic conditions."[16]

One hundred years after the beginning of the "Nadir Period" and African American advocacy of socialism, the triumph of conservative politics in the United States made Marxism impracticable. The fall of Marxist regimes in Eastern Europe made Marxism impossible. Under Reaganism, Nehemiah was remembered not for socialist reforms but for an entrepreneurial ethic of urban renewal. In the early 1980s black Evangelical Christian activist John Perkins delineated a strategy for the development of the impoverished black communities that had become tragic grist for the mill of endless public policy debates. Rather than a theoretical treatment, Perkins offers "a practical strategy by which American evangelicals can do the work of biblical justice in our own land." [17] The church-sponsored self-help initiatives described by Perkins require a special kind of leadership, and Perkins finds the paradigm for such leadership in the pragmatic piety of Nehemiah.

In his reading of the book of Nehemiah, Perkins delineates "principles that guided Nehemiah's response to the need of his people," [18] among which he includes a balanced propensity for planning and prayer, a good sense of timing, and a willingness to face unfavorable consequences. In addition, Nehemiah exercised responsible, successful leadership because he "did his homework," "identified with his people," "inspired a spirit of cooperation," and "refused to let his enemies distract him."[19]

Eschewing government action, Perkins makes his appeal to potential Nehemiahs to rescue the perishing inner cities. He calls upon Americans of means to bring their skills, education, and expertise back to devastated inner-city communities. "Where are those Nehemiahs among us," he challenges, "who will focus the attention of the people on God's power and promise and thus inspire a spirit of wholehearted cooperation?" For Perkins, they are among the educated and affluent: "young black lawyers and doctors; experienced nurses and educators; affluent white suburban managers and financiers; skilled builders and architects; middle-class plumbers and electricians; trained secretaries and journalists; students and time-tested retirees."[20] The vocation described by Perkins is a clarion call of conscience and at the same time a kind of preferential option for the middle class, in that, like Nehemiah, those of education, means, and advantage are called by God to invest their cultural and other capital into Christian community development. The crisis of the black poor is to be joined by an inspired, bourgeois voluntarism.

Perkins argues that the civil rights movement was ultimately inadequate because of its reliance on government legislation and enforcement. Reflecting on Martin Luther King, Jr.'s "I Have a Dream" speech, Perkins writes, "[King's] dream was my dream, too. Yet at that very time God was at work in my heart, shaping a dream bigger than the American dream, a dream rooted in the very gospel of Jesus Christ."[21] Perkins asserts that he has a dream that transcends, even supplants the dream that King articulated in his famous 1963 address. The new commonwealth Perkins seeks is not a utopian vision of America as a great, idealized land of justice and freedom. Instead Perkins has a grass-roots vision of the restoration of the local, quotidian ruins of black inner-city communities, some literally "burned with fire," as the biblical report to Nehemiah puts it, in the urban conflagrations that followed King's assassination. Perkins's plan for community uplift suggests the fatigue of the systemic analysis of discrimination and its legal remedies that had constituted the rationale for civil rights activism and antipoverty legislation. "By the 1980s the problem of inequality had been recast. . . . social scientists (and ultimately the public) . . . concluded that the culture of the black poor was the main factor contributing to high unemployment, low educational achievement, high rates of out-of-wedlock births, and rising crime rates."[22] For America at large, but especially for some post-civil rights black intellectuals, the *Zeitgeist* rejected legal interventions and political analyses in favor of social and moral causality. "Conservatives, and a growing number of liberals, were content to exhort African Americans to somehow transcend social and economic inequalities that beset their race. The call went out for a community of heroes."[23]

Thus in Perkins's proposed political economy it is the voluntary redistribution of economic resources by inspired individuals, not government intervention, that achieves distributive justice. "Justice is achieved by working with God to share His resources with the disenfranchised of the earth." [24] It is this distributive justice that social welfare programs and other government interventions have failed to achieve. The pursuit of this justice does not mandate socialism or some other form of collectivist economy. The proper economic context for economic justice, according to Perkins, is the free market, provided its operation is guided by an authentic Evangelical piety that restrains acquisitiveness and directs entrepreneurship: "serious failures" notwithstanding, writes Perkins, "I don't want to throw out the free enterprise system. The freedom which many use to satisfy their greed can also be used to develop economic enterprises not based on greed." [25] Welfare, on the other hand, squanders human resources by incapacitating the poor: "Though conceived in compassion, most of the poverty programs do not develop people, but cripple them." [26] His activist exegesis recommends self-help, entrepreneurial initiative, and a spirited and spiritual private sector as an antidote to the dependency and decadence inspired by the welfare state. Perkins asserts that the hope of the poor, especially the black poor, is to be found in grass-roots activism organized through the church, which "holds the key to justice in our society." [27] Indeed, the drastic curtailment of social programs, begun under Reagan, "offers the church a golden opportunity as never before. . . . The only institution in America with the human resources adequate to meet the needs of the poor is the church." [28]

The decade of the 1980s witnessed the incarnation of John Perkins's dream of church action and community restoration informed by the biblical figure of Nehemiah's postexilic project. In New York City a consortium called the East Brooklyn Churches developed and implemented a plan to build 5,000 homes amid the boarded-up and burned-out residential properties of East Brooklyn. Led by Reverend Johnny Ray Youngblood and inspired by a series of sermons he preached on the book of Nehemiah, the project was dubbed Nehemiah Homes. Youngblood's Saint Paul's Baptist Church was galvanized by the text of Nehemiah, in which they read a gospel that proclaimed a labored restoration for themselves and their ruined community. "We're going to build taproots into the rubble of East Brooklyn," promised Youngblood, "so we can't be moved."[29] "Our roots," Youngblood preached in the fall of 1980, "are deep in this city."[30] In the 1996 *Report of the National Task Force on African American Men and Boys*, Dr. Harry Boyte, director of the Hubert H. Humphrey Center for Democracy and Citizenship, cites the Nehemiah Homes project as a paragon of public work and responsible citizenship. He highlights the importance of the biblical story of Nehemiah, "a very political organizing story,"[31] as illustrative of the kind of civic activism that promises to be an effective response to the present urban crisis.

Perkins reads Nehemiah in the early years of Reaganism. His principled vision informs a strategy of working within the political order without changing it: Perkins himself had served on Reagan's Task Force on Hunger during the president's first term. Overtly political solutions are rejected in favor of an evangelical crusade of good works, a strategy advocated by some conservative black politicians and pundits. "Riding the wave of popular conservativism that put Ronald Reagan in the White House in 1980, . . . black conservatives applauded legislation that eliminated state-imposed racial barriers, but they decried group-based social policies and remedies, citing the worsening condition of poor and undereducated blacks as evidence of flawed liberal social policies."[32] Rhetoric on the left and the right, however, remained at the level of effects. Little public discussion illumined the root cause of the plight of the poor: the progressive mechanization of Southern agriculture and the recent deindustrialization of the urban North and Midwest. Millions of the working poor, whose semiskilled and unskilled labor made them peripheral to the economy, had now become economically superfluous. This profound structural transformation of the American economy rendered obsolete not only older forms of labor but older forms of analysis. The activism of traditional black liberal leadership did not address the new realities of the American economy, in which "white racism . . . cannot fully explain the socioeconomic position of the majority of black Americans."[33] In 1963 Perkins, then the pastor of a small church in rural Mississippi, reflected prophetically on the ecomonic crisis in progress as well as the intellectual crisis to come. "Mechanization was displacing Mississippi sharecroppers, driving them even deeper into poverty. Racial tensions were rising. The problems plaguing our little community were so great, and we were so few. What could we do?"[34] His query in 1963 anticipated what West describes as the "crisis of black liberalism" a generation later, that is, "its inability to put forward visions, analyses, and programs that can ameliorate the plight of the black working poor and underclass."[35] "The new black conservatives," West adds, "highlight this crisis."

The Nehemian figuration of John Perkins and other black Christian intellectuals takes form in a new historical moment, one witnessing the demise of the liberal consensus on civil rights and the remedies of racial discrimination. For African Americans it suggests both the frustrated aspiration and its territorial realization of the Promised Land. The people of God are not called to march around the walls of the Promised Land, but to rebuild them. The metaphor of the long march is no longer apropos; taking up one's staff has given way to rolling up one's sleeves. African Americans are no longer looking for a city in the heavens, beyond history. Their city, like Nehemiah's Jerusalem, is a city made with hands.

Nehemiah's troubled memoir recounts how he rebuilds the earthly Jerusalem brick by brick. Unlike Abraham leaving Ur, Nehemiah leaves the imperial capital of Susa en route to Jerusalem knowing exactly where he is going. Abraham, and the sojourners of faith he exemplifies desire not "the land they had left behind," to which they could presumably hope to return, but "a better country, that is, a heavenly one"[36] (11:14-16). Theophus Smith has pointed out that in the book of Hebrews the desire for a heavenly homeland "transcends the possibility of fulfillment by any temporal country" and that "desire must seek fulfillment beyond history."[37] "Diaspora," Smith asserts, "*replaces* the desire for a temporal homeland with an orientation and yearning toward world-transcending citizenship."[38] But for the Diaspora we meet at the beginning of Nehemiah's story (Neh 1:8), the return of the Jews to their ancestral homeland, "the land they had left behind," is the antithesis of the long march to the transcendental territory of Hebrews 11. The desire of Diaspora to return to a temporal homeland is not replaced; it is intensified. They do not dream of a heavenly commonwealth. It is a homeland in history that constitutes the Diaspora dream come true: "When the Lord restored the fortunes of Zion, we were like those who dream" (Ps. 126:). This is the difference between the biblical sojourner and the denizen of Diaspora: the former, like his spiritual forefather Abraham, never knows where he is going, the latter always does. The denizen of Diaspora knows where he is going because he knows the way home. Through previous experience or vicarious vision, he knows precisely where home is. Nehemiah is not a visionary who glimpses the New Jerusalem, as does the writer of the Epistle to the Hebrews (Heb. 11:22) and as the exile John of Patmos would do from his solitary confinement on a rocky island in the Aegean (Rev 1:9; 21:1–12). Nehemiah's Jerusalem is the old Jerusalem, the Old City, as it were, not coming down from God out of heaven but raised up by Nehemiah and his colleagues out of the dust and ashes.

James Weldon Johnson memorialized in verse the anonymous authors of the Negro spirituals, "untaught, unknown, unnamed." W. E. B. Du Bois, however, remembered these singers of the Sorrow Songs as "exiled Africans."[39] With poignant insight, Du Bois understood the Bards as they understood themselves: they were singing their song in a strange land, never to return home. Like Daniel, the three Hebrew Boys, and Ezekiel, their life was an ordeal of faith and their vision of a distant freedom. But their figurations did not take them beyond the Exile. That act of imagination and political will remained for their descendants; it was left to them at a later time to sink their roots deep into the rubble of the ruins that they now claimed as their own. They would call to mind neither Exodus nor Exile, for they were neither going out to freedom nor going into captivity. Theirs was not a way out, but a way up: they would go up to their earthly Zion. They would see that it lay in ruins with its gates burned. They would rebuild its walls so that they might no longer suffer disgrace. And they would remember Nehemiah for good.

Notes

1. Michael A. Knibb, "The Exile in the Literature of the Intertestamental Period," *Heythrop Journal* 17, (1976), 255, 258.
2. Knibb, "The Exile," pp. 262–263.
3. Canticles Rabbah 2:12.
4. B. Sukkoth 20a.
5. B. Megillah 3a, b. Sanhedrin 21b.
6. B. Berakot 15a, see Joseph Blenkinsopp, p. 39.

7. B. Sanhedrin 93b.

8. Blenkinsopp, *Ezra-Nehemiah*, (London: SCM Press, 1988), Ezra-Nehemiah, p. 59.

9. Theophus Smith, *Conjuring Culture* (New York: Oxford University Press, 1994), p. 251.

10. Charles Shelby Rooks, "Toward the Promised Land: An Analysis of the Religious Experience of Black America," *The Black Church* II: 1, (September 1973), p. 9.

11. Carl J. Anderson, "Ezekiel and the Vision of Dry Bones," in Linda Goss and Marian E. Barnes, eds., *Talk That Talk: An Anthology of African American Storytelling* (New York: Simon and Schuster/Touchstone, 1989), pp. 199–205.

12. Knibb, "The Exile," p. 255.

13. George Washington Woodbey, "The Bible and Socialism" (1904), repr. in Philip Foner, ed., *Black Socialist Preacher* (San Francisco: Synthesis Publications, 1983), p. 122.

14. Woodbey, "The Bible and Socialism," p. 125.

15. Ibid., 123.

16. Woodbey, "The Bible and Socialism," pp. 122, 125.

17. John Perkins, *With Justice for All* (Ventura, Cal.: Regal, 1982), pp. 12–13.

18. Ibid., pp. 191–92.

19. Perkins, *Justice*, pp. 191-195.

20. Ibid., p. 196.

21. Ibid., p. 52.

22. William M. Banks, *Black Intellectuals* (New York: W. W. Norton, 1996), p. 235.

23. Ibid.

24. Perkins, *Justice*, p. 14.

25. Ibid., p. 170.

26. Ibid., p. 15.

27. Ibid., 12.

28. Ibid., p. 165.

29. Quoted in Harry Boyte, "Citizenship and Young African Americans," in Bobby William Austin, ed., *Repairing the Breach* (Dillon, Col.: Alpine Guild, 1996), p. 267.

30. Samuel G. Freedman, *Upon This Rock* (New York: HarperCollins, 1993), p. 339.

31. Boyte, "Citizenship," p. 267.

32. Banks, *Black Intellectuals*, p. 230.

33. Cornel West, "Assessing Black Neo-conservatism," in Floyd W. Hayes, III, ed., *A Turbulent Voyage: Readings in African American Studies* (San Diego, Cal.: Collegiate Press, 1992), p. 653.

34. Perkins, *Justice*, p. 52.

35. West, "Assessing Black Neo-conservatism," p. 653.

36. Smith, *Conjuring Culture*, p. 252.

37. Ibid. Emphasis the author's.

38. W. E. B. Du Bois, *The Souls of Black Folk* (Chicago: A. C. McClurg, 1903; repr. New York: Penguin, 1989), p. 208

8

Theological Affinities in the Writings of Abraham Joshua Heschel and Martin Luther King, Jr.

Susannah Heschel

THE PHOTOGRAPH OF Abraham Joshua Heschel walking arm in arm with Martin Luther King, Jr., in the front row of marchers at Selma has become an icon of American Jewish life, and of black-Jewish relations. Reprinted in Jewish textbooks, synagogue bulletins, and studies of ecumenical relations, the picture has come to symbolize the great moment of symbiosis of the two communities, black and Jewish, which today seems shattered. When Jesse Jackson, Andrew Young, Henry Gates, or Cornel West speaks of the relationship between blacks and Jews as it might be, and as they wish it would become, they invoke the moments when Rabbi Heschel and Dr. King marched arm in arm at Selma, prayed together in protest at Arlington National Cemetery, and stood side by side in the pulpit of Riverside Church.

The relationship between the two men began in January 1963 and was a genuine friendship of affection as well as a relationship of two colleagues working together in political causes. As King encouraged Heschel's involvement in the civil rights movement, Heschel encouraged King to take a public stance against the war in Vietnam. When the Conservative rabbis of America gathered in 1968 to celebrate Heschel's sixtieth birthday, the keynote speaker they invited was King. Ten days later, when King was assassinated, Heschel was the rabbi Mrs. King invited to speak at his funeral.

What is considered so remarkable about their relationship is the incongruity of Heschel, a refugee from Hitler's Europe who was born into a Hasidic rebbe's family in Warsaw, with a long white beard and *yarmulke*, involving himself in the cause of civil rights. Today, looking back from a generation more accustomed to African American leaders such as Louis Farrakhan, King's closeness to Heschel seems beyond belief. What drew the two men together? What formed the basis of their close friendship?

A comparison of King and Heschel reveals theological affinities in addition to shared political sympathies. The preference King gave to the Exodus motif over the figure of Jesus certainly played a major role in linking the two men intellectually and religiously; for Heschel, the primacy of the Exodus in the civil rights movement was a major step in the history of Christian–Jewish relations. Heschel's concept of divine pathos, a category central to his theology, is mirrored in King's understanding of the nature of God's involvement with humanity. For both, the theological was intimately intertwined with the political, and that conviction provided the basis of the spiritual affinity they felt for each other.

The bond between Heschel and King was a religious bond nurtured by the surprising spiritual connections informing their understandings of the Bible. Here was a Jewish theologian, born and raised in Warsaw to a distinguished family of religious leaders within the unworldly, deeply pietistic environment of East European Hasidism, who joined with a minister from the theologically conservative, pietistic African American church. Both had left the worlds of their family as young men, Heschel to study at the Reform movement's rabbinical seminary in Berlin while completing his doctorate in philosophy at the University of Berlin, King to study for the ministry at the liberal Protestant Crozer Theological Seminary and then complete his doctorate at Boston University. Heschel's exposure to Christian thought came during the 1930s in Germany, at a time when Protestant theologians were debating whether to eliminate the Old Testament and declare Jesus an Aryan in order to modify Christian theology to accommodate the Nazi regime.[1] King's exposure to Judaism was undoubtedly limited during his childhood years, and the Protestant theological tradition he studied had not yet rid itself of the anti-Jewish bias permeating its view of Jesus and the Hebrew Bible. Given that context, it is striking to read King's unusually positive depiction of the relationship between Jesus and Judaism in a student essay he wrote at Crozer Seminary in 1949:

> Jesus was a Jew. It is impossible to understand Jesus outside of the race in which he was born. The Christian Church has tended to overlook its Judaic origins, but the fact is that Jesus of Nazareth was a Jew of Palestine. He shared the experiences of his fellow-countrymen. So as we study Jesus we are wholly in a Jewish atmosphere. . . . There is no justification of the view that Jesus was attempting to find a church distinct from the Synagogue. The gospels themselves bear little trace of such a view. Throughout the gospels we find Jesus accepting both the Temple and the Synagogue.[2]

Heschel's evaluation of Christianity reflected a similarly positive affirmation. In a 1964 address he wrote that Jews "ought to acknowledge the eminent role and part of Christianity in God's design for the redemption of all men."[3]

What linked Heschel and King theologically was their reading of the Bible, particularly of the prophets, and the understanding of God they drew from their biblical readings. Everything else grew out of that understanding: the nature of morality, the nature of prayer, as well as the centrality of political commitments. The theological position of each is usually described in similar terms: the writings of Heschel and King are said to echo the neo-orthodox theological traditions represented by Karl Barth and Reinhold Niebuhr, but also the liberal theological traditions expressed in historical-critical analyses of biblical texts and in social and political involvements of religious leaders. Whatever the influences of formal theological arguments, it is clear that each represents the spirit of his own religious tradition. King was shaped by the religious traditions of the black church, while Heschel gave voice to the spiritual teachings of East European Hasidic piety, and for that reason the parallels between them are all the more interesting.

How did King manage to seize the imagination of America, to inspire and move to tears even the most secular among his followers, and to soften the hearts of so many of his opponents? King's work has been identified as intellectual heir to Gandhi, Niebuhr, Anders Nygren, Paul Tillich, Henry Nelson Wieman, and Walter Rauschenbusch, but the powerful impact he achieved on his listeners was derived from the spiritual traditions of his church. Clayborne Carson, James Cone, and Keith Miller, among others, argue for the primacy of black religiosity in shaping King, rather than his formal training in white theology. Cone writes, "The faith of the Black experience began to shape King's idea of God during his childhood, and it remained central to his perspective throughout his life."[4] The religiosity prevalent in much of the black church is supposed to transform the congregation; Miller, for example, notes, "In the experience of the ring shout, some slaves became, so to speak, their counterparts from the Bible."[5] Listening to a sermon or hymn could not occur without a response. Moreover, suffering was neither private nor inconsequential; by one's merging oneself with the biblical narrative, the Bible took on cosmic proportions. In Memphis, the night before he was assassinated, King described civil rights activists as the burning bush: "Bull Connor next would say, 'Turn the firehoses on.' And as I said to you the other night, Bull Connor didn't know history. He knew a kind of physics that somehow didn't relate to the transphysics that we knew about, and that was the fact that there was a certain kind of fire that no water could put out."[6]

Yet as leader of the civil rights movment, King also departed from his church in significant ways, even while retaining its spiritual teachings, just as Heschel left his Hasidic milieu even while transmitting Hasidism's teachings in the modern language of his theological writings.[7] The relationship both had as adults to the religious communities of their childhoods was similar. For example, the attitude of the black church toward the civil rights movement was ambivalent. While urban churches became an early focal point of organizing activity, rural churches, as Charles Payne notes, were more reluctant to become involved: "Those who joined the movement in the early days ordinarily did so in defiance of their church leadership. Nonethelesss, if the church as an organization did not lead people into the movement, the religiosity of the population may have been much more important."[8] Some of the difference between urban and rural church communities may be attributed to the white patronage of black churches in the rural South.[9] Religion could serve as a force of political accommodation or of rebellion against the established order, and elements of the black church allied themselves with each side. King, Carson notes, "fought an uphill struggle to transform the Black church into an institutional foundation for racial struggles."[10] To accomplish that goal, King also carefully shaped the religious teachings he emphasized.[11]

The revival of Jewish religiosity and social activism that Heschel promoted in his post–World War II career in the United States encountered similar ambivalences from the religious community in which he had been raised. Once he departed the pietistic, Hasidic world of his childhood for an academic career, he did not return. Just as the church as an institution did not lead African Americans into the civil rights movement, Hasidism turned its members away from the political work Heschel led, and he received no public support from Orthodox colleagues. Indeed, two of the leading Orthodox figures in postwar America, Norman Lamm and Joseph Soloveitchik, attacked him for his ecumenical work. Yet despite their opposition, it was the very religiosity of both many Jews and many African Americans that inspired their political activism and the nature of the political stances they took.

The affinities between King and Heschel emerge in the language they used to explain their political positions, but even more unexpectedly in the religious mood they evoked through their religious language. There are three themes that are shared by Heschel and King. First and most striking is the commonality between the spirituality taught by Heschel and King, rooted in the emphasis King gave to the Hebrew Bible and the Exodus narrative and in Heschel's emphasis on the prophets. King and Heschel return their political activities to the biblical narrative. King's comparison of what is occurring in Alabama with the Exodus from Egypt, for instance, is not simply a politically astute use of a biblical story, but an effort to transfigure the participants into the biblical realm, in which actions have consequences for the divine plan of history. Political activism is not simply history, but *Heilsgeschichte*, salvation history occurring within the realm of God. That same tone is found in Heschel's political writings, in which he transfers the questions of the day into a biblical schema, so that they are occurring not only on a human plane, but within the life of God as well, in a tradition well established within the Jewish mystical tradition.

Second, permeating King's words, the responses of his listeners, and the hymns of the movement is a fundamental assumption of divine concern with the events that are transpiring in the civil rights struggle. God is involved and engaged in that struggle, because God is not remote and transcendent but possesses subjectivity and is affected by the treatment human beings accord one another. That conviction is central to Heschel's major theological claim, that the God of the Bible is not impassive but is a God of pathos who responds to human deeds, suffering with us. The idea of a divine responsiveness to human activity is central to Kabbalah, the Jewish mystical tradition, but in reference solely to commandments between humans and God. Heschel expanded the tradition, as Arthur Green has recently pointed out, to include the ethical commandments regulating behavior between human beings. When I injure a fellow human being, Heschel wrote, I injure God. Similarly, the good deeds performed by human beings give strength to God. Green explains that "the urgency and cosmic vitality the Kabbalists associated with religious action was re-assimilated [by Heschel] to the religion of the Biblical prophets and the absolute demands they made for justice, care for the needy, and compassion for a God who ultimately depends upon man to do His bidding."[12]

Third, King speaks not as an observer of society but as a spokesperson for God, conveying a divine perspective. He is never simply a messenger; his words carry an urgency that indicates his own deep engagement as a person standing in the presence of God. Such a stance is precisely what characterizes the nature of the prophet, Heschel argues. It is not simply the message of the prophets that the Bible wishes to convey, according to Heschel, but the prophet's own subjectivity and religious consciousness. To understand the nature of prophecy, it is crucial to understand the nature of the prophet.

While it has long been recognized that King spoke within the biblical narrative, there has not been a consensus regarding within which narrative he should be understood. Two of the most important books about King that were published during the 1980s each identified him with a different Bible: *Parting the Waters*, by Taylor Branch, saw King primarily as the Hebrew Bible's Moses, liberating his Israelites; *Bearing the Cross*, by David Garrow, evoked the image of the New Testament Christ, viewing King as a Jesus figure of vicarious and redemptive suffering. Garrow remains insistent on what he views as King's emphasis upon Christianity and Jesus, and Vincent Harding identifies Black Power with the "autonomous action" of the Old Testament, whereas King's efforts reflect the "demonstration of power in weakness" of the New.[13] It is not surprising, of course, that King speaks of himself as a Christian preacher or urges his audience, "Let us be Christian in all of our action." On the other hand, the story of the civil rights movement is not the story of Jesus, nor are any of his teachings invoked as central guideposts. Instead, the dominant narrative is the Exodus, and the most important single verse from the Bible is taken from Amos. The Christian theologian H. Richard Niebuhr explains, "In distinction from the Book of Amos and from most of the other prophets, Jesus does not address the strong and influential in the community, demanding of them that they do justice to the poor; he directs his address to the latter. Hence there are no such injunctions to turn from oppression of the poor as we find in Amos."[14] While King referred often to the figure of Jesus in his sermons, his most important public addresses rarely mention him, turning much more frequently to Moses and the prophets of the Hebrew Bible. That focus is not unexpected; Lawrence Levine, among others, has noted the centrality of Moses and the Old Testament in black slave religion, which interprets the story as a proto-theology of liberation.[15] The story of the Exodus became the leitmotif of the civil rights movement, with the South identified as Egypt, blacks as the Children of Israel, and King as Moses.[16] This continued an earlier tradition; Malinda Snow notes, "In the story of the children of Israel in Egypt, . . . [slaves] discovered the central type of their experience, which prefigured their own deliverance from slavery. They merged biblical and contemporary time."[17] Still, King's sometimes deliberate shift from Jesus to Moses or one of the biblical prophets is striking in a Christian preacher, from whom we might expect greater stress on the figure of Jesus as the liberator. For example, in "The Negro and the Constitution," written in 1944 when he was fifteen, he concludes, "We cannot be truly Christian people so long as we flaunt the central teachings of Jesus: brotherly love and the Golden Rule. . . . My heart throbs anew in the hope that inspired by the example of Lincoln, imbued with the spirit of Christ, [Americans] will cast down the last barrier to perfect freedom." Nearly twenty years later, in his famous speech, "I Have a Dream," modeled, as Keith Miller and Emily Lewis argue,[18] after the rhetorical scheme and thematic substance of "The Negro and the Constitution," King shifts from the New Testament to the Hebrew Bible, supplanting Jesus with Amos and Isaiah: "No, we . . . will not be satisfied until justice rolls down like waters and righteousness like a mighty stream."

That particular verse, Amos 5:24, became a kind of anthem of the movement, cited frequently by King and engraved at his memorial in Atlanta. It is worth noting that the translation King used does not appear in the standard translations of the Bible used by Christian theologians, the King James Bible and the Revised Standard Version, but is identical to Heschel's own translation in his study, *The Prophets*, published in 1962, a book that was widely read by civil rights leaders. Let us compare:

King James Bible: "But let judgment run down as waters, and righteouness as a mighty stream"

Revised Standard Version: "But let justice roll down like waters, and righteousness like an everflowing stream"

Jewish Publication Society: "But let justice well up like water, righteousness like an unfailing stream"

Heschel's translation: "Let justice roll down like waters, and righteousness like a mighty stream."[19]

Heschel's study of the prophets, which originated as his doctoral dissertation at the University of Berlin, completed in 1933, brought a new direction to biblical studies. Beginning with Martin Luther, Protestant scholars had seen the prophets as interpreters of the law of Moses. By the mid-nineteenth century the message of the prophets was detached from the law by Christian commentators, and prophetic religion was viewed as the great last flowering of biblical religion, before its decline into what was viewed as the priestly and rabbinic legalistic religion of Judaism. Jesus, it was argued, was heir to the prophets, whereas Judaism represented a degenerate religion that had forsaken the prophetic teachings. Throughout the literature of European biblical scholarship until the post-World War II era there is little mention of the social critique formulated by the prophets. Under the influence of the History of Religions school that took shape in Germany during the first decades of this century, biblical scholars revived an old tradition of interpreting prophecy as "ecstatic." That view diminished the significance of the prophet's actual words by viewing the prophet as speaking while under a kind of trance. The implication was that the prophet was so transfixed by the experience that he or she did not fully comprehend what he or she was saying. The originality of the prophets also tended to be diminished in German biblical circles. Gerhard von Rad, one of the most influential twentieth-century interpreters of the prophets, placed them within the context of ancient Near Eastern traditions, explaining, "Now once that is granted, any definition of the prophet as a brilliant religious personality, standing close to God, falls to the ground. So, too, does the whole concept of 'prophetic religion,' which was set up as a spiritual counter-balance to the priestly religion of the cult."[20]

American Protestant traditions, by contrast, had long identified biblical religion with commitment to political protest and social activism. The social gospel movement, associated primarily with the theologians such as Walter Rauschenbusch, Howard Thurman, and Harry Emerson Fosdick, articulated the social concern of the prophets and presented it as central to the biblical message, and their influence on King is clear. Their impact on biblical scholarship, however, began only much later. Yet while King ultimately came to present the prophets as great social critics, in line with the social gospel traditions, his earliest writings from his student years described them otherwise. For instance, in a paper on Jeremiah, written in 1948 when he had just entered Crozer Seminary, King presented the prophet primarily as a critic of religion, not of society.[21]

From the outset of his career, Heschel emphasized the social critique of the prophets, in striking contrast to the prevailing biblical scholarship in Germany, where he completed his doctoral dissertation in 1933 on "Prophetic Consciousness." Published in 1935 as a book in German, his study was later expanded, and it appeared in English in 1962, at the same time that he began his engagement in political work. Heschel's achievement was to bring to the fore the centrality of the prophetic critique of social injustice without neglecting the religious experience underlying their passions. He writes, for example:

> "We and the prophet have no language in common. To us the moral state of society, for all its stains and spots, seems fair and trim; to the prophet it is dreadful. So many deeds of charity are done, so much decency radiates day and night; yet to the prophet satiety of the conscience is prudery and flight from responsibility. Our standards are modest; our sense of injustice tolerable, timid; our moral indignation impermanent; yet human violence is interminable, unbearable, permanent. . . . The prophet's ear perceives the silent sigh."[22]

His central category of divine pathos was derived from Hasidic thought and constituted his modernized version of the traditional kabbalistic term *zoreh gavoha*, divine need.

The primacy of the Exodus and the prophets and the relative absence of references to Jesus lent the civil rights movement an ecumenical, and even a philosemitic image in the eyes of major segments of the Jewish community. Heschel, for example, was particularly touched during the march from Selma to Montgomery by King's references to the Exodus in his sermon, describing three types among the Israelites who left Egypt, and he viewed King's choice of the Exodus over Jesus as a significant moment in Christian–Jewish relations. Shortly after returning from the march, he wrote to King:

> The day we marched together out of Selma was a day of sanctification. That day I hope will never be past to me—that day will continue to be this day. A great Hasidic sage compares the service of God to a battle being waged in war. An army consists of infantry, artillery, and cavalry. In critical moments cavalry and artillery may step aside from the battle-front. Infantry, however, carries the brunt. I am glad to belong to infantry! May I add that I have rarely in my life been privileged to hear a sermon as glorious as the one you delivered at the service in Selma prior to the march. [23]

For Heschel, the march had spiritual significance; he wrote that he felt "as though my legs were praying."

For Heschel, the centrality of the Exodus in the civil rights movement was a sign of Christian theological affirmation of its Jewish roots, an issue he considered pivotal to the contemporary ecumenical efforts in which he was involved. The Second Vatican Council, which met from 1961 to 1965, promulgated its statement concerning the Jews, *Nostra Aetate*, on October 28, 1965. Heschel was consulted on numerous occasions by leaders of the Council, including Cardinal Bea and Pope Paul VI, and he considered its work of great importance. Believing that King's use of the Exodus would be strengthened if he were to participate in a Passover celebration, Heschel invited King and his wife to his family's seder, to take place on April 16, 1968: "The ritual and the celebration of that evening seek to make present to us the spirit and the wonder of the exodus from Egypt. It is my feeling that your participation at a Seder celebration would be of very great significance." King was assassinated just days before Passover.

Selma was a major event in Heschel's life. A few days before the march was able to take place, in mid-March 1965, Heschel led a delegation of 800 people protesting the brutal treatment the demonstrators were receiving in Selma to FBI headquarters in New York City. There had been violence against the demonstrators in Selma, and for two months they had been prevented from beginning the march. The New York delegation was not permitted to enter the FBI building, but Heschel was allowed inside,

FIGURE 8.1. *Martin Luther King, Jr., Abraham Joshua Heschel, and civil rights marchers in Selma, Alabama, 1965. Courtesy of the Ratner Center for the Study of Conservative Judaism, Jewish Theological Seminary.*

surrounded by 60 police officers, to present a petition to the regional FBI director. On Friday, March 19, two days before the Selma march was scheduled to begin, Heschel received a telegram from King inviting him to join the marchers in Selma. Heschel flew to Selma from New York on Saturday night and was welcomed as one of the leaders into the front row of marchers, along with King, Ralph Bunche, and Ralph Abernathy (fig. 8.1). Each of them wore flower leis, brought by Hawaiian delegates. In an unpublished memoir Heschel wrote upon returning from Selma, he described the extreme hostility he encountered from whites in Alabama that week, from the moment he arrived at the airport, and the kindness he was shown by Dr. King's assistants, particularly the Reverend Andrew Young, who hovered over him with great concern during the march.

Upon his return, Heschel described his experience in a diary entry:

> I thought of having walked with Hasidic rabbis on various occasions. I felt a sense of the Holy in what I was doing. Dr. King expressed several times to me his appreciation. He said, "I cannot tell you how much your presence means to us. You cannot imagine how often Reverend [C.T.] Vivian and I speak about you." Dr. King said to me that this was the greatest day in his life and the most important civil-rights demonstration. . . . I felt again what I have been thinking about for years—that Jewish religious institutions have again missed a great opportunity, namely, to interpret a civil-rights movement in terms of Judaism. The vast majority of Jews participating actively in it are totally unaware of what the movement means in terms of the prophetic traditions.[24]

Just before the march began, a service was held in a chapel, where he read Psalm 27, "The Lord is my light and my salvation; whom shall I fear?"[25] Heschel's presence in the front row of marchers was a visual symbol of religious Jewish commitment to civil rights and "stirred not only the Jewish religious community but Jews young and old into direct action, galvanizing the whole spectrum of activists from fundraisers to lawyers."[26] Not everyone reacted as positively to the marchers; the *New York Times* carried a report that Republican Representative William L. Dickinson asserted that the march was a communist plot and that "drunkenness and sex orgies were the order of the day."[27]

King's identification of the movement with the Exodus drew on a long tradition in black slave religion and the black church, in which the most significant biblical figure was Moses. In spirituals and sermons Moses was described as the liberator from Egypt rather than the lawgiver at Sinai, and Jesus, viewed as a figure of suffering, tended to be merged with Moses. At best, Jesus was a derivatory figure whose purpose and significance were not original but derived from the prophets, in a theological tradition stemming from Rauschenbusch.[28] The identification of the movement with the Exodus continued in King's work, Keith Miller makes clear, in sermons and in formal addresses such as "I See the Promised Land," which he delivered to a group of striking Black sanitation workers in Memphis the night before he was assassinated. In that speech, King merges his listeners, but also all civil rights activists, with the Israelite slaves under Pharaoh: "You know, whenever Pharaoh wanted to prolong the period of slavery in Egypt. . . . He kept the slaves fighting among themselves. . . . When the slaves get together, that's the beginning of getting out of slavery. Now let us maintain unity."[29]

Heschel used similar imagery when writing about civil rights, but he used the imagery to rebuke white audiences for their racism. American Jews, too, were Egyptians, in Heschel's retelling. At his first major address on the subject, at a conference on Religion and Race sponsored by the National Conference of Christians and Jews in Chicago on January 14, 1963, the occasion where Heschel and King first met, Heschel opened his speech by returning the present day to biblical history: "At the first conference on religion and race, the main participants were Pharaoh and Moses. . . . The outcome of that summit meeting has not come to an end. Pharaoh is not ready to capitulate. The exodus began, but is far from having been completed. In fact, it was easier for the children of Israel to cross the Red Sea than for a Negro to cross certain university campuses."[30] In February 1964, at another conference, held at a time when white resistance in America was increasing, Heschel reminded his audiences that Israelites, just after leaving Egypt, had complained of the bitter water they found at Marah, asking Moses, "What shall we drink?" Chiding his audience, Heschel writes:

> This episode seems shocking. What a comedown! Only three days earlier they had reached the highest peak of prophetic and spiritual exaltation, and now they complain about such a prosaic and unspiritual item as water. . . . The Negroes of America behave just like the children of Israel. Only in 1963 they experienced the miracle of having turned the tide of history, the joy of finding millions of Americans involved in the struggle for civil rights, the exaltation of fellowship, the March to Washington. Now only a few months later they have the audacity to murmur: "What shall we drink? We want adequate education, decent housing, proper employment." How ordinary, how unpoetic, how annoying! . . . We are ready to applaud dramatic struggles once a year in Washington. For the sake of lofty principles we will spend a day or two in jail somewhere in Alabama. . . . The tragedy of Pharaoh was the failure to realize that the exodus from slavery could have spelled redemption for both Israel and Egypt. Would that Pharaoh and the Egyptians had joined the Israelites in the desert and together stood at the foot of Sinai![31]

Few in the Jewish community have achieved the moral stature of Heschel, able to chastise American Jews in a prophetic voice for their racism. During his lifetime, many in the community were openly critical of Heschel, arguing that he had established himself as a leader without having been selected. He had no right to speak to the Vatican on behalf of Jewry, many claimed, as if he spoke on behalf of other Jews. At the same time, Heschel quickly was recognized on the national level as a major voice in the civil rights struggle. For example, when President John F. Kennedy wanted to convene religious leaders to discuss civil rights at a meeting at the White House in June 1963, Heschel was one of those invited to attend. In response to Kennedy's telegram inviting him to the meeting, Heschel telegraphed:

> I look forward to privilege of being present at meeting tomorrow four pm. Likelihood exists that Negro problem will be like the weather. Everybody talks about it but nobody does anything about it. Please demand of religious leaders personal involvement not just solemn declaration. We forfeit the right to worship God as long as we continue to humiliate Negroes. Church

> synagogue have failed. They must repent. Ask of religious leaders to call for national repentance and personal sacrifice. Let religious leaders donate one month's salary toward fund for Negro housing and education. I propose that you Mr. President declare state of moral emergency. A Marshall plan for aid to Negroes is becoming a necessity. The hour calls for moral grandeur and spiritual audacity.[32]

Both Heschel and King have been viewed as falling under the influence of the two most important theological tendencies of the century, the neo-orthodoxy associated with Barth and Niebuhr, and the liberal trends known either as ethical monotheism within the Jewish tradition or as culture Protestantism within Christian tradition. Both saw the limitations of each tradition, suspicious of Barth's assertion of God's utter and complete transcendent otherness, according to which human beings are unable to affect the divine realm, while at the same time uncomfortable with liberalism's diminution of divine power and action within the world and with what they saw as its naive optimism regarding human nature. Instead, both spoke of God in similar terms, as deeply involved in the affairs of human history, yet at the same time as other than the worldly realm. For both, God has a subjective life that is affected by human deeds; human beings constitute an object of divine concern.

Heschel developed a theology of what he termed "divine pathos" that he claimed was rooted in the teachings of the biblical prophets. In the experience of the prophets, God was not remote, nor simply a commanding force that expects obedience. Rather, God responds to human beings "in an intimate and subjective manner," experiencing "joy or sorrow, pleasure or wrath." Humanity and God do not inhabit detached realms, because God "has a stake in the human situation. . . . Man is not only an image of God; he is a perpetual concern of God."[33] Central to the prophets is the conviction that "the attitudes of man may affect the life of God, that God stands in an intimate relationship to the world."[34] Such a theology, by assuming that a dynamic encounter between human beings and God is possible, testifies to some degree of analogy between God and people, thereby elevating the moral significance of human life. Divine pathos, as Heschel defines it, bears the religious implication "that God can be intimately affected" and the political implication that "God is never neutral, never beyond good and evil."[35]

King's own dissatisfaction with theological liberalism's understanding of the nature of God was clear, beginning in his student writings. In his dissertation on Tillich and Wieman he criticized the impersonality of God characteristic of both theologians' work. Commentators have stressed King's affirmation of neo-orthodoxy's contention that God acts in history, as well as his rejection of the essentially passive role of human beings in neo-orthodox theology. James McClendon has commented, "Man on his own loses his way, grows weary, discouraged, while passive dependence on God alone is disobedience to God."[36] The pathos of God is not described or argued by King in the same language that Heschel uses but is invoked in the images of his language. Indeed, essential to the power of King's words is the implication that God has compassion for human beings and is sympathetic to human suffering. During the Montgomery boycott, he declared, "God is using Montgomery as His proving ground," assuring his followers, "Remember, if I am stopped, this movement will not stop because God is with the movement." Later, in 1968, he said, "It is possible for me to falter, but I am profoundly secure in my knowledge that God loves us; He has not worked out a design for our failure." God's involvement in the struggle was an important component in solidifying the identity of the movement with biblical *Heilsgeschichte*.

According to Heschel's theology, human history is God's history too, because, as he entitled one of his books, "man is not alone." King used similar language in *Strength to Love*: "However dismal and catastrophic may be the present circumstances, we know that we are not alone, for God dwells with us in life's most confining and oppressive cells."[37] In his doctoral dissertation King had criticized Tillich for the impersonality of his God. The "ground of being," King wrote, was "little more than a sub-personal reservoir of power, somewhat akin to the impersonalism of Oriental Vedantism."[38] Heschel, in a television interview, used humor to describe Tillich: "One of the most popular definitions of God common in America today was developed by a great Protestant theologian: God is the ground of being. So everybody is ready to accept it. Why not? Ground of being causes me no harm. Let there be a ground of being, it doesn't cause me any harm, and I'm ready to accept it. It's meaningless."[39] The absence of a commanding voice and of divine concern for human life, which were central, in Heschel's view to the biblical message, renders Tillich's God unsatisfying.

Using language that is strikingly similar, both Heschel and King assert that God is not the "unmoved Mover" of the Aristotelian tradition, unconcerned with the joys and troubles of human life, but is in fact deeply affected by earthly affairs. King writes, "The God that we worship is not some Aristotelian 'unmoved mover' who merely contemplates upon Himself; He is not merely a self-knowing God, but an other-loving God Who forever works through history for the establishment of His kingdom."[40] Heschel used similar language, arguing that in Judaism, God is the "most moved Mover," responsive to human suffering and challenging us to respond to the divine initiative: "To be is to stand for, and what human beings stand for is the great mystery of being God's partner. God is in need of human beings."

God's need of human beings is a prominent tradition within classical Jewish mysticism. Human actions affect the divine realm, according to the mystics, strengthening the forces of mercy or judgment within God, who responds in kind. The divine realm itself is dependent upon human actions, because God is understood to have gone into exile with the Jewish people, sending the divine presence to reside in the earthly realm. As much as human beings are in need of redemption, God too awaits redemption and exists in a measure of dependence upon human deeds. King writes something similar: "By endowing us with freedom, God relinquished a measure of his own sovereignty and imposed certain limitations upon himself."[41] Divine concern is an assumption that pervades the black church. Lewis Baldwin writes, "The concept of a personal God of infinite love and undiluted power 'who works through history for the salvation of His children' has always been central to the theology of the Black Church."[42]

Theologically as well as politically, King and Heschel recognized their own strong kinship. For each there was an emphatic stress on the dependence of the political on the spiritual, God on human society, the moral life on economic well-being. Indeed, there are numerous passages in their writings that might have been composed by either one. Consider, for example, Heschel's words: "The opposite of good is not evil, the opposite of good is indifference," a conviction that he translated into a political commitment: "In a free society, some are guilty, but all are responsible." [43] King writes, "To accept passively an unjust system is to cooperate with that system." In so doing, he went on, "the oppressed becomes as evil as the oppressor." Not to act communicates "to the oppressor that his actions are morally right." Social activism was required by religious faith, both Heschel and King argued, particularly when society had developed immoral institutional structures: "Your highest loyalty is to God and not to the mores, or folkways, the state or the nation or any man-made institution."[44]

Their common understanding of the prophets and of the connections between faith and political engagement was the motivation that brought both men to speak out against the war in Vietnam, despite the political consequences. Heschel was the founder, together with Richard John Neuhaus and John Bennett, of an antiwar organization, known as Clergy and Laymen Concerned About Vietnam, which he established in the fall of 1965.[45] Even as social protest was for him a religious experience, religion without indignation at political evils was also impossible: "To speak about God and remain silent on Vietnam is blasphemous," he wrote. Over and over, in speeches at universities, synagogues, and antiwar rallies, he denounced the murder of innocent people in Southeast Asia. However difficult it may be to stop the war today, he said, it will be even more difficult tomorrow; the killing must end now.

Whether or not Dr. King should speak out publicly against the war in Vietnam was a topic that preoccupied Heschel during the years between 1965 and 1967. Would his public opposition to the war hurt the civil rights movement? Which was the better political course, and which was the greater moral good? Lacking widespread support even within the SCLC for a public position against the war, King came under severe attack for his opposition. Major newspapers within both the black and white communities editorialized against him, and civil rights leaders including Ralph Bunche, Whitney Young, Roy Wilkins, Jackie Robinson, and Senator Edward Brooke publicly criticized him.[46]

Heschel remained deeply engaged in antiwar efforts during the last years of his life. He lectured frequently at antiwar rallies and made his opposition to the war an integral part of his public lectures and of his classes at the Jewish Theological Seminary, where he served as professor of Jewish ethics and mysticism in the department of philosophy. The atrocities committed by U.S. forces in Vietnam, and the obvious political futility of a war against guerillas, were vigorously condemned by Heschel, who was placed under FBI surveillance; he was branded an anti-American subversive by supporters of the war. But the real subversiveness, Heschel said, came from the policies of the American government:

> Our thoughts on Vietnam are sores, destroying our trust, ruining our most cherished commitments with burdens of shame. We are pierced to the core with pain, and it is our duty as citizens to say no to the subversiveness of our government, which is ruining the values we cherish. . . . The blood we shed in Vietnam makes a mockery of all our proclamations, dedications, celebrations. Has our conscience become a fossil, is all mercy gone? If mercy, the mother of humility, is still alive as a demand, how can we say yes to our bringing agony to that tormented country? We are here because our own integrity as human beings is decaying in the agony and merciless killing done in our name. In a free society, some are guilty and all are responsible. We are here to call upon the governments of the United States as well as North Vietnam to stand still and to consider that no victory is worth the price of terror, which all parties commit in Vietnam, North and South. Remember that the blood of the innocent cries forever. Should that blood stop to cry, humanity would cease to be.[47]

The crimes committed in Vietnam were destroying American values and were also undermining our religious lives, he insisted. Someone may commit a crime now and teach mathematics an hour later. But when we pray, all we have done in our lives enters our prayers.[48] As he had articulated in his early essays of the 1940s, the purpose of prayer is not petitionary. We do not pray in order to be saved, Heschel stressed in his writings, we pray so that we might be worthy of being saved. Prayer should not focus on our wishes but is a moment in which God's intentions are reflected in us.[49] If we are created in the image of God, each human being should be a reminder of God's presence. If we engage in acts of violence and murder, we are desecrating the divine likeness.

King delivered a formal statement opposing the war in a major address sponsored by Clergy and Laymen Concerned, on April 4, 1967, in New York's Riverside Church. Echoing themes similar to those articulated by Heschel, he reminded his audience that the motto of the SCLC was "To save the soul of America," and he said, "If America's soul becomes totally poisoned, part of the autopsy must read Vietnam. . . . A nation that continues year after year to spend more money on military defense than on programs of social uplift is approaching spiritual death."[50] He went on to call for a "revolution of values" in American society as the best defense against communism, and for removal of "those conditions of poverty, insecurity and injustice which are the fertile soil in which the seed of communism grows and develops."

The anguish that Heschel felt over the war in Vietnam was relentless and often left him unable to sleep or concentrate on other matters. Throughout those years he received warnings and complaints from some members of the Jewish community, who felt his protests were endangering American government support for the State of Israel. Similarly, King was attacked for endangering President Lyndon Johnson's support for the civil rights movement, and his outspokenness against the war did not win approval from the major black organizations. SNCC and CORE opposed the war, but the Urban League and the NAACP defended it. Whitney Young said, "the greatest freedom that exists for Negroes . . . is the freedom to die in Vietnam."[51]

Both Heschel and King spoke of each other as prophets. On March 25, 1968, just ten days before he was assassinated, King delivered the keynote address at a birthday celebration honoring Heschel, convened by the Rabbinical Assembly of America, an umbrella organization of rabbis in the Conservative movement. In his introduction of King to the audience, Heschel asked, "Where in America today do we hear a voice like the voice of the prophets of Israel? Martin Luther King is a sign that God has not forsaken the United States of America. God has sent him to us. His presence is the hope of America. His mission is sacred, his leadership of supreme importance to every one of us." In his address, King said that Heschel "is indeed a truly great prophet." He went on, "here and there we find those who refuse to remain silent behind the safe security of stained glass windows, and they are forever seeking to make the great ethical insights of our Judeo-Christian heritage relevant in this day and in this age. I feel that Rabbi Heschel is one of the persons who is relevant at all times, always standing with prophetic insights to guide us through these difficult days."[52]

It is clear that their relationship carried profound meaning for both Heschel and King. They seem to have been aware of the symbolic significance of their friendship, and they used it as a tool to foster further alliances between Jews and blacks. Heschel worked on joint projects with Jesse Jackson and Wyatt T. Walker, among others, while many of King's closest advisors were Jews. The opposition of most Jewish organizations to affirmative actions programs, beginning in the 1970s, never won support from Heschel, who died in 1972, and it is likely he would have mediated the tensions arising from the Jewish community's hostility toward Andrew Young and Jesse Jackson that developed in the late 1970s and 1980s. Yet while Heschel gave his political support to a wide range of African American leaders, it was the theological affinity he experienced with King that lent their relationship a particularly strong and profound intimacy.[53]

Neither community today has voices of moral leadership comparable to the voices of King and Heschel. The prophetic mood they created has been replaced by voices of witness that speak about the racism and anti-Semitism of our society, but without offering the transcendent religious vision they provided. The moments of transcendence that predominated in the civil rights era have shifted to moods of cynicism. Perhaps if the memory of that era and the symbolism of the friendship between Heschel and King survives, it will one day inspire the transformation that remains so badly needed.

NOTES

1. Doris L. Bergen, *Twisted Cross: The German Christian Movement in the Third Reich* (Chapel Hill: University of North Carolina Press, 1996); Susannah Heschel, "Nazifying Christian Theology: Walter Grundmann and the Institute for the Study and Eradication of Jewish Influence on German Church Life," *Church History* 63, no. 4 (December 1994): 587–605.

2. Martin Luther King, Jr., "Who Was Jesus of Nazareth?" in *The Papers of Martin Luther King, Jr.*, ed. Claryborne Carson, vol. 1 (Berkeley: University of California Press, 1992), p. 245.

3. Abraham J. Heschel, "No Religion Is an Island," *in Moral Grandeur and Spiritual Audacity: Essays of Abraham Joshua Heschel*, ed. Susannah Heschel (New York: Farrar, Straus and Giroux, 1996), p. 242.

4. James Cone, *Martin and Malcolm and America: A Dream or a Nightmare* (Maryknoll, N.Y.: Orbis Books, 1991); cited by Michael Eric Dyson, *Reflecting Black: African-American Cultural Criticism* (Minneapolis: University of Minnesota Press, 1993), p. 256.

5. Keith D. Miller, "Alabama as Egypt: Martin Luther King, Jr., and the Religion of Slaves," in *Martin Luther King, Jr., and the Sermonic Power of Public Discourse*, ed. Carolyn Calloway-Thomas and John Louis Lucaites (Tuscaloosa: University of Alabama Press, 1993), p. 21. For a discussion of influences of the black church on King's thought, see Lewis Baldwin, *There Is a Balm in Gilead: The Cultural Roots of Martin Luther King, Jr.* (Minneapolis: Augsburg Fortress Press, 1991), and Fred Downing, *To See the Promised Land: The Faith Pilgrimage of Martin Luther King, Jr.* (Macon, Ga: Mercer University Press, 1986). For contrary interpretations that place King's intellectual development within the context of Rauschenbusch, Niebuhr, and Gandhi, see Kenneth Smith and Ira G. Zepp, *Search for the Beloved Community: The Thinking of Martin Luther King, Jr.* (Valley Forge, Pa: Judson Press, 1974), and John J. Ansbro, *Martin Luther King, Jr.: The Making of a Mind* (Maryknoll, N.Y.: Orbis Books, 1983).

6. Cited by Michael Osborn, "The Last Mountaintop of Martin Luther King, Jr.," in Calloway-Thomas and Lucaites, *Sermonic Power of Public Discourse*, p. 153.

7. See Arthur Green, "Three Warsaw Mystics," *Jerusalem Studies in Jewish Thought* 13 (1996), 1–58.

8. Charles M. Payne, *I've Got the Light of Freedom: The Orgonizing Tradition and the Mississippi, Freedom Struggle* (Berkeley: University of California Press, 1995), p. 272.

9. Hans A. Baer and Merrill Singer, *African-American Religion in the Twentieth Century: Varieties of Protest and Accommodation* (Knoxville: University of Tennessee Press, 1992), p. 39.

10. Clayborne Carson, "Rethinking African-American Political Thought in the Post-Revolutionary Era," in *The Making of Martin Luther King and the Civil Rights Movement*, ed. Brian Ward and Tony Badger (New York: NYU Press, 1996), p. 117.

11. David Garrow has warned that some of King's sermons and lectures were substantially revised before being published. Nonetheless, I am assuming that his writings published after 1957 remain valid expressions. David Garrow, "The Intellectual Development of Martin Luther King, Jr.: Influences and Commentaries," *Union Seminary Quarterly Review* 40 (January 1986): 5–20; reprinted in *Native American Religion and Black Protestantism*, ed. Martin E. Marty (Munich: K. G. Saur, 1993), pp. 206–21.

12. Green, "Three Warsaw Mystics," p. 48.

13. Ibid. See also Vincent Harding, "The Religion of Black Power," in *The Religious Situation*, ed. D. Cutler (Boston: Beacon Press, 1968), pp. 3–38.

14. W. Beach and H. Richard Niebuhr, eds., *Christian Ethics* (New York: Ronald Press, 1955), p. 34; cited by Preston N. Williams, "James Cone and the Problem of a Black Ethic,"

Journal of the History of Ideas 65, no. 4 (October 1972): 483–94; reprinted in Marty, *Native American Religion and Black Protestantism*, p. 280.

15. Lawrence Levine, *Black Culture and Black Consciousness* (New York: Oxford University Press, 1977). See also Iain MacRobert, "The Black Roots of Pentecostalism," in *African-American Religion: Interpretive Essays in History and Culture*, ed. Timony E. Fulop and Albert J. Raboteau (New York: Routledge, 1997), pp. 295-309.

16. See, for example, Martin Luther King, Jr., *Strength to Love* (New York: Harper and Row, 1963), pp. 71–81; idem, *Where Do We Go from Here: Chaos or Community?* (New York: Harper and Row, 1967), pp. 23, 31, 89, 124, 170. I do not agree with the assertion of the primacy of Jesus over Moses in King's writings by James H. Smylie, "On Jesus, Pharaohs, and the Chosen People: Martin Luther King as Biblical Interpreter and Humanist," *Interpretation* 24 (January 1970): 74–91.

17. Malinda Snow, "Martin Luther King's 'Letter from Birmingham Jail' as Pauline Epistle," *Quarterly Journal of Speech* 71 (1985), 319.

18. Keith D. Miller and Emily M. Lewis, "Touchstones, Authorities, and Marian Anderson: The Making of 'I Have a Dream,' " in Ward and Badger, *The Making of Martin Luther King*, pp. 147–61.

19. Abraham J. Heschel, *The Prophets* (New York: Harper and Row, 1962), pp. 212 and passim.

20. Gerhard von Rad, *The Message of the Prophets*, trans. D. M. G. Stalker (New York: Harper and Row, 1962), pp. 13-14.

21. Carson, *Papers*, vol. 1, pp. 181–95.

22. A. J. Heschel, *The Prophets*, p. 9.

23. Dated 29 March 1965.

24. Cited in S. Heschel, "Introduction," *Moral Grandeur and Spiritual Audacity*, pp. xxiii–xxiv.

25. He writes in an unpublished memoir that he had originally intended to read Psalm 15, "O Lord, who shall sojourn in thy tent?" but changed his mind after he arrived in Selma.

26. Murray Friedman with Peter Binzen, *What Went Wrong? The Creation and Collapse of the Black–Jewish Alliance* (New York: Free Press, 1995), p. 191.

27. *The New York Times*, 22 March 1965.

28. Walter Rauschenbusch, *Christianity and the Social Crisis* (New York: Macmillan, 1908).

29. Martin Luther King, Jr., "I See the Promised Land," in *A Testament of Hope: The Essential Writings and Speeches of Martin Luther King, Jr.* (San Francisco: HarperCollins, 1986), pp. 280–81.

30. Abraham J. Heschel, "Religion and Race," in *The Insecurity of Freedom: Essays on Human Existence* (New York: Farrar, Straus and Giroux, 1966), p. 85.

31. Abraham J. Heschel, "The White Man on Trial," in *The Insecurity of Freedom*, 101-3.

32. The telegram from Kennedy was dated 12 June 1963: "At four o'clock on Monday, June 17, I am meeting with a group of religious leaders to discuss certain aspects of the nation's civil rights problem. This matter merits serious and immediate attention and I would be pleased to have you attend the meeting to be held in the East Room of the White House. Please advise whether you will be able to attend. John F Kennedy"; Heschel's reply was dated 16 June 1963.

33. A. J. Heschel, *The Prophets*, 226.

34. Ibid., p. 229.

35. Ibid., pp. 224, 231.

36. James McClendon, *Biography as Theology* (New York: Abingdon Press, 1974), pp. 80–86; cited by John H. Patton, "'I Have a Dream': The Performance of Theology Fused with the Power of Orality," in Calloway-Thomas and Lucaites, *The Sermonic Power of Public Discourse*, p. 112.

37. King, *Strength to Love*, p. 86.

38. King, CCG, dissertation, p. 271; cited by Ansbro, *The Making of a Mind*, p. 60.

39. Abraham J. Heschel, "Carl Stern's Interview with Dr. Heschel," in S. Heschel, *Moral Grandeur and Spiritual Audacity*, p. 408.

40. 1957 Prayer Pilgrimage for Freedom address at the Lincoln Memorial; quoted in Ansboro, *The Making of a Mind*, p. 47.

41. King, *Strength to Love*, p. 64.

42. Lewis V. Baldwin, "Martin Luther King, Jr., the Black Church, and the Black Messianic Vision," in *Martin Luther King, Jr., and the Civil Rights Movement*, ed. David J. Garrow, vol. 1 (Brooklyn: Carlson, 1989), p. 7.

43. Heschel used that phrase frequently; cf. "The Reasons for My Involvement in the Peace Movement," in S. Heschel, *Moral Grandeur and Spiritual Audacity*, p.225, "A Prayer for Peace," op. cit., 231.

44. King, *Strength to Love*, 128.

45. The name was changed in the late 1970s to Clergy and Laity Concerned.

46. Frederick J. Antczak, "When 'Silence Is Betrayal': An Ethical Criticism of the Revolution of Values in the Speech at Riverside Church," in Calloway-Thomas and Lucaites *The Sermonic Power of Public Discourse*, pp. 134–35.

47. Text reprinted in Susannah Heschel, "Introduction," in *Moral Grandeur and Spiritual Audacity*, p. xxiv. See also Robert McAfee Brown, Abraham J. Heschel, and Michael Novak, *Vietnam: Crisis of Conscience* (New York: Association Press, 1967).

48. Abraham J. Heschel, "The Holy Dimension," in S. Heschel, *Moral Grandeur and Spiritual Audacity*, pp. 318–27.

49. A. J. Heschel, "Prayer," in ibid., pp. 340–53.

50. Martin Luther King, Jr., "A Time to Break Silence," in *A Testament of Hope*, pp. 234, 241.

51. Adam Fairclough, "The Southern Christian Leadership Conference and the Second Reconstruction, 1957–1973," *Southern Atlantic Quarterly* 80, no. 2 (spring 1981), 177–94; reprinted in Marty, *Native American Religion and Black Protestantism*, p. 200.

52. The texts of both speeches are reprinted in King, *A Testament of Hope*, pp. 657–79.

53. For their thoughtful comments and suggestions, I would like to thank my colleagues Jacob Aronson, Richard Cogley, and Constance Parvey.

9

This Is the Gateway to the Lord

The Legacy of Synagogue Buildings for African American Churches on Cincinnati's Reading Road

Karla Goldman

THE CLASSICAL STONE-FACED edifice of the Southern Missionary Baptist Church stands imposingly at the corner of Lexington Ave. and Reading Road in Cincinnati's Avondale neighborhood, an area of old-world apartment buildings and detached homes, some stately and some more modest (fig. 9.1). About a mile further up Reading in North Avondale, the Zion Temple First Pentecostal Church, with its distinctive facade of massive rough-hewn stones occupies the corner of Reading and North Crescent[1] with retiring dignity and solidity. Although these two thriving African American Christian congregations reflect the current ethnic character of the Avondale and North Avondale neighborhoods, both church buildings were dedicated as synagogues in 1927, the centerpieces of a proud, prosperous, and dynamic urban Jewish community. While that community is all but gone from Avondale, these churches remain as physical reminders of its existence and offer an intriguing point of connection between two communities which in today's Cincinnati find few moments of vital contact.

From the first decade of the twentieth century through the early 1960s Avondale was home to a dense and dynamic ethnic neighborhood crowded with Jewish business, cultural, and religious institutions. Today, although a number of Jews continue to live in the substantial and comfortable homes of North Avondale, the only active remnant of Avondale's once rich and diverse Jewish institutional life is the Weil Funeral Home.[2] As in many such neighborhoods across the United States, the end of this singularly rich moment of Jewish urban life and culture was marked by transformative demographic changes for both American Jews and African Americans. Among Jews, growing affluence, rising expectations, and the dominance of the automobile prompted a push toward suburbanization, especially among young people, which undermined the vitality of the urbanized Jewish center. At the same time, many African Americans, displaced by the restructuring of Cincinnati's downtown areas, found their way to Avondale. As elsewhere, the growth of Avondale's African American population ultimately accelerated Jewish departures from the area.[3]

As in many American cities, the Jewish community of Cincinnati left their African American successors with the physical infrastructure of a dense institutional life. The phenomenon of black and Jewish congregations sharing the same religious structures at different points in time is a common one, having roots as far back as the nineteenth century.[4] In 1826 the second Jewish congregation in New York City purchased the former premises of the First Coloured Presbyterian Church on Elm Street. The pattern has been repeated whenever immigrant Jews have moved into formerly black neighborhoods. In Boston, for instance, when Jews joined an influx of white immigrant groups into Boston's West End in the late nineteenth century, the black residents relocated, leaving their religious structures behind. In the process, three African American churches in the West End became synagogues, with two of these black congregations moving into former synagogues in Boston's South End.[5]

The more common pattern has been the one in which blacks have replaced Jews, transforming neighborhoods in cities across the country and converting hundreds of synagogue building to new uses. Clearly the substantial synagogue buildings of America's urban residential neighborhoods proved an attractive feature for the new residents of these neighborhoods as they provided homes for the churches which were as central to the black community as synagogues had been for the Jewish community. Appropriately, the buildings that had been built in Avondale and many other Jewish communities in the first decades of the twentieth century were constructed very much on a model that would be desired by growing churches, anxious to contain many activities within their walls. Jewish synagogues of the 1920s were built to serve their communities not just with sanctuaries for worship but with extensive institutional facilities that could serve the diverse concerns of increasingly complex communities.[6]

The Isaac M. Wise Center building, now the home of Zion Temple First Pentecostal Church, was intended as a satellite to the magnificent Plum Street Temple in downtown Cincinnati. The new Wise Center offered members access to a religious school and communal life on a site closer to their homes than the Plum Street Temple, which had been built in 1866 at a time when most congregants lived in the downtown area. Thus while the new Wise Center included a modest sanctuary, the building design emphasized the social and educational needs of the congregation more than it did worship. The earliest proposal for a new Wise Center in North Avondale included "a large auditorium . . . with proper stage facilities for Wise Center forums and plays . . . . suitable and sufficient class-rooms for our religious schools . . . a school library, a study for the Rabbi and a large office—proper cloak rooms . . . . a large gymnasium, which would be used for Wise Center dances . . . and for congregational dinners. Kitchen facilities should also be included. . . . We also consider the erection of a swimming pool."[7] The building, dedicated in 1927, eschewed the swimming pool but otherwise provided a home for an expansive version of congregational life.

Congregation Adath Israel's 1927 building, commonly referred to as the Lexing-

FIGURE 9.1. *Southern Missionary Baptist Church, building exterior. Photograph by Karla Goldman.*

ton Avenue Synagogue until it became the Southern Missionary Baptist Church in 1964, combined a grand sanctuary with extensive congregational facilities.[8] Behind the monumental facade of the sanctuary, which dominates the view of the building from Reading Road, looms an extensive institution with meeting rooms, an institutional kitchen, a smaller chapel, a large school building, and a fellowship hall which doubled as auditorium and gymnasium. Both Wise Center and the Lexington Avenue Synagogue were built to house the expanding activities of growing and prosperous congregations at the height of a prosperous age. The buildings themselves were meant to be both homes to these congregations and testimony to the solidity and permanence of their communities. They did in fact provide valued institutional homes during the unsettled years of depression and World War II which followed their construction. Throughout the vicissitudes of these times, these synagogue buildings, along with many others in the Avondale and North Avondale neighborhoods, remained the public religious face of a Jewish community defined by shared institutions, geography, and a vibrant cultural and neighborhood life.

It might have seemed that the end of World War II and the coming prosperity of the 1950s would mark the full flowering of an established Jewish community and its institutions. And in fact, the Jews of Cincinnati did enjoy an energetic institutional religious life in the postwar years as Americans turned to religion as embodied in congregational affiliation and membership. Yet even as their religious institutions brimmed over with activity, the dissolution of Avondale's Jewish culture was clearly underway. Change in the neighborhood of the Lexington Avenue Synagogue in the 1950s was explosive. Small streets that had been completely Jewish for years often became, within the space of a single year, exclusively African American. The Jewish Community Relations Council reported that from 1948 to 1958 the Jewish population of Southern Avondale declined from 6,500 to 450. This transition from a predominantly Jewish to a predominantly African American neighborhood happened more quickly in the southern end of the neighborhood closer to downtown than in the northern sections of Avondale. Although some synagogues in South Avondale were sold to black churches in the 1950s, the Isaac M. Wise Center building in North Avondale remained a synagogue until 1973.

This rapid transition indicates the tension and panic which must have prevailed among Jewish residents who feared falling property values and various urban ills they associated with African American neighborhoods. Still, most Jewish and African American residents of the time who were consulted for this article seem to remember the transition with little rancor. One African American recalls that her new neighbors were very gracious, assured her family that they were pleased to have them as neighbors, but very soon moved away.[9] Former Jewish residents certainly recall the fear of falling housing values as neighborhoods became African American, but many seem to feel that the anxiety only precipitated moves that they probably would have made anyway. Many Cincinnati Jews, remembering the purchase of their first homes as young adults in the 1940s and 1950s, recall that, for a number of reasons, including the inappropriateness of Avondale-sized homes for small families, they did not even consider remaining in Avondale at that time. One former resident reported that by 1948 when she and her husband looked for a new home, "you could just feel the push of people moving out."[10]

The transference of many of Cincinnati's synagogues to African American congregations seemed to advance with a similar lack of bad feeling. By the fall of 1950, the Adath Israel congregation had already begun to hold regular services in the Roselawn Theater and to plan for the expansion of "cultural and religious activities" for the benefit of those members of the congregation who had moved further north along Reading Road into Roselawn.[11] Through the 1950s, the congregation steadily increased its presence in Roselawn as the community's rabbi tried to win the support of the synagogue's younger members in his efforts to liberalize the congregation's ritual practices by promising to offer a religious school program and to pursue the construction of a congregational facility in the Roselawn area. The congregation purchased one site in Roselawn for a religious school and in 1958 purchased a second Roselawn property (built as a nightclub) for $237,000 with the expectation of using it first as a branch religious school and sanctuary and later as a site for a new synagogue building.[12]

According to many long-time Adath Israel members, by the time representatives of the Southern Missionary Baptist Church first came to look at the synagogue property in 1962, the congregation's membership was gone from Avondale. The oft-repeated claim that all of the congregation's Jews had already moved may be an exaggeration, yet it is clear that the area around the synagogue had become predominantly African American, and the board was determined to go forward with a Roselawn building because "most of our people live here."[13] In fact, congregational leaders believed that "Southern" was the last large black congregation in need of a new church with the financial ability to purchase and maintain a facility the size of the Lexington Avenue Synagogue.[14] So when representatives of the Southern Baptist Church, anticipating the destruction of their own church in Cincinnati's West End as part of the city's redevelopment plans, came looking for a new building, there does not seem to have been much agitation within the Jewish congregation over the decision to sell and move the congregation permanently in the direction of Roselawn.

Southern leaders at first had hoped to build a building of their own but quickly realized that a new structure would be far more costly than the purchase of an existing property. Hoping to find a site that would be convenient to their dispersed members, many of whom, like their church, had been displaced by government redevelopment plans, church representatives scouted out numerous sites around the city including another former synagogue with a smaller sanctuary space slightly farther south on Reading Road. Ultimately, when the church committee returned to the Lexington Avenue Synagogue six months after their first visit, they were surprised to learn that the purchase price had been substantially reduced by synagogue leaders who had already committed themselves to building a new synagogue on their Roselawn site and who were hoping to avoid greater losses as, from their perspective, the neighborhood continued to decline. A contract to purchase the synagogue building for the sum of $238,000 was approved and completed in September 1962.[15]

The building purchased by the Southern Missionary Baptist Church was built in the style of a classical Greek temple with an impressive portico and Corinthian columns. As historian Lance Sussman has observed of the many similarly designed synagogues of this era, Adath Israel declared to the world passing by on Reading Road, Avondale's main avenue, "that Judaism was an ancient and integral part of Western civilization." Its massive and dignified presence quietly indicated that "the Jewish heritage was based on lofty, noble ideals that contributed to the strength and stability of society."[16] The Adath Israel building, built to serve immigrants from Eastern Europe and their children, was strikingly similar in design to Avondale's first substantial synagogue edifice, built in 1906 on Rockdale Avenue for one of Cincinnati's exceedingly prosperous and Americanized Reform temples whose members were identified with the mid-nineteenth-century wave of German-Jewish migration.

The synagogue dedicated by Adath Israel in 1927 was even designed by a member of Rockdale Temple,[17] but it represented a declaration by Adath's Israel's chiefly Eastern European constituency of their own substance and success. Still, there was to be no mistaking the nature and identity of their institution. Adath Israel's classical edifice was marked by a profusion of Jewish symbols on both its interior and exterior that was quite characteristic of the way in which Eastern European immigrants and their children used their grand synagogues during this era to celebrate and illustrate their Americanized prosperity and taste, together with their particular Jewish identity.

While the earlier Rockdale Temple's pediment had been adorned with a universalistic biblical English phrase, "My House Shall Be a House of Prayer for All Peoples," the Adath Israel pediment was inscribed in similarly lofty but Hebrew letters with the full name of the congregation. In the pediment's prominent central circle, passersby would note a proud stone Star of David. At the corners of the building stood large brass menorahs, and large Stars of David adorned the buildings' front and side walls. The interior decorations matched the exterior in terms of the prominence of Jewish symbols and emblems. The elaborate gilded central chandelier was constructed out of a series of Stars of David. The skylight from which it hung was also marked by a massive stained-glass Jewish star. Numerous smaller chandeliers replicated the star motif. Either a menorah or Star of David adorned the side of each seat adjacent to the aisles. Sconces for smaller lights in the style of candles also appeared in the form of six-sided stars. There were more stars at the summits of the many decorative interior columns that lined the walls and crowned the arches above each tall stained glass window. The stained glass windows themselves each contained a large pane devoted to a different Jewish holiday, offering some visual image of the holiday along with the holiday name inscribed in Hebrew. Around the base of the interior dome were painted Hebrew selections, chosen by the congregation's rabbi, drawn from various Jewish sources ranging from the Bible to modern Hebrew poetry. The above description only begins to describe the profusion of Jewish emblems evident in the sanctuary—even the grates for the radiators were in the form of Stars of David.

The sale of this building to the Southern Missionary Baptist Church created an unusual situation. Since the Jewish congregation was not yet prepared to establish itself elsewhere, the two congregations occupied the building together for thirteen months. Not too many Adath Israel members seem to have distinct memories of this period, most observing that they used the synagogue sanctuary on Saturday and the church used the auditorium space on Sundays. Reverend Henry Larkins, who was a member of the church committee that worked on the purchase of the building, recalls this period as one in which the congregations were forced together by circumstance: "We were forced from the West End, they were forced to stay with us." According to Larkins, the period of dual occupancy turned into a great experience for both congregations. He recounts that despite what he perceived as negative feelings from both sides at the outset, shaped by the many "stigmas of that time," once the two congregations were in the same space, they "learned to respect each other" as they created unanticipated connections. He believes that the members of the synagogue community who came in with very low opinions of blacks as a group were surprised to find themselves dealing with church members who "sat down like gentlemen and did business in a dignified way." According to the reverend's account, the two groups "learned to respect each other" and to coexist peacefully and productively.[18]

As the Jewish congregation prepared to leave Reading Road, they set about the process of "deconsecrating" the synagogue space. The contract of sale in fact stipulated that the synagogue would remove the congregation's two eight-branched candelabras, the eternal light, the Torah ark with the Ten Commandments engraved in stone, and the large table on the pulpit. In addition, the contract provided that the Jewish congregation would remove "all glass containing Hebrew words and Jewish religious symbols." Gaps left in the stained glass would be replaced with "leaded art stained glass harmonious with the remaining windows" but would "not include special lettering or symbols."[19] The deconsecration process involved a systematic attempt to remove many of the symbols that marked the building as a place of Jewish worship. Some of the Orthodox Jewish congregations in the city, anxious to avoid the transformation of their synagogues into churches, which they believed was prohibited by Jewish law, were careful to sell their buildings only to groups that would not make them into churches. The Adath Israel congregation was willing to accept a church as its best customer but still sought to reduce the building's Jewish character by removing many of the signs of its religious orientation. In addition to removing the particular items stipulated in the contract, the congregation saw to it that much of the Hebrew lettering on the inside of the sanctuary was painted over and that the markings on the building exterior were covered over or obliterated. Cement was used to cover up the congregation's Hebrew name and the various particularistic Jewish emblems on the building's exterior. The Star of David in the middle of the entrance pediment disappeared, as did the Hebrew words inscribed over the door. The process of deconsecration culminated in the Jewish congregation's final service on November 1, 1964, at which time congregational leaders carried the community's Torah scrolls out of the building.

Despite all this work to hide or remove so much of the building's heritage, the space bequeathed to the African American congregation was still marked by a profusion of Jewish emblems and symbolism. Until they yielded to disrepair, two large brass menorahs continued to stand at the corners of the entrance portico. Inside, the Star of David chandeliers and the endless series of six-sided stars and menorahs continue to dominate the space. Those who worked to adapt the sanctuary space to the needs of the Southern Missionary Baptist Church did not touch these many details of design. What redesign there was focused upon the relatively limited specific needs of the church. The most substantial change came in removing the synagogue's pulpit area, replacing it with a larger platform that could accommodate the church's large choir and those church members who needed to be on the pulpit during services. The elaborate design at the front of the sanctuary, with its small columned portico balcony surmounted by a painted arch of a cloudy blue sky, remained as it had been, with the addition of the motto, "One Lord, One Faith, One Baptism."

The major requisite for a Baptist church that is not supplied in a standard synagogue building is a baptismal pool. Although there was a desire to put this essential symbolic and functional element at the center of the proceedings at Southern's new church, practical considerations made it too difficult to incorporate the pool into the choir space. The old baptismal pool from Southern's downtown church was transferred to the stage of the new church's fellowship hall. This location was meant to be temporary, but although the original pool has since been replaced, the new pool remains in the fellowship hall.

One other innovation required by the church upon purchase of the building was the addition of a parking lot. Because Jewish religious law forbids driving on the Jewish Sabbath and holidays and because Adath Israel was built at the center of a walking neighborhood, the synagogue had only a small parking area for most of its existence, even after many of the congregants who had moved away began to drive to synagogue. Southern, therefore, purchased an adjoining property to turn into a parking lot. Apart from these changes, and the later additions of new school buildings, the church, especially the sanctuary, appears much as it did at the time of Adath Israel's deconsecration service.[20]

By the time the Wise Center was sold, a decade after the Adath Israel transaction, the city and the nation had gone through a period of social unrest and violence that in Cincinnati had manifested itself chiefly in Avondale. Riots in 1967 and 1968 had destroyed much of Avondale's business districts. Many white-owned enterprises, including those belonging to Jews, departed. Little replaced them, and eventually many business blocks were entirely demolished by the city. Most of the Jewish community's synagogues and institutions had left for the suburbs, including Rockdale

Temple, the closest counterpart to Wise in numbers, religious orientation, and status in the community. The utter collapse of the neighborhood's Jewish character was graphically illustrated when the once-grand Rockdale Temple building was firebombed in September 1970. Although the congregation had already departed, and black community groups had been occupying the building for some time, many in both the Jewish and African American communities understood this act as a pronouncement by black militants that Jews had no place in Avondale.[21]

Meanwhile Wise Center, positioned at the southern edge of North Avondale, where many white residents were committed to the creation of a sustainable integrated community, was largely untouched by the violence and tumult that had capped the departure of so many other institutions from Avondale. Still, although a large number of Jews were among those determined to resist the cycle of panic selling and white flight which had transformed South Avondale, it was difficult for a major institution to resist the pressures that were sending Jews and Jewish communal expectations to the north of the city. Congregational leaders worried about declining religious school enrollments and could only expect that the trend would continue. Many believed the tide turned irrevocably when the congregation's elderly senior rabbi was mugged at a bank across the street from the Center.[22]

In 1957 the First Pentecostal Church of Cincinnati, like other congregations anticipating the destruction of their church in the face of expressway construction in the West End, had moved north to the Walnut Hills area, next to Avondale, where they constructed a church building of their own. By 1972 the modest one-story structure they were able to build had become inadequate. The church community had prepared plans for an expansion of their facilities and secured the necessary financing, but it was clear that the building they could afford would not meet the needs and hopes of their congregation. Pastor Jasper Phillips, the church's spiritual leader, heard that the Wise Center building on Reading Road, about a mile away, had become available and, although he was skeptical of his congregation's financial ability to acquire such a substantial edifice, he made up his mind to look into the possibility. When Phillips first visited Wise Center in the winter of 1972–1973, the initial gruff response he recalls receiving from the congregation's rabbi ("have you got a million dollars?") was less than welcoming. He persisted, however, and in contacting the congregation's president, John Benjamin, found that his interest was received with seriousness and respect.[23] Rabbi Goldman, who had gone to Selma during the civil rights movement to participate in the work of Martin Luther King, Jr., believed that the congregation should stay in its urban setting. Many others committed to staying in North Avondale also hoped to keep the Center in the neighborhood. Still the will of the congregation was clear, and Goldman and others came to accept the board's decision to sell and to construct a new facility to the north in Amberley Village. Ultimately it was John Benjamin, president of the North Avondale Neighborhood Association, the group dedicated to the stabilization of North Avondale as an integrated community, who, as congregational president, presided over the sale of the synagogue facility to Pastor Phillips and his congregation. Despite his North Avondale home, Benjamin believed that the best interests of the congregation clearly lay in the suburbs.[24]

In the four months between the sale agreement in February 1973 and the actual transfer of the building on July 1, Pastor Phillips, his wife Beulah, and other members of their church community became a familiar presence at the Wise Center building as they attended some synagogue events, held some of their own meetings at the temple building, and generally checked out the premises. Mrs. Phillips recalls that in an effort to make her feel more comfortable on the new premises, she was invited to help serve tea along with members of the temple Sisterhood. As at Adath Israel, many at Wise Center were impressed by the seriousness and congeniality of the church's members.[25]

Like the Southern congregation, Pastor Phillips's church made few initial changes in the physical structure of the facility. While not as grand as Adath Israel's sanctuary, the Wise auditorium was also clearly marked as a Jewish space. In the words of Beulah Phillips, the many Stars of David displayed in the sanctuary were "engraved in the wall" in gratings and other patterns. Most notably, a series of large stained glass windows display distinct images of various Jewish motifs along with Hebrew inscriptions. As at the Southern Baptist congregation, the members of the First Pentecostal Church felt no dissonance in maintaining the display of these symbols within their church sanctuary. Members of both churches today observe that although the various symbols do not carry the same meaning for them that they would for those of the Jewish faith, they do nothing to take away from the goals of the church. Church members look upon the design details as accentuating the beauty of spaces that have become their spiritual homes.

Members of both churches commonly emphasize that the physical structure of their church buildings is subordinate to the importance of the worship of God and the gathering of God's community that goes on within them. Many members of the church, in fact, when questioned about the meaning of the details of their building to the community, indicate their own awareness of its origin but question whether many other church members are equally aware. Ozell Davis of Southern, like many others, recalls being struck by the sheer size of the building, at the same time that she felt disoriented by all the doors and exits and entrances. Like many of her fellow congregants, and members of other former-synagogue churches, she emphasized that the building itself was much less important than what went on inside it. One young man pointed out that the church's building was a suitable building for his congregation because it was big and stable enough to handle the church and its many activities.

Beyond aesthetics, church leaders point to the ways in which the presence of emblems of the Jewish faith connect the churches to the biblical heritage of their own communities. Pastor C. Dennis Edwards I, the current pastor at Southern, observes that "everywhere you look you are reminded of the Lord." In an interview focused on the church's past as a synagogue, Pastor Edwards readily expressed his sense of the many ways in which the distinctive atmosphere created by the former synagogue building provides an enriching context for the religious experience he hopes to engender during worship.[26] Reverend Edwards, even more than many members of his church, pointed to the importance of the congregation's grand edifice; he has made restoration to its former glory one of the central emphases of his new pastorship.

Bishop Jasper Phillips and his wife likewise take the import of their physical setting very seriously. When the First Pentecostal Church of Cincinnati moved into the Wise Center building, one of the ways in which the church marked the transition to the new space was to adopt the name Zion Temple First Pentecostal Church of Cincinnati. It is not unusual for African American churches to use either "Zion" or "Temple" in naming themselves, yet in this case, as Bishop Phillips acknowledges, the resonance of the new name with the building's past made it seem a fitting title for this particular place of worship of the Lord.[27]

The Phillipses point to the utility of the Zion Temple building in offering their members physical representations of the lessons they are studying in the Scripture. They cite especially in this regard the stained glass image of the Jewish harvest festival, which they take as a representation of the Feast of the Pentecost, the celebration of which in the New Testament is fundamental to adherents of modern-day Pentecostalism.[28]

Those who have paid the most attention to the legacy of these buildings find the form of the ancient Jerusalem Temples in the synagogue architecture erected by American Jews of the 1920s. A study of the history of Southern church building conducted for the benefit of the community by Eartell Brownlow, a life-long church member, lays out quite clearly how the building's "guidelines came from the original temple in Jerusalem." Her study details how the plaza and steps leading to the entrance, the three entry doors, the entrance vestibule, and the decorative pillars of the sanctuary all replicate the design of the ancient temple.[29]

The Phillipses, leaders of Zion Temple, readily make the connection between the holiness that inhered in the synagogue community and the ancient Temple and that which prevails in their own church. Asked about the baptismal pool which in their church occupies the space that was taken up by the ark containing the Torah scrolls at Wise Temple, Bishop Phillips explained that it is extremely important to have baptism, the moment of spiritual transformation when candidates unite with the church and the body of Christ, at the center of their proceedings in a place where everyone can see and recognize its centrality. Mother Phillips acknowledged the striking symmetry of having this sacred space where so many accept the faith of the church in the very site which in the synagogue, she notes, drawing upon biblical descriptions of Solomon's Temple in Jerusalem, was the "holy of holies."[30] While the Torah ark in modern synagogue is not technically thought of as the "holy of holies," the presence of the Torah within the ark does harken back to the ark of the covenant constructed to carry God's words as conveyed to Moses and to the Temple with its

Holy of Holies, built to contain the ark of the covenant. It is in these connections, where church members experience the enriching consciousness of the presence of the Old Testament, that their buildings become more than simply grand and beautiful spaces.

The Phillipses, who have been the leaders of the Zion Temple congregation for almost fifty years and have been married more than sixty, have a quite learned appreciation of the ways in which their temple resonates with a biblical past. Others in their church are less informed yet they too seek out the connections and seem to draw pride from the extra layers that are present in their church. One member, seeking to understand his church's building in its biblical context, asked some Jewish visitors about the outdoor structure remaining from the Wise Temple days, which had been used to construct the festive and ritual sukkah, a temporary symbolic dwelling during the fall harvest festival of Sukkot. He inquired whether Wise Temple members had used this "grill" for the ritual sacrifices that he knew had been carried on in the ancient Temple in Jerusalem. Members often inquire of Jewish visitors whether the aspects of their church that seem to them distinctive, like the way light enters the sanctuary, were designed with some special religious or Jewish intent.

Those who now occupy these buildings have become keepers of their stories and oral traditions. Mother Beulah Phillips proudly affirms that the church is still serving as "a beacon like it was for the Jewish nation," when "Rabbi Sally [Priesand]," America's first woman rabbi, worked at Wise Center while she was a student at Cincinnati's Hebrew Union College. Many Zion Temple members recount that the building had been constructed of stone imported from Palestine. And in fact, the cornerstone of the Wise Center was brought from Palestine as a reflection of the Zionist ideology of its rabbi in 1927. Members of the maintenance staffs at both Southern and Zion Temple, in addition to being aware of the history of their churches, also speak with justifiable pride about the special work and creativity that it takes to keep these old buildings in working order.

Most of the church members consulted for this study maintained that the space in which their congregations exist is extraneous to the encounter with God which goes on there. Indeed, these congregations demonstrate little need to impose emblems of their own upon the former synagogue spaces beyond those few essentials necessary to the practice of their faith. Still, although these church members deny the importance of physical space, most do seem to take great pride in the structures of their church homes as something out of the ordinary. They give the impression that these spaces, with their suggestion of grandeur and their notable attention to detail, are appropriate spaces to dedicate to God. All agree that the extra touches add a measure of beauty to the church environment.

The particular religious pedigree of these church buildings appears to have had no impact upon the expression of worship and belief acted out in their sanctuaries. In fact, Jewish observers familiar with the formality and restraint typical of most American Jewish worship settings can only be struck by the contrast between the driving percussion, the rocking choir, the powerful almost singsong sermonic intonation, and the congregants sometimes being overcome by the spirit of God which mark the worship in these sanctuaries today, and the staid and restrained behavior characteristic of the Jewish worshippers who once occupied these pews. Similarly it is jarring for Jewish visitors to Zion Temple to see (or even think about) the space of the Torah ark, which holds so much meaning in Jewish religious expression, being used as a baptismal pool.[31]

The contrast between these two modes of worship behavior carried on in the same place, although at different times, raises intriguing questions about the religious and social experience of African Americans and American Jews in this country. As home first to some of Cincinnati's Jewish congregations and now to these black churches, these buildings have provided the setting for two different groups both seeking to define a religious and ethnic identity that can give positive meaning to their distinctive, minority presence in American society. That these groups have found such different modes of religious expression speaks powerfully to the very different economic, social, and political experiences that have informed the ways in which African American and American Jews have chosen to express their religiosity in an American religious setting.

Given the difference in religious expression across these two groups, together with the conflictual context in which we have become accustomed to understanding the relationship between blacks and Jews, the positive interest that so many of today's church members show toward the Jewish past of their church buildings becomes that much more noteworthy. The meaning of these buildings for their current occupants varies from individual to individual, but the words and analysis of Eartell Brownlow provide an illuminating guide to understanding the ways in which these buildings, built as the expression of another group's identity and status, have become a source of pride and meaning for the African American congregations that have adopted them.

Eartell Brownlow's connection to the history of her church's physical home is both personal and theological. In "The Building We Call Home," Brownlow points out that the three buildings that served the congregation for the first 46 years of its existence "no longer exist." In a series of interviews, Mrs. Brownlow has explained that in addition to the loss of these one-time church buildings, all the homes in which she has lived have also fallen victim to the continuing municipal restructuring of Cincinnati, which has often brought demolition to African American neighborhoods. She has nowhere to return to in search of reminders of her personal and spiritual past. This lack of a physical past of her own prompted her to invest herself in the investigation of the history of the building that had become her church home. With no access to her own material past, she began to find personal connection and meaning to a building whose history of in many ways she has adopted as her own.[32]

In sharing the results of her investigation with those in her church, Brownlow helped many members to reflect with even more appreciation upon the church's physical space and to look upon every detail of its decor as layered with significance. For many, her work tangibly added to the conviction that their church "is a special place."[33] In addition to providing historical information about the former synagogue, Brownlow also offered a metaphysical rendering of the relationship between the Southern congregation and the "building [they] call home." In her paper, Brownlow points out that the years when their congregation was being founded were the very years in which the Adath Israel congregation planned construction of the Lexington Avenue Synagogue: "God was providing a place for Southern's home while we as a church body w[ere] still in the infant stage." The basic Christian premise that the New Testament and dispensation came to displace and build upon the Old is explicit in her observation that "the builders of this building had no knowledge that they were preparing a place where the Son of God, Jesus Christ, would be worshipped."

In a somewhat similar vein, Mother Beulah Phillips of Zion Temple relates that in the 1950s, before their church had even moved out of its storefront space in the West End, she would come up to North Avondale with her son for music lessons at the home of his teacher, Mr. Goldberg. On their journey they would pass the corner of Reading and North Crescent, and she recalls that often when she saw the Wise Center building she would speculate to herself, "What couldn't we do if we had a church?" Though she never dreamed that her church would ever be able to afford anything like the Wise Center, her idle thoughts of the time reinforce her perception now that there was something miraculous in the course of events that brought her community to Reading and North Crescent.[34]

Bishop Phillips is quite clear in expressing his sense that the "hand of God" was present in the transactions that brought his church to their particular corner. Relating to the biblical story that in Canaan the Israelites found "wells that they did not dig and homes that they did not build," he recalls with a kind of wonder how everything that his congregation needed but did not have the resources to build for themselves—classrooms, a fellowship hall, a parking lot, a kitchen—were to be found at Wise Center. Everything that they "had in mind to do" but could not afford, when they came to Wise Center, they found "it was all in place." And somehow "it came to pass" that the congregation was able to secure the funding to acquire it for themselves.[35]

Without speculating on the degree of involvement of God's hand in the events that brought these congregations to these particular buildings, it is striking to note how well these facilities suit their current occupants. With a grandeur and solidity peculiar to economic and social conditions of the times in which they were built, they stand in an urban setting, by and large abandoned by the Jews of Cincinnati. Their large sanctuaries meet the needs of their well-attended Sunday worship but would be too big for the usual Sabbath attendance at today's Adath Israel and Wise Center. Both churches, having added additional school buildings and conducting regular day schools as part of their diverse programming, take full advantage of the institutional facilities they purchased from the Jewish congregations, filling them with a vital religious energy and life. These are buildings that both congregations rightfully call home.

Like Eartell Brownlow, Bishop Phillips and his wife as well as probably most members of these congregations believe that their presence is helping to uncover the true purpose of these buildings in serving in the worship of Jesus Christ. But this theological conviction in no way dampens the rich appreciation, expressed by Eartell Brownlow, for a community that dedicated the Lexington Avenue Synagogue "to the glory of God and [as a] place to be reverent."[36] Indeed the sanctity of these buildings as synagogues has been enriched by the respect and appreciation accorded to their Jewish past by many at the Southern Baptist Church and Zion Temple.

When the Adath Israel congregation left Avondale, they eradicated, or took with them, many of the physical markers of the building's Jewish identity. One of their final acts was to cover the Hebrew inscription, engraved in stone, which surmounted the building's central doorway with cement. Fittingly perhaps, in recent years the cement of 1964 has fallen away, again revealing the words from Psalm 118 which Mrs. Brownlow has translated for her fellow congregants. Today's Avondale is no longer Jewish, street crime is a constant problem, businesses are struggling to find a foothold, cars dominate the environment—much has changed. Yet at the central entry to Cincinnati's Southern Missionary Baptist Church, the old inscription at least remains as true as it ever was: "This Is the Gateway to the Lord."

Notes

1. In April 1998 the Cincinnati City Council voted to rename North and South Crescent Avenues in honor of Fred Shuttlesworth, veteran of the civil rights movement and ally of Martin Luther King, Jr, whose church is further up the street.

2. The small Orthodox North Avondale Synagogue closed in November 1997.

3. For a description of this process in Boston, see Hillel Levine and Lawrence Harmon, *The Death of an American Jewish Community: A Tragedy of Good Intentions* (New York, 1992).

4. For more on this phenomenon see, Karla Goldman and David Kaufman, "Unwitting Commonality," *Boston Globe*, August 1, 1994, p. 11; Albert Ehrenfried, "A Chapter in the Evolution of the Boston Synagogue," *Jewish Advocate*, September 30, 1943.

5. Gerald H. Gamm, "In Search of Suburbs, Boston's Jewish Districts, 1843–1994," in *The Jews of Boston*, ed. Jonathan D. Sarna and Ellen Smith (Boston, 1995), p. 141.

6. For development of the synagogue-center, see David Kaufman, "'Shul with a Pool': The Synagogue-Center in American Jewish life, 1875–1925," Ph.D. dissertation, Brandeis University, 1994.

7. K. K. Bnai Yeshurun, *Year Book*, 1921–22 (Cincinnati, 1921), p. 8.

8. This building was also informally referred to as "Feinberg's Shul," after Louis Feinberg, who served as the congregation's beloved rabbi from 1918 until his death in 1949.

9. Interview with Cheryl North, December 18, 1997.

10. Interviews with Louis Jacobs, Morris Fogel, Betty Levine, Walter Hattenbach. Quotation from interview with Elaine Bloom, April 2, 1998. Real estate advertising in *American Is-*

raelite which began to appear regularly in December 1953 featured numerous listings for "modern" and "up-to-date" homes in Bond Hill, Roselawn, and Amberley village.

11. *American Israelite*, August 10, 1950, p. 1; William Hirschfeld to Adath Israel congregation, August 22, 1950, Adath Israel Nearprint file, Marcus Center of the American Jewish Archives, Cincinnati [AJA].

12. Adath Israel Minutes, April 30, 1958, Microfilm #2198, AJA; interview with Walter Hattenbach, February 6, 1998.

13. Adath Israel Minutes, January 31, 1962.

14. Interview with Walter Hattenbach.

15. Interview with Reverend Henry Larkins, August 10, 1997; Adath Israel minutes, August 29, 1962; September 10, 1962.

16. Lance J. Sussman, "The Suburbanization of American Judaism as Reflected in Synagogue Building and Architecture, 1945–1975," *American Jewish History* 75:1 (1985): 32.

17. Interview with Ted Schwartz, February 18, 1998.

18. Interview with Reverend Harry Larkins.

19. Adath Israel minutes, September 10, 1962.

20. Interview with Morris Fogel, January 5, 1998; see photographs of "Deconsecration Service" in possession of Adath Israel congregation.

21. Interview with Eartell Brownlow, April 1, 1998; interview with Elaine Bloom.

22. Interview with John Benjamin, August 20, 1997; interview with Rabbi Albert Goldman, June 30, 1997.

23. Interview with Bishop Jasper Phillips and Beulah Phillips, February 20, 1998.

24. Interviews with Benjamin, Phillips, Goldman.

25. Interview with Florence Arenstein, March 31, 1998; interviews with Benjamin, Phillips. *American Israelite*, February 1973, June 1973.

26. Interview with Pastor C. Dennis Edwards I, November 4, 1997.

27. Interview with Jasper and Beulah Phillips.

28. Ibid.

29. Eartell Jeter Brownlow, "The Building We Call Home," unpublished paper written for the Southern Baptist Missionary Church, November 21, 1993.

30. Interview with Jasper and Beulah Phillips.

31. Florence Arenstein, former administrator of Wise Temple, remembers that she was taken aback when she learned of the church's plans for the ark: "It's a strange feeling when something you're very familiar with and is part of you is used for such a kind of an alien thing." Interview with Arenstein.

32. Various interviews with Eartell Jeter Brownlow.

33. Interview with Ozell Davis, August 5, 1997; interview with Eartell Brownlow, April 1, 1998.

34. Interview with Jasper and Beulah Phillips.

35. Ibid.

36. Brownlow, "The Building We Call Our Home."

"The Jew" in the Haitian Imagination

Pre-Modern Anti-Judaism in the Postmodern Caribbean

Elizabeth A. McAlister

Europe and the Jews: A Mythological Blueprint for Demonization

Each year in Haiti the Holy Week of Easter sets the stage for spiritual dramas of remembrance, performed in carnivalesque street theater throughout the country. While Catholics reenact the Passion of Jesus and enter with him into his tribulation and resurrection, some practitioners of the Afro-Haitian religion called Vodou organize enormous musical parades called Raras and take to the streets for the spiritual warfare that becomes possible when the angels and saints remove to the underworld, along with Jesus, on Good Friday. The cast of characters who have a hand in the week's events include the deities of Vodou—especially Baron Simitye, the Vodou "Lord of the Dead"—the *zonbi* (recently dead) who are his wards, and also Jesus, the two thieves crucified with him, a couple of Haitian army officers who secretly witnessed the resurrection, Pontius Pilate and the Romans, Judas, and "the Jews." The week's ritual events combine the plots and personae of the Christian narrative with the cosmology of various African religions and rehash them in local ritual dramas whose elements draw from the entire history of the Atlantic world, from the European Middle Ages to the contemporary condition of global capitalism in the Americas.[1]

The Haitian Lenten Rara season remembers a certain history of the Americas. Said by Haitians from the town of Leogane to be "an Indian festival," the Raras provide a fleeting yearly remembrance of the 250,000 Tainos who died in the first two years after Christobal Colon's (Christopher Columbus) fateful 1492 arrival in Haiti, known as Aiyti-Kiskeya, the "mountainous land."[2] But this is only the first of many fragmented historical memories. Harnessing the spiritual power of the deities in the Petwo, Lemba, and Kongo branches of Vodou, the Raras also recall and activate religious principles from the African kingdom of Kongo that flourished in the fourteenth and fifteenth centuries. The festival carries Creole memories also, layers of American-side history. Rara parades come to their climactic finish in Easter week precisely because Holy Week was mandated (in 1685, under the Code Noir) to provide a respite from labor for enslaved Africans of the colony. Slavery and the distinctions between freedom and servitude are themes in the Raras and in Vodou, as they are in the Christian story.[3]

Besides remembrances of the Indians, the Africans, and the enslaved Creoles, however, Haitian Holy Week is also an heir to the anti-Judaism of medieval European popular thought. After all, Christobal Colon and the early colonists were products of the religious worldview of the late Middle Ages, when the Inquisition was in full force. In a telling coincidence of history, Colon set sail for what he would call the *outro mondo* (other world) in August of 1492, only three days after the final departure of the Jews from Spain.[4] This was the era during which Spain expelled its entire Jewish population, and the Inquisition reserved special tribunals for any *anusim*, or *conversos*, converted Jews, who were suspected of "Judaiizing."[5] As figures to be manipulated, demonized, or embraced, "the Jews" are marked as the original "Other" of Europe, the very first object of Christendom's projection, marginalization and demonization. Europe's demonization of Jews became a mythological blueprint for the encounter with Native peoples and Africans in the Americas.

Easter week in Haiti tells many histories, then, but it is this last one that interests us here: the demonization by European Christianity of two groups—Jews and black Africans. This work is about how some black Africans (Haitians) have inherited, used, and manipulated European Christian anti-Judaism. I will suggest here that many of the negative images of Vodou draw from and elaborate upon medieval European images of Jews. These flexible popular tropes hinge on the figure of the devil and link the devil first with "the Jews" and then, in colonial Saint Domingue, with the Africans and Afro-Creole Vodouists.[6]

An anthopologist who specializes in Haiti, I was studying the Rara festivals throughout Haiti and came upon a series of obscure rituals and conceptions revolving around notions of "the Jews." In contemporary Haiti, local dramas replay the Christian ritual cycle of death and resurrection at Holy Week and represent the symbolic presence of Judas and of "the Jews." The way their present-day descendants portray and perform "the Jew," however, tells a complicated and ambiguous story.

The story is not simply about a one-directional process of "Othering" and demonizing a conquered people. I am also interested in the agency of the disenfranchised, in their expressions, reactions, and representations. Some present-day practitioners of Vodou manipulate the inherited, demonized images of "the Jew" in both alarming and creative ways. In the course of Easter week, "Jews" are demonized and burned in effigy by some—but they are also honored and claimed by others as forefathers and founders of the Rara bands. Various Rara leaders embrace the identity of "the Jew" and claim a sort of mystical Jewish ancestry. In accepting the label of "Jew, "these Rara leaders might be understood as taking on a mantle of denigration as a kind of psychic resistance. In carving out a symbolic territory as "Jews," they symbolically oppose the powers that historically have sought to exploit them—the Haitian Catholic elite.

Through the image of Jews in the Haitian imagination, we can interpret the process of domination that married Christianization and anti-Semitism to a process of racialized capitalist expansion in the Americas. The imaginary reserved for European "demonic" Jews is portable and easily transferred into the Indian and African peoples of the Atlantic world. But myths, by their nature, create imminent and shifting imaginaries, less easily controlled by orthodoxy. Exploited peoples embraced the image of the Jew and creatively performed oppositional dramas in which they critique the morality of Christianity and their own place in the class structure.

Postmodern Peasants: Rara and Class in Haiti

The entire Lenten season is politically charged for Haitian society as the annual period in which peasant-class people are sanctioned by tradition to parade and sing. Rara begins right after Carnival on Ash Wednesday and builds throughout Lent until Easter weekend. Occurring in multiple localities, Rara's Easter week parades represent the largest popular gatherings of Haitian *pèp-la*, (the people, the folk). Groups of fifteen to several hundred people play drums and bamboo horns, dance along the roads, and stop traffic for miles in order to perform rituals for Vodou deities at crossroads, bridges, and cemeteries. Rara underscores the opposition of Vodou and Catholicism because of Rara's boisterous public presence during the period of Lent, a Catholic time of solemnity and self-deprivation.

Given the drastic disparity of wealth in Haiti, the appearance of thousands of peasant-class people in public space is inherently a deeply charged moment, considered "dangerous" both culturally and politically by dominant groups. For members of the educated enfranchised classes, hundreds of noisy people celebrating in the streets conjure an image of their nightmarish fantasies about mass popular uprising. As a large-scale popular festival, Rara is structurally oppositional to the dominant classes who make up the Haitian enfranchised minority: the literate, monied classes in their various aspects, who have historically depended on the Haitian army and U.S. support to maintain power.

It has long been routine to speak of Haiti as being a "divided society" comprised of two major classes: the rural "peasants" and the French-identified "elite." This cliché oversimplifies a complex historical process and the resulting heterogeneities of the various class actors in that country. The opposition also obscures the intimacy that characterizes the contact between the powerful and those they dominate.[7] It *does*, however, refer to a definite and blatant divide in Haitian society: between a politically and economically enfranchised minority and a disenfranchised, exploited majority. The root of Haitian inequality began in colonial plantation slavery and subsequent devastating economic policies after independence in 1804. Agricultural goods produced with the simplest technology by a growing peasantry were and still are taxed at customs houses and provide the bulk of government revenues. This basic scenario of an overtaxed, unrepresented nonliterate peasantry exploited by an urban bourgeoisie remains unchanged to the current time. An estimated .8 percent of the Haitian population currently owns 44.8 percent of the wealth.[8]

The classes who have historically performed Rara and who still make up the majority of Rara participants are the mass of the black peasantry and, recently, the urban poor. Not unlike other peoples of the so-called developing world, their essentially premodern peasant condition now lies embedded in the postmodern context of global capital. The Haitian nation-state is a virtually powerless entity on the international stage, and the peasantry and urban poor are caught in a system that constitutes them as the lowest link in a globalized capitalism. Perhaps the most crucial factor in upward mobility today is access to family and resources from *lòt bò dlo* (the other side of the water)—New York, Miami, or other points in the Haitian diaspora. Haitian transmigrants send home an estimated $100 million a year to families and small businesses.[9] Following the realities of transnationalism, Rara parades are also dotted with *djaspora*, (literally, "diasporas"), the returning townspeople from abroad who come to participate in the festival during precious vacation weeks off from work.

"Heat Up the Rara": Mystical Contracts and Community

Most Rara bands are affiliated with *ounfo* (temples) of Afro-Haitian religion, as well as with secret societies called Bizango and Shanpwel. Rara can be read as an annual ritual period when the spiritual work of the *ounfo* is taken into public space. In this sense, Rara is a peripheral branch of Afro-Haitian religion known nowadays as Vodou. This religious culture of the Haitian majority consists of a fluid, inherited, oral tradition of relationships with deities from various African societies, as well as relationships with ancestors.

The major historical contributors to the creolized system called Vodou were the cultures of Dahomey, Yoruba, and Kongo, with pockets and influences from numerous other ethnic groups among the enslaved Africans who began to arrive in Hispaniola as early as 1512. When the French gained control of the territory in 1697, the French style of Catholicism of the later colony was superimposed onto the Spanish Catholicism of the early period. The Africans re-created their beliefs and practices in a complex process of creolization, embracing parts of Catholicism as well as elements of Freemasonry, French occultism, and African Islam.[10]

Vodou is concerned most fundamentally with the healing arts, in physical, psychological, and spiritual realms. Anthropologist Karen McCarthy Brown convincingly argues for the centrality of healing to Vodou and that healing must in turn be understood in terms of a cultural definition of personhood. As individuals are defined by their relationships both to ancestors and to those living in the community, illness is always approached through a careful consideration of imbalance in relationships. Treatment is effected by attending to the webs of relationships that define a person in the Haitian context. The spiritual work of Vodou has to do with *chofe* ("heating") life energy and restoring it to balance.[11] There is also an established set of practices related to the forcible manipulation of relationships with others. Vodouists and anthropologists alike distinguish between a *fran Ginen* (literally, "true African") moral system and the immoral practices of the *boko* (sorcerer).[12]

Rara bands parade through public thoroughfares using music, song, small bonfires, and other ritual techniques of Vodou, in order to *chofe* relationships with Vodou *lwa* (deities) who protect and direct the bands. Most Rara bands are under the patronage of a Vodou *lwa*, and participation in a band is a form of spiritual service. Bands visit local cemeteries and serenade the ancestors, sometimes enticing any interested *zonbi* (souls) of the recently dead to join the Rara in a spiritual attachment that will *chofe* the drummers and mystically work to *kraze* ("crash") other neighborhood bands. Rara bands think of themselves as small armies, out on maneuvers to perform mystical work and carve out territory. The bands are often *angaje*, or under a mystical contract to parade for seven years in a row. This serious spiritual engagement strengthens the relationship of the whole community with the *lwa* of Vodou and enhances good fortune and health.[13]

Bwile Jwif: "Burning the Jew" in Effigy

> It was Holy Thursday night in 1993, and my research team and I were out recording and filming a Rara band in the narrow back-streets of Port-au-Prince. We were dancing along down the dark hilly streets at a good clip, on our way to a small cemetery to try to get some *zonbi* to *chofe* ("heat up) the band for the season's climax on Easter. We stopped while the band paid a musical salute to the invisible guardian of the cemetery gates in Vodou. I looked up and noticed a straw dummy sitting on the roof of the house across the street. It was a "Jew" (fig. 10.1).
>
> He was sitting in a chair in the open air, on top of this one-story tin-roofed house. Made of straw and dressed in blue jeans, a shirt, suit jacket, and sneakers, this "Jew" wore a tie and had a pen sticking out of his shirt pocket. His legs were crossed, and over them sat what looked to be a laptop computer fashioned out of cardboard. A cord seemed to run from the computer down into a briefcase that sat by his chair.
>
> I asked around for the *mèt Jwif-la*, its owner. An older man missing a few teeth came forward, offering a calloused, muscular handshake that revealed a life of hard physical labor. He was from the countryside in the South of the island, a migrant to Port-au-Prince. I found myself in the ridiculous position of having to complement him on his work. "Nice Jew you've got there," I said, "*Ou gen yon bèl Jwif la, wi.*" "Oh yes, we leave it up for the Rara band to pass

FIGURE 10.1. *Effigy of a "Jew" waiting to be burned in a Port-au-Prince neighborhood, 1993. Photograph by Elizabeth McAlister.*

by. Tomorrow afternoon we'll burn it," he said. "Aha . . . well . . . great . . . " said my research partners and I, flaring our eyes at each other. I guess nobody told the guy that Jean-Claude Duvalier banned the practice in the 1970s, around the time of a rush of tourism and foreign industrial investment. I bet other people still do it, here and there.

The Easter ritual of burning "the Jew" or burning "Judas" in effigy was practiced until recently by all classes in Haiti. There were many local variations, but usually by Maundy Thursday an effigy was erected in some central location, and at 3:00 on Good Friday it was burned by the local community.[14] This was done in a ritual retaliation against Judas, who betrayed Jesus, or against "the Jews" who "killed Jesus."

The symbol of the Jew surfaced around Easter among all classes in most regions of Haiti. Local peasant communities enacted this carnivalesque theater and so did wealthy plantation households. Thérèse Roumer, a writer from the provincial city of Jérémie, remembered the *Juifs errants*, the "wandering Jews" of her childhood. Her father owned expansive tracts of land in the region and maintained a large family home. A "Jew" was erected at the beginning of Lent. He had stuffed pants and shirt, with a pillow for a head, and he sat in a chair on the veranda by the front door. The idea, said Madam Roumer, was to kick the Jew whenever you went in or out of the door, "say any bad words you had," and scold him for killing Jesus. On the Saturday morning before Easter all of the children from town would find wooden sticks, come to the house to beat him, and then burn him up in a bonfire.[15] Children were exhorted by the grownups to "pray for the conversion of the Jews."[16] The family would then go off to church for some holy water and wash down the verandah.[17]

Most of those intervened remembered that the Jew in effigy was part of a child's game, in which the "Jew" represented Judas himself and was hidden by the adults in the neighborhood. William Seabrook, whose book *The Magic Island* has sustained many critical blows since its publication in 1929, wrote this tongue-in-cheek account, worth reproducing in its entirety:

> On the last bright Easter morning which I spent in Port-au-Prince—this was only a year ago—the Champs de Mars, a fashionable park adjacent to the presidential palace and new government buildings, resembled an untidied battlefield on which scenes of wholesale carnage had been recently enacted.
>
> It was impossible to drive through it without swerving to avoid mangled torsos; it was impossible to stroll through it without stepping aside to avoid arms, legs, heads, and other detached fragments of human anatomies.
>
> It was impossible also to refrain from smiling, for these mangled remains were not gory; they exuded nothing more dreadful than sawdust, straw and cotton batting. They were, in fact, life-sized effigies of Judas and Pontius Pilate's soldiers—done to death annually by naive mobs bent on avenging at

> this somewhat late day an event which occurred in Palestine during the reign of Tiberius.
>
> . . . I had made the acquaintance, so to speak, of one Judas before he betrayed our Lord and fled to the woods. All the little community had contributed toward his construction. He sat propped in a chair outside the doorway. They had stuffed an old coat, a shirt, and a long pair of trousers with straw, fastened old shoes and cotton gloves, also stuffed, to the legs and arms, and had made ingeniously a head of cloth, stuffed with rags, with the face painted on it and a pipe stuck in its mouth. They introduced me to this creature very politely. They were rather proud of him. He was Monsieur Judas, and I was expected to shake hands with him. You see—or perhaps you will not see unless you can recall the transcendental logic which controlled the make-believe games you used to play in childhood—that Judas had *not yet* betrayed Jesus. He was, therefore, an honored guest in their house, as Peter or Paul might have been.
>
> And so their righteous wrath will be all the more justified when they learn on Saturday morning that Judas has turned traitor. Then it is that all the neighbors, armed and shouting, the men with machetes and *coco-macaque* bludgeons, the women with knives, even more bloodthirsty in their vociferations, invade the habitation where Judas has been a guest, demanding, "*Qui bo' li*?" (Where is the traitor hiding?)
>
> Under the bed they peer, if there is a bed; behind doors, in closets—I happened to witness this ceremony in a city suburbs, where they do have beds and closets—while members of the household aid in the search and make excited suggestions. But nowhere can Judas be found. It seems that he has fled. (What has really occurred is that the head of the house has carried him off during the night and hidden him, usually in some jungle ravine or thicket close on the city's edge. Judas usually takes to the forest as any man would, fleeing for his life. But this is not always predictable. A Judas has been known to hide in a boat, in a public garage yard, even under the bandstand in that Champs de Mars whither so many of them, wherever found, are dragged for execution.)
>
> So tracking Judas becomes a really exciting game. A group collects, shouting, beating drums, marching in the streets, racing up side-alleys; meeting other groups, each intent on finding the Judas planted by its own neighborhood, but nothing loath to find some other Judas and rend him to pieces *en passant*. Crowds may be heard also crashing and beating through the jungle hillsides. It is rather like an Easter-egg hunt on a huge and somewhat mad scale.[18]

Other cultures practice the tradition of burning Judas in effigy at Easter week, notably in Mexico and other parts of Latin America.[19] The practice may stem from the liturgical dramas, or "evangelizing rituals," practiced by early Jesuit missionaries to the Americas. The Jesuits are known to have staged elaborate dramas in the communities where they worked, playing out scenes from Jesus' life.[20] Passion Plays spread the idea of Jews as "Christ-killers." According to this ritual logic, Judas, who betrayed Jesus, is conflated with "the Jews" who "mistreated Jesus," making all Jews into "Judases."[21] The supposed role that the Jews played in the Crucifixion, as described in the New Testament, embellished in legend, and potrayed on the stage, was familiar to both cleric and layman. It was a good starting point for moral teaching.

The idea that "the Jews killed Jesus" is rooted, of course, in the New Testament, which can be read as a polemic that displays the anti-Judaism of the early Church toward the Jews. Sander Gilman has argued that the negative image of the difference of the Jew found in the Gospels (and especially, we might note, the figure of Judas) became the central referent for all definitions of difference in the West.[22] During the medieval period European Christianity produced the image of "the demonic Jew," an inhuman creature working directly for Satan. Joshua Trachtenberg writes in his classic work *The Devil and the Jews* that "the two inexorable enemies of Jesus, then, in Christian legend, were the devil and the Jew, and it was inevitable that the legend should establish a causal relation between them."[23] By the medieval period the devil was cast as the master of the Jews, directing them in a diabolical plot to destroy Christendom.

In the medieval Passion Plays that set the tone for the popular Christianity of Christobal Colon's Europe and the colonial Jesuit missions, the Jews are handed the entire weight of blame for Jesus' death, and Pontius Pilate and the Roman participants in the narrative fade into the background.[24] Medieval European Mystery Plays were popular liturgical dramas, reenacting various scenes from scripture. They grew into village festivals performed in marketplaces and guildhalls, taking on the "secular, boisterous, disorderly and exuberant life of the folk."[25] In *Le Mystere de la Passion*, a fourteenth-century French play depicting the Crucifixion, the Jews are the villains of the piece, egged on by devils. In the climax the devils instigate Judas to betray his master, and they howl with glee when they are successful.[26] The idea of Jews as demonic "Christ-killers" is enhanced throughout the medieval period, forming a central theme of anti-Judaism that will authorize the persecution of Jews during the Inquisition.

The clergy of the Spanish period, like the French that followed them, were small in number and faced the overwhelming project of establishing and maintaining Christianity. It is likely that the Jesuit, Dominican, and Franciscan missionaries in Hispaniola made use of the theatrical tactics deployed by their colleagues in New Spain to convert the Native Americans. In that colony, large-scale popular dramas were modeled after the Mystery Plays of Spain and France, depicting the winners and losers in the Christian story and making clear parallels to the colonists and the conquered. Judas, "the Jews," Jesus, and the apostles made for casts of characters that would illustrate the larger drama of power relations at the start of the colonial enterprise.[27] The Christian story and theatrical public rituals generated narratives meant to authorize and display the technologies—chains and whips—of servitude. European Christendom dramatically set itself up as a sole civilizing force against the barbaric and demonic forces of Jews, Native Indians, and Africans.[28]

The historical antecedents of the Haitian *bwile jwif* ("Jew burning") rituals may well be in these sorts of Passion Plays that referenced the events of the Spanish Inquisition. In the late fifteenth and sixteenth centuries—as the Spanish were establishing the slave trade to the colonies—*conversos* believed to have secretly practiced Judaism were sentenced to be burned alive in Spain. Jews in hiding were sentenced in absentia and burned in effigy.[29] These auto-da-fé practices were likely the model upon which the Latin American rituals are based. Although the Inquisition was never organized in Hispaniola, the Easter effigy burnings are most likely rooted in Inquisition symbolism and its attendant public ritual terror.[30]

Other bits of cultural flotsam and jetsam may have trickeld down from Inquisition history. The *lwa* Papa Gede, in his own code language, calls the pig "Jwif." Surely Papa Gede is remembering one of the most common caricatures of the Jew in the Middle Ages, the the notorious figure of the *Judensau*, in which a sow feeds her Jewish offspring with the devil looking on.[31] Perhaps the expression is an inverted survival of the fifteenth-century term for the Spanish *conversos,* who were called *marranos* (swine; pig) after the Christians conquered the Moors.[32]

Anti-Jewish sentiment was an implicit part of the ruling process of the French colony of Saint-Domingue. The Church itself was among the largest of the slave-owning landholders in the colony, and it won an advantage with the establishment of the Code Noir.[33] This edict by King Louis XIV mandated the planter class to baptize and Christianize the slaves, just as it simultaneously outlawed the exercise of any religion other than Catholicism. The Jesuits, working as an order before the 1704 official establishment of their mission, manifested a marked dislike of Jews and their religion. In 1669 they appealed to the Crown representative to take actions against "tavern keepers, undesirable women and Jews."[34] In 1683 the Church induced King Louis XIV to expel all Jews from the colony and to impose a religious test on new immigrants.[35]

It would have been only logical, then, for the colonial clergy to take the image of the Jews as an evil, anti-Christian force and hold them up in comparison with early forms of Vodou—the real threat to Christianity in the colony. Although the Christianization of the Africans in colonial Saint Domingue was a halfhearted and badly organized enterprise, enslaved people were mandated by the Code Noir to be baptized, and they sporadically attended mass, married, and were directed in catechism.[36] In their efforts to control the enslaved, the clergy preached Paul's letters to the Ephesians and other biblical passages exhorting slaves to obey their masters.[37] Most of their practical worries revolved around the "superstition" of the Africans, their magical abilities, and their knowledge of poison, for greater than the fear of diabolism was the more imminent threat of uprising and rebellion. Numerous regulations were passed in the colonial period and after, making various religious and magical practices illegal. Underlying anti-Vodou sentiment was the notion that the Africans, like the Jews before them, were acting in consort with the devil.

The litany of charges that were leveled against Jews in medieval Europe were transferred wholesale onto the Vodouist. The list of devilish crimes that were attributed to European Jews was an elaborate series of evil activities aimed at destroying Christendom. Jews were accused of a range of magical crimes, from superstition, sorcery, and desecration of the host, all the way to ritual murder, the drinking of Christian blood, the eating of human flesh, and poisonings.[38] It is striking that this list is replicated in the colony, targeting Africans and Creoles of Saint Domingue.

Like the *marranos*—converted Jews constantly under suspicion of "Judaizing"—African converts to Christianity were suspected of sorcery. Joan Dayan writes of the late eighteenth century, "It seemed as if the more Christian you claimed to be, the more certainly you could be accused of conniving with the devil."[39] A decree passed in 1761 complained that slaves' religious meetings at night in churches and their catechizing in houses and plantations were actually veiled opportunities for prostitution and marronage. Slaves who had taken on roles of "cantors, vergers, churchwardens, and preachers" were charged with "contamination" of sacred relics with "idolatrous" intentions.[40] Africans requested to be baptized over and over, believing in the mystical properties of the rite, or wishing to attend the accompanying feast.[41]

The legal codes from the colony to the present criminalize numerous practices of sorcery, linking the devil with the Africans and Creoles. A decree passed in 1758, for example, prohibited the use of "*garde-corps* or *makandals*."[42] Still in use today as *pwen* (literally "points"), these "body-guards" were objects infused with spiritual force, directed to protect their wearers. Makandal was also the name of the famous maroon leader in the Haitian revolution. An adept botanist as well as a revolutionary, Makandal was convicted of instigating a campaign of poisoning planters' wells in 1757, during which more than 6,000 whites were poisoned.[43] Besides being labeled superstitious, sorcerers, poisoners, and false Christians, Africans and Creoles were accused of stealing and desecrating the host, drinking blood, and cannibalism, charges that rounded out and replicated the litany of anti-Christian charges against Jews.

Satan's Slaves: Vodouists in the Catholic Imaginary

Throughout Haitian history, the Catholic clergy and the enfranchised classes have cast Vodou as a cult of Satan, a complex of African superstitions to be purged from the beliefs of the Haitian majority. In cycles of violent repression, Vodou practitioners have been jailed, tortured, and killed, and sacred objects have been burned. Using the image of slavery so salient to a population once enslaved and perpetually negotiating its sovereignty, the Church's antisuperstition campaigns targeted Vodouists as slaves of Satan, who is himself working to contaminate and destroy Christianity. Consider this rhetoric from a Haitian catechism of the antisuperstition campaigns of the 1940s:

—Who is the principal slave of Satan?

The principal slave of Satan is the oungan. [Vodou priest]

—What names do the oungan give to Satan?

The names the oungans give to Satan are the lwa, the angels, the saints, the dead, the twins.

—Why do the oungan take the names of the angels, the saints, and the dead, for Satan?

The oungan give the names angels, the saints, and the dead, to Satan to, deceive us more easily.

—Do we have the right to mix with the slaves of Satan?

No, because they are evil-doers and liars like Satan.[44]

In Haitian cultural politics, Catholicism has positioned itself against Vodou as an official, European, legitimate, orthodox tradition associated with ruling power and authority. Vodou occupies an oppositional space which is Creole, home-grown, unorthodox, diverse, and by extension illegitimate, impure, evil, and satanic. Politically, then, the two traditions have been constructed as polar opposites. The Lenten period becomes an interesting and tense time during which Catholic and Vodou practices clash. The performance of Rara during Lent, within the Roman Catholic yearly calendar, reveals its historical evolution as a festival celebrated in a world dominated by Catholicism. The Rara festival unfolded in an Afro-Creole cultural space juxtaposed against a Catholic order, and its performance each year underscores the political oppositions between the two symbolic systems.

The political uses each tradition makes of the other is only the most public face of culture, however, and obscures the complex interactions between the traditions, the ways they combine themselves, and the ways individual people combine them in practice. Focusing on their political opposition obscures the dialectic figuring and reconfiguring inherent in historical processes of creolization. Writing on Afro-Cuban religion, David H. Brown points out that "An overemphasis on 'religion,' the binary positioning of 'African' and 'European/Catholic' systems, and the stark racial opposition of 'white' and 'black' limits our comprehension of the multiplicity of experiences, influences, and roles Afro-Americans *chose* in complex Caribbean creole societies. 'African' and 'European' interacted less as static capsules than as historical processes."[45]

American cultures evolved through processes of creolization, wherein cultural tropes and symbols shift and reconfigure themselves within unequal power relations. Both the Afro-Haitian religion and the Catholicism that evolved in Haiti were constructed in dialectical relation to each other. To a significant degree, Vodou and Catholicism each has incorporated the other into its philosophies and practices. Each tradition is constitutive and revealing of the other.

Cultural complexes that evolve in unequal relations of power take on a process similar to the culture wars between "high" and "low" culture articulated by Stallybrass and White:

> A recurrent pattern emerges: the "top" attempts to reject and eliminate the "bottom" for reasons of prestige and status, only to discover, not only that it is in some way frequently dependent upon the low-Other . . . but also that the top includes that low symbolically, as a primary eroticized constituent of its own fantasy life. The result is a mobile, conflictual fusion of power, fear, and desire in the construction of subjectivity; a psychological dependence upon precisely those others which are being rigorously opposed and excluded at the social level.[46]

Institutional Catholicism depends on its opposition to Vodou, for it is its position against what is impure and illegitimate that strengthens Catholic virtue in Haiti. In the Christian story, the trope of the Jew is used by the enfranchised classes as a kind of fantasy "low-Other" that authorizes Catholic bourgeois superiority. The equation of non-Christians with Jews gave bourgeois Haitians one more cultural difference between themselves and the nonliterate Vodouists. Besides being dark-skinned, nonliterate, Creole-speaking peasants, they also were pagans, and anti-Christians. Symbolically, they were Jews. Haitian Catholics came to depend, in a sense, on the trope of the Vodouist-Jew as a force to oppose and exclude, a way to define the Catholic self through a negative referent.

The myths and rituals that surface at Easter yield particularly illustrative readings for the way in which both "high" and "low" culture groups reach for symbols and embrace, perform, and transform them in the ongoing process of negotiating power. The performances of Easter myths range from the strictest Catholic mass to the popular Easter rituals sanctioned by Catholicism, all the way to the oppositional readings of Rara bands.

Theologically, Easter is the most important holiday in the Catholic calendar, celebrated in Haiti both in official church mass and in popular rituals. One of the Easter traditions practiced by all classes is the reenactment, after church on Good Friday, of *Les Chemins de la Croix*, the stations of the cross. For this Passion Play a series of ritual stations are set in place, and barefoot pilgrims, some dressed in burlap, visit each station, fasting, without water, reciting prayers before each spot. A local man plays the role of Jesus, and other actors portray other figures in the story. The Passion Play was honed as a genre in medieval Europe, and this somber drama drawn from the four gospels still enacts itself in numerous locations on Good Friday all over the Christian world.[47]

At the same time that Catholics engage in these Easter rituals, Rara bands are busy parading through public thoroughfares. In fact, some Raras deliberately plan to walk past churches on Sunday to annoy the Christians. In 1993 a priest in Pont Sonde ended mass with the admonishment, "Don't go in the Rara," worried he might lose some parishioners to this "devil's dance." In the imaginary of the Haitian bourgeoisie, Vodouists have been cast as evil slaves in Satan's army. As anti-Christians, they became symbolic Jews.

> "If you go in the Rara, you are a Jew."
>
> A Rara band called "Ya Sezi" ("They will be surprised") walked for miles all day on the Good Friday of 1993, along the banks of the Artibonite River. They were on their way to the compound of Papa Dieupe, a wealthy landowner in the region, and also the "Emperor" of a Shanpwèl society. My team and I had chosen Papa Dieupè's as the best place to be for Rara; we figured we could comfortably stay put in one place and watch the bands come to salute the "big man."
>
> Ya Sezi's entrance was spectacular for a sleepy country day. We could hear the *banbou* blowing for miles, and children would run through and breathlessly announce that the band was coming to salute the Emperor. They came up the path, and did the ritual salutes for the Vodou spirits living in the trees in the compound, and then turned to salute Papa Dieupe's "children" in the society. Finally, after they'd played until about midnight, Papa Dieupe himself emerged from his small house and received them.
>
> After playing music in the compound for much of the night, the group slept, and awoke early Saturday morning to play and "warm up" before they left. While the musicians played, each of the dancers (who were all women) took turns holding the whip belonging to the leader, and ran in circles through the compound. The other dancers set off in hot pursuit, their dresses streaming out behind. Papa Dieupe told me they were taking turns being Jesus, running from the "Jewish soldiers." Pilate's Roman soldiers were nowhere in evidence, but rather had been collapsed into a new bloodthirsty figure of "Jewish soldiers." Comically enacting Jesus' suffering on his walk to Calvary, the Rara members were amusing themselves by portraying both Jesus and his "killers," "the Jews." [48]

During the Easter Rara festivals, the story of Jesus' life and death replays itself in the churches and streets of the country, and Jesus, Judas, and the Jews join the spirits of Vodou as dramatic characters to be performed and interpreted. Good Friday in particular becomes a day of stark contrasts between the *fran Katolik,* who pray, fast, and walk the stations of the cross, and the Rara bands, who parade noisily through the streets singing and working to *chofe* ("heat up") relationships with Vodou spirits and the recently dead. Catholic Haitians make a clear connection between the exuberant celebrations of Rara on the anniversary of Jesus' death, and "the Jews who killed him." A popular expressions is, *Ou al nan Rara, se Jwif ou ye*, "If you go in the Rara, you are a Jew."

Haitian Catholicism equates Vodou, the devil, and "the Jews who killed Christ," and we can see how celebrating Rara in the streets on the day Christ died "makes you a Jew" in the Catholic view. Even some university-educated Haitians have a vague concept that "Rara is a Jewish festival." At a fancy cocktail party in the wealthy enclave above Petionville I was introduced to a young Haitian architect from the mulatto class. "Studying Rara?" he asked incredulously. "Well, you'll find that it's a Jewish thing." Pressed on how a Jewish festival could have found its way through history to be adopted by the Haitian peasantry, the man shrugged his shoulders and reached for his rum punch.

Every Rara member I interviewed, on the other hand, remembered that Rara "came from Africa," with the slaves. This seems a clear historical fact: Rara continues and extends a number of African cultural principles, including the centrality of community enterprise, relationships with the ancestors and the deities, a kind of politics of "big-man-ism," the use of natural sites for spiritual work, as well as the performative African-based drumming, call-and-response singing, and dance in public festival.

After establishing the African roots of the festival, however, Rara leaders would invariably go on to articulate the idea that Rara was linked to the Jews. Many of them cited the precise origin of Rara as the celebration of the Crucifixion itself. "It was the Jews who crucified Christ who made the first Rara." One *oungan* explained it this way:

> Long ago, after they finished nailing Jesus to the cross, the soldiers who did that saw that it would be even more satisfying to put out a Rara to show that they were the winners. They put out a Rara, they made music. They were rejoicing, singing and dancing.[49]

This idea that "the Jews who crucified Christ" rejoiced and made the first Rara was related to me over and over by Rara members. The historical genealogy of the notion is obscured here, as is the cultural history of most dispossessed groups. Yet one returns to the Passion Plays of the early church, modeled after the ones in medieval France, England, and Germany. The Jews are the central villains of these stories and are directed by demons and devils hovering in the background. Together the devils and the Jews convince Judas to betray his master, and celebrate when they are successful. Joshua Trachtenberg describes it thus: "Around the cross on which Jesus hangs the Jews whirl in a dance of abandon and joy, mocking their victim and exulting in their achievement." This explicit scenario of a crucified Christ surrounded by joyful, dancing Jews celebrating their victory makes its way from the popular European imaginary to become a memory of former African slaves.[50] Another Rara president reiterates:

> Rara is what they did when they crucified Jesus, on Good Friday. At that point, all the Jews were happy. They put the Rara out, they masked, they danced, they dressed in sequins, they drank their liquor and had fun.[51]

The link between Rara and "the Jews who killed Christ" was strong enough in the Haitian imagination that Rara members became Jews in their own rememberings. A *oungan* told me that "It was the Jews who came with this tradition. Now it's become our tradition."[52] Another *oungan* provided an explanation that implicitly described how the Africans could have inherited this celebration of the ancient Hebrews. "Rara is something that comes from the Jewish nation. So, mystically speaking, Haitians are descended from Africa. The Africans always kept their mystical rites."[53] In this logic, Africans are equated with the Jews of antiquity, and it is this linkage that explains how Haitians have inherited Rara from the Jews. Through Rara, these Haitians embraced the subversive identity of "the Jew" and see Jews somehow as forerunners of their African ancestors.

When Rara members embrace the negative cultural category of the Jew, the mythology they generate may be understood as a repressed people's subversion of the ruling order. This class resistance to Catholic hegemony is a form of theatrical positioning on the part of the peasants that says "We are the Jews, the enemy of the French Catholic landowners." Like other groups that take on the negative terms ascribed to them by the powerful, Haitians take on a mantle of denigration in the face of a hostile dominant class. Just as "high culture" includes "low culture" symbolically in its self-construction, so here does the "popular culture" include the "elite" in its turn. Laënnec Hurbon understands this dynamic historically as a creative appropriation of cultural goods:

> ... [the slaves'] diverting of Christianity to their own ends ... had nothing to do with the systematic denial of Christianity, nor was it a sign of inadequacy of evangelization, but a process of making off with those elements of Christianity which could be useful in the struggle and in the construction of their new culture.[54]

Vodouists' interpretations of biblical stories can be understood as creative subversions of official discourse. Like the Rastafari of Jamaica, Vodouists are adept orators and creative interpreters of myth and Scripture. Every imaginative Vodou practitioner may offer a new visionary interpretation of Bible and of history. These versions allow Vodouists and Rara members to authorize their own history while positioning themselves, for themselves, in terms of the dominant class and its religious ideology.

Jesus Christ is the subject of much theorizing on the part of Vodouists. In one myth, God created the twelve apostles just after he created the earth and the animals. The apostles were rebellious and challenged God. In punishment, God sent them to *Ginen*, the mythical Africa of Vodou's past and future. The apostles and their descendants became the *lwa*, while a renegade apostle who refused to go to *Ginen* became a sorcerer and took the name Lucifer.[55] Throughout the oral mythologies of Vodou is a clear theme of morality and a distinction between working with the Ginen spirits and working with the forces of sorcery. Usually the sorcerer is also a slave master of captured spirits and souls, and so themes of morality are bound together with philosophical issues of slavery and freedom.

One story I was told creatively posits Jesus as the first *zonbi*, a soul that has been captured and sold in order to work for its owner. Although I have written of this elsewhere, it bears reiterating here. This myth positions Jesus and God as the innocent victims of two unscrupulous Haitian soldiers who secretly witnessed the resurrection. It was related to me by a sorcerer who confided that he knew the techniques of capturing the spirit of the recently dead (*zonbi*) and ordering it to work:

> The whole reason that we are able to raise people after they die goes back to when they crucified Jesus Christ. Christ was sent by Gran Jehovah, by *Gran Mèt* [literally "Great Master"]. He also sent Mary Magdelene, along with two bodyguards for Jesus from the Haitian Armed Forces. When Jehovah gave the password to raise up Jesus from the dead, the soldiers stole the password and sold it. It's been handed down from father to son, which is how I could get it.[56]

Vodou takes what it can use theologically and constantly re-creates itself with fresh material. The Vodouist fits biblical figures into an already existing Afro-Creole scheme. Jesus is problematic for the Vodouist: the heavy catholicizing of the French and, later, the Haitian elite makes Jesus the god of the dominant classes. This story subtly acknowledges the teller's opposition to Christianity: a worker (a Haitian foot-soldier) stole something from Jesus (the god of the elite). The stolen knowledge now becomes a tool for the subordinates, since it is Vodouists who now control the resurrection secrets of God. This tale illustrates how the Vodouist uses oppositional mythology as one of the ongoing weapons in everyday Haitian class warfare.

Rara leaders I interviewed accepted the Catholic label of pagan, Satanist, and Jew and theorized their position in a specific Vodou theology. This view agrees that Rara is anti-Christian. As one leader explained, "Rara is basically against the power of God. Because Rara is what they did when they crucified Jesus, on Good Friday." This view understands Rara to be "against the power of God," in Catholic terms.[57]

On some level, however, God has abandoned Haitians. The president of *Rara Mande Gran Moun* in Léogane explained: "God made the king Lucifer. God commands the sky, and the king Lucifer commands the earth. Everybody who is poor on this earth is in hell."[58] In this interpretation, God rules the heavens but has given Lucifer control over the earth, and humans are actually the political subjects of the king Lucifer. In the face of a class structure divided by access to the means of production but marked in many ways by religious affiliation, the response of the Vodouist is to embrace and creatively rework the identity given them by Catholics.

Commenting directly on the suffering generated by extreme economic exploitation, the figure of Lucifer stands as a kind of moral commentary on the state of Haitian government and its history of class inequality.

Rara leaders construct theology through the appropriation of "high" cultural elements into allegories of empowerment. The stories of the "Jewish Rara" and the "*zonbi* Christ" construct a sort of engagement with the texts of the Catholic dominant classes in which the power of the Vodouists or Rara members is hidden inside the images of demonization. Haitian sorcerers construct themselves as active enemies of the Catholic order, as Jews, or as allies of thieves who stole from God. The narratives support Hurbon's statement that "In the eyes of the Voodooist, his mysticism is his power. Thus it may be correct to say that the Voodoo cult, since its inception with a Creole coloration, is used by Voodoo believers as a power base from which to deal with the power elite."[59]

These myths can be seen as antihegemonic counternarratives that reconfigure histories and genealogies to cast power with the popular classes. It is a common result of repressive contexts that cultural expression will generate double-voiced, allegorical strategies so that the dominant culture is turned back on itself, transformed by the subordinate. The myths generated and performed by Rara reveal how "high" Catholic culture and the "low" Vodou culture are constructed in relation to one another, each mystically exoticizing the other in the ongoing performance of class in Haitian society. Each end of the class spectrum reaches for the figure of "the Jew" to authorize its own power in the imaginary of Haitian class warfare. "The Jew" in Haiti remains largely a figure constructed from the leftovers of medieval Christianity and sustained through Catholic popular culture. Inherited by Afro-Haitians, "the Jew" is creatively re-presented as a figure allied in opposition to the Church, to the landowners, and to the Franco-Haitian elite.

Conclusion

A popular expression of surprise in Haiti roughly corresponds to the phrase "I'll be damned!" It says, simply, *Jesu, roi des Juifs!* "Jesus, king of the Jews." "The Jews" are a stock figure in Haitian popular culture, inherited in the process of Catholic European missionizing that was part and parcel of the Latin American plantation enterprise. A figure used at once as scapegoat and mystical forebear, "the Jew" can also be a comedian who speaks the unspeakable. He shows up in Carnival as *Papa Jwif*, a *Juif errant* (wandering Jew) who delivers satirical political commentary or enacts problematic issues in the community. In Port-au-Prince during the coup that ousted President Aristide, Papa Jwif was both a signal of the AIDS pandemic and a symbol of the corrupt military rulers, diseased beyond redemption. He showed up as a carnival character dying of AIDS. He was surrounded by an entourage of doctors perpetually treating him with useless remedies, coded as U.S. political forces propping up a violent and corrupt regime.

FIGURE 10.2. *Statue of "Saint Moses" holding the tablet containing the ten commandments sits on a Vodou altar in Petite Riviere de l'Artibonite. Photograph by Phyllis Galembo.*

"The Jew" and Judas are most often negative markers, and to be a *jouda* (Judas) is to betray one's friends through gossip. I have heard particularly violent army officers or tonton makoutes described in low tones as *yon Jwif* (a Jew) in their cruelty or barbarism. To be greedy or stingy is to be *kras pase Jwif* (cheaper than a Jew). While most of the negative images of the Jew center on the premodern anti-Judaism focusing on Jews as betrayers and "Christ-killers," the anti-Semitic vocabulary of Jews as hoarders and usurers has crept secondarily into the Haitian cultural vocabulary.

In Vodou, "the Jew" represents a particularly potent magic, centered on the figure of Moses. Haitians have canonized Moses as a Vodou spirit of their own, and handmade ceramic figures of *Sen Moyiz* (Saint Moses) clutching the tablets containing the Ten Commandments sit on the occasional altar (fig. 10.2). With Moses long pictured in popular Christianity as the most famous magician of all time, who transformed serpents into staffs and parted the Red Sea, his magic intrigues Haitian mystics. His magic and the magic of "the Jews" in general is an attractive source of power for disenfranchised Vodouists.

All of the myths, symbols, and rituals centered on the Jew raises the question: What was the historical Jewish presence in Haiti? While Jews never established a lasting community, it is nevertheless possible to discern a thin strand of Haitian

Jewish history. It starts with the genesis of the modern Americas: at least one known recently converted *converso* was aboard Cristobal Colon's ship in 1492, and five others are suspected by historians.[60] Although the forces of the Inquisition excluded Jews, Moors, and other non-Christians from the colonies, "Jews slipped through and managed to live unmolested in loosely organized communities."[61] Most colonial Jews were Sephardim, Iberian Jews of Spanish or Portuguese origin. They often came under false identities, many of them to Hispaniola, which was settled first.[62] Some came directly from France, but others made a circuitous route from initial settlements in Dutch territories, or from Spanish and Portuguese colonies after they established the Inquisition.[63] In a study on Jews in Saint Domingue, Zvi Loker has located Jewish settlements in four zones of Haiti, including 80 Jewish families from Curaçao who settled as traders in Cap François and brought with them a prayer leader.[64]

The relationships between most Christians and the Jews in Saint Domingue were friendly, and Jews became a subgroup of the planter and business class. As a result, the efforts of the Church to create an anti-Jewish popular feeling were not too successful. The demonized images of the biblical Jews do not seem to have been converted into explicit anti-Jewish violence.

In the late nineteenth century, Ashkenazi Jewish families arrived in the country. The pattern for these arrivals and for the descendants of colonial Jews was to assimilate and convert to Catholicism, although many today acknowledge their Jewish ancestry. There were also Jews among the Middle Eastern diaspora of the early twentieth century, who settled in Haiti to become known as *Siryen*, "Syrian," regardless of their nationalities as Syrian, Lebanese, or Palestinian.[65] Later, during the Holocaust, some French and German Jews made their way to Haiti on steamship. While most moved on to North America or Israel, a handful stayed in Haiti to live out the rest of their lives. In perhaps the most delightful symbolic reversal of all, the Haitian legislature in the 1930s declared all Jews to be of African ancestry, since they came from Egypt at the time of the Exodus with Moses. This justified permitting European Jews to settle in Haiti as enfranchised citizens, since the Haitian Constitution had made land ownership possible only to those of African descent.

Despite the small but constant Jewish presence in Haiti, there is no evidence that a synagogue ever existed. Only one Jewish cemetery was established, long ago in the colonial period; it has long since been abandoned.

As Haitians spread further abroad in their own diaspora, the founding of the State of Israel and subsequent gathering of Jews have given Jews a positive image. The Aristide government contracted for a study of Israel and its politics of returning citizenry, viewing Israel as a possible model for recouping the human potential lost in the brain drain of outmigration.

Despite the recent positive valence given to Jews in Haitian thought, the original anti-Judaic tropes of Christianity remain. As this essay has rehearsed, Easter season has always set the stage for the resurfacing of the image of "the Jew," both in popular theater and in the official church. Throughout Christendom, references to Jews were most numerous in sermons delivered during Easter, and the clergy used the Crucifixion story as the moment to illustrate the demonic nature of the "Jew". The rituals of Holy Week provided the clergy with a clear narrative to fix in the minds of the faithful the enormous crime that the Jews had committed against Jesus.[66]

The symbolism of Christianity is extremely powerful; its emergence and predominance as a major religious and political force make this obvious. It is the narrative quality of Christianity that is so powerful, a symbolic progression that makes its way into popular thought from sermons and church services to the Passion Plays, stations of the cross, Carnival parodies and, in Haiti, Vodou myth and Rara theater. These popular, dramatic manifestations demonstrate that Christianity is not just a theological system: "It is also a structure of the imagination; its most striking feature, by which it has gained its hold on a great portion of humanity, is its narrative."[67]

Bruce Lincoln admonishes us that examining "world religions without considering the way they came to enjoy that status is a serious methodological and moral error. In contrast, to probe that history is to understand how a relatively small set of religions have expanded their territory and power at the expense of others."[68] In Haiti, the site of the first American colony, the African survivors of plantation slavery have inherited the anti-Judaism of medieval Europe. At the same time the same Africans and their Creole descendants became targets of a brutal campaign of cultural violence that used anti-Judaism as its blueprint. Today, layers upon layers of historical symbolic residue swirl around together, as "Jews" are both saints and ancestors, pigs and Judases. They can be at once ancient wisdom and global capital, but are always a mystical and exotic power in the Haitian imagination.

Notes

1. This work is indebted to Phyllis Mack and her faculty research seminar at the Rutgers Center for Historical Analysis, where I began this essay as a postdoctoral fellow, and to Albert J. Raboteau and the Northeastern Seminar on Black Religions at Princeton University. I also wish to thank my research partners in Haitian fieldwork: Chantal Regnault, photographer extraordinaire; my assistant, Phenel Colastin; and our driver, Blanc Bazle. Thanks also to Father Antoine Adrien and Holly Nicolas, and to Leslie Desmangles, Joel Dreyfuss, Henry Goldschmidt, Leon-Francois Hoffman, Glenn Ingram, Alan Nathanson, Judith Weisenfeld, and Jeremy Zwelling. I am also most grateful to Deborah Dash Moore and the Young Scholars Program in American Religion and Betsy Trauble and the Wesleyan University Center for the Humanities, and wish that space permitted me to name the participants in these seminars who generously helped me think this story through.

2. Bartolome de las Casas, *History of the Indies* (New York: Harper & Row, 1971). Cited in Catherine Keller, "The Breast, the Apocalypse, and the Colonial Journey," in Charles B. Strozier and Michael Flynn, eds., *The Year 2000: Essays on the End* (New York: NYU Press, 1997), pp. 42–58. Haiti has various name changes: The Amerindian "Aiyti-Kiskeya" was changed by Colon to "Hispaniola," "Little Spain." Later, in 1697, the French named their

colony Saint Domingue, and in 1804, newly independent slaves and people of color returned the land to its original name of Haiti.

3. These themes are taken up in my dissertation; see Elizabeth A. McAlister, "'Men Moun Yo,' 'Here Are the People': Rara Festivals and Transnational Popular Culture in Haiti and New York City." Ph.d. dissertation, Yale University, 1995.

4. Ronald Sanders, *Lost Tribes and Promised Lands: The Origins of American Racism* (1978) (New York: Harper Perennial, 1992), p 90.

5. Cecil Roth, *A History of the Marranos* (Philadalphia, Jewish Publication Society of America, 1932). *Anusim*, Hebrew for "forced ones," has now replaced the English "Crypto-Jews" or the Spanish *conversos*, or "converted Jews," and the more derrogatory *marranos*, or "swine," in Jewish studies literature. See also David M. Gitlitz, *Secrecy and Deceit: The Religion of the Crypto-Jews.* (Philadelphia: The Jewish Publication Society, 1996).

6. Christendom also links the Jews, the devil, and the peoples of the First Nations in New Spain and the United States. See Fernando Cervantes, *The Devil in the New World: The Impact of Diabolism in New Spain* (New Haven, Conn.: Yale University Press, 1994).

7. Michel-Rolph Trouillot, *Haiti, State Against Nation: The Origins and Legacy of Duvalierism* (New York: Monthly Review Press, 1990), p. 81.

8. World Bank, "Memorandum on the Haitian Economy. May 13. Latin American and Caribbean Regional Office, 1981. Cited in Linda Basch, Nina Glick Schiller, and Cristina Szanton Blanc, *Nations Unbound: Transnational Projects, Postcolonial Predicaments and Deterritorialized Nation-States* (Langhorne, Pa: Gordon and Breach, 1994), p. 159.

9. Basch, Schiller and Blanc, *Nations Unbound*, p. 161.

10. See, for example, Joan Dayan, *Haiti, History, and the Gods* (Berkely: University of California Press, 1995), Leslie Desmangles, *The Faces of the Gods: Vodou and Roman Catholicism in Haiti* (Chapel Hill: University of North Carolina Press, 1992); LeGrace Benson, "Some Breton and Muslim Antecedents of Vodou Drapo," in *Sacred and Ceremonial Textiles* (Chicago: Textile Society of America, 1996), pp. 68–75.

11. Karen McCarthy Brown, *Mama Lola: A Vodou Priestess in Brooklyn* (Berkely: University of California Press, 1991).

12. See Serge Larose,. "The Meaning of Africa in Haitian Voodoo," in *Symbols and Sentiments: Cross-Cultural Studies in Symbolism*, ed. I. M. Lewis (London: Academic Press, 1977), pp. 85–116.

13. In Vodou, the soul is made up of different overlapping parts. The *zonbi* is a part of the soul that lingers near the grave. It retains the personality of the living person and can be captured and manipulated. This *zonbi*, the *zonbi astral*, is not connected to a body and is different from the living-dead figures in the popular Haitian and U.S. imagination, so often portrayed by Hollywood. For an elaboration on the uses and construction of *zonbi astral*, see Elizabeth McAlister, "A Sorcerer's Bottle: The Art of Magic in Haiti," in Donald J. Cosentino, ed., *Sacred Arts of Haitian Vodou* (Los Angeles: UCLA Fowler Museum, 1995), pp. 304–21.

14. This is the time of Jesus' death noted in Scripture.

15. Therese Roumer, interview, Petionville, February 16, 1993.

16. George Fouron, personal communication, New Haven, Conn. November 1997.

17. Therese Roumer, interview, Petionville, February 16, 1993.

18. W. B. Seabrook, *The Magic Island* (New York: Literary Guild of America, 1929), pp. 270–72.

19. See, for example, Muriel Thayer Painter, Edward H. Spicer and Wilma Kaemlein, eds., *With Good Heart : Yaqui Beliefs and Ceremonies in Pascua Village* (Tuscon: University of Ari-

zona Press, 1986), and James S. Griffith, *Beliefs and Holy Places: A Spiritual Geography of the Primeria Alta* (Tuscon: University of Arizona Press, 1992), p. 95.

20. See Marilyn Ekdahl Ravicz, *Early Colonial Religious Drama in Mexico: From Tzompantli to Golgotha* (Washington, D.C.: Catholic University of America Press, 1970), and Richard C. Trexler, "We Think, They Act: Clerical Readings of Missionary Theatre in 16th Century New Spain" in Steven L. Kaplan, *Understanding Popular Culture: Europe from the Middle Ages to the Nineteenth Century* (New York: Mouton Publishers, 1984), p. 189–227.

21. In *Judas Iscariot and the Myth of Jewish Evil* (New York: The Free Press, 1992), Hyam Maccoby points out the consistent use of Judas by Christian myth as a symbol for all Jews. "Of all Jesus' twelve disciples, the one whom the Gospel story singles out as traitor bears the name of the Jewish people."

22. Sander Gilman, *The Jew's Body* (New York: Routledge, 1991), p. 18.

23. Joshua Trachtenberg, *The Devil and the Jews: the Medieval Conception of the Jew and Its Relation to Modern Antisemitism.* (1943) (New York: Harper Torchbooks, 1966), p. 20.

24. Trachtenberg, *Devil and Jews*, p. 20.

25. Painter, Spicer and Kaemlein, *With Good Heart*, p. 352.

26. Trachtenberg, *Devil and Jews*, p. 22.

27. Trexler, "We Think, They Act."

28. For a discussion of the conflation of British, Protestant, and Civilized into one identity against Native American "heathens," see James Axtell, *The Invasion Within: The Contest of Cultures in Colonial North America* (New York: Oxford University Press, 1996).

29. See Roth, *History of the Marranos*. The anti-Judaism taught by the Catholic clergy in Haiti bears the characteristics of a classically premodern Jew-hatred centering on the betrayal of Judas. In this logic, Jews are primarily polluters and traitors; there is little reference to the modern anti-Semitic tropes of a Jewish conspiracy of exploitation hinging on issues of capital or usury. See the chapter "From Anti-Judaism to anti-semitism" in Gavin I. Langmuir, *History, Religion and Antisemitism* (Berkeley: University of California Press, 1990), pp. 275–305.

30. On the Inquisition and the Jews in Mexico, see Seymour B. Liebman, *The Jews in New Spain: Faith, Flame and the Inquisition* (Coral Gables, Fla.: University of Miami Press, 1970).

31. Trachtenberg, *Devil and Jews*, p. 26.

32. See Marc Shell, "Marranos (Pigs), or from Coeistence to Toleration," *Critical Inquiry* 11, no. 2 (Winter 1991), 306–35.

33. Carolyn E. Fick, *The Making of Haiti: The Saint Domingue Revolution from Below* (Knoxville: University of Tennessee Press, 1990), p. 278.

34. George Breathett, *The Catholic Church in Haiti (1704–1785): Selected Letters, Memoires and Documents* (Salisbury, N.C.: Documentation Publications, 1982), p. 4.

35. Anne Grene, *The Catholic Church in Haiti: Political and Social Change* (East Lansing: Michigan State University Press, 1993), p. 76.

36. G. Debien, "La Christianisation des esclaves des Antilles francaises aux XVIIe et XVIIIe siecles." *Revue d'histoire de l'Amerique francaise*, 21 (1967), 99–11.

37. Ephesians 6:5.

38. see Joshua, *Devil and Jews*.

39. Dayan, *Haiti, History, and the Gods*, p. 252.

40. Dayan, *Haiti, History, and the Gods*, p. 253.

41. Moreau de Saint Mery [1797] 1958, 1:55. Cited in Desmangles, *Faces of The Gods*, p. 27.

42. Dayan, *Haiti, History, and the Gods*, p. 252.

43. Dayan, *Haiti, History, and the Gods*, p. 252.

44. Cited in Laënnec Hurbon, *Dieu dans le Vaudou Haïtien* (Port-au-Prince: Editions Deschamps, 1987), p. 21.

45. David H. Brown, "Garden in the Machine: Afro-Cuban Sacred Art and Performance in Urban New Jersey and New York," Ph.D. Dissertation, Yale University, 1989, p. 16.

46. Peter Stallybrass and Allon White, *The Politics and Poetics of Transgression* (Ithaca, N.Y.: Cornell University Press, 1986), p. 3.

47. I witnessed such a Passion Play by African American Catholics at Saint Ann's shrine in New Orleans, for example, in 1998.

48. The band Ya Seizi can be heard playing in Papa Dieupe's compound on track 19a of the recording compiled by this author: "Rhythms of Rapture: Sacred Musics of Haitian Vodou," Smithsonian/Folkways Recording SF 40464, 1995.

49. Interview with Papa Mondy Jean, Port-au-Prince, April 1992.

50. A few Rara presidents told me that there was a game, a noisemaker, that the Jews held in their hands and spun at the Crucifixion. This made a noise that came to be called "Rara." Interview with Papa Telemarque, Darbonne, Léogane, March 6, 1993. One notices the possible connection with the noisemakers of Purim. This connection seems obscure; at any rate, it is yet impossible to locate.

51. Rara costumes are elaborately sequined in parts of Haiti. Interview with Simeon, Bel Air, Port-au-Prince, July 30, 1993.

52. Interview with Simeon, Bel Air, Port-au-Prince, March 20, 1993.

53. Interview with Simeon, Bel Air, Port-au-Prince, July 30, 1993.

54. Laënnec Hurbon, *Culture et Dictature en Haiti*: l'imaginaire sous controle (Paris: L'Harmattan, 1979), p. 43.

55. Alfred Metraux, *Voodoo in Haiti* (1959) (New York: Schocken Books, 1972), p. 326.

56. Interview with Papa Dieupe, Artibonite, Easter Sunday 1993.

57. A smiliar symbolics works in Afro-Cuban religion, Lukumi. Unbaptized ritual objects and "working" charms are called *judeo*, "Jewish."

58. Interview with Mayard, Rara Mande Gran Moun, Léogane, March 20, 1993. David H. Brown reports an interesting parallel in the Kongo-derived Palo Monte practices in Cuba. As he constructs a *prenda*, a "working" object, on Good Friday, a Mayombero comments to Brown, "On the day of the week, the week of the year when they are quiet—Good Friday—we are doing our thing." Says Brown, "As spiritual opposites of Christ and the Saints of Olofi and the orichas, they are 'driving nails' on the day of the Crucifixion." Brown, "Garden in the Machine, " p. 375.

59. See Hurbon, *Culture et Dictature en Haiti*, p. 133.

60. Seymour Liebman, *The Jews in New Spain: Faith, Flame and the Inquisition* (Coral Gables, Fla.: University of Miami Press, 1970), p. 31.

61. Clarance Haring, *The Spanish Empire in America*, p. 29. Cited in Liebman, *The Jews in New Spain*, p. 42.

62. Liebman, *The Jews in New Spain*, p. 42.

63. Zvi Loker, "Were There Jewish Communities in Saint Domingue (Haiti)?" *Jewish Social Studies* 44, no. 2 (Spring 1983), 135–46.

64. Loker, "*Jewish Communities*," p. 137.

65. The residence of the Israeli ambassador, at the time of this writing, is at the center of Jewish activities in the country. He invites any practicing Jews and Jewish visitors to Haiti to holiday seders at his home.

66. Bernard Glassman, *Anti-Semitic Stereotypes Without Jews: Images of the Jews in England 1290–1700* (Detroit: Wayne State Press, 1975), 25.

67. Maccoby, *Judas Iscariot,* p. 1.

68. Bruce Lincoln, "Religious Imperialism and Its Victims: Resisting the Erasure of Those Who Resist," conference paper, UC Davis, March 1996.

Selected Bibliography

Akbar, Na'im. *Light from Ancient Africa*. Tallahassee, FL: Mind Productions, 1994.

Ansah-Owusu, David. *Islamic Talismanic Tradition in Nineteenth-Century Asante*. Lewiston, ME: Edwin Mellen Press, 1991.

Ansbro, John. *Martin Luther King, Jr.: The Making of A Mind*. Maryknoll, NY: Orbis Books, 1983.

Asante, Molefe Kete. *Kemet, Afrocentricity and Knowledge*. Trenton, NJ: Africa World Press, 1990.

Austin, Bobby William, ed. *Repairing the Breach*. Dillon, Colorado: Alpine Guild, 1996.

Baer, Hans, and Merrill Singer. *African-American Religion in the Twentieth Century: Varieties of Protest and Accommodation*. Knoxville: University of Tennessee Press, 1992.

Baldwin, James. *The Fire Next Time*. New York: Dell, 1962.

Baldwin, Lewis. "Martin Luther King, Jr., the Black Church, and the Black Messianic Vision." David Garrow, ed., *Martin Luther King, Jr., and the Civil Rights Movement*. Brooklyn, NY: Carlson, 1989.

———. *There Is a Balm in Gilead: The Cultural Roots of Martin Luther King, Jr.* Minneapolis: Augsburg Fortress Press, 1991.

Baron, Salo. "Ghetto and Emancipation." *Menorah Journal* 14, 1928.

Bellah, Robert, et al. *Habits of the Heart: Individualism and Commitment in American Life*. Berkeley: University of California Press, 1985.

Ben-Avdi, Herbert. "Witness 17 Describes Black Hebrew's Fight." *The Jerusalem Post*, February 22, 1972.

Ben-Jochannan, Yosef A. A. *We the Black Jews: Witness to the "White Jewish Race" Myth*. Baltimore: Black Classic Press, 1993.

Benson, LeGrace. "Some Breton and Muslim Antecedents of Vodou Drapo," *Sacred and Ceremonial Textiles*. Chicago: Textile Society of America, 1996.

Bergen, Doris. *Twisted Cross: The German Christian Movement in the Third Reich*. Chapel Hill: University of North Carolina Press, 1996.

Berger, Graenum. *Black Jews in America: A Documentary with Commentary*. New York: Commission on Synagogue Relations, Federation of Jewish Philanthropies of New York, 1978.

Berman Paul., ed. *Blacks and Jews: Alliances and Arguments*. New York: Delacorte Press, 1994.

Black Anti-Semitism and Jewish Racism. Introduction by Nat Hentoff. New York: Schocken, 1970.

Bleich, David. "Black Jews: A Halakhic Perspective." *Tradition* 15, 1972.

Blenkinsopp, Joseph. *Ezra–Nehemiah*. London: SCM Press, 1988.

Bloom, Harold. *The American Religion: The Emergence of the Post-Christian Nation*. New York: Simon & Schuster, 1992.

Blyden, Edward Wilmot. *The Jewish Question*. Liverpool: Lionel Hart and Company, 1898.

Boyarin, Daniel. *Intertextuality and the Reading of Midrash*. Bloomington: Indiana University Press, 1990.

Brackman, Harold. *Ministry of Lies: The Truth Behind the Nation of Islam's "The Secret Relationship Between Blacks and Jews."* New York: Four Walls Eight Windows, 1994.

Breathett, George. *The Catholic Church in Haiti (1704–1785): Selected Letters, Memoires and Documents*. Salisbury, NC: Documentation Publications, 1982.

Brotz, Howard. *African-American Social and Political Thought, 1850–1920*. New Brunswick, NJ: Transaction, 1992.

———. *The Black Jews of Harlem: Negro Nationalism and the Dilemmas of Negro Leadership*. New York: Schocken, 1964.

Brown, Karen McCarthy. *Mama Lola: A Vodou Priestess in Brooklyn*. Berkeley: University of California Press, 1991.

Burkett, Randall. *Garveyism as a Religious Movement: The Institutionalization of a Black Civil Religion*. Metuchen, NJ: Scarecrow Press, 1978.

Burroughs, Nannie Helen. "Unload Your Uncle Toms." *The Louisiana Weekly*, December 23, 1933; repr. in Gerda Lerner, *Black Women in White America*. New York: Vintage, 1973.

Carson, Clayborne. "Rethinking African-American Political Thought in the Post-Revolutionary Era." Brian Ward and Tony Badger, eds., *The Making of Martin Luther King and the Civil Rights Movement*. New York: New York University Press, 1996.

Clarke, John Henrik, ed. *Marcus Garvey and the Vision of Africa*. New York: Vintage Books, 1974.

Clegg III, Claude Andrew. *An Original Man: The Life and Times of Elijah Muhammad*. New York: St. Martin's Press, 1997.

Cone, James. *Martin and Malcolm and America: A Dream or a Nightmare*. Maryknoll, NY: Orbis Books, 1991.

Diner, Hasia. *In the Almost Promised Land: American Jews and Blacks, 1915–1935*. Baltimore: Johns Hopkins University Press, 1995.

Downing, Fred. *To See the Promised Land: The Faith Pilgrimage of Martin Luther King, Jr.* Macon, GA: Mercer University Press, 1986.

Drake, St. Clair. "African Diaspora and Jewish Diaspora: A Convergence and Divergence." Joseph Washington, ed., *Jews in Black Perspectives: A Dialogue*. Boston: University Press of America, 1989.

———. *The Redemption of Africa and Black Religion*. Chicago: Third World Press, 1970.

Drake, St. Clair, and Horace Cayton. *Black Metropolis*. New York: Harper, 1945.

DuBois, W. E. B. *The Souls of Black Folk*. Chicago: A. C. McClurg, 1903; repr. New York: Penguin, 1989.

DuPree, Sherry Sherrod. *African American Holiness Pentecostal Movement: An Annotated Bibiography*. New York: Garland Publishing, 1996.

Ehrenfield, Albert. "A Chapter in the Evolution of the Boston Synagogue." *Jewish Advocate*, September 30, 1943.

Essen-Udom, E. U. *Black Nationalism*. Chicago: University of Chicago Press, 1962.

Farrakhan, Louis. "Farrakhan on Anti-Semitism." *The Final Call*, February 16, 1994.

Fauset, Arthur Huff. *Black Gods of the Metropolis*. Philadelphia: University of Pennsylvania Press, 1971.

Festinger, Leon, Henry Rieken, and Stanley Schachter. *When Prophecy Fails*. New York: Harper and Row, 1956.

Foxman, Abraham. "Farrakhan's True Colors Always Emerge," Letter to the Editor, *Forward*, February 13, 1998.

Freedberg, Sydney. *Brother Love: Murder, Money and a Messiah*. New York: Pantheon, 1994.

Friedman, Murray, with Peter Binzen. *What Went Wrong? The Creation and Collapse of the Black–Jewish Alliance*. New York: Free Press, 1995.

Freedman, Samuel G. *Upon This Rock*. New York: HarperCollins, 1993.

Forman, Seth. *Blacks in the Jewish Mind: A Crisis in Liberalism*. New York: New York University Press, 1998.

Gamm, Gerald. "In Search of Suburbs, Boston's Jewish Districts, 1843–1994." Jonathan D. Sarna and Ellen Smith, eds., *The Jews of Boston*. Boston: Northeastern Univ. Press, 1995.

Gardell, Mattias. *In the Name of Elijah Muhammad: Louis Farrakhan and the Nation of Islam*. Durham, NC: Duke University Press, 1996.

Gates, Jr., Henry Louis. "The Charmer." *The New Yorker*, April 29 and May 6, 1996.

Gavriel HaGadol, Prince, with O. B. Israel. *The Impregnable People: An Exodus of African Americans Back to Africa*. Washington, DC: Communicators Press, 1993.

Geertz, Clifford. *The Interpretation of Cultures*. New York: Basic Books, 1973.

Genovese, Eugene. *Roll Jordan Roll*. New York: Vintage Books, 1974.

Gerber, Israel. *The Heritage Seekers: American Blacks in Search of Jewish Identity*. Middle Village, NY: Jonathan David, 1977.

Gilman, Sander. *The Jew's Body*. New York: Routledge, 1991.

Gilroy, Paul. *The Black Atlantic: Modernity and Double Consciousness*. Cambridge, MA: Harvard University Press, 1993.

Gitlitz, David. *Secrecy and Deceit: The Religion of the Crypto-Jews*. Philadelphia: Jewish Publication Society, 1996.

Glassman, Bernard. *Anti-Semitic Stereotypes Without Jews: Images of the Jews in England 1290–1700*. Detroit: Wayne State Press, 1975.

Goldman, Karla, and David Kaufman. "Unwitting Commonality." *Boston Globe*, August 1, 1994.

Good, Byron. *Medicine, Rationality and Experience*. Cambridge: Cambridge University Press, 1990.

Green Arthur. "Three Warsaw Mystics." *Jerusalem Studies in Jewish Thought*, vol. 13, 1996.

Gregory, Dick. *No More Lies: The Myth and the Reality of American History*. New York: Harper and Row, 1971.

Grene, Anne. *The Catholic Church in Haiti: Political and Social Change*. East Lansing: Michigan State University Press, 1993.

Griggs, Tony. "Angry Black Jews Return Here." *The Chicago Defender*, September 27, 1972.

Haddad, Yvonne Yazbeck, and Jane Idleman Smith. *Mission to America: Five Islamic Sectarian Communities in North America*. Gainesville: University Press of Florida, 1993.

Hanson, Paul. *Isaiah 40–66*. Louisville: John Knox, 1995.

Harding, Vincent. "The Religion of Black Power." D. Cutler, ed., *The Religious Situation.* Boston: Beacon Press, 1968.

Hare, Paul, ed. *The Hebrew Israelite Community*. Lanham, MD: University Press of America, 1998.

Herskovits, Melville. *The Myth of the Negro Past.* Boston: Beacon Press, 1945.

Heschel, Abraham Joshua. *The Prophets.* New York: Harper and Row, 1962.

———."Religion and Race." *The Insecurity of Freedom: Essays on Human Existence.* New York: Farrar Straus and Giroux, 1966.

Heschel, Susannah, ed. *Moral Grandeur and Spiritual Audacity: Essays of Abraham Joshua Heschel.* New York: Farrar, Straus and Giroux, 1996.

Hitchens, Christopher. "The False Messiah Who Hates Jews." *The Spectator*, January 25, 1986.

Jacobs, Steven. *The Hebrew Heritage of Black Africa.* Philadelphia: Boldlee Publishing, 1976.

Jones, Charisse. "Thousands Rally at United Nations on 'Day of Atonement.'" *The New York Times*, October 17, 1996.

Jones, Le Roi. *Blues People: Negro Music in White America.* Westport, CT; Greenwood Press, 1963.

Jones-Farajaje, Elias. *In Search of Zion: The Spiritual Significance of Africa in Black Religious Movements.* Berlin: Peter Lang, 1990.

Jordan, Winthrop. *White Over Black: American Attitudes Toward the Negro.* New York: W. W. Norton, 1968.

Kardiner, Abram, and Lionel Ovesy. *The Mark of Oppression.* Cleveland: World Publishing, 1962.

Khanga, Yelena. *Soul to Soul.* New York: Basic Books, 1990.

King, Kenneth. "Some Notes on Arnold J. Ford and New World Black Attitudes to Ethiopia." Randall Burkett and Richard Newman, eds., *Black Apostles: Afro-American Clergy Confront the Twentieth Century.* Boston: G. K. Hall, 1978.

King, Jr., Martin Luther. "I See the Promised Land," in *A Testament of Hope: The Essential Writings and Speeches of Martin Luther King, Jr.* San Francisco: HarperCollins, 1986.

———.*Strength to Love.* New York: Harper and Row, 1963.

———.*Where Do We Go from Here: Chaos or Community?* New York: Harper and Row, 1967.

Korn, Bertram. "Jews and Negro Slavery in the Old South 1789–1865." *Publications of the American Jewish Historical Society* 1, 1961.

Landes, Ruth. "The Negro Jews of Harlem." *Jewish Journal of Sociology* 9, 1967.

Langmuir, Gavin. *History, Religion and Antisemitism.* Berkeley: University of California Press, 1990.

Larose, Serge. "The Meaning of Africa in Haitian Voodoo." I. M. Lewis, ed., *Symbols and Sentiments: Cross-Cultural Studies in Symbolism.* London: Academic Press, 1977.

Lerner, Michael, and Cornel West. *Jews and Blacks: A Dialogue on Race, Religion and Culture in America.* New York: Penguin, 1996.

Leslau, Wolf. *Falasha Anthology: The Black Jews of Ethiopia.* New Haven, CT: Yale University Press, 1951.

Levine, Hillel, and Lawrence Harmon. *The Death of an American Jewish Community: A Tragedy of Good Intentions.* New York: Free Press, 1992.

Levine, Lawrence. *Black Culture and Black Consciousness.* New York: Oxford University Press, 1977.

Liebman, Seymour. *The Jews in New Spain: Faith, Flame and the Inquisition.* Coral Gables, FL: University of Miami Press, 1970.

Lincoln, C. Eric. *The Black Muslims in America*, Boston: The Beacon Press, 1973.

Loker, Zvi. "Were There Jewish Communities in Saint Domingue (Haiti)?" *Jewish Social Studies* XLV, 1983.

Long, Charles. *Significations: Signs, Symbols and Images in the Interpretation of Religion.* Philadelphia: Fortress Press, 1986.

Lounds, Jr., Morris. *Black Hebrews: Black Americans in Search of Identity.* Washington, DC: University Press of America, 1981.

Lynch, Hollis. "A Black Nineteenth-Century Response to Jews and Zionism: The Case of Edward Wilmot Blyden." Joseph Washington, ed., *Jews in Black Perspectives: A Dialogue.* Boston: University Press of America, 1989.

———. *Edward Wilmot Blyden, Pan-Negro Patriot, 1832–1912.* New York: Oxford University Press, 1967.

MacCahill, Delores. "Black Hebrews Cook Up a Land of Promise in Liberia." *Chicago Sun Times*, April 11, 1969.

Maccoby, Hyam. *Judas Iscariot and the Myth of Jewish Evil.* New York: Free Press, 1992.

Magida, Arthur. *Prophet of Rage: A Life of Louis Farrakhan and His Nation.* New York: Basic Books, 1996.

Malcion, Jose. *How the Hebrews Became Jews.* New York: UB Productions, 1978.

Marable, Manning. "Black Self-Help, Entrepreneurship, and Civil Rights," in *The Crisis of Color and Democracy.* Monroe, ME: Common Courage Press, 1992.

———.*Blackwater: Historical Studies in Race, Class Consciousness and Revolution.* Dayton: Black Praxis Press, 1981.

Marcus, Jacob. The Colonial American Jew, 1492–1776. Detroit: Wayne State University Press, 1970.

Marsh, Clifton. From Black Muslims to Muslims: The Transition from Separatism to Islam, 1930–1980. Metuchen, NJ: Scarecrow Press, 1984.

Meier, August. "The Emergence of Negro Nationalism." *The Midwest Journal* IV, 1952.

Melnick, Ralph. "Billy Simons: The Black Jew of Charleston." *American Jewish Archives* 32, 1980.

Metraux, Alfred. *Voodoo in Haiti.* New York: Schocken, 1972.

Michaeli, Ethan. "Ben Ammi Proclaims Political Alignment." *The Chicago Defender*, July 8, 1996.

———."Hebrew Israelites Settle into Modern Israel." *The Chicago Defender*, June 3, 1996.

Moses, Wilson. *Black Messiahs and Uncle Toms: Social and Literary Manipulations of a Religious Myth.* University Park: Pennsylvania State University Press, 1982.

———.*The Golden Age of Black Nationalism, 1850–1925.* Hamden: Archon Books, 1978.

Muhammad, Elijah. *How to Eat to Live.* Chicago: Muhammad's Temple of Islam No. 2, 1967.

———.*How to Eat to Live, Book Two.* Chicago: Muhammad's Temple of Islam No. 2, 1972.

———.*Message to the Blackman in America.* Newport News, VA: United Brothers Communications Systems, 1992.

———.*Our Saviour Has Arrived.* Chicago: Muhammad's Temple of Islam No. 2, 1974.

Muhammad, Jabril. *Farrakhan, the Traveler.* Phoenix: Phoenix and Co., 1985.

Neusner, Jacob. *The Way of Torah.* Belmont, CA: Wadsworth, 1993.

Perkins, John. *With Justice for All.* Ventura, CA: Regal, 1982.

Raboteau, Albert. "African Religions in America: Theoretical Perspectives." Joseph Harris, ed., *Global Dimensions of the African Diaspora.* Washington, DC: Howard University Press, 1993.

———. "Ethiopia Shall Stretch Forth Her Hands: Black Destiny in Nineteenth-Century America," in *A Fire in the Bones: Reflections on African American Religious History.* Boston: Beacon Press, 1995.

———. "Exodus, Ethiopia, and Racial Messianism: Texts and Contexts of African American Chosenness." William Hutchinson and Hartmut Lehmann, eds., *Many Are Chosen: Divine Election and Western Nationalism.* Minneapolis: Fortress Press, 1993.

———. *Slave Religion: The Invisible Institution in the Antebellum South.* New York: Oxford University Press, 1978.

Rad, Gerhard von,. *The Message of the Prophets*, trans. D. M. G. Stalker. New York: Harper and Row, 1962.

Redkey, Edwin. *Black Exodus.* New Haven, CT: Yale University Press, 1969.

Reznikoff, Charles, and Uriah Engleman. *The Jews of Charleston.* Philadelphia: Jewish Publication Society, 1950.

Roberts, John. *From Trickster to Badman: The Black Folk Hero in Slavery and Freedom.* Philadelphia: University of Pennsylvania Press, 1989.

Robinson, James, ed. *The Nag Hammadi Library in English.* San Francisco: Harper San Francisco, 1988.

Rooks, Charles Shelby. "Toward the Promised Land: An Analysis of the Religious Experience of Black America." *The Black Church* II:1, 1973.

Roth, Cecil. *A History of the Marranos.* Philadelphia: Jewish Publication Society, 1932.

Salzman, Jack, ed. *Bridges and Boundaries: African Americans and American Jews: A Resource Guide.* New York: The Jewish Museum, 1994.

———. and Cornel West, eds. *Struggles in the Promised Land: Toward a History of Black–Jewish Relations in the United States.* New York: Oxford University Press, 1997.

Sanders, Ronald. *Lost Tribes and Promised Lands: The Origins of American Racism.* New York: Harper Perennial, 1992.

Scott, William. "Rabbi Arnold Ford's Back-to-Ethiopia Movement: A Study of Black Emigration, 1930–1935." *Pan African Journal* VIII, 1975.

Seabrook, W. B. *The Magic Island.* New York: Literary Guild of America, 1929.

The Secret Relationship Between Blacks and Jews, Nation of Islam (NOI) Research Department, 1991.

Shapiro, Deanne Ruth. "Double Damnation, Double Salvation." MA Thesis, Department of Philosophy, Columbia University, 1970.

———. "Factors in the Development of Black Judaism." C. Eric Lincoln, ed., *The Black Experience in Religion.* Garden City, NY: Anchor Doubleday Press, 1974.

Singer, Merrill, "Life in a Defensive Society: The Black Hebrew Israelites." Jon Wagner, ed., *Sex Roles in Contemporary American Communes.* Bloomfield: Indiana University Press, 1982.

———. "'Now I Know What the Songs Mean!': Traditional Black Music in a Contemporary Black Sect." *Southern Quarterly* 23, 1985.

———. *Saints of the Kingdom: Group Emergence, Individual Affiliation, and Social Change among the Black Hebrews of Israel.* Doctoral Dissertation, Department of Anthropology, University of Utah, 1979.

———. "The Social Context of Conversion to a Black Religious Sect." *Review of Religious Research* 30, 1988.

Singer, Merrill, Freddie Valentìn, Hans Baer, and Zhongke Jia. "Why Does Juan Garcìa Have a Drinking Problem? The Perspective of Critical Medical Anthropology." *Medical Anthropology* 14, 1992.

Smith, Jonathan. "What a Difference a Difference Makes." Jacob Neusner and Ernest Frerichs, eds., *"To See Ourselves as Others See Us": Christians, Jews, "Others" in Late Antiquity.* Chico, CA: Scholars Press, 1985

Smith, Kenneth, and Ira Zepp. *Search for the Beloved Community: The Thinking of Martin Luther King, Jr.* Valley Forge, PA: Judson Press, 1974.

Smith, Theophus. *Conjuring Culture: Biblical Formations of Black America.* New York: Oxford University Press, 1994.

Smith, Timothy. "Slavery and Theology: The Emergence of Black Christian Consciousness in Nineteenth-Century America." *Church History* 41, 1972.

Smylie, James. "On Jesus, Pharaohs, and the Chosen People: Martin Luther King as Biblical Interpreter and Humanist," *Interpretation* 24, 1970.

Snow, Malina. "Martin Luther King's 'Letter from Birmingham Jail' as Pauline Epistle," *Quarterly Journal of Speech* 71, 1985.

Sobel, Mechal. *Trabelin On: The Slave Journey to an Afro-Baptist Faith.* Princeton, NJ: Princeton University Press, 1979.

Stallybrass, Peter and Allon White. *The Politics and Poetics of Transgression.* Ithaca, NY: Cornell University Press, 1986.

Sussman, Lance. "The Suburbanization of American Judaism as Reflected in Synagogue Building and Architecture, 1945–1975." *American Jewish History* 75, 1985.

Suttner, Immanuel. "Members of the Tribe." *The Jerusalem Report*, July 15, 1993.

Tinney, James. "Black Jews: A House Divided," *Christianity Today*, December 7, 1983.

Tov, Emmanuel. *Textual Criticism of the Hebrew Bible.* Minneapolis: Fortress Press, 1992.

Trachtenberg, Joshua. *The Devil and the Jews: The Medieval Conception of the Jew and Its Relation to Modern Antisemitism.* New York: Harper Torchbooks, 1996.

Trouillot, Michel-Rolph. *Haiti, State Against Nation: The Origins and Legacy of Duvalierism.* New York: Monthly Review Press, 1990.

Uya, Okon Edet. "Life in a Slave Community." *Afro-American Studies* 1, 1971.

Vincent, Theodore. *Black Power and the Garvey Movement.* Berkeley CA: Ramparts Press, 1971.

Waitzkin, Howard. "Black Judaism in New York." *Harvard Journal of Negro Affairs* 1, 1967.

Weisbord, Robert. *African Zion: The Attempt to Establish a Jewish Colony in the East African Protectorate.* Philadelphia: Jewish Publication Society, 1968.

Wigoder, Emmet. "America's Black Jews in Israel." *Israel Magazine* 3, 1970.

Williams, Joseph. *Hebrewisms of West Africa: From Nile to Niger with the Jews.* New York: Biblo and Tannen, 1930.

Wilmore, Gayraud. Black Religion and Black Radicalism. Maryknoll, NY: Orbis Books, 1998.

Windsor, Rudolph. *From Babylon to Timbuktu*. New York: Exposition Press, 1969.

Windsor, Rudolph, and Steven Jacobs. *The Hebrew Heritage of Our West African Ancestors*. Wilmington, DL: Rose-Lee, Inc., 1971.

Wolfson, Bernard. "The Soul of Judaism," *Emerge*, September 1995.

Wynia, Elly. *The Church of God and the Saints of Christ: The Rise of Black Jews*. New York: Garland Publishing, 1994.

X, Malcolm. *The Autobiography of Malcolm X, As Told to Alex Haley*. New York: Ballantine Books, 1965.

York, Malachi, Z. *360 Questions to Ask a Hebrew Israelite*. Parts 1–4, 1994–1995.

———.*360 Questions to Ask the Israeli Church*. Part 1, 1995–1996.

———.*Does Dr. Malachi Z. York Try to Hide the Fact That He Was Imaam Issa?* 1996.

———.*Man from Planet Rizq*. (n.d.)

———.*Nuwaubu and Amunnubi Rooakhptah: Fact or Fiction?* (n.d.)

———.*The Scroll of Malachi*. 1994.

———.*The Wisemen*. 1995/1989.

Index

Abernathy, Ralph, 176
Abeta, 60–61, 63
Abraham, 67, 119, 121–122, 130, 133, 136, 165–166
Adam and Eve, 58, 103, 106–107, 123, 126–127
Africa, 34, 44; as black homeland, 25, 26; Hebrew Israelite view of, 55, 60, 73, 82, 86; Nubian Islaamic Hebrew view of, 120; as symbol for African Americans, 20, 89. *See also* Ethiopia
African Methodist Episcopal Church, 44
Ahmadiyyah, 104
Akhmatova, Anna, 108
Alliance of Black Jews, 4, 38, 39, 49
ancient Israelites. *See* biblical Hebrews
Ansaaru Allah Community. *See* Nubian Islaamic Hebrews
Anti-Defamation league, 37, 38, 74, 109–110
anti-Semitism, 91, 109–110, 205
apocalyptic, 64, 75, 93, 124, 135–136, 156, 160
Apocryphon of John, 103
Arabs, 85
Arad, 66, 69, 74

baptism, 59, 194
Bar/Bat Mitzvah, 131
Baron, Salo, 5
Barth, Karl, 170, 179
Ben Ammi, 61, 65–69, 75–87, 119; in Chicago, 76–77; rise to leadership, 61, 66–69; views of Israel, 78, 81–82; views of the Nation of Islam, 84–85
Ben Israel, Prince Asiel, 74, 78
Benjamin, Walter, 108
Ben Yahweh, Yahweh, 119
Beta Yisroel. See Ethiopian Jews
Bible. *See* Hebrew Bible
biblical Hebrews, 56, 59, 156, 172, 178; and Hebrew Israelites, 61, 63, 65, 76; and Nation of Islam, 95, 111; and Nubian Islaamic Hebrews, 133, 136
Black Hebrew Israelites. *See* Hebrew Israelites
black Jews, 21, 33–51
Bloom, Harold, 105
Blyden, Edward Wilmot, 15–16
Boyarin, Daniel, 107, 124
Brotz, Howard, 57

Carson, Clayborne, 170
Carter, Ben. *See* Ben Ammi
Catholicism, 9, 206
Cherry, Prophet F. S., 10, 21, 58–60
Chicago, 33–51, 177; and Hebrew Israelites, 55, 60–61, 73–75, 78, 82, 83, 87
Chicago Defender, 73, 76–77
children of Israel. *See* biblical Hebrews
Chosen People, 14; African American self-definition, 19–20; biblical doctrine, 19; Hebrew Israelites as, 63, 81; Nation of Islam as, 91; whites' false claim as, 106
Christ. *See* Jesus
Christianity, 6, 9, 34, 40, 51, 56, 90–93, 94–99, 103–104, 111–112, 119–120, 123–124, 128, 135, 153, 158, 162, 169, 172, 179, 203–223

Christmas, 131
Church of God and Saints of Christ, 58, 119
Church of the Living God, 57–58
Cincinnati, 9, 61, 187–201
circumcision, 59, 131
civil rights movement, 168–183
Civil War, 55, 57, 60
Commandment Keepers Congregation, 7–8, 25, 47, 119
Cone, James, 170
Congregation Adath Israel, 188, 192–194, 196, 200–201
conversion to Judaism: rejection by Hebrew Israelites, 66–67
Couliano, Ioan, 102
Crowdy, William, 21, 58–60

David (King), 69, 121
Day of Atonement, 84, 112, 129–131. *See also* Yom Kippur
Dead Sea Scrolls, 160
Detroit, 78, 79, 93
diaspora, 7, 10, 16, 22, 158–160, 166, 206
Dimona (Israel), 66–68, 73, 75, 77–80, 82, 84, 87
Du Bois, W. E. B., 166

Easter, 203–205, 209–212
eating, 49; Hebrew Israelite view of, 75; Nation of Islam views of, 95–101
Egypt, 57, 59, 61, 76, 120, 122, 124, 132, 171–172, 175, 177–178, 222
Enoch, 156, 160
Ethiopia, 7, African American emigration to, 26–27; and Bible, 20; and racialist discourse, 20, 48
Ethiopian Hebrews. *See* Commandment Keepers Congregation
Ethiopianism, 15, 20
Ethiopian Jews, 25, 48, 56, 79, 86, 118, 123
exile. *See* diaspora
Exodus, 19, 59, 122, 129–133, 158, 166, 168–169, 171–172, 175, 177–178, 222; as inspiration for Hebrew Israelites, 61, 76

Falashas. *See* Ethiopian Jews
Fard, W. D. *See* Muhammad, Fard
Farrakhan, Louis, 4, 36–37, 49, 89, 91, 168; attitudes toward Jews, 89, 109–113; and Hebrew Israelites, 74, 78, 84–86. *See also* Nation of Islam
Fishbane, Michael, 104
Five Percent Nation of Gods and Earths, 8, 90, 118
Ford, Arnold J., 10, 23, 24, 25–28, 47, 119
Foxman, Abraham, 109–110
Funnye, Capers, 4, 34, 39, 42–49

Garden of Eden, 75, 107
Garvey, Marcus, 10, 19, 20, 23, 47, 86. *See also* UNIA
Gates, Henry Louis, Jr., 111–112
Geertz, Clifford, 61
Genesis Rabah, 101, 125
Genovese, Eugene, 56
Gnosticism, 94, 101–103, 105, 108
Green, Arthur, 171

Haiti, 203–223
Hasidism, 9, 168–170, 175, 177
Hatzaad Harishon, 10
Hebrew Bible, 7, 55–56, 101, 105, 128, 154, 192; African American interpretations of, 18; book of Amos, 172–173; book of Chronicles, 132; book of Daniel, 156–160; book of Deuteronomy, 131, 133; book of Ezekiel, 77, 121; book of Ezra, 153–156; book of Genesis, 75, 94, 102–103, 105–109, 121–123, 125–127; book of Haggai, 155–156; book of Isaiah, 136, 159; book of Jeremiah, 174; 130; book of Kings, 132; book of Nehemiah, 8, 154–156; book of Numbers, 133; book of Psalms, 76, 201; book of Samuel, 132; book of Zechariah, 155–156; Hebrew Israelite interpretations of, 65, 75–77; interpretations by Martin Luther King and Abraham Joshua Heschel, 169–173; Nation of Islam's interpretation of, 94–95, 97, 102, 108; Nubian Isaamic Hebrew interpretation of, 124–125, 136; themes in, 7

Hebrew Israelites, 4, 55, 62, 86–87, 90, 119; choir, 74; in Israel, 66–68, 73, 78–82, 86–87; in Liberia, 63–65; origins, 60–61; rituals and beliefs of, 75–76; symbols of, 69–70
Hebrew Union College, 198
Herman, Mordechai, 22, 119
Heschel, Abraham Joshua, 4, 9, 10, 170, 183; Hasidism and, 168–170, 175, 177; march at Selma, 168, 175–177; opposition to Vietnam War, 181–182; study of the prophets, 173–174; theology of, 171, 179–181; view of Christianity, 169
Holocaust, 50–51
Holy Tabernacle Ministries. *See* Nubian Islaamic Hebrews
How to Eat to Live, 95–101

Inquisition, 204, 212, 222
Isaac, 122
Isaac M. Wise Center, 188–189, 194–196, 198, 200
Ishmael, 122–124, 131
Islam, 56, 89–90, 95, 99, 106, 108–109, 118–119, 121, 123–124, 128, 130, 134–135, 206
Israel, 4, 6, 55–56, 119; and Hebrew Israelites, 66–68, 73, 78–82, 86–87

Jackson, Jesse, 112, 183
Jacob, 122
Jerusalem, 69, 73, 75, 153, 155, 160, 165–166, 197
Jesus, 49, 51, 59–60, 77, 93, 121, 168, 172–173, 177, 200, 209, 211; as Aryan, 169; as black, 58; as Jewish, 169; as *zonbi*, 219
Jewish Theological Seminary, 181
Jews, 6, 33–51, 109, 123, 171, 177–178, 204, 207, 211–212, 215–216, 220–223; Ashkenazic, 39, 42, 48, 118, 122–123, 222; in Cincinnati, 187, 189–201; Conservative, 6, 33, 168, 176; demonized, 204, 217–218; desire to imitate, 59; Ethiopian, 48; Hebrew Israelite understandings of, 67, 76, 78, 81–82, 87; images of, 211, 215–216; and Judaism, 44–45, 55–56, 90–91, 97, 101, 110, 119–120, 123, 126, 128; as imposters, 58, 122; Nation of Islam's view of, 97–101, 112–113; Orthodox, 6, 40, 98; Reform, 33, 45; Sephardic, 42, 118, 122–123, 204, 222. *See also* black Jews
Joshua, 56

Kabbalah, 135, 171–172
Kashrut, 49, 98, 101, 113
King, Martin Luther, Jr., 9, 10, 92, 170, 183, 195; assassination of, 175; march at Selma, 168, 175–177; opposition to Vietnam War, 181–182; theology of, 179–181; view of Jesus as a Jew, 169
Kugel, James, 101
Ku Klux Klan, 37

Lamm, Norman, 171
Law of Return, 66
Levine, Lawrence, 17–18, 172
Leviticus, 75, 95, 97, 130, 133
Liberia, 55, 61, 63–67, 119
Long, Charles, 18
Luther, Martin, 173

Maccabees, 155
Malcolm X, 5–6, 86, 92, 105
Marable, Manning, 56
Marx, Karl, 161
Matthew, Wentworth, 24, 27, 47, 119. *See also* Commandment Keepers Congregation
Mecca, 105–106, 131
Melchizedek. *See* York, Malachi Z.
Message to the Blackman in America, 92–95, 102, 105–108
messiah, 75, 135–136
Midrash, 90, 101, 103–104, 107, 109, 124–127
Million Man March, 36, 112
Moorish Science Temple, 31 n. 17, 118
Moorish Zionist Temple, 8, 58, 118–119
Moses, 19, 56–57, 95, 97–99, 122–123, 125–126, 129, 156, 161, 173, 197, 221–222; as black, 67; identified with Martin Luther King Jr., 172

Moses, Franklin J., 57
Muhammad, 121, 123, 128, 130
Muhammad, Elijah, 4, 89, 91, 93, 103–106, 109; attitude toward Jews, 89, 94, 97–101, 112–113; attitude toward white Muslims, 97, 99–100; attitude toward whites, 89, 92, 94, 97, 107; biblical interpretation, 97, 102, 105–109; views of Christianity, 94–97, 100
Muhammad, Fard, 93–96, 104
Muhammad, Warith, 109
Muslims, 6, 10, 85, 96, 97–98, 100, 103, 112, 122. *See also* Islam

NAACP, 5, 183
Nation of Islam, 4, 8, 10, 36, 89–93, 101, 104–105, 107, 109, 112, 118; and Hebrew Israelites, 74, 84–85; ideology of, 4–5; and Jews, 91, 97, 109–113
New Testament, 77, 121,124, 159, 173, 197, 200, 211; book of Acts, 97; book of Hebrews, 156, 165–166; book of Revelation, 121, 128, 131, 133, 135–136, 166; Gospel of John, 92–93
New York City, 38, 80, 175–176, 206
Niebuhr, Reinhold, 170, 179
Nubian Islaamic Hebrews, 8, 10, 89–90; celebration of holidays, 128–132; dress and iconography, 132–136; origins, 118–120; relationship to Judaism, 118–136
Nuwaubu, 124, 136

Old Testament. *See* Hebrew Bible
Our Saviour Has Arrived, 108

Passover, 7, 59, 175; and Hebrew Israelites, 61, 65, 80; and Nubian Islaamic Hebrews, 129
Paul, 111
Perkins, John, 162–165
Priesard, Sally, 198
Promised Land, 165
Protestantism, 83, 92, 169, 174, 179
Protocols of the Elders of Zion, 49

Qumran, 156
Quran, 97, 100, 120, 123–124, 129–131, 134

Raboteau, Albert, 56
Rastafarianism, 10, 86
Reconstruction, 59, 161
Riverside Church, 168, 182
Rosh Hashanah, 129

Sabbath, 33–34, 59; Hebrew Israelite celebration of, 76; Nubian Islaamic Hebrew celebration of, 128–131
Sinai, 51, 177–178
Sirah, 155
slavery, 18, 22, 4795, 109, 129, 157–158, 204, 212
Smith, Jonathan Z., 91
Smith, Theophus, 165
Soloveitchik, Joseph, 171
Southern Missionary Baptist Church, 187, 189–194, 201
Spirituals, 17–18, 153, 157–158
Star of David, 55, 133–134, 192–194
Sudan, 122–123
Sufi, 120, 133
synagogues, 33–34; 169; in Cincinnati, 187–201

tallit, 131
Talmud, 156
Tanner, Benjamin Tucker, 59
Targum, 124–125
tefillin, 131
Temple (Jerusalem), 75, 130–133, 136, 155, 157, 159, 197–198
Temple of the Gospel of the Kingdom, 118
Tillich, Paul, 170, 180
Turner, Bishop Henry M., 59–60
Turner, Nat, 56–57

Universal Negro Improvement Association (UNIA), 10, 23, 86. *See also* Garvey, Marcus.

Vodou, 203–223
von Rad, Gerhard, 174

Washington, Booker T., 47, 59
Woodbey, George Washington, 161–162

Yakub, 92, 99, 105, 107–109
Yamassee Native American Nuwaubians, *See* Nubian Islaamic Hebrews
Yom Kippur, 76, 84, 112, 129–131
York, Dwight Z. *See* York, Malachi Z.
York, Malachi Z., 122; biblical interpretation, 125–126; different names of, 120, 133, 135–136
Young, Andrew, 176, 183
Youngblood, Johnny Ray, 164

Zion, 85, 119, 166, 197
Zionism, 80, 86
Zion Temple First Pentecostal Church, 187–188, 195, 197–201